Indigenous Participation in Australian Economies II

Historical engagements and current enterprises

Indigenous Participation in Australian Economies II

Historical engagements and current enterprises

Edited by Natasha Fijn, Ian Keen, Christopher Lloyd and Michael Pickering

Australian
National
University

E PRESS

ANU
E PRESS

Published by ANU E Press
The Australian National University
Canberra ACT 0200, Australia
Email: anuepress@anu.edu.au
This title is also available online at: http://epress.anu.edu.au/

National Library of Australia Cataloguing-in-Publication entry

Title: Indigenous participation in Australian economies, II : historical engagements
              and current enterprises [electronic resource] / Natasha Fijn ... [et al]

ISBN: 9781921862830 (pbk.) 9781921862847 (ebook)

Notes: Includes bibliographical references and index.

Subjects: Aboriginal Australians--Economic conditions.
              Business enterprises, Aboriginal Australian.
              Aboriginal Australians--Employment.
              Australia--Economic conditions.

Other Authors/Contributors:
              Fijn, Natasha.

Dewey Number: 306.30994

Cover design and layout by ANU E Press

Cover image: Gudurr with photo of Dave Rust and Scotty Salmond 2008. Courtesy State Library
of Western Australia image number 007852D

Contents

Indigenous Enterprises and Employment Schemes

Figures

Maps

Tables

Foreword

Jon Altman

This book is part of a bold intellectual quest to re-envisage and re-theorise the nature of Indigenous participation in the Australian colonial economy. It has arisen out of an Australian Research Council (ARC) Linkage project between scholars at The Australian National University, the University of New England and the National Museum of Australia that was completed in 2011. This book is the second substantive publication from the project, following on from *Indigenous Participation in Australian Economies: Historical and anthropological perspectives*, edited by Ian Keen and published by ANU E Press in 2010. The title of this volume—*Indigenous Participation in Australian Economies II: Historical engagements and current enterprises*—suggests to me that the research project has grown beyond its original intent.

The project's key goal—to revisit historical, spatially diverse and now contemporary articulations of Indigenous and settler-state and settler-capitalist social and economic forms—is long overdue. It is an ambitious interdisciplinary collaboration; its team of researchers deploys the disciplinary lenses of anthropology, history, economic history, material culture and prehistory (or archaeology). Participating in the public conference held at the National Museum of Australia in November 2009, I was struck that the topic attracted an even wider set of perspectives than originally anticipated, as well as more scholarly interest. And just as the disciplinary perspectives grew so did the time frame under consideration. This raises important questions about how we characterise the temporal and spatial boundaries of the Australian colonial economy: is there still a colonial frontier out there? From an Indigenous perspective, is Australia post colonial or still colonial? As the project has expanded and evolved, it strikes me that it has been well managed by the lead researchers who have been happy not to steer any tight predetermined course.

In his recent article 'Settler colonialism and the elimination of the native', Patrick Wolfe (2006) draws on his earlier work to make three points of great pertinence to this project. First, he notes that the colonial invasion and its transformative capitalist system were predicated on wholesale expropriation of the land and resources—the principal settler-colonial logic to eliminate native societies was to gain unrestricted access to territory. Quoting Deborah Bird Rose from her book *Hidden Histories* (1991), Wolfe reminds us that in order to get in the way of settler colonisation all Indigenous hunter-gatherers had to do was to stay at home. Second, Wolfe notes that settler colonisers came to stay: invasion is structural; it is not some historical event that can be isolated to a particular place and time such as Sydney in 1788. And third, Wolfe suggests that settler colonialism has both negative and positive dimensions. Negatively, it strives for the dissolution of native societies—a dissolution that in the past included the summary massacre of Indigenous people, as new histories of frontier conflict now document. Positively, a new colonial society is created and a range of new options emerges from the logic of elimination, including integration or assimilation of Indigenous people as citizens—what is referred to today as mainstreaming, with its goal of normalisation or 'Closing the Gap' in socioeconomic status according to the norms of the dominant settler-colonial society.

It is not surprising under such circumstances that a diversity of Indigenous participations in Australian economies has resulted, and I note a growing propensity to use plurals to denote this. Such diversity has been documented in research beginning 40 years ago, especially in the series Aborigines in Australian Society under the general guidance of political scientist Charles Rowley, as Ian Keen and Chris Lloyd note in their Introduction to this volume. Two theoretical developments in recent years positively influence the current project of economic reinterpretation and expanded possibilities.

The first is the path-breaking work of Ian Keen in his major study, *Aboriginal Economy and Society: Australia at the threshold of colonisation* (2004). Here Keen meticulously examines available sources to ask to what extent Aboriginal economy and society varied across Australia at the time of British colonisation. This exhaustive work employs a tripartite classification, ecology, institutions and economy, summarises similarities and differences and provides explanation for variation. Having this work on hand provides a frame of reference for understanding from a structural-functionalist perspective the endogamous explanations for diversity of participations. We have clearly moved beyond any crude universalising of the pre-colonial hunter-gatherer mode of production continent wide.

The second development is the broad reflexive shift in the social sciences in recent decades to more inclusively consider economic and social relations from the perspective of those marginalised, subordinated and dominated on the frontier, whose way of life was, and is, challenged and often destroyed. From the earlier writings of Talal Asad and Eric Wolf to more recent translations into English of the works of Michel Foucault and Pierre Bourdieu, we are now far more comfortable in theoretically incorporating workings of power, conflict and agency into structural analyses. There is a more nuanced engagement today with different logic and a greater acceptance of inevitable contestation over economic values. The writings over a long time of James Scott make it clear that the weak or subordinate will not meekly acquiesce to some predetermined pathway to modernity proposed for them; the weak can strategically deploy many forms of resistance. Similarly, while in the past social scientists might have overemphasised dualities like kin-based versus market-based economic regimes or customary versus Western economic norms, recent scholarship is moving beyond such essentialised binaries to a greater recognition of ongoing contestation and associated new forms of economic mixture, accommodation, adaptation, adoption, interdependence and even symbiosis. To return to Patrick Wolfe's ideas and terms, the contributors to this volume ask how native elimination has been challenged by the natives or the natives and their allies at the local and regional levels.

* * *

I was honoured to be invited to give the opening keynote address to the conference on which this volume is based. I had participated in an earlier conference in Auckland in December 2008 reported in *Indigenous Participation in Australian Economies: Historical and anthropological perspectives* and so could already see the project's potential to provide insights deploying these new perspectives and fresh empirical case material.

I was asked by the conference organisers to speak about my particular conceptualisation of the hybrid economy. I chose to highlight its role as a political project, with political being used in a broader sense than the usual conflicts over the ownership and distribution of resources; I had also developed this notion for discursive conflicts that have rapidly escalated in Australian society in the early twenty-first century, although structurally they had always been there, it was just an issue of degree.

My address was titled 'The hybrid economy as political project: reflections from the Indigenous estate', and I was especially keen to launch the conference with some provocation around the notion of scholarship as political and of economic hybridity as not just being geographically limited to the very remote areas where I do most of my research. Owing to unforeseen circumstances, my opening address was further developed for publication in *Culture Crisis: Anthropology and politics in Aboriginal Australia* (2010), a volume that I co-edited with Melinda Hinkson. I would have liked to include my essay here as it resonates with so many others and I could have doubled my Higher Education Research Data Collection (HERDC) points, but this did not seem proper.

I was hopeful that participants at the conference would critically engage with the notion of economic hybridity that I have been promulgating as a conceptual tool for properly understanding the diverse and at times very complex forms of production regime informed by intercultural social norms. I was especially keen to advocate for the rejection of a host of crude dualities like market/non-market, formal/informal, Indigenous/non-Indigenous, real economy/welfare economy that take us nowhere in understanding the empirically grounded complexity of diverse Indigenous economies.

At the same time, I have become increasingly aware that despite the failure of the neo-liberal ascendancy and the free market to actually deliver much to Indigenous Australia, there is a dominant ideological, discursive, intellectual and even policy commitment to this form of development. And yet it seems to me that any hasty adherence to neo-liberal globalisation during a time of great global uncertainty is an extremely risky venture. This is a view shared by many Indigenous people living culturally and geographically beyond the mainstream. For them, economic plurality and cultural diversity might be less risky than some imagined seamless, conflict-free integration into the mainstream—as if the asymmetry of power relations in Australian society and a history of neglect, marginalisation and racism can magically be wished away.

The political project that I am promoting is for scholarship to be deployed to challenge the dominance of a discourse that focuses only on the capitalist economy and notions of Indigenous deficiency as defined by statistics that reflect Western social norms. The very project of improvement, to use the language of Tania Murray Li in *The Will to Improve* (2008), looks to reshape any Aboriginal values, beliefs, social relations and practices that remain distinct from mainstream norms. This project needs to be questioned. This is partly because it is not new in the Australian context; it revisits earlier failed attempts to shape Aboriginal subjectivities, to sedentarise, civilise, normalise, to 'develop' Aboriginal people, to transform them into subjects of the global project of modernity, to become responsible citizens of a multicultural, liberal democratic state, to be hardworking labourers or profit-driven entrepreneurs in a free market, to be capitalist consumers of mass culture. It is also because it does not accord with principles articulated in the UN Declaration on the Rights of Indigenous Peoples that the Australian Government endorsed in April 2009.

The contributions within this book take on this challenge admirably by properly integrating people and agency and differing cultural perspectives into an elaborate scholarly mosaic of analyses, interpretations and reinterpretations. This is a key strength of this volume: the consistent purpose of authors not to pre-empt any economic development pathway for Indigenous people, but to question an emerging monolithic view of what Aboriginal economic futures should be, by providing a more complex appreciation of what has gone on, and continues to go on, at the frontier.

* * *

One wants to open a conference with challenges but not with undue pessimism. And so I ended my keynote address by quoting from the poem and song *Anthem* by Leonard Cohen:

> Ring the bells that still can ring
>
> Forget your perfect offering
>
> There is a crack, a crack in everything
>
> That's how the light gets in.

Loic Wacquant's recent reading and translation of Pierre Bourdieu in *Punishing the Poor* (2007) provides grounds for optimism. Bourdieu's proposition is that the state cannot be construed as monolithic but rather as a splintered space of forces vying over the definition and distribution of public goods in what he terms 'the bureaucratic field'. Today in Indigenous affairs the bureaucratic field is locked in struggle between the dominant Right Hand of the state promulgating normalisation and the subordinate Left Hand promulgating greater choice. Cohen's words might be invoked as a means of exploiting cracks in the bureaucratic field to support Indigenous aspirations and desires that are not currently accommodated by the Australian state and its current 'Closing the Gap' policy obsession.

Cohen's poem is open to another metaphoric adaptation here: there can be cracks too in how we challenge previously dominant intellectual interpretations of the past and the present. In my view, this volume and its contributions do just that: they allow the light in so that we can see more clearly the emergence of local and regional 'hybrid economies' involving articulations of Indigenous and settler social and economic forms, and the emergence of new complexes of transactions and relations over the past two centuries. This is a very worthwhile project that will, in my view, make significant contributions to our understandings of the forms of Indigenous participations in Australian 'frontier' economies.

References

Altman, J. 2010. What future for remote Indigenous Australia? Economic hybridity and the neoliberal turn. In J. Altman and M. Hinkson (eds), *Culture Crisis: Aboriginal politics in Aboriginal Australia*. Sydney: UNSW Press.

Keen, I. 2004. *Aboriginal Economy and Society: Australia at the threshold of colonisation*. Oxford: Oxford University Press.

Keen, I. 2010. *Indigenous Participation in Australian Economies: Historical and anthropological perspectives*. Canberra: ANU E Press.

Li, T. M. 2008. *The Will to Improve: Governmentality, development and practice of politics*. Durham, NC: Duke University Press.

Rowley, C. 1968. *Aborigines in Australian Society*. Canberra: Commonwealth Office of Aboriginal Affairs.

Wacquant, L. 2007. *Punishing the Poor: The neoliberal government of social insecurity*. Durham, NC: Duke University Press.

Wolfe, P. 2006. Settler colonialism and the elimination of the native. *Journal of Genocidal Research* 8 (4): 387–409.

Introduction

Ian Keen and Christopher Lloyd

The changing and fraught participation of Indigenous people in the Australian economy since the first European settlement until the present are issues of great significance to Indigenous people themselves and to the wider society and polity. The story of conquest, decimation and marginalisation, while being the fundamental reality, tells only part of the story of the impact on Indigenous Australians of being forcibly incorporated into the worldwide settler-capitalist revolution of the eighteenth and nineteenth centuries (Belich 2001). Another significant part of the story involves the accommodation, adaptation and incorporation of Indigenous people into that new world. Indigenous and non-Indigenous scholars have been attempting recently to increase our knowledge and understanding of this history and of the present complex situation. Part of the context of this re-examination has been the debate since Prime Minister Kevin Rudd's 2008 apology speech (Rudd 2008) and the associated 'Closing the Gap' policy of the Australian Federal Government. The Rudd Government, together with the States and Territories, developed the National Indigenous Reform Agenda (NIRA; 'Closing the Gap') in 2008, much of which is focused on remote Australia. 'Closing the Gap', while well intentioned, envisages a top-down and interventionist approach that arises from a modernisation ideology that effectively sees the problem of Indigenous disadvantage as solvable through the 'mainstreaming' of Indigenous economic activity. An alternative view stresses the complexity, variety, agency and relative autonomy of Indigenous participation in the Australian economy historically and today, and thus provides a different perspective for the present debates.

This is the second volume to emerge from a significant project on Indigenous participation in the Australian economy, funded by an Australian Research Council (ARC) Linkage Grant (grant number LP0775392) involving the cooperation of the School of Archaeology and Anthropology at The Australian National University and The National Museum of Australia. The present volume arises out of a conference in Canberra on Indigenous Participation in Australian Economies at the National Museum of Australia on 9–10 November 2009. The conference attracted more than 30 presenters. The themes were diverse, comprising histories of economic relations, the role of camels and dingoes in Indigenous–settler relations, material culture and the economy, the economies of communities from missions and stations to fringe camps and towns, the transitions from payment-in-kind to wage economies and Community

Development Employment Projects (CDEP), the issue of unpaid and stolen wages, local enterprises, and conflicts over development. Professor Jon Altman presented the keynote address at the conference.

Sixteen of the conference presentations have developed as chapters of this book, which stands as a companion volume to the earlier *Indigenous Participation in Australian Economies: Historical and anthropological perspectives* (ANU E Press, 2010). We have organised the chapters in this volume under three main headings: Indigenous people and settlers, labour history and stolen wages, and Indigenous enterprises and employment schemes.

The Introduction to the earlier volume noted the invisibility of Indigenous Australians in many economic histories in the light of the very considerable body of research on the participation of Indigenous people in many sectors of the Australian economy, including marine industries, early settlements and farms, the pastoral industry and mining, and research on Indigenous labour history more generally. It sketched a number of anthropological approaches to the analysis of Indigenous economic relations and of the articulation of Indigenous economies and market capitalism in Australia. Approaches to internal economic relations have included obligations to kin, reciprocity and demand sharing. Approaches to economic relations between Indigenous people and the wider Australian economy have included the concepts of internal colonialism, welfare colonialism and the hybrid economy.

In this volume, we take up the central theme addressed by Jon Altman in his keynote address, concerning the use and significance of the hybrid economy model for the analysis of Indigenous economic participation. This concept has been widely used in the social sciences (Kraidy 2005). Altman's refinement and application of the concept to Australian Indigenous economic history, especially in remote Australia in recent times, have proven fruitful to research and policy debates (see his recent restatement in Altman 2009). In his keynote address at the conference, Altman explained that he had developed the hybrid economy model because of the inadequacy of a market/non-market dualism, which underestimates the role of the state and under-theorises the process of governmentality. He was also motivated by the history and cultures wars, which he saw as manifestations of 'the neo-liberal ascendancy'. This ascendancy emphasises, in effect, the agenda of moving Indigenous Australians further into the capitalist market economy as the only way forward. But people on the ground, rather than in Canberra, have a growing recognition of the inability of private capital to deliver development opportunities in remote Australia. These regions appear, through economic-rationalist eyes, to be essentially unproductive regions but this ignores their potential as sites of Indigenous culturally based, hybrid production activity.

Altman takes the hybrid economy model to be dynamic and flexible, both spatially and temporally, and to be more complex than is immediately apparent. The model is able to reflect Aboriginal agency, and to challenge the blindness of state and private interests to what happens in the non-monetised informal sector. The fruitfulness of the model is shown by its use in several chapters in this volume, including Christopher Lloyd's chapter, in which he attempts to show its relevance to historical as well as contemporary analysis, about which more is said below.

Indigenous communities in remote areas are non-mainstream, and there is no evidence that larger communities—as present Federal Government policy dictates—would provide better economic prospects. As Altman suggested in his address: 'the state project is to homogenise communities and discourage small dispersed settlements and mobile populations that are hard and expensive to govern.' The state 'looks to eliminate non-state spaces and to meet the labour and resource needs of mature capitalism'. The smaller remote communities, however, provide opportunities for alternative life-worlds and livelihoods.

Altman regards the NIRA ('Closing the Gap') as worrying from the perspective of remote communities, for several reasons. First is the intention to incorporate those living in remote locations into mainstream education and training, and the market economy, 'encouraging' residents to move to larger communities 'where to-be-delivered education and job opportunities exist for an imagined gap-free future'. Second is the oversimplification of complex development issues as mere technical problems. Third is the locking in of resources to the detriment of those living in small communities who are in greatest need.

Altman has used the hybrid economy model to suggest some development alternatives for people living culturally and geographically beyond the mainstream. First, some mining companies have recently recognised the economic hybridity of Indigenous communities. Second, a grassroots 'caring for country' movement has seen the use of Indigenous and local knowledge in the paid provision of environmental services—for example, on lands at risk of species contraction and threats from feral animals, exotic weeds and pollution (see chapters in this volume by Concu, Dalley, Memmott and Stolte). The institution of Indigenous Protected Areas has facilitated the maintenance of hybrid economies and the commodification of culture. In sum, as Altman said, 'the politics of the hybrid economy project aims to empirically demonstrate sectoral overlaps and intersections that can be used by Indigenous interests to advance arguments for more equitable access to resources in the quest for substantive, not statistical equality'.

There is a need, Altman argued, to recognise customary and communal rights over resources on Aboriginal lands (and waters) in areas as diverse as climate change, the carbon economy, water rights, the arts industry and wildlife harvesting. The diversity of the hybrid economy is a less risky and more hopeful option than the imagined economic integration of remote-living Aboriginal people into the mainstream.

Several of the chapters in this volume take up the hybridity theme, particularly those in the third section, although not all focus on remote communities. The chapters begin with perspectives on Indigenous people in Australian economic history.

Economic Histories

In Chapter One, Christopher Lloyd takes up the challenge of the hybrid economy model, along with two other concepts applied in settler economic history: 'conquest' and 'production regimes'. Distinguishing between the hybrid economy model and the concept of hybridity more generally, Lloyd argues that hybridity needs to be part of a larger set of concepts if it is to carry the weight placed on it. It is a useful concept, but potentially overly general and misleading in its application. Not all examples of socioeconomic articulation, blending, merger and fusion are hybridisations. Moreover, generalising concepts of this kind need to be tempered by detailed descriptions of particular cases. A major difference between biological and social hybridity, he suggests, is that the former is of closely related species and subspecies, whereas the latter occurs between social forms of very different types. The essential point about social hybridity is that of combining elements from the 'parental' contributors in ways that produce new, emergent entities, processes and structures, and that these are viable—which is to say that they reproduce themselves through time. Hybrid forms are not simple articulations but have emergent properties.

The utility of the concept of hybridity, Lloyd argues, depends on its implicit or explicit relations to a field of other concepts including 'conquest', 'articulation', 'fusion' and 'agency'. Lloyd traces the importance of processes of conquest in colonial history, for conquest and transformation were common features of settler colonies. Hybridity might be seen as a survival strategy on the part of Indigenous peoples, for hybrid forms had to be developed if local autonomy was to be maintained to some degree.

Lloyd constructs a model of alternative historical pathways, from conquest or articulation to mestizoisation, hybridisation, creolisation and other outcomes. In the settler economies a variety of outcomes between settler and indigenous peoples resulted in the emergence of new production regimes of many kinds, and these were usually different from the 'mainstream' settler-capitalist economies. Indigenous-based hybrid production forms have to be understood, Lloyd argues, within larger capitalist production regimes—a concept with Marxian and Polanyian origins. The idea of a regional or national production regime points to the interconnections between the forms of production, each with its own particular structure. In the settler economies, there developed an increasing degree of systematic integration of local forms of production, resulting in the emergence of an integrated system of capitalist dominance by the early nineteenth century. The possibilities of non-capitalist and non-globalising forms and zones were increasingly closed off and the space for indigenous and other local autonomy began to disappear.

Lloyd examines two particular cases: Van Diemen's Land in the early nineteenth century, where Aboriginal people supplied kangaroo meat and hunting dogs to European bushrangers and shepherds who sold on these products to the state and the free market, and the case of the Bawinanga Aboriginal Corporation as analysed by Jon Altman. He goes on to address the overall conditions for hybrid economies in the light of ultra-modernism and globalisation. He concludes that the scope of societalisation through hybridity has greatly narrowed, and is perhaps closing. Social change will take place to an increasing degree through endogenous local processes of evolution within the global system. This conclusion has implications for the possibilities of hybrid economic solutions to development as envisaged by Jon Altman, and is taken up in the last section of this book. The next four chapters illustrate some of the conditions within which hybrid economic formations could develop or were inhibited on the Australian colonial frontier.

Chapter Two, written by John White, is set in colonial New South Wales and details the reactions of Yuin people to colonial incursions, intended or unintended. White argues that Yuin people incorporated settlers into their social relations by means of exchange. Drawing on Taussig's writing, he suggests that the fear of Aboriginal people beyond the frontier precipitated a 'culture of terror'. Rumour had it that Yuin were 'hostile savages' and indeed cannibals, so rationalising the violence inherent in settler society. In contrast with such rumours, on several occasions Yuin people came to the rescue of non-Indigenous survivors of shipwrecks between 1797 and 1841, and provided seafood to people at Broulee between shipments of supplies. White interprets the help given to survivors as an extension of Indigenous sociality—of obligations based on 'relatedness' (drawing on Myers' [1986] use of the term). It could be, however, that survivors rescued at Tuross were believed to be ghosts of the (Aboriginal) dead. Later episodes of so-called 'begging', when work and fish were scarce, are further evidence of the incorporation of settlers into Indigenous patters of mutual obligation and the extension of demand sharing. This particular experience of colonisation, White argues, was highly localised. His chapter is thus an account of hybrid economic relations in which Aboriginal people incorporated settlers into their own network of exchange and mutual obligation.

In Chapter Three, Anthony Redmond discusses the incorporation of aspects of settler society into traditional exchange relations. He addresses first the dichotomy drawn in twentieth-century anthropology between economic and ritual/cultural relations between Aboriginal groups and country, reflected in the *Aboriginal Land Rights (Northern Territory) Act* (1976). He links this dichotomisation to the distinction between 'ceremonial exchange' and barter or trade. The *wurnan* exchange network of the Kimberley involves both ritual and everyday objects including food and implements. This network links patrilineal clans and individuals in customary paths of exchange in which trade may be through trading partners or 'private' between individuals, and integrates trade with relations through initiation rituals and marriage exchange. Individual leaders control segments of the *wurnan* routes, which now incorporate clothing, vehicles and money. *Wurnan* has become a symbol of a continuing desire for autonomy in relation to the 'corporatisation' of Aboriginal political life, Redmond argues. A condition for this continuity, however, is the recognition of Indigenous rights to trade in the resources of native title claim areas by the courts. Rather than 'hybridity', this case illustrates the articulation of a traditional mode of exchange with the market economy.

Petronella Vaarzon-Morel's discussion of the mediating role of camels in the eastern Western Desert (Chapter Four) encompasses a lengthy time frame. These introduced animals played a pivotal role in the colonisation of the desert and in the development of the settler economy, Vaarzon-Morel argues. The use of camels by explorers, surveyors and prospectors among others was pivotal to colonial development in the region, due to their capacity to survive in the hot and arid environment, and they played a part in the incorporation of Indigenous people into the encapsulating society. The animals were in turn gradually incorporated into the domestic economy of the Pitjantjatjara people and their neighbours. Indigenous engagement with camels in the Australian desert changed over time, however, and was more varied and complex than has been recognised hitherto. The chapter covers Indigenous responses to camels in early encounters with Europeans, and during the transition to mission and pastoral stations, and then discusses engagement with the market for camels and camel products during the 1980s and 1990s. Vaarzon-Morel thus outlines a complex set of economic relations in which the customary sector intersected with a wide variety of market sectors and the state through its support of missions and stations, through the bounty for dingo scalps, and through more recent programs.

Alan O'Connor (Chapter Five) traces changes in the economy of Anangu people of the Ernabella region (Pitjantjatjara, Yangunytjatjara and Ngaanyatjarra languages); the Ernabella mission was established in 1937. Here, engagement in the trade for dingo scalps (enabled by the government bounty) was combined with hunting and gathering and work as shepherds. The commercial craft industry began in 1948, with Anangu women learning to adapt their own spinning techniques to wool, and learning to weave the yarn to make floor rugs and other items. Men worked as shepherds and in wool production, and made artefacts for sale. O'Connor states that 'in the early years of the mission, Anangu were moving between the customary and market economies with the mission authorities gradually assuming the roles of the state in areas such as education, health services and rations'. Indigenous, market and state/mission sectors came together at this time.

Some men were also employed off the mission on cattle stations and in mines, and fruit picking provided employment at least for a period in the late 1960s. There was also an internal mission economy, with men employed, for example, in gardening, construction and maintenance of infrastructure, the last underpinned by an industrial training school. The state was increasingly involved in the local economy from the 1970s following the incorporation of the Ernabella community; O'Connor reports limited employment for a growing population, however, and a decreased ability to rely on hunting and gathering for subsistence. Unemployment benefits and other transfer payments became available.

O'Connor reports the growth of a number of small businesses run by Anangu following the incorporation of Ernabella, and in the late 1970s a number of community employment programs were in place. Meanwhile the outstation movement began in the late 1970s, encouraged by policies introduced by the Whitlam Government, but now languishing due to lack of government support and service delivery. The state sector dominates the current economy, in O'Connor's view, and the market sector is very limited, although new enterprises around tourism, the recycling of vehicles and clothing as well as existing arts and crafts enterprises are under development. The next five chapters turn to the history of Indigenous labour in Australia, including the issue of stolen wages.

Labour History and Stolen Wages

The concept of a hybrid economy tends to be silent about the coercive relations involved in economic relationships in which the customary sector plays a major role. The theory of internal colonialism (Hartwig 1978) depicts as exploitative the relationship between, for example, the pastoral industry on the one hand, and, on the other, Indigenous people who partly met the costs of social reproduction of the labour force through hunting, gathering and fishing, who were paid in kind or with very low wages, and whose labour in effect subsidised the pastoral industry. From this point of view, at the extreme end of exploitation were Aborigines captured on the frontier and who became convict labourers. Resistance to invasion was classified as criminal because colonial authorities did not recognise the existence of a state of war on the Australian frontier.

The colony of New South Wales began, of course, as a penal colony, and, as Krystyn Harman points out in Chapter Six, it is generally overlooked that a small but significant proportion of convicts were Indigenous. The chapter begins with the recent perspective of the convict era as an integral part of Australian economic history rather than as 'an unsavoury aberration that preceded free settlement', in the words of Bob Hawke. Aboriginal convicts possessed few marketable skills, and, except for trackers, were usually relegated to the status of 'labourer', though with a wide range of occupations. The chapter examines in some detail the cases of Musquito and Bull Dog, who were involved in actions to repel the colonial incursions on the Hawkesbury River and shipped to Norfolk Island, and who were put to work as charcoal burners. Musquito was later assigned to settlers as their convict servant. Duall or Dewal was captured during the punitive expedition ordered by Governor Lachlan Macquarie in 1816 following conflict to the west of Sydney. He was repatriated to Cowpastures to work as a translator for an expedition to find a direct route to Bathurst. A similar process occurred in Victoria, where Harman traces the case of Yanem Goona, sent to Norfolk Island and then to the coalmine at Saltwater River. The aim from mid-century was to Christianise and civilise Aboriginal people, as well as to make examples of them.

Indigenous convicts were relatively few in number; far more common in Australia was the incorporation of Indigenous people into mission economies. Gwenda Baker (Chapter Seven) argues that Yolngu workers on Methodist missions in north-east Arnhem Land were not only vital to the development and survival of the missions, but also that over time 'they became an increasingly skilled, competent and reliable workforce'. By the end of the mission era, Indigenous participation in mission economies had led to an increase in the skill base (meaning skills outside the customary sector) among most workers, but they were 'to be a skilled labour force lost'. This skill base was lost after the end of the mission era in the early 1970s, she argues. Baker traces the history of the mission and township economies from the beginning of the north-east Arnhem Land mission in the 1920s through to the 1970s.

Yolngu leaders now see the period of transition at the end of the mission era as a 'government takeover', according to Baker, and Yolngu see the mission past as a joint enterprise between Yolngu and the Methodist (later Uniting Church) mission. Baker argues that Yolngu strove to develop working skills within the mission system. A large number of industries were closed, however, and the workforce drastically reduced with the creation of award wage positions at the end of the mission era (in the early to mid-1970s). The uptake of social service benefits made creating a new Indigenous economy more difficult. At the end of the mission era, when the councils became incorporated, fledgling industries faltered, proposals for Indigenous-run enterprises were rejected and the Aboriginal workforce shrank.

In Chapter Eight, Fiona Skyring addresses the introduction of equal wages for Aboriginal pastoral workers in the Kimberley region in 1968–69. This event has usually been interpreted (for example, by Bill Bunbury) as the main factor leading pastoral stations to lay off Aboriginal workers and to evict Aboriginal communities. Skyring shows, however, that the extension of award wages to Aboriginal workers was but one factor in a much more complex story. Other factors, including the introduction of helicopter mustering, led to the lay-off of Aboriginal workers. But there is more to the story than that. Stolen wages and pension moneys were crucial factors in the economic collapse in the Kimberley from the late 1960s, Skyring argues. The pastoral industry had benefited from what was in effect a tripartite subsidy. The first was cheap Aboriginal labour. The second was very low pastoral lease rents, and the third was the misappropriation of Commonwealth pension cheques intended for Aboriginal people. The end of these three modes of subsidy coincided, with devastating effects on the Kimberley economy.

This tripartite subsidy ended by the 1970s with the introduction of award wages and realistic lease rents. The effect was devastating, and the decline of the local economy affected Aboriginal people most, with the eviction of Aboriginal communities from stations and the creation of what Skyring terms 'refugee camps', coinciding with the right to consume alcohol. Aboriginal people had little money and food, and lived in abysmal conditions. Thus, it was not only the introduction of award wages that led to the evictions of Aboriginal workers, but also a more complex conjunction of circumstances.

Turning to Queensland, Ros Kidd (Chapter Nine) shows that each State government, and the Federal Government with regard to the Northern Territory from 1911, enacted legislation controlling Indigenous lives and labour, and put in place surveillance systems to force individuals to abide by them. If you were a person of Aboriginal descent, governments 'could dictate where and when you worked, the type and conditions of that work, what you might be paid and if you could spend it'. In Queensland until 1979 with respect to government settlements, Aboriginal and Torres Strait Islander legislation overrode industrial protections enjoyed by all other Australian workers. With the enactment of the *Aboriginals Protection and Restriction of the Sale of Opium Act* of 1897, what Ros

Kidd calls a 'system of enforced labour' was introduced into Queensland. The legislation was intended to protect Aboriginal people from abuses, but in doing so it granted the Government powers to control their lives. Kidd argues that the resulting settlements in Queensland were not closed institutions but were essential to the development of the State in providing pools of rural labour. The needs of rural industries were 'the prime motivator for the Aboriginal labour market'. By 1907 there were more than 3000 contracted Aboriginal workers across the State.

Kidd traces abuses both in conditions of work and in the control and appropriation of Indigenous wages. Not only were wages for Indigenous workers lower than those for white employees but also workers were systematically cheated out of a substantial proportion of those wages, Kidd argues. Successive governments appropriated moneys from trust funds, and Commonwealth child endowment paid to Aboriginal mothers after 1941 was also appropriated. The history of attempts to recover stolen wages is equally dismal in Kidd's account.

Andrew Gunstone (Chapter 10) relates a similar story for the State of Victoria in his review of Victorian Government legislation, regulations and inquiries relating to Indigenous wages and employment for the period of the Board for the Protection of Aborigines from 1869 to 1957. The *Aborigines Protection Act* of 1869 created the Board for the Protection of Aborigines (BPA), and established controls, including over employment and wages. Under 1871 regulations, the board and employers could negotiate contracts and the BPA could order wages to be paid to a third party such as a guardian. People on Coranderrk, for example, were paid only one-third of the going rate from 1874, and Aboriginal people at Lake Condah received only a nominal wage and were unable to obtain certificates to work off the reserves. Aboriginal people in private employment off the reserves, Gunstone shows, were often paid less than non-Indigenous workers. Gunstone reports an absence of accountability and poor financial administration of reserves, and indeed inadequate accountability of the BPA to the Victorian Parliament, and for many years it rarely convened. Abuses continued to occur in the era of the Aborigines Welfare Board and the Ministry for Aboriginal Affairs.

The six chapters of the third section of this volume examine a range of Indigenous enterprises, past and present. They provide examples of economic structures in remote and semi-remote areas, which have had some success in linking Indigenous skills and values to the market and to government funding. Several of these chapters describe development alternatives for those living culturally and geographically beyond the mainstream, as discussed by Jon Altman. The section begins with a focus on art and craft.

Indigenous Enterprises and Employment Schemes

Peter Thorley and Andy Greenslade (Chapter 11) trace the history of the Papunya art movement in the Western Desert. In the initial phase of desert art, the market was smaller and more restricted geographically than it is today; prices were low and there were few investors. Their main interest lies in how the paintings came into being, and the dynamics of their production in terms of interpersonal relationships—through what they call 'interpersonal histories'. The establishment and maintenance of valued relationships by means of which artists were able to exchange paintings for cash and other desired items were crucial. These relationships were investments, and were protected. Production has been a collective process involving providers of materials, the documentation of artists' stories and packaging for the market. The authors focus on one particular artist, Kaap Tjampitjinpa, and his relationship with Gwen and Owen Daniels, who were Papunya residents from 1976 to 1977. Gwen Daniels became a collector of Kaapa Tjampitjinpa's work as his broker and sponsor, provided space for him to paint, recorded stories and supplied materials during a lull in Papunya Tula activity. Thorley and Greenslade relate the importance to museum collections of documenting such relationships. One of the challenges for museums is the incorporation of a sense of the personal and interpersonal into their collections and exhibitions, they argue.

In Chapter 12, Maria Nugent provides a history of decorative shell-work produced by Indigenous women of La Perouse in Sydney, and situates her discussion within the context of the debate about the relationship between 'tourist art' and 'fine art'. Shell-work has no clear link to 'traditional' art practice and its aesthetic value has not been universally accepted, but the work has become collectible. Some of this work involved collaboration between shell-workers and art collectors or curators, and has been exhibited as urban Aboriginal art. Nugent argues that the 'new celebratory accounts about shell-work's development from tacky souvenir to art object' rely on 'staging a break between past and present'. The work no longer counts as souvenirs for tourist consumption, but as artworks worthy of collection and discussion. The break is not sustainable, Nugent argues, and she traces the development of markets for shell art to support this argument, demonstrating continuities between past and present. Aboriginal women have negotiated changes in taste and in markets, which have been diverse and ever changing, with subtle changes to their work. Art and craft production was thus a key to a degree of economic independence for Aboriginal families living on the fringes of Sydney.

Gretchen Stolte (Chapter 13) echoes Altman's critiques of the one-size-fits-all tendency in Federal Government policy—here in relation to Indigenous art centres, especially the tendency to seek a uniform model for such centres.

She does so by examining a section of the 2007 report of the Senate Standing Committee on Environment, Communications, Information Technology and the Arts, *Indigenous Art—Securing the future*. The committee investigated the size, sustainability and future needs and opportunities of the Indigenous visual arts and crafts sector. Stolte is particularly concerned with the 'one size fits all' model. Indigenous art centres, she suggests, go beyond being simple service providers; some have become 'the cultural hub' of a community, fostering the renewal and continuation of language, ceremonies and other traditions. Their roles have been defined in many ways, she argues, and they do more than engage in art production. Some art centres are run as commercial enterprises, while others have a development focus. A single business model is therefore inappropriate.

In particular, Stolte compares Papunya Tula Artists (PTA) with Maningrida Arts & Culture (MAC). The Senate Committee appears to have favoured PTA as a model, for its commercial success and 'aggressive and disciplined approach' to the market. This financial success, Stolte argues, is not readily reproduced elsewhere, for Papunya art has a unique history and is in high demand, and PTA sponsors a limited number of artists. To force MAC into the PTA model would reduce the number of people involved in the arts and compromise the reproduction of cultural knowledge. The search for a 'one size fits all' model is therefore misdirected.

In Chapter 14, Paul Memmott begins with the challenge for remote Indigenous communities to generate economies that are embraced by the Indigenous communities themselves, are grounded in Aboriginal culture and social capital, and that reconcile viable enterprise with the motivation to participate voluntarily. Such motivation, he argues, can arise from the demand for and provision of services, and he takes the Myuma Group based in western Queensland as a model. This is a group of three interlinked Aboriginal corporations established by Indjalandji-Dhidhanu people, and based in Camooweal and Mount Isa. Like Thorley and Greenslade, Memmott gives attention to the personal qualities and relations behind the enterprise—namely, the background of members of the Saltmere family who have been instrumental in setting up the Myuma Group. One might argue that the Myuma Group represents an example of a hybrid economic structure embedded in the wider economy, for it has been supported by government funding, engages in the market economy across northern Australia, provides support for the local Indigenous community, and the Myuma Group's practice, Memmott writes, is based on a strong commitment to Aboriginal law and culture. It is an intercultural organisation with both Indigenous and non-Indigenous people in senior positions—an important mix in negotiating in both Aboriginal and non-Aboriginal domains.

In her study of Indigenous environmental rangers at Mornington Island in the Gulf of Carpentaria, Cameo Dalley (Chapter 15) raises the question of how autonomous Indigenous culture can be in a context of intercultural relations. Rangers' perceptions of dugong management, she argues, do not always match those of the Federal Government through which they are employed. Dalley traces some of the changes the 'Working on Country' program has brought to the lives of the rangers and their families, especially through the more than doubling of the rangers' incomes from those available in the existing CDEP scheme. Major items of expenditure include four-wheel-drive vehicles, which are used to access remote parts of country and gather bush foods.

Rangers have been critical of local hunting practices, especially over-hunting for social status, using outboards and speedboats, and the failure to share meat along traditional lines. They have been constrained, however, by a desire not to infringe on the autonomy of hunters. The use of 'management speak' such as 'monitoring' has facilitated a stance against direct interference. At a communal level, there is some resistance to any government control of dugong hunting, with a desire to gain private funding for rangers, but Dalley sees the idea of total autonomy as unrealistic. She surmises, however, that were the Government to increase restrictions on hunting, the relationship of rangers to their community would change radically.

Moving to Arnhem Land, Nanni Concu (Chapter 16) examines in detail the working of the Payments for Environmental Services (PES) program in remote Australia—a scheme that is linked to Indigenous natural resource management (NRM) carried out by traditional owners and custodians and Indigenous land and sea management groups, and increasingly formalised through Indigenous Protection Areas (IPAs)—a program established in 1996 and based on voluntary agreements between the Commonwealth and traditional Aboriginal owners. Concu describes in particular the workings of two IPAs: those of Dhimurru in north-east Arnhem Land and Djelk in north-central Arnhem Land.

Concu argues that in remote areas job opportunities are limited, and economic participation of the kind envisaged by government would require relocation or increased mobility, potentially resulting in further economic disadvantage. The low agricultural potential in many parts of the Indigenous estate inhibits investment in the sector. Furthermore, Indigenous people often have distinct sets of incentives and cultural demands that preclude the direct transfer of non-Indigenous models of entrepreneurship and employment. PES schemes, Concu argues, provide an alternative form of Indigenous participation, based on the commercialisation of environmental goods and services and through government-supported NRM activities. By trading environmental goods and services through market exchange and public funding, Indigenous communities would be able to access financial resources for the creation of culturally appropriate NRM employment. As well as combating environmental degradation, the IPAs have economic, educational, social and health benefits for Indigenous communities, and their outcomes compare more than favourably with other NRM initiatives. Dhimurru Aboriginal Corporation and Djelk Rangers both have experience in PES schemes, and both manage important IPAs. His chapter outlines their structure and activities in detail.

Several factors have contributed to the success of the IPA program, Concu suggests, including the support of government funding and the role of Indigenous knowledge in guiding conservation. The IPA programs, however, need to be coordinated with other government programs and overarching policy frameworks. There are also limitations: there is a need for projects to fit Indigenous values and responsibilities, and modes of Indigenous governance; and there have been limitations in government policies.

The Introduction to the first volume concluded that the chapters contributed to the body of research and writing on the engagement of Indigenous people in the economy of the colonial era and through the twentieth and early twenty-first centuries, and expressed the hope that research and writing of the kind presented therein would foster a dialogue between the perspectives of economic history, ethnography and historical anthropology on Indigenous participation in Australian economies. Such dialogue was certainly fostered during the 2009 conference on which the present volume is based. This volume adds considerably to that body of research and writing, and links empirical studies both to theoretical frameworks and to pressing policy issues.

References

Altman, J. C. 2009. *Beyond closing the gap: valuing diversity in Indigenous Australia*. CAEPR Working Paper 54/2009, Centre for Aboriginal Economic Policy Research, Australian National University, Canberra.

Belich, J. 2001. *Paradise Reforged: A history of the New Zealanders from the 1880s to the year 2000*. Honolulu: University of Hawai'i Press.

Hartwig, M. C. 1978. Capitalism and Aborigines: the theory of internal colonialism and its rivals. In T. Wheelwright and K. Buckley (eds), *Essays in the Political Economy of Australian Capitalism*, pp. 119–41. Sydney: Australia and New Zealand Book Company.

Kraidy, M. W. 2005. *Hybridity, or the Cultural Logic of Globalization*. Philadelphia: Temple University Press.

Myers, F. 1986. *Pintupi Country, Pintupi Self: Sentiment, place and politics among Western Desert Aborigines.* Canberra: Australian Institute of Aboriginal Studies.

Rudd, K., 2008. Apology to Australia's Indigenous peoples, House of Representatives, Parliament House, Canberra. Speech as Prime Minister of Australia, Canberra, 13 February, <http://www.pm.gov.au/media/speech/2008/speech_0073.cfm>

1. Settler Economies and Indigenous Encounters: The dialectics of conquest, hybridisation and production regimes

Christopher Lloyd

Against Over-Generalisation: For description in social science history

The socioeconomic histories of settler societies with their conquests, impacts, articulations, fusions and hybridisations are a fraught field for research, with a wide range of conceptualisations and debates, and one with significant material effects in the present. Few areas of contemporary social science history have more direct social significance. History wars, governmental Indigenous policies, socio-anthropological research and political debates are all directly affected by conceptual/scientific and ideological debates. Furthermore, the literature on settler economic history, in contrast with that of social and cultural history, has been somewhat lagging in this conceptual debate.[1] This chapter is a discussion of the development, meaning, use and usefulness of the central but controversial concepts of 'conquest', 'hybridity' and 'production regimes' to the field of settler–Indigenous economic relations and their consequences. I argue we need all these concepts and several more and that the concept of 'hybridity' must be part of this bigger set of concepts—depending on how it is specified and used—if it is to carry the weight placed on it. In particular, it is argued here that the concept of 'hybridity'—now extensively used in cultural studies and especially post-colonial studies—is useful for this field but also potentially over-generalising and misleading in its application. The danger is, I argue, that the use of 'hybridity' could obscure as much as it illuminates if it is too generalised. Surely not all socioeconomic articulations, blendings, mergers or fusions are hybridisations. If they are then the concept loses specificity and power because of over-generalisation.

The problems of over-generalisation and reification bedevil the socio-historical sciences, especially those branches, such as economics and sociopolitical 'science', that rely overly on aggregated statistical data series (most of which are

1   The research for this chapter has been supported by Australian Research Council Linkage Grant LP0775392, in association with the National Museum of Australia. I thank Jon Altman for comments on an earlier draft.

compiled by official agencies and via processes devoid of real research), flawed statistical techniques (devastatingly criticised in Ziliak and McCloskey 2008), and very general concepts that are used as substitutes for detailed examination of cases. The aggregating socio-historical sciences pay far too little attention to the empirical 'field' research that is necessary to description and understanding. On the other hand, those branches of socio-historical research, particularly history and sometimes cultural studies, that concentrate only or mainly on description and make insufficient generalisations based on quantitative data, comparison and general concepts are not able to provide adequate analyses. One essential task, then, is to combine general concepts, such as 'hybridity' and 'production regimes', with detailed descriptions of particular cases. As W. G. Runciman argued and demonstrated persuasively in his *Treatise on Social Theory*, description is a fundamental task of social science. How descriptions are generated and framed is essentially via the formulation and use of ideal typical concepts whose meaning is fixed by being

> intelligible by reference both to what 'their' experience is like to themselves and to the analogous experience of others to which it is being likened. It can however, equally well be done from either end. It can be formulated either as a hypothetical set of circumstances, or form of behaviour, or mode of attitude or feeling from which an adjectival concept is then derived, or as an adjectival concept implying an extreme instantiation which would be applicable if, and only if, a hypothetical state of affairs, etc. were to be observed. (Runciman 1983:291)

The descriptive ideal type must be such that while being ideal, it contains nothing impossible in the sense of being simply an explanatory abstraction but rather is a general-limit case of what actually is possible. 'Hybridity' should be used in such a manner—as a descriptive generalisation that aids in describing and understanding the nature or characteristics of a particular real social form. An explanatory abstraction, on the other hand, such as 'production regime', is a concept that is used to explain the causal processes of particular cases.

The General Meaning of Hybridity

The original use of the concept of 'hybridity'—a word of ancient Latin origin— as developed in the genetics of animal and plant breeding and the biological sciences more widely, refers generally to the mixing or blending of organisms through interbreeding to produce new, sometimes very vigorous, organisms. But in some cases one consequence of such selective breeding is infertility— that is, the inability of the new, artificially created organism to reproduce itself, often because of slightly incompatible chromosomal structures of the parents.

This is often the case with hybrid crop species and sometimes with interspecies breeding among closely related animals such as horses and donkeys, lions and tigers, goats and sheep. On the other hand, hybrid breeding within animal species, such as cattle, does not usually result in infertility because the breeding is only to select certain characteristics of alleles through crossbreeding and even through a degree of deliberately incestuous selective breeding. It is also important to know that hybridity is a naturally occurring phenomenon in the plant kingdom, especially at species boundaries and among members of a genus. In this case, the resulting plant species are not able to reproduce through sexual processes but simply by spreading through rhizomes so that all the supposedly different organisms in a specific area are actually the same organism.

A specific form of hybrid is a chimera, which is the transgenic result of the genes of one organism or species, such as a bacterium, being transposed into the germ line of another, such as a plant, which produces a specific genetic innovation, which, in artificial breeding, has a desirable effect on that organism's survivability or behaviour.

The transfer of 'hybridity' into the social sciences—a sort of hybridisation of research concepts in a sense—has been influential but controversial. The concept of 'hybridity' is now widely and centrally employed in the broad field that includes Indigenous studies, post-colonial studies, diaspora studies and settler-society studies. Use is also made in literary studies, management theory, economic theory, geographical theory, technological theory, car technologies, robotics and, most strikingly, in conceptualisations of human–technological convergence through the development of cyborgs. In all these areas it seems the basic assumption—often without much conceptual explication—is that the mixing or blending of types, genres, structures, logics or processes results in something that is not just novel but also has emergent properties and even existential vigour that surpasses the parents. Of course, strictly speaking, many of the entities described as 'hybrids' do not actually fit the specific definition, being rather syncretics, such as cyborgs, rather than true hybrids.

A fundamental difference between biological and social hybridity is in the degree of difference in the nature of the 'parent' entities. Biological hybridity is of closely related species and subspecies. Social hybridity, on the other hand, occurs between very different social forms. This is crucial to the concept. Articulations and fusions of closely related social forms do not usually result in hybridity but simply fusions or mergers. Hybridity often has the connotation of partial overlap for specific purposes between very different social forms while much of the 'parent' formations remains apart from the hybridised area of activity and the distinct contributions by the parents can be identified, at least while it remains a hybrid activity or form. That of course raises the key issues of stability and the persistence of hybrids. Are they relatively stable structures or dynamic and perhaps unstable transitional forms?

Therefore, the key implicit ideas in all these areas of the social sciences that claim to be dealing with hybridity are about 'adaptation', 'viability', 'emergence' and even 'dialectic'. Hybridity is taken to be a state or outcome of mixing and blending of hitherto distinct and often very different entities and structures that combine elements from the parental contributors in ways that produce sometimes surprising or divergent but certainly viable new entities, processes and structures. Viability is essential to the concept and description of cases, for without it the new entities and structures would obviously not exist. This is not simply a tautology, for viability carries the idea of continuous existence and some degree of autonomous power through time. A hybrid outcome becomes a new practice or structure and so takes on a life of its own with a degree of autonomy in the sense of enabling human agency and structural reproduction. Hybrid outcomes are not simply syncretic entities or systems that simply cobble together features of the parents, like famous mythical chimeras such as centaurs, mermaids and minotaurs. Furthermore, hybrids are not simply articulations, which are usually exchange relationships through which more or less independent societies enter relations of greater or lesser co-dependence. Such articulations might lead to hybridisations but not necessarily, at least in the short run (cf. Austin-Broos 2003).

Thus, for a genuine hybrid to come into being there must be emergent properties that arise from but are not reducible to particular characteristics of the parents. Hybrids are indeed real things with properties and powers of their own, which have to be described in their own particularities. Sooner or later, we can surmise, most hybrids cease to be such and become simply new, integral formations, cultures or production regimes. This, we can say, is one of the fundamental logics of socioeconomic history in the sense of the evolutionary process of societalisation in the very long run.

Two further general issues about hybridity need to be raised: degeneracy and the possibly metaphorical nature of the concept. Natural plant hybrids could be viewed as degenerates in the sense that the new species has lost its power of sexual reproduction. On the other hand, this can be seen as a viable evolutionary strategy. Of course, judgments of 'degeneracy' are unwarranted in biology for that idea implies a natural teleology, which is a false step. The idea of progress has bedevilled biology and should also be avoided in the social sciences, especially if it springs from a pernicious teleology. 'Degeneracy' in social science has roots in racism and manifest destiny. The essential point about hybridity is its adaptiveness and agency. These are not metaphorical ideas. 'Hybridity' and its associated concepts are descriptive-analytical in force and seem to be necessary to social explanation.

Conquest, Articulation, Fusion, Survival, Agency

The usefulness and power of 'hybridity' in social description and explanation depend, then, I argue, on its implicit or explicit integral connection with other key concepts or ideas, especially 'conquest', 'articulation', 'fusion', 'survival' and 'agency'.

Conquest has been a fundamental force of human history ever since the relation of objective property emerged from what Marx called the 'historic process' of production, which led to the separation of the primordially unified inorganic conditions of human existence from the active being of humanity. The original form of communal human sociality was a natural (that is, not historical) presupposition of existence (Marx 1986:411–13). But ever since the advent of pastoral and agricultural societies and therefore of social classes, human societal evolution has been driven to a significant degree by collective violence over the conditions of production. Large-scale resource competition, class divisions and conflict led to imperialism and the near universality of slavery. Conquests of land, people and cultures and the resulting destruction, massacres, fusions and hybridisations have been long-running themes of millennia throughout the world. The history of English social structure, language, culture and governance from even earlier than the Roman conquest is a good example of this process. Conquests can have many outcomes, from complete annihilation of peoples and cultures to absorptions and fusions (such as has occurred many times in England), including mestizoisations, hybridisations and accommodations that permit relative autonomy of the conquered. All of these processes occur over extended time scales. In every case, key questions concern the specific contexts and processes that lead to specific outcomes and the degree of autonomy and agency of subordinated peoples. In all outcomes from conquest there is, of course, a hierarchy of dominance and subjection.

The imperial conquest, settlement and local historical processes of what became the settler, creole and mestizo societies of the European empires from the early sixteenth century onwards (to say nothing about Asian and African empires in medieval and early modern times) produced many varied social outcomes by the twentieth century. Not all indigenous peoples of the settler world were either exterminated or enslaved, but many who were not were at least marginalised, especially in the sparsely populated temperate zones that became settler societies. Settler–indigenous conflict and outcomes evolved in many ways; nevertheless, the facts of conquest and transformation were shared by all.

Perhaps hybridisation can best be understood as a strategy—an agential strategy of survival and adaptation and even progress in response to processes of collision, conquest and domination. Thus, key questions are of self-activation, domination, subjectivity and universal logic of cultural and economic adaptation and survival. Is hybridity perhaps often the only possible strategy for cultural and social survival under imperialism and globalisation? This is probably so, for the power of imperial/global forces is such that the whole world is now enmeshed into a single economic system and the hegemony of 'global culture' is very strong. The logic of a global world is the logic of universality and sameness. Hybrid forms have to be developed if local autonomy is to be maintained to some degree. This applies to all societies, not just indigenous ones.

Is the concept of 'hybridity' too general in its application? If the development of hybrid socio-cultural-economic formations is a phenomenon of such universality, its application to a particular case might not tell us much about it beyond a truistic description. Hybridisation, it can be argued, is a universal consequence of societal evolution because the evolutionary process of societalisation in the long run has always resulted in hybridisation through the conquest or merger of societies (what can collectively be described as social collisions). Unlike the evolution of species, which is a one-way process of separation that cannot be reversed once the process has resulted in new species, the evolution of societies through both evolutionary drift and societalisation is sometimes 'reversible' in the sense of reversion leading to something like the previous state and, moreover, societies can merge (often through conquest) to form new societies that incorporate features and components of the previous separate formations. These merged forms are often described as hybridisations, which is a particular form of merger that preserves essential features of the previous forms. In other words, the issue is not whether hybrid formations emerge from social collisions, which they often do, it is to do with the forms and features of the merged outcomes.

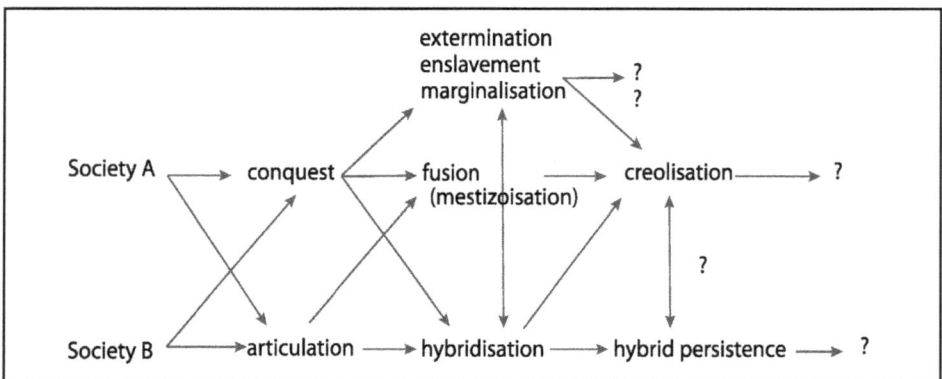

Figure 1.1 Conceptual matrix of conquest and articulation

From Settler Production Regimes to Globalisation

Kraidy (2005) has described hybridisation as 'the cultural logic of globalization'. Can we extend this idea to say that hybridisation is a (not 'the') logic of the economic history of all settler–indigenous relations within settler societies, at least, and perhaps within all economies undergoing globalisation? If globalisation is the process of global integration such that local differences and local autonomies become hybridised or fused then indigenous communities and peoples and other marginalised groups and regions might have little choice about their futures. Resisting globalisation today is as difficult as resisting settler invasions in earlier times.[2]

In the neo-European settler domains[3] from the eighteenth century onwards, various outcomes between settlers and indigenous people were experienced that resulted in the emergence of new production regimes involving the articulation of settlers and indigenous people. These articulations were usually quite distinct from the dominant relations of production between land, capital and wage labour in the 'mainstream' settler-capitalist economies. Indigenous people were at best marginalised by the conquest of their lands in 'the great land rush' (Weaver 2003), and out of their marginalised state certain hybrid forms sometimes emerged. Numerous cases of what can be described as creole and hybrid economic and cultural processes can be identified in the historical and contemporary literature on North America, southern South America and Australasia.

Settler societies have certain special characteristics that have set them apart over the past couple of centuries (cf. Belich 2009; Denoon 1983; Lloyd and Metzer 2012; Weaver 2003). A fundamental characteristic has been and is still the settler–indigenous relationship, which is quite different from other intercultural and interracial relationships in other forms of colonial and post-colonial society of the modern European imperial age.[4] This characteristic, which resulted from

---

2 Indigeneity is not just a phenomenon of settler societies. First peoples still exist as hybridised societies within many European, Asian, Middle Eastern and African states.
3 These regions in the temperate zones—mainly in the Americas, Australasia and Southern Africa—are distinguished by their particular interconnection of land, capital and labour of an emergent and then developed capitalist kind by the mid-nineteenth century. They contrast with tropical colonial zones where coerced plantation labour was the dominant form and colonial zones where indigenous peasantries remained the dominant economic form. In settler societies, the settler-capitalist form became dominant with strong articulation to the world market via large flows of capital, free labour and commodities. Here indigenous people were initially marginalised or even exterminated (cf. Belich 2009; Denoon 1983; Lloyd 2012; Lloyd and Metzer 2012).
4 The relatively sharply defined ethnic distinction between the descendants of settlers (or immigrants) and indigenous people that we find today in the United States, Canada, Argentina, Australia, New Zealand and Israel is not found in other parts of Latin America where mestizoisation has been the norm. But it could be the case that the degree of mestizoisation is greater in the United States, Canada and Australia than is generally recognised. An interesting case is Chile, a typical settler society in many respects, in which the majority of people are now of mixed settler–indigenous lineage but only a minority self-identifies as indigenous.

the dispossession of indigenous people and the expropriation of most of their lands, has been the foundation of a distinct capitalist production system within the capitalist world economy. In tropical plantation colonies until the late nineteenth century, the labour supply system was typically one of full coercion of imported slaves, such as in the Caribbean/Gulf of Mexico and northern Brazilian regions, or enslaved indigenous people, such as in the Andean region, or semi-coerced, indentured labour systems as in the Pacific and Indian oceans regions. In the settler societies, indigenous peoples who survived were usually highly marginalised, surviving on remnant reserved lands and attempting to maintain traditional ways of life. The majority was not proletarianised. As the twentieth century progressed, they became increasingly state dependent. Reassertion of traditional rights and development of hybrid production became a global movement in the late twentieth century.

'Production regime' is a useful concept with Marxian and Polanyian ancestry that refers to the complex formation of a whole society's economic and regulatory structure and processes, particularly its labour control, management and technological subsystems, and how these all interconnect. A production regime has several levels of complexity and integration, including various economic sectors, industries and regions, and state regulatory systems. The whole is integrated and regulated by state and private formal control, by physical infrastructure, as well as by substantive social processes (cf. Lloyd 2002, for more detail on regulatory regimes of political economy).

The idea of a regional or national 'production regime' is of the interconnections between the various forms of production, each of which has a substructure of technical, organisational, social and cultural arrangements that is necessary for the production and distribution of the means of material life and of commodities. In turn, each form of production is connected to a series of other forms of production in some sort of cluster or hierarchy, which together constitute a whole regional, national and even global system of economic interdependence. Capital, labour, materials, commodities, ideas and even institutional forms flow within and between them. Each form of production has its own structure, dynamic and trajectory. But within the whole regional or national economy, as regions and nations grew in strength and integration over recent centuries, there developed an increasing degree of systemic integration of local forms of production so that an integrated system of capitalist dominance emerged by the early nineteenth century within settler societies, predicated strongly on a world market. These zones and new colonial and nation-states became very intermeshed into the world commodity, capital and labour flow systems. The possibilities of non-capitalist and non-globalising forms and zones within these societies were increasingly closed off as the nineteenth and twentieth centuries wore on. The space for indigenous and other local autonomy began to disappear. It seems there were only three possibilities left for most peoples by the mid-twentieth century: complete absorption into the dominant society and culture, albeit in an impoverished and marginal way; some form of creolisation in marginal areas; and hybridisation. All these forms can be found within settler societies today.

Indigenous-based hybrid production forms have to be understood, then, as subordinate and dependent modes within larger capitalist production regimes. Rapidly changing capitalism and the world market determine the possibilities. Nevertheless, socio-cultural and economic hybridisations by indigenous people have to be understood as strategies for adaptation, survival and agency. The impetus must spring largely from the needs and aspirations of indigenous peoples, for the globalised capitalist context in which they must move contains no such imperative.[5]

Hybridity in Australian Indigenous Contexts: Two descriptions re-examined

The use of 'hybridity' to describe and analyse Australian Indigenous social situations and processes has been fruitful and we can say that a research-based policy program has now emerged, centred on Jon Altman's and others' works.[6] There have also been other instances of settler–Aboriginal accommodations that we can perhaps redescribe as cases of hybridity (cf. Lloyd 2010b). Of the latter kind, one in particular stands out as worthy of re-examination in this mode: James Boyce's *Van Diemen's Land* (2009). In the light of the foregoing discussion, we can make some constructive commentary about Boyce's historical account and also Altman's research and policy program.

The story described in Boyce's *Van Diemen's Land* (2009) was of an emergent frontier and unofficial 'occupation' of areas beyond the narrow confines of state-directed settlement in the early decades of Van Diemen's Land history. A kangaroo and dog economy emerged from about 1808 in the grasslands and woodlands of the Midlands region. Boyce describes an overlapping and technologically convergent economy of convicts and bushrangers, on the one hand, and Aborigines on the other. By 1813, cattle and sheep grazing began to replace kangaroo hunting as the main source of meat for the rapidly growing colony. By 1820 an export trade in meat and even limited numbers of livestock was flourishing. The livestock-owning and management system was largely one of free-ranging stock proprietors or share farmers herding their own animals on

---

5   This seems to be the contention of Noel Pearson in his recent writings (Pearson 2009).
6   See Altman (especially 2005a, 2005b, 2005c, 2007).

extensive and rich grazing lands (Boyce 2009:68–72). Before the early 1820s, the power of the local state authorities was very weak or even non-existent in the frontier pastoral areas that were effectively controlled by bushranging gangs and Aboriginal clans. While it seems from Boyce's work that there was ongoing but limited miscegenation and violence between Europeans and Aborigines, in the period after 1808 there was an emergent structure of commercial interactions between four groups—bushrangers and convicts (sometimes indistinguishable), Aborigines, the emergent stock-owning capitalist elite, and the state—that could be described as hybridity. The hybridity seems to have existed essentially at the intersection of the Aboriginal system of supplying kangaroo products and later hunting dogs and the European bushrangers and shepherds who were interested in on-selling these products to the state and to the free market. These Aboriginal people became, we could hypothesise at least, hybridised in their economic relationship with the European colony in these early decades of settlement, and it seems a rough modus vivendi existed on the frontier of what is now eastern and Midlands Tasmania.

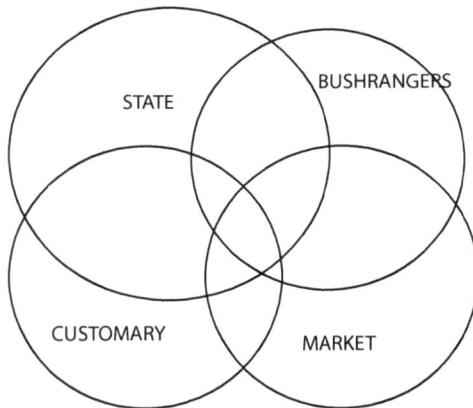

Figure 1.2 The production system of Van Diemen's Land (inspired by Altman and Boyce)

The hypothesised hybrid production regime of early Van Diemen's Land—supplying kangaroo products and dogs—existed within and was made possible by the nature of the parent societies. Clearly, the European society had commodities that Aboriginal people came to desire—tools, blankets, other cloth and dogs—and the Aboriginal people had access to large quantities of game to supply the new colony with food. The establishment of a state market for kangaroo meat opened this possibility and Aboriginal people soon came to see the 'technological' benefit of dogs for hunting—which were hitherto absent in Tasmania, unlike mainland Australia—and quickly adopted this means and also began breeding dogs for sale. Dogs were essential for large-scale hunting since firearms were relatively primitive and not in good supply.

Nevertheless, the essential nature of Tasmanian Aboriginal society, while obviously strongly impacted at this boundary with the European world, remained a foraging, subsistence production system until the growing settler colony began to assert its power into wider areas of the island and the state moved to seize the full potential of the land resource. Then Aboriginal people were completely marginalised or massacred and survived only as a mestizo population. There is scant evidence of proletarianisation of the original population.

Thus, some Aboriginal people were able to adapt for a period to the powerful presence of European groups and their production system by, in effect, innovating a hybrid form of production based on exchange. This hybrid form developed and evolved for about 15 years until swept away from the mid-1820s by the Tasmanian settler state and its capitalist coalitionists. This story has similarities with cases of hybrid production on the grasslands and in the forests of North America and Argentina[7] in the eighteenth and early to mid-nineteenth centuries.

Jon Altman has done much to describe cases of hybridity within contemporary 'remote' Australia. His description of the Bawinanga Aboriginal Corporation (BAC), for example, and its Indigenous context in central Arnhem Land, is a case of the intersection of customary, market and state sectors in which the customary zone of economic activity is adapted in part to the demands of market and state.

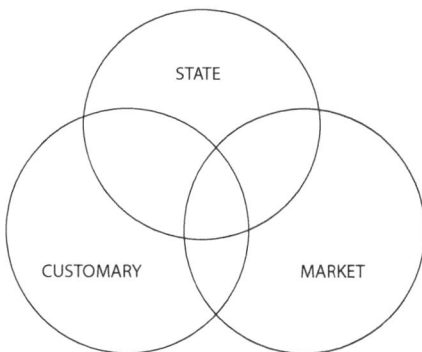

Figure 1.3 Altman's Venn diagram of hybridity[8]

---

7 The Argentine case of frontier cattle hunting is particularly striking, in which a large-scale trade developed on the basis of vast herds of feral cattle on the pampas that became the chief resource of indigenous and mestizo groups. The militarisation of the frontier through the competition for this rich resource and later the settler conquests of indigenous lands played a crucial role in Argentine nation building, politics and civil wars until the present. The indigenous inhabitants of Argentina were decimated by settler conquests and today they are largely marginalised and impoverished, representing less than 1 per cent of the total population.
8 The most recent articulation of the construct is in Altman (2010).

Altman provides an ideal-typical description of the three-sector intersection of state, market and customary domains, as in Figure 1.3. A static description of such a regime would concentrate on the areas of intersection, why and how they came about, and how they operate and are regulated.

While there is in reality no 'pure' market, state or customary sector in such contexts as these two cases, each of the segments contains, at least in theory, a partially distinct form of activity with varying combinations of customary, state and market-based determination. The point of the idealisation is to focus attention on the central issues about such hybrid production forms, as indicated previously, which are their agential and dynamic characters: to what extent were/are Indigenous people able to innovate, develop and remain in control of these articulations in a context of powerful external forces; and are they more or less stable forms or rapidly changing transitional forms? The historical record varies, of course, but the roles of the state and the market in settler societies are obviously crucial. In the case of the BAC, Altman shows that there have been vicissitudes in its prosperity and capacity but it has shown resilience over recent decades and the future outlook seems positive (Altman 2005b).

We have to be fully cognisant of a fundamental fact about all modern societies generally and especially settler societies from the eighteenth century onwards, which is that these are very dynamic and fluid, rapidly evolving capitalist societies with a powerful impetus to proletarianisation and economic development on the basis of the world market. The roles of traditional and local (non-capitalist or quasi-capitalist peasant-based) socioeconomic structures were essentially non-existent within the settler domains, once they became established as such from the eighteenth century, unlike in either their European or their indigenous backgrounds. Settler processes were land-grab 'clearances' and rapaciously profitable resource-extraction economies. The capacity of indigenous resistance in a socioeconomic sense was very limited and insofar as it happened it was only in 'remote' and 'difficult' regions that were less desirable to capitalist metropolitan interests.

On the Dialectic of Historical Evolution in Settler Societies: From description to explanation?

What we have with Boyce's and Altman's accounts are perceptive descriptions of Indigenous hybrid agency in the face of enormous difficulty in 'hard places' (Pearson's 2009 term). But 'hard places' do not always remain 'hard', as the rapid penetration of pastoral capitalism into the Van Diemen's Land Midlands showed and as the development of tourism in the Central Australian desert shows. While hybridity might be the only viable response by Pearson's 'serious'

Aboriginal people to the bad choices that confront them in remote areas, in other areas—older country towns, new mining towns and inner suburbs—where marginalisation rules, the hybridisation possibility is no longer open. Other responses and outcomes are occurring.

In the particular case of hybrid forms, our theoretical approach must be able to reveal the dynamics of the shifting boundaries between the three sectors and the actual or likely outcome of a severe erosion or collapse between the boundaries with the decline or disappearance of the customary sector in many cases. Once severely eroded, is the customary sector able to be reactivated sufficiently in order to form the cornerstone of a new hybridity? Without a vibrant customary sector, such a production form is not possible, of course. The possibility and strength of customary activity depend on many local factors. In the BAC case that Altman discusses, it seems that its capacity to remain viable and strongly supported by its inhabitants is in fact somewhat tenuous. He identifies several corrosive factors or potentials. And even if it does thrive it is perhaps the exception that helps to prove the rule of customary erosion throughout remote Australia to the extent that viable hybrid forms might no longer be able to be reactivated in many locales. On the other hand, the strength of some particular market-focused activity in some contexts, such as the Central Australian Indigenous art movement, could provide (and perhaps is providing) the necessary foundation for the survival and even revival of the customary sector in some places.[9] But as Marx said long ago, trade and capital are solvents that erode all non-capitalist forms that enter into the orbit of capital. The power of the income and thence capital flowing from the art movement and from mining royalties has a significant impact on Australian Indigenous communities.

Beyond description, then, we must have theory in all areas of social science. The most fundamental aspect of theory is about the forces of social change or historicity. At its most abstract is the theory of dynamics and evolution of all social forms; the constancy of fundamental and rapid social change, and the often bewildering experience of it, is the central reality of ultra-modernity today. Can any socio-cultural-economic form—especially Indigenous, local, regional forms—remain integral and resistant to these forces? The long-run process of social change and transformation or, to put it another way, the history of societalisation, is a history of social evolution via complex processes of reproduction, divergence, adaptation, collapse, conquest, hybridisation and fusion. Indigenous people are necessarily no more or less subject to these forces than any other communities. The issues are about the degree and capacity of individual and collective agency and how those can be sustained and developed under the difficult circumstances of global capitalism.

---

9   As Jon Altman has pointed out recently: 'The indigenous visual arts sector in remote Australia is probably the best documented exemplar of intercultural production in the hybrid economy…The production and marketing of art sits squarely in the intersection of customary, state and market sectors' (Altman 2010).

All of the adaptations, collapses, conquests, hybridisations and fusions of history have produced the evolutionary tree of societalisation. But there is a marked contrast between biological and social evolution: the first is through genetic drift due to mutation combined with the separation of alleles so that they diverge over millions of years; the second is through the dialectical processes of transformation through imperfect social reproduction leading variously to supersession, separation, conquest, hybridisation and fusion. In the modern world, separations become impossible, so the scope of societalisation via hybridity has greatly narrowed and is perhaps closing. Henceforth societalisation as the world has known it for millennia might no longer be possible. This is a momentous consequence of capitalist globalisation. This does not mean that rapid social change will not occur but it has to be via endogenous local processes of evolution within the global system.

The dialectics of the global system of ultra-modernity, with its massive interconnectedness, its powerful systems and hierarchies of self-understanding, education and knowledge, and its growing devolution and even collapse of agency downwards from the interstate system, are such that transformations and supersessions become increasingly processes of local collective agency and design. In this context, the meaning of indigeneity changes and new alliances between groups can be constructed on the basis of the creation of new local institutions and new local practices. That they will be hybrids of the old customary-based kind seems doubtful but the future is always largely unknown.

References

Altman, J. 2004. Economic development and Indigenous Australia: contestations over property, institutions, and ideology. *The Australian Journal of Aboriginal and Resource Economics* 48 (3): 513–34.

Altman, J. 2005a. Development options on Aboriginal land: sustainable Indigenous hybrid economies in the twenty-first century. In L. Taylor, G. K. Ward, G. Henderson, R. Davis and L. A. Wallis (eds), *The Power of Knowledge*. Canberra: Aboriginal Studies Press.

Altman, J. 2005b. Economic futures on Aboriginal land in remote and very remote Australia: hybrid economies and joint ventures. In D. Austin-Broos and G. Macdonald (eds), *Culture, Economy and Governance in Aboriginal Australia*. Sydney: University of Sydney Press.

Altman, J. 2005c. *The Indigenous hybrid economy: a realistic sustainable option for remote communities?* Paper, 26 October, Australian Fabian Society, Melbourne.

Altman, J. 2007. Alleviating poverty in remote Indigenous Australia: the role of the hybrid economy. *Development Bulletin* (72).

Altman, J. 2009. *Beyond closing the gap: valuing diversity in Indigenous Australia.* CAEPR Working Paper No. 54/2009, Centre for Aboriginal Economic Policy Research, Australian National University, Canberra.

Altman, J. 2010. What future for remote Indigenous Australia? Economic hybridity and the neoliberal turn. In M. Hinkson and J. Altman (eds), *Culture Crisis: Anthropology and politics in Aboriginal Australia.* Sydney: UNSW Press.

Altman, J., Buchanan, G. and Biddle, N. 2006. The real 'real' economy in remote Australia. In B. H. Hunter (ed.), *Assessing the Evidence onIndigenous Socioeconomic Outcomes: A focus on the 2002 NATSISS.* CAEPR Research Monograph 26. Canberra: ANU E Press.

Austin-Broos, D. 2003. Places, practices, and things: the articulation of Arrernte kinship with welfare and work. *American Ethnologist* 30 (1): 118–35.

Belich, J. 2009. *Replenishing the Earth: The settler revolution and the rise of the Anglo-world, 1783–1939.* Oxford: Oxford University Press.

Blaser, M., Feit, H. A. and McRae, G. (eds) 2004. *In the Way of Development: Indigenous peoples, life projects and globalization.* London: Zed Books.

Boyce, J. 2009. *Van Diemen's Land.* Melbourne: Black Inc.

Denoon, D. 1983. *Settler Capitalism: The dynamics of dependent development in the southern hemisphere.* Oxford: Oxford University Press.

Howitt, R., Connell, J. and Hirsch, P. (eds) 1996. *Resources, Nations, and Indigenous Peoples.* Melbourne: Oxford University Press.

Jentoft, S., Minde, H. and Nilsen, R. (eds) 2003. *Indigenous Peoples: Resource management and global rights.* Delft: Eburon.

Kapchan, D. A. and Strong, P. T. 1999. Theorizing the hybrid. *Journal of American Folklore* 122 (445): 239–53.

Kraidy, M. K. 2005. *Hybridity, or the Cultural Logic of Globalization.* Philadelphia: Temple University Press.

Levitus, R. 2009. Aboriginal organisations and development: the structural context. In J. Altman and D. Martin (eds), *Power, Culture, Economy: Indigenous Australians and mining.* Canberra: ANU E Press.

Lloyd, C. 2002. Regime change in Australian capitalism: towards a historical political economy of regulation. *Australian Economic History Review* 42 (3): 238–66.

Lloyd, C. 2010a. The coming of the Anglo-world; a critical appreciation of Belich's 'Replenishing the Earth'. *New Zealand Journal of History* 44 (1).

Lloyd, C. 2010b. The emergence of Australian settler capitalism in the nineteenth century and the disintegration/integration of Aboriginal societies: hybridisation and local evolution within the world market. In I. Keen (ed.), *Indigenous Participation in Australian Economies: Historical and anthropological perspectives.* Canberra: ANU E Press.

Lloyd, C. 2012. Institutional patterns of the settler societies: hybrid, parallel, and convergent. In C. Lloyd, J. Metzer and R. Sutch (eds), *Settler Economies in World History.* Leiden: Brill.

Lloyd, C. and Metzer, J. 2012. Settler colonization and societies in world history: patterns and concepts. In C. Lloyd, J. Metzer and R. Sutch (eds), *Settler Economies in World History.* Leiden: Brill.

Lulka, D. 2009. The residual humanism of hybridity: retaining a sense of the earth. *Transactions of the Institute of British Geographers* [NS] (34): 378–93.

Marx, K. 1986. Outline of the Critique of Political Economy (Rough Draft of 1857–58). In K. Marx and F. Engels, *Collected Works. Volume 28.* London: Lawrence and Wishart.

Moran, A. 2005. White Australia, settler nationalism and Aboriginal assimilation. *Australian Journal of Politics and History* 51 (2): 168–93.

Nairn, T. 2009. Hybridity, not district 10. *open Democracy*, 10 September 2009, <http://www.opendemocracy.net/>

Nederveen Pieterse, J. 1998. Hybrid modernities: mélange modernities in Asia. *Sociological Analysis* 1 (3): 75–86.

Nederveen Pieterse, J. 2001. Hybridity: so what? *Theory, Culture and Society* 18 (2–3): 219–45.

Pearson, N. 2009. *Radical Hope: Education and equality in Australia.* Quarterly Essay 35. Melbourne: Black Inc.

Peers, D. M. 2007. Gunpowder empires and the garrison state: modernity, hybridity, and the political economy of colonial India, circa 1750–1860. *Comparative Studies of South Asia, Africa and the Middle East* 27 (2): 245–58.

Rock, D. 1985. *Argentina: From Spanish colonization to the Falklands War*. Berkeley: University of California Press.

Runciman, W. G. 1983. *A Treatise on Social Theory.Volume I: The methodology of social theory*. Cambridge: Cambridge University Press.

Salomons, C. 2006. Hybrid historiography: pre- and post-conquest Latin America and perceptions of the past. *Past Imperfect* 12: 1–33.

Stewart-Harawira, M. 2005. *The New Imperial Order: Indigenous responses to globalization*. London: Zed Books.

Stross, B. 1999. The hybrid metaphor: from biology to culture. *Journal of American Folklore* 122 (445): 254–67.

Weaver, J. 2003. *The Great Land Rush and the Making of the Modern World, 1650–1900*. Montreal: McGill–Queen's University Press.

Whatmore, S. 2002. *Hybrid Geographies: Natures, cultures, spaces*. London: Sage.

Ziliak, S. T. and McCloskey, D. N. 2008. *The Cult of Statistical Significance*. Ann Arbor: University of Michigan Press.

Indigenous People and Settlers

2. Before the Mission Station: From first encounters to the incorporation of settlers into Indigenous relations of obligation

John M. White

Introduction

By the end of the twentieth century, Aboriginal people of the Eurobodalla region of the NSW South Coast were broadly incorporated into the expanding settler economy.[1] With ongoing labour shortages impeding economic development, Aboriginal labour became critical to the success of the forestry and fishing industries and to the emergence of seasonal horticultural industries. Shortfalls in income were supplemented with the continuance of subsistence fishing. These patterns of seasonal employment were characteristic of the hybrid economy of the Eurobodalla until the 1970s (see White 2010, 2011). Altman (2001) employs the hybrid economy model to counter perspectives on the marginalisation of Aboriginal people from the settler-capitalist (or 'real') economy. His model comprises the intersection of customary, market and state sectors of economic activity. Altman applies this concept to contemporary Aboriginal communities in remote northern Australia. As Keen (2010:8) notes, however, the model is 'readily adaptable to capture the variety of local economies that emerged on the frontier'.[2] On the southern NSW coastal frontier, local Aboriginal people were forced off their country by the expansion of small-scale landholdings, and subsequently moved variously between estuarine camps close to sources of employment and the government-administered station at Wallaga Lake. Rather than examining the processes of incorporation into the settler economy, this chapter aims to invert the question and will explore how Aboriginal people came to incorporate the presence of settlers into pre-existing, seasonal and dynamic patterns of economy and sociality. In doing so, this chapter will wind the clock back to a critical juncture in the region's history of intercultural

---

1   This chapter is indebted to the Eurobodalla Aboriginal Cultural Heritage Study steering committee and to the excellent research conducted by Goulding and Waters (2005) in compiling an Aboriginal history of the Eurobodalla.

2   Elsewhere (White 2011), I have problematised the application of Altman's model to past-focused studies and have suggested that the nature of exclusion, social control and exploitation also needs to be taken into account when discussing the articulation between customary and settler modes of production.

relations: the initial four decades of contact that resulted in Aboriginal groups moving from social and spatial distance to incorporating settlers into relations of obligation. Through an examination of the documentary record, the chapter also suggests that the Eurobodalla experienced a highly localised process of European colonisation.

The recent edited volume by Jolly et al. (2009) provides interesting points of comparison regarding early or initial intercultural encounters in the Pacific that encompassed both extreme violence and exchange. In Papua New Guinea, several writers have discussed emergent relationships with Australian patrols (Bonnemère and Lemonnier 2009; Strathern 1992). Marilyn Strathern (1992) described the exchange of shells in the Mount Hagen region as part of a revelatory moment in which the distinction between Hageners and the Australian strangers was collapsed. Strathern argues that 'above all, they were recognisable as human because they contained within them the capacity to transact' (Strathern 1992:251). In Australia, there is a considerable body of literature dealing with general themes of massacre, theft and reprisals in the initial encounters between settlers and Aboriginal people in a variety of spatial and temporal locations. For example, in analysing depictions of Aboriginal people in violent conflicts on the Macleay River pastoral runs, Barry Morris gave legitimacy to Taussig's term 'the culture of terror' (Taussig 1987). Elsewhere in New South Wales (and more generally throughout Australia), conflict on the pastoral frontier was an ongoing concern for the colonial administration (see Loos 1982; Reece 1974; Reynolds 1981; Robinson and York 1977).[3] Literature dealing with congeniality or exchange in the initial encounters between Aboriginal people, explorers and settlers is sparse, although there are several accounts of Europeans being saved from starvation when they were lost in the bush (see Flannery and Morgan 2002; Morrill 2006). Henry Reynolds provides a range of Aboriginal 'first encounters' with Europeans (as well as with introduced animals and new material goods), and considers how Aboriginal people attempted to 'explain the newcomers in traditional terms and to assimilate them within kinship networks' (Reynolds 1981:3).

In view of the available archival material on the Eurobodalla region, this chapter will argue that the most compelling reason for the rapid tempering of intercultural violence, theft and reprisals, and the rapid incorporation of Aboriginal labour in the emerging settler economy, is the relationship between exchange and relatedness. In approaching the concepts of exchange and relatedness, I am following Strathern's example of the Mount Hagen encounter insofar as the human/non-human binary was collapsed by the Anglo-Australians' ability to exchange culturally meaningful shells. As Strathern noted, 'this gave them a

---

3   Prevailing accounts of violence in the Australian context reflect the specific mode of production in the dominant pastoral sector of the settler economy. The forcible alienation of Aboriginal people from their country was both a question of economic viability and a question of survival.

dimension in time. Or to put it another way, this made relationship possible' (Strathern 1992:249). I suggest that it is precisely the breakdown of these self/ other binaries that is required if we are to approach the inverted question of socioeconomic incorporation. In this chapter, I am using the notion of relatedness as a flexible category rather than as a bounded polity defined by kin relations. Myer's (1986) conceptualisation of relatedness (as opposed to 'differentiation') is instructive in this respect. In a structural-functionalist, 'bubble' notion of culture (described by Redmond as the 'culture gardens' approach), relatedness is rigidly dialectical to differentiation and tends to obfuscate the range of interactions and identifications in an intercultural context (Redmond 2005:234). I argue here that Yuin relations with non-kin co-residents (settlers) cannot be viewed in terms of 'either' or 'or', but rather as being incorporated into a relatively open sociality not necessarily defined in terms of kin relations. Following Strathern, I argue that *exchange* between individuals gave Europeans a tangible, temporal dimension for the Yuin.

Early History of Intercultural Relations

William Drew's reflections on the early days of the European colony at Sydney— 'the first seeds of which were sown amid the sighs and groans and tears of the wicked and worthless, and the swish of the dreadful cat and the clank of iron gyves'—provide an important insight into the shaping of colonial subjectivities through violence and suffering (Sergeant William Drew in Becke and Jeffery 1896:140). Referring to the lashing of several convicts, Drew describes the 'spectacle' as 'a very dreadful one', and remarks that he would 'never forget the feeling of horror' that he 'experienced in witnessing their punishment' (p. 70). Following the arrival of the First Fleet in Sydney, Drew observed several encounters between Aboriginal people and Europeans and concluded: 'there is no doubt in my mind the savages of this country are a treacherous race' of 'murderous inclinations' (p. 128). This is perhaps what Taussig refers to as 'the reciprocating yet distorted mimesis' of the 'colonial mirror which reflects back onto the colonists the barbarity of their own social relations, but as imputed to the savage or evil figures they wish to colonise' (Taussig 2002:9).[4] The fear of Aboriginal people precipitated certain kinds of interactions in the dialectic described by Taussig (2002) as a 'culture of terror'. Taussig urges that

> we would be most unwise to overlook or under-estimate the role of terror.
> And by this I mean us to think through terror, which as well as being a

---

4   This is also reminiscent of the kind of dichotomous order posited by post-colonial theorists such as Franz Fanon (1970) and Homi Bhabha (1993), in which the colonised (to borrow the phrase from Biber) become the 'dark doppelgänger of their new imperial masters' (Biber 2005:623).

physiological state is also a social fact and a cultural construction whose baroque dimensions allow it to serve as the mediator *par excellence* of colonial hegemony. (Taussig 2002:1)

These 'baroque dimensions' of terror are explicit in the late eighteenth and early nineteenth-century rumours that Aboriginal people south of Botany Bay were 'hostile savages' and 'were generally believed to be cannibals' (Bowden 1952:37). This image was later distributed in Maclehose's (1838) *Picture of Sydney and Stranger's Guide in New South Wales for 1838*, which sought to inform new arrivals to the colony of the barbarous practices of Aboriginal people, including the widespread phenomenon of cannibalistic infanticide amongst Aboriginal men. The *Sydney Herald* was also complicit in promulgating the image of savagery and cannibalism during the late 1830s (see Reece 1974:93). In her discussion of cannibalism in Australian colonial discourse, Biber (2005) draws on the 1826 case of a shepherd, Henry Preston, who became lost near Wollondilly (on the southern outskirts of the colony at Sydney). Allegations of cannibalism were laid against several Aboriginal people in the district and were reported to Governor Ralph Darling. A few days later, 'Preston walked out of the bush unharmed' (Biber 2005:622).

Pickering's research into the available archival sources on cannibalism in Australia led him to the conclusion that 'there is no reliable evidence to support the claim that Australian Aboriginal societies practiced institutionalised cannibalism' (Pickering 1999:51). In retrospect, however, Pickering's findings would have provided little comfort to the European settlers at Wollondilly. In the case of Henry Preston, the allegation of cannibalism was a product of a historical moment of mythologised characterisation. As Biber remarks, this kind of 'cannibal discourse is the product of colonial anxiety', the origins of which 'lay in childhood fantasies of cannibalistic savages roaming the darkest corners of the Empire' (Biber 2005:629).[5] On a localised level, terror as a social fact existed in a dialectic that created, and was created by, mediated narratives of violence beyond Sydney and the Cumberland Plain that served to fashion a phantasmic image of South Coast Aboriginal people in the 'space of death'. By projecting the image of terror onto Aboriginal people (Taussig's 'victims'), Europeans could rationalise their own acts of violence. Further, in the 'epistemic murk' of these mediated narratives documenting atrocities committed by Aboriginal people, the actions of soldiers, sealers, sailors and settlers were motivated, retold and reconstituted.

Documentary records suggest that Europeans and Aboriginal people initially came into physical contact in the Eurobodalla region of New South Wales in 1797. A ship, the *Sydney Cove*, foundered on a beach at Gippsland and the crew

---

5   For a more general analysis of these types of discourses, see Lindenbaum (2004).

began the long journey by foot up the coast to the colony at Sydney. Of the 17 men who survived the wreck, only four made it back to Sydney, encountering several 'hostile' groups of Aboriginal people along the way (Goulding and Waters 2005:24). One of the survivors, W. Clarke, recalled meeting with Aboriginal people in the vicinity of the Tuross River estuary:

> Met fourteen natives who conducted us to their miserable abodes in the wood adjoining to a large lagoon and kindly treated us with mussels, for which unexpected civility, we made them some presents. These people seem better acquainted with the laws of hospitality than any of their countrymen…for to their benevolent treat was added an invitation to remain with them for the night…As far as we could understand these natives were of a different tribe from those we had seen and were then at war with them. They possessed a liberality to which the others were strangers and freely gave us a part of the little they had. (Clarke, cited in Gibbney 1989:14)

Provisioning of this type is not without precedent, as the famous accounts of James Morrill and William Buckley suggest. Aboriginal people saved Morrill from starvation after he was shipwrecked off the Great Barrier Reef in the 1840s and he continued to live in camp for nearly two decades (Morrill 2006). Similarly, Buckley, an escaped convict, was given food in his initial encounter with Wautharong people and continued to live and travel with them for many years (Flannery and Morgan 2002).

Following Clarke's encounter, there is no documentary evidence of interactions between Europeans and Aboriginal people in the Eurobodalla region until 1806. Wesson, however, identified that a woman of mixed descent was reported to be living in the Bodalla area in 1842 and approximates the year of her birth as 1804. This date, Wesson argues, predated both the arrival of the first pastoralists and the advent of onshore whaling at Twofold Bay (Wesson 2002:18). Although there is little documentary evidence of their activities, sealers were clearly travelling along the South Coast by the end of the eighteenth century. As Wesson suggests, sealers were probably illiterate and would have had little reason to document their activities (Wesson 2002). As Amery and Muhlhausler further noted, 'many of the sealers were runaway convicts and sailors who had left their ships in Sydney' (Amery and Muhlhausler 1996:48). It appears that the practice of abducting Aboriginal women was also common among sealers. Captain Kelly wrote in 1815 that it was 'customary' for sealers based in Bass Strait to 'have from two to five of those native women for their own use and benefit' (Henley and Plomley 1990). Kelly also refers to adult children of mixed descent, which again places the sealers on the south-eastern coastline prior to 1806. In March 1806, Governor Philip King reported that a number of Aboriginal people had been killed by sealers at Twofold Bay (Governor King, cited in Organ 1990:30).

Two later articles appeared in the *Sydney Gazette* referring to the terror experienced by European seamen encountering Aboriginal people at Batemans Bay (*Sydney Gazette*, 15 May 1808, 26 May 1821). The second account, in 1821, provides macabre details of the events and is consistent with the reporting style of the era:

> The next morning (Easter Sunday) at daylight, they were suddenly attacked by about twelve natives, with a discharge of 50 or 60 spears, followed up by a continued volley of stones. James Brock was thrice speared; one entered a thigh, another slightly grazed his breast, and the third perforated the chest; which produced instantaneous death...The unfortunate men were now in a truly pitiable and forlorn condition; Block was lying in the boat a corpse; Whittaker was sorely wounded; and Thorn beheld nothing but a horrid and cruel death, at the hands of the savages, ready to meet him, or else the dread expectancy of being entombed in the ocean's vast abyss. (*Sydney Gazette*, 26 May 1821:3)

By way of the prominence of the two articles in Australia's first newspaper, the reputation of the ferocity of Aboriginal people at Batemans Bay was broadly circulated in Sydney, reinforcing rumours of terror and cannibalism in the south.

The 1821 voyage of the *Snapper* encountered Aboriginal people as it entered Batemans Bay and explored the Clyde River. The leader of the exploratory party, Lieutenant Robert Johnson, reported to the *Sydney Gazette* that '[a]t one Place I landed, taking with me the two Natives who accompanied me from Sydney, upon which we were met by a Tribe of them, who shewed [sic] no Symptoms of Hostility towards us, but entered freely into Conversation' (*Sydney Gazette*, 10 December 1821:1).

Johnson was able to gain information about the loss of another ship further south in which Captain Stewart's group of survivors was 'cut off by the Natives of Two-fold Bay', and of an escaped convict who had, it was asserted, capsized his boat in the middle of Batemans Bay and had not made it to shore (*Sydney Gazette*, 10 December 1821:1). Johnson concluded that the convict, Briggs, and his companions had 'suffered the same fate' as the shipwrecked party at Twofold Bay. While Johnson had personally experienced no hostility from Aboriginal people at Batemans Bay, his report still emphasised the perils of southward journeys, and it was assumed that the attack was motivated by cannibalism (Reece 1974:102). Once again, the image of terror on the southern maritime frontier was circulated in Sydney by the *Gazette*. The following year, 1822, a member of Charles Throsby's overland exploration party ventured towards Batemans Bay but lost his nerve 'because of the reputed hostility of the natives in this area' (Perry 1963:100).

Four years later a Wesleyan missionary led an expedition to the South Coast in the hope of finding a suitable location to base a mission. In October 1826, John Harper arrived at Batemans Bay and for the next two weeks encountered, without hostility, a number of Aboriginal people in the area who, in his words, had not been 'contaminated by the whites' (Harper 1826). Importantly, Harper initiated contact by offering an Aboriginal man blankets and biscuits, which were reciprocated with 'several presents' once he was led to shore (Harper 1826). Harper clearly believed that friendly relationships could be forged with Aboriginal people as long as Europeans acted with integrity:

> No man of pure motives need be afraid of travelling with the blacks, even in the most obscure place. Alltho' [sic] this assertion is not credited in the Colony by some people, yet I know from experience more than thousands who would object to it…Let the whites reform their conduct and they need never be afraid. (Harper 1826)

The Wesleyan Missionary Society, of which Harper was a leading figure in the new colony, held the view that their ministries (their 'saving plan of redemption') needed to be separate from European settlement, at the 'uttermost bounds of their scattered, uncivilised, unsociable and cannibal tribes' (Walker n.d.). The 'contamination' that Harper refers to in his journal reflected his view that the colony was a place of 'vile infamous and libidinous conduct' (Harper 1827). Harper's mentor, Reverend Walker, also believed that missions would have most success 'at a proper distance from the theatre of temptation' (Walker 1821). While Harper intended to return to Batemans Bay to establish the mission, his request was denied by Governor Darling, who concluded that allowing the selection of land by the Wesleyan Missionary Society 'would have been prejudicial to the interests of the settlers' (Darling 1827). In the same year, the government surveyor, Thomas Florance, was given the task of providing a detailed survey of the coastal region between Jervis Bay and Moruya in 1828. Florance compiled a report on possible regions for settlement, based on the proximity of sheltered ports or potential harbours to land suitable for agricultural production (Dowd 1972). Harper's desire to Christianise Aboriginal people at Batemans Bay, at a distance from the contaminating influence of settler society, paradoxically led to the widespread settlement of the region. His genuine effort to create a mission coupled with his reports of friendly, rather than hostile 'savages' inspired a new confidence in the possibility of settlement in the south. Following Harper's unsuccessful application to Governor Darling, the Eurobodalla region was settled within three years.[6]

---

6   Gibbney wrote that 'wandering cattlemen had penetrated south of the Bay by about 1826', but does not provide any sources for the claim (Gibbney 1989:18). Presumably, these cattlemen would have originated from the expansion of pastoralism on the Monaro plain during this period and had come down to the coast via the Araluen Valley.

The first settler at Murramarang, William Morris, wrote a number of letters to the Governor reporting the spearing of cattle and threatening of settlers by Aboriginal people, and requested permission to be given to shoot those responsible and for soldiers to be sent to ensure the settlers' safety (Morris, 24 September 1830, cited in James 2001:5). In response, Lieutenant Macalister was sent to the Batemans Bay area and concluded that Aboriginal people from the mountains (rather than the coastal Yuin) were responsible for the violence. Macalister proposed that the conflict was a result of mountain groups missing out on blankets that were distributed by Morris on behalf of the colonial administration. In response, blankets were distributed evenly to both the mountain people and the coastal Yuin. Macalister's report in 1831 concluded that the incidents were anomalous and that his mediations had settled the matter once and for all (Macalister 1831, cited in Organ 1990:170). Gibbney's account gives credit to Macalister as an 'unusually intelligent officer' for seeking 'pacification not punishment' and that his efforts were so successful that 'even Morris ceased to complain and the Aboriginal people never again attempted resistance' (Gibbney 1989:22). Organ rightly noted, however, that Gibbney's 'account glosses over the more unsavoury aspects of this affair—it does not describe the European atrocities' (Organ 1990:164).

A year after Macalister's report, a shooting party led by Joseph Berrymen murdered two men, a pregnant woman and an older woman at Murramarang. Organ (1990) provides a documentary record of the killings that offers conflicting accounts of the events, ranging from the complainant, Mr Thompson, to the accused, Joseph Berryman. In the end, Berryman escaped without charge. While there is no direct evidence implicating Morris of Murramarang with recruiting the shooting party, Morris was clearly dissatisfied with Macalister's approach to resolving the matter. In both of his letters, Morris calls for permission to be given to shoot the ringleaders as his desired form of reprisal. It is unclear, however, whether or not Morris decided to take the matter into his own hands. By 1845 it appears that, in general, the hostilities had ceased and the prevalence of livestock theft had been ameliorated by Macalister's mediations (Gibbney 1989:21–8; James 2001:7). In the absence of further documented conflicts, it appears that the initial era of intercultural relations had come to an end. Memories of frontier violence remain in the oral history of Aboriginal people on the South Coast today. A prominent narrative implicates one of the first settlers to arrive in the region in the 1840s, Alexander Weatherhead. In various accounts, Weatherhead has been described as deliberately poisoning Aboriginal people through the use of flour or cream laced with strychnine. In other oral testimonies, Weatherhead is also remembered as forcing Aboriginal people to work as slaves when he was serving as manager at Nugatta Station. An unrelated account refers to atrocities being committed in the vicinity of Coila Creek. It is likely that many further incidences of violence occurred but were not documented.

Exchange, Provisioning and Heroism at Broulee

The original settlement at Broulee was heavily reliant on provisions shipped from Sydney. In between shipments, the small community of settlers was saved from starvation on several occasions during the 1830s by local Aboriginal people who provided them with seafood (Rose 1923:375). Later, in 1841, a heroic story emerges of Aboriginal people saving the survivors of the shipwrecked *Rover* at Broulee in a daring rescue operation. With the settlers unable to swim out through the surf, several Aboriginal people risked their own lives to rescue the seamen. Two accounts of the rescue provide conflicting details as to the number of Aboriginal people involved and the mode of rescue. Robinson's second-hand account of the saga gives reference to two men:

> I was happy to find that the other Aborigines along the Coast were equally well spoken of several persons by their instrumentality had been saved. The most striking instance (brought under notice) was the Wreck of a Steamer in a Storm at Broole [sic] when all hopes of saving the white persons were given up, and when no Individual would venture, two Aboriginal natives at the imminent risk of their own lives boldly plunged into the Breakers and rescued the sufferers who but for them must have perished. (Robinson 1844, cited in Mackaness 1978:23)

In contrast, an account from 1849 increases the number of rescuers to 15 and details a highly coordinated rescue effort:

> Some of the tribe…greatly distinguished themselves, three or four years since, by saving the crew of a schooner which was wrecked in the surf. The white by-standers stood aghas [sic], and could not contrive means to render any assistance; but fifteen of the aborigines formed a line, hand in hand, and went into the surf and saved all on board. (Townsend 1849, cited in Cleary 1993:39)

Regardless of the conflicting details, the actions of the heroes at Broulee are remarkable. But is it enough to view these events, and the earlier provisioning of Clarke's party, as evidence that Yuin people were, as Gibbney suggests, 'clearly a kindly folk who welcomed travelers' (Gibbney 1989:14). The hostility towards seamen on the maritime frontier contradicts that assumption, despite the actions probably being in retaliation to earlier atrocities committed by the marauding sealers.

In his analysis of provisioning in Aboriginal systems, Keen identified that 'people invested in the productivity of others through their own generosity, and expected recipients to be generous in return. Indeed, continuing relatedness required constant affirmation through giving' (Keen 2004:354). Therefore, underlying systems of reciprocal giving are a fundamental premise of the existence of relatedness. A. W. Howitt (1904) provided a key early ethnography of the South Coast region, detailing forms of sociality and exchange practices in the late 1800s. Howitt observed that Yuin people were intermarrying and trading with groups from the Shoalhaven in the north, the Braidwood district in the west, and with groups from Twofold Bay and the coastal range in the south.[7] These transactions included sister exchange and the trade of weapons, food and other goods. Reciprocal giving occurred within a network of relatedness reinforced by cycles of transactions. This framework is useful in examining the provisioning of settlers at Broulee in the 1830s because relationships had already been formed between the first settlers and Aboriginal people. The earliest written record identifying individual Aboriginal workers was provided by John Hawdon, who, along with Francis Flanagan, had taken up land in the Moruya area by 1830. Presumably, Hawdon was exchanging rations for labour and it is clear that he was highly regarded by Aboriginal people in the region, as the following passage suggests: 'They always regarded Mr. Hawdon's word as law, and he was called upon to settle many a dispute' (Buck n.d.).[8]

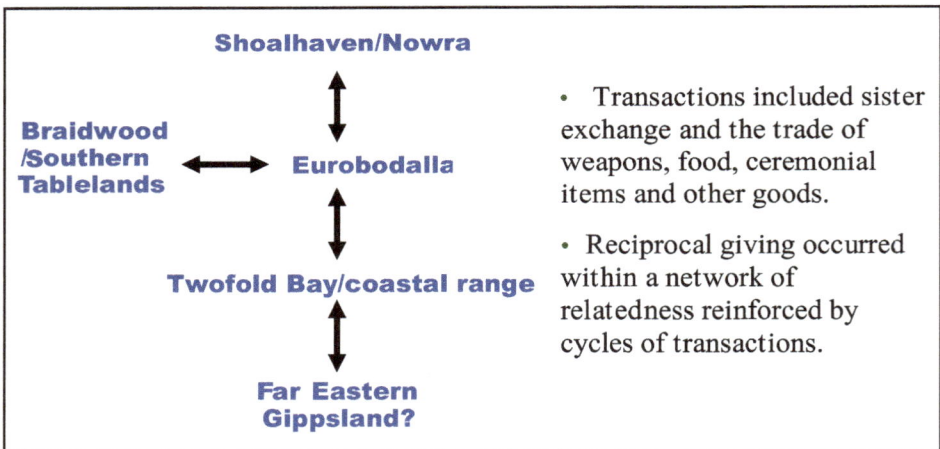

Figure 2.1 Howitt's (1904) evidence of Yuin exchange practices

Source: Boundaries of intermarriage and trade networks from Howitt (1904).

Broulee was also a hub for the distribution of blankets during a period in which the Aboriginal population was in rapid decline—most likely due to an influenza epidemic (Wesson 2000:130). Both Francis Flanagan and Captain Oldrey were

---

7   Robinson's journals push this southern boundary further to describe customary journeys to far east Gippsland (Robinson 1844).

8   It is evident that patron–client relations developed between Hawdon and several Aboriginal people who returned seasonally to work for him over a number of years. Aboriginal people were motivated to work for the settlers on a seasonal basis, preferring to wander off in the warmer months when resources were plentiful along the coast.

responsible for distributing blankets and providing a census of the number of Aboriginal people in the district. As Wesson (2000:131) identified, Oldrey's 1842 census was unusual because it included 'family groups and the names and ages of all members of a family'. Oldrey also detailed the country in which each family usually camped, with the greatest number of families clustered around the settlement at Broulee (Oldrey 1842). The comprehensive detail in Oldrey's blanket returns entails an intimate knowledge of the individual family groups that could have been achieved only through close relationships extending over a number of years. In contrast, Morris's census provided only the number of people to which blankets were distributed and the names of the adult male family members (Wesson 2000:131). Through the provisioning of blankets and establishing close relationships with Aboriginal people in the area, Oldrey (along with Hawdon) can be credited with narrowing the social and spatial distances between Aboriginal people and the broader community of settlers at Broulee. In the absence of kin terms being used for individual settlers, however, it is impossible to argue that this relatedness was extended to kin relations in the manner in which Redmond describes the relationship between Ngarinyin workers and white stock owners in the Kimberley, where 'relative strangers' became 'strange relatives' (Redmond 2005:234).

Understanding the rescue of the survivors of the *Rover* in terms of relations of obligation based on relatedness is also instructive in this respect. I suggest that the rescue was a projection of relations of obligation onto the strangers in the boat, who were probably thought to be part of the local settler community. Oldrey petitioned the colonial administration to provide a reward for the heroes involved but his requests were refused. Taking the matter into his own hands, Oldrey had several brass gorgets fabricated for the rescuers. Oldrey is also credited as 'pleading the cause' of an Aboriginal man held in captivity at the police office (Townsend, cited in Cleary 1993:39). Once again, Oldrey was involved in maintaining relatedness through exchange. In 'sticking up' for the man in captivity, the object of exchange exists as much in the material form of gorgets as it does in providing a service of the type that Keen describes as creating 'a more diffuse obligation'. Keen adds that the effects of a service on a relationship could be enduring, depending on the perceived value of the action' (Keen 2004:354). These 'gifts of service' are also reminiscent of Sansom's four orders of 'signal service' in which 'bailing out'—or acts of rescue—'transforms the relationship between heroic rescuer and saved victim for as long as they both shall live' (Sansom 1988:169).

Provisioning of Strangers?

Sansom's schema is problematic if we return to the provisioning of Clarke's party in 1797, keeping in mind they were probably the very first Europeans any of the people at the Tuross camp had met. Stumbling out of the bush, starved and dishevelled, they must have had curiously white skin. Did they resemble a *Tulungul*, the spirit or ghost of a dead relative described by Howitt (1904:463)? Why would gift giving be triggered with absolute strangers? This is a puzzle for which I have no definitive answers. I suspect that it had something to do with a belief that Clarke and his men were physical manifestations of supra-natural beings; or, as evidence that information about the colony in Sydney had spread to the South Coast via the 'bush telegraph'; or, with a more generalised (or perhaps even locally defined) predisposition towards generosity as Les Hiatt's 'highest secular value' in Aboriginal Australia (Hiatt 1982:14).

The first rationale (based on misunderstanding) is certainly not without its problems. Sahlin's (1995) view that Hawaiians perceived Captain Cook as a physical manifestation of the god *Lono* has been greatly disputed (see Borofsky 1997 for a review of the debate). William Buckley's experience in Victoria, however, lends some credibility to this premise. In Morgan's account collected in 1852, Buckley stated that the Wautharong people thought he was the returned spirit of a dead relative and gave him the name Murrangurk, 'meaning literally, returned from the dead' (Flannery and Morgan 2002:45).

> They called me Murrangurk, which I afterwards learnt, was the name of a man formerly belonging to their tribe, who had been buried at the spot where I had found the piece of spear I still carried with me. They have a belief, that when they die, they go to some place or other, and are there made white men, and that they then return to this world again for another existence. They think all the white people previous to death were belonging to their own tribes, thus returned to life in a different colour. (Flannery and Morgan 2002:38–9)

Based on this section of Buckley's account, it seems that the incorporation of Buckley into the Wautharong 'tribe' was more of a case of 'reincorporation' based on reincarnation beliefs. Prior to being given the name Murrangurk, however, Buckley had been provided with seafood on his initial encounter with Wautharong men in which he feared that he was going to be cannibalised: 'At length my suspense ended, by their taking the fish, fairly dividing them, and handing to me the first and best portion' (Flannery and Morgan 2002:31). In view of the available evidence, it appears that provisioning preceded the reincorporation of the dead relative's spirit (manifested in the white skin of William Buckley) into the Wautharong network of kin relations.

The second rationale assumes that information about the presence and activities of Europeans had spread south from Sydney in the nine years between 1788 and 1797. It is possible that the 'bush telegraph' had conveyed news about both the wealth of new and desirable goods at the colony and the violence and terrifying new technologies. In the Townsville region of northern Queensland, James Morrill's account gives precedence to this rationale, as information was systematically spread about the presence of the white people who had come from the sea:

> When they had done, they came and fetched us into their midst as on the previous evening, to show us to them. This was continued evening after evening for about six or eight evenings successively, as representatives from the more distant tribes came in to see the wonderful people, til the most distant known to them had seen us. (Morrill 2006:33)

Later, Morrill's party was again exhibited to a much larger gathering, involving up to 1000 representatives of 10 'tribes'.[9] In the case of the NSW South Coast, the existence and efficacy of a 'bush telegraph' hinge on questions of communicability—whether Yuin networks of relatedness extended north towards Sydney and if there was some overlap between the language groups in these regions.

Howitt's observations of the Bunan male initiation ceremonies involved groups from as far north as the Shoalhaven and west to the Braidwood district, and it is likely that these gatherings involved the exchange of information about the settlers (Howitt 1904:519–20).[10] This question also relies on shared languages or bilingualism in the regions between the Eurobodalla and Tharawal-speaking groups near Botany Bay. In her analysis of language ranges in south-eastern New South Wales, Wesson suggests that people in the Ulladulla region were 'bilingual, that both Thoorga and Tharawal were typically spoken in the region, or that an indeterminate form of the two languages was in use in the area' (Wesson 2000:157). Based on the evidence of communicability, it is therefore possible that information about the Europeans had been circulated between groups as far south as the Tuross River by 1797. Yet two questions remain that are impossible to answer with any degree of certainty: did reports of violent new technologies outweigh the allure of desirable goods? And, should encounters with Europeans be feared or welcomed with the anticipation of reciprocity?

Expanding on the third rationale, it seems that the idea of relatedness being prior to, or essential for, exchange could be inverted so that exchange itself facilitates relatedness. In any case, it is the predisposition towards exchange (as

---

9   The evidence suggests that this gathering was a male initiation ceremony.
10   Reynolds suggested that news about Europeans was spread rapidly throughout Australia along 'traditional trade routes' (Reynolds 1981:11).

a function of maintaining relatedness) that was characteristic of the nonviolent interactions between Aboriginal people and the first wave of settlers on the NSW South Coast. It is this predisposition that also led to the amelioration of conflict, as a cycle of theft and reprisals, and the rapid incorporation of Aboriginal labour to fill the critical labour shortage in the primary-sector industries; however, I do not want to overstate relatedness in terms of the social incorporation of Aboriginal people into settler society. Indeed, increases in the scale of settlement were concomitant with the increasing marginalisation of Aboriginal people from town life. Racial attitudes were reinforced by government policies and rhetoric designed to segregate and exclude Aboriginal people from interacting with settler society. Accounts of the subsequent years bemoan Aboriginal people 'begging' around the coastal towns during periods when work was scant and the fish were off the bite. I suggest that a more accurate reflection on this period would view these actions as evidence that the settlers had become incorporated into the Indigenous social and economic worlds of mutual obligation, and demand-sharing expectations had been extended, through relatedness, onto relative strangers (Peterson 1993).[11]

Conclusion

A final point that I want to emphasise is that the early colonial history of the Eurobodalla points to a highly localised and specific experience of colonialism. Through the course of my examination of the maritime frontier, I have argued that the pervasiveness of violence and terror as a self-reproducing social fact correlates well with Taussig's (1987) notion of a 'culture of terror'. Yet, despite what appears to have been a unified colonial mind-set, several individuals (including the missionary Harper, Captain William Oldrey and John Hawdon) showed some openness to Indigenous difference and socio-cultural complexity and, in doing so, facilitated the incorporation of settlers into Indigenous relations of obligation. It is always tempting to view colonialism as a totalising, monolithic process accompanied by a unified discourse; however, I agree with Nicholas Thomas's suggestion that 'only localised theories and historically specific accounts can provide much insight into the varied articulations of colonizing and counter-colonial representations and practices' (Thomas 1994:ix). Colonialism (in much the same way as 'frontier') unfurls itself in a variety of places and times, economic circumstances and modes of production. Yet it also encompasses myriad individual-level predilections, epistemes and

---

11   Both Reynolds (1981) and Broome (1982) briefly allude to the notion that begging (as an emergent practice) was related to Indigenous domestic moral and economic systems, although neither author provides a theoretical elaboration of that relationship. While I also suggest here the possibility of a link in certain contexts, a detailed discussion of evidentiary and theoretical perspectives is necessary and is beyond the scope of this chapter.

interactions. Despite mythologised characterisations of South Coast Aboriginal people as 'cannibalistic savages', the racialised and terrified subjectivities that were generated in the convict context were not always projected onto relations with the Indigenous 'other'. Indeed, by resisting claims on their subjectivities by the notion that colonialism inexorably consists of perilous and luridly violent encounters, some individuals were able to find a measure of redemption outside the colonial imaginary.

Acknowledgments

This chapter owes a special debt to Ian Keen, Nic Peterson and Tony Redmond for their constructive feedback. I would also like to acknowledge and express my gratitude to Philip Taylor for his incisive thoughts and comments on an earlier version of this chapter.

References

Altman, J. 2001. *Sustainable Development Options on Aboriginal Land: The hybrid economy in the twenty-first century*. Canberra: Centre for Aboriginal Economic Policy Research, Australian National University.

Amery, R. and Muhlhausler, P. 1996. Pidgin English in New South Wales. In P. Muhlhausler, D. Tryon and S. Wurm (eds), *Atlas of Languages of Intercultural Communication in the Pacific, Asia, and the Americas*. Berlin: Mouton de Gruyter.

Becke, L. and Jeffery, W. 1896. *A First Fleet Family: A hitherto unpublished narrative of certain remarkable adventures compiled from the papers of Sargeant W. Dew of the marines*. London: T. Fisher Unwin.

Bhabha, H. 1993. *The Location of Culture*. New York: Routledge.

Biber, K. 2005. Cannibals and colonialism. *Sydney Law Review* 27: 623–37.

Bonnemère, P. and Lemonnier, P. 2009. A measure of violence: forty years of 'first contact' among the Ankave-Anga (Papua New Guinea). In M. Jolly, S. Tcherkézoff and D. Tryon (eds), *Oceanic Encounters: Exchange, desire, violence*. Canberra: ANU E Press.

Borofsky, R. 1997. Cook, Lono, Obeyeskere and Sahlins. *Current Anthropology* 38: 255–65.

Bowden, K. 1952. *George Bass 1771–1803: His discoveries, romantic life and tragic disappearance*. Melbourne: Oxford University Press.

Broome, R. 1982. *Aboriginal Australians: Black Response to White Dominance, 1788-1980*. Sydney: George Allen and Unwin.

Buck, M. n.d. *Old Colony Days: John Hawdon's letters. Volume II*. Moruya, NSW: Moruya and District Historical Society.

Cleary, T. 1993. *Poignant Regalia: 19th century Aboriginal breastplates & images*. Sydney: Historic Houses Trust of New South Wales.

Darling, G. 1827. Governor Darling to Earl Bathurst, despatch no. 32. *Historic Records of Australia* XIII (1).

Dowd, B. 1972. Thomas Florance, 1783–1867. *Journal of the Royal Australian Historical Society* 58: 89–100.

Fanon, F. 1970. *Black Skin, White Masks*. St Albans, UK: Paladin.

Flanagan, F. 1845. Response to circular letter from Francis Flanagan. In *Report from the Select Committee on the Condition of the Aborigines with Appendix, Minutes of Evidence and Replies to a Circular Letter*. Sydney: Government Printing Office.

Flannery, T. E. and Morgan, J. 2002. *The Life and Adventures of William Buckley; 32 years a wanderer amongst the Aborigines of the then unexplored country around Port Phillip, now the Province of Victoria*. Melbourne: Text Publishing.

Gibbney, H. J. 1989. *Eurobodalla: History of the Moruya district*. Sydney: in association with the Shire of Eurobodalla.

Goulding, M. and Waters, K. 2005. *Eurobodalla Aboriginal Cultural Heritage Study South Coast New South Wales*. Carlton North, Vic.: Goulding Heritage Consulting Pty Ltd.

Harper, J. 1826. Mr. Harper's Journal [October 1826]. Wesleyan Mission House Despatches, Bonwick Transcripts Missionary, 1824–1829, Mitchell Library, Sydney.

Harper, J. 1827. Harper to Rev. J. Newstead, 25 April 1827. In Wesleyan Mission House Despatches, Bonwick Transcripts Missionary, 1824-1829, Mitchell Library, Sydney.Henley, K. and Plomley, B. 1990. *The Sealers of Bass Strait and the Cape Barren Island Community*. Hobart: Blubber Head Press.

Hiatt, L. 1982. Traditional attitudes to land resources. In R. M. Berndt (ed.), *Aboriginal Sites, Rites and Resource Development*. Perth: University of Western Australia Press.

Howitt, A. W. 1904. *The Native Tribes of South-East Australia*. London: Macmillan.

James, A. 2001. *Batemans Bay: Story of a town*. Batemans Bay, NSW: Self-published.

Johnson, R. 1821. Report from Robert Johnson, 10th December 1821. *Sydney Gazette*.

Jolly, M., Tcherkézoff, S. and Tryon, D. (eds) 2009. *Oceanic Encounters: Exchange, desire, violence*. Canberra: ANU E Press.

Keen, I. 2004. *Aboriginal Economy and Society: Australia at the threshold of colonisation*. South Melbourne: Oxford University Press.

Keen, I. 2010. Introduction. In I. Keen (ed.), *Indigenous Participation in Australian Economies: Historical and anthropological perspectives*. Canberra: ANU E Press.

Lindenbaum, S. 2004. Thinking about Cannibalism. *Annual review of Anthropology* 33: 475-98.

Loos, N. 1982. *Invasion and Resistance: Aboriginal–European relations on the north Queensland frontier 1861–1897*. Canberra: Australian National University Press.

Maclehose, J. 1838. *Picture of Sydney and Stranger's Guide in New South Wales for 1838*. Sydney: J. Spilsbury.

Mackaness, G. (ed.) 1978. *George Augustus Robinson's Journey into South-Eastern Australia, 1844*. Australian Historical Monographs 19 [NS]. Dubbo, NSW: Review Publications.

Morrill, J. 2006. *17 Years Wandering Among the Aboriginals*. (Originally published 1864, with photographs published by Eric Mjoberg, 1918). Australian Aboriginal culture series 1. Virginia, N.T.: Welch.

Myers, F. 1986. Reflections on a meeting: structure, language, and the polity in a small-scale society. *American Ethnologist* 13 (3): 430–47.

Oldrey, W. 1842. Return of Aboriginal Natives taken at Broulee the 6th day of May 1842. Colonial Secretary Special Bundles: Aborigines 1837–44: Papers dealing with the issue of blankets, and including returns of the native population in the various districts, State Records of New South Wales, Sydney.

Organ, M. 1990. *A Documentary History of the Illawarra and South Coast Aborigines*. Wollongong, NSW: Aboriginal Education Unit, Wollongong University.

Perry, T. M. 1963. *Australia's First Frontier: The spread of settlement in New South Wales 1788–1829*. Melbourne: Melbourne University Press in association with The Australian National University.

Peterson, N. 1993. Demand sharing: reciprocity and the pressure for generosity among foragers. *American Anthropologist* 95: 860.

Pickering, M. 1999. Consuming doubts: what some people ate? Or what some people swallowed? In L. Goldman (ed.), *The Anthropology of Cannibalism*. Westport, Conn.: Bergin & Garvey.

Redmond, A. 2005. Strange relatives: mutualities and dependencies between Aborigines and pastoralists in the northern Kimberley. *Oceania* 75: 234–46.

Reece, R. 1974. *Aborigines and Colonists*. Sydney: Sydney University Press.

Reynolds, H. 1981. *The Other Side of the Frontier: An interpretation of the Aboriginal response to the invasion and settlement of Australia*. Townsville, Qld: History Department, James Cook University.

Robinson, F. and York, B. 1977. *The Black Resistance*. Camberwell, Vic.: Widescope International Publishers.

Robinson, G. A. 1844. Field journals April 13 – May 11 1844. Unpublished transcription by I. D. Clark [1998], Mitchell Library, Sydney.

Rose, C. 1923. Recollections of the early days of Moruya. *Journal and Proceedings of the Royal Australian Historical Society* VIII.

Sahlins, M. 1995. *How 'Natives' Think. About Captain Cook, for example*. Chicago: University of Chicago Press.

Sansom, B. 1988. A grammar of exchange. In I. Keen (ed.), *Being Black: Aboriginal cultures in 'settled' Australia*. Canberra: Aboriginal Studies Press.

Strathern, M. 1992. The decomposition of an event. *Cultural Anthropology* 7: 244–54.

Taussig, M. 1987. *Shamanism, Colonialism and the Wild Man*. Chicago: University of Chicago Press.

Taussig, M. 2002. Culture of terror—space of death: Roger Casement's Putumayo Report and the explanation of torture. In J. Vincent (ed.), *The Anthropology of Politics. A reader in ethnography, theory and critique*. Oxford: Blackwell.

Thomas, N. 1994. *Colonialism's Culture: Anthropology, travel and government*. Cambridge: Polity Press.

Walker, W. 1821. Walker to Watson, 8 November 1821. Wesleyan Mission House Despatches, Bonwick Transcripts Missionary, 1824–1829, Mitchell Library, Sydney.

Walker, W. n.d. Walker to General Secretaries. Wesleyan Mission House Despatches, Bonwick Transcripts Missionary, 1824–1829, Mitchell Library, Sydney.

Wesson, S. 2000. *An Historical Atlas of the Aborigines of Eastern Victoria and Far South-Eastern New South Wales*. Melbourne: School of Geography and Environmental Science, Monash University.

Wesson, S. 2002. The Aborigines of eastern Victoria and far south-eastern New South Wales, 1830 to 1910: an historical geography. Unpublished PhD thesis, School of Geography and Environmental Science, Monash University, Melbourne.

White, J. M. 2010. Peas, beans and riverbanks: seasonal picking and dependence in the Tuross Valley. In I. Keen (ed.), *Indigenous Participation in Australian Economies: Historical and anthropological perspectives*. Canberra: ANU E Press.

White, J. M. 2011. Histories of Indigenous–settler relations: reflections on internal colonialism and the hybrid economy. *Australian Aboriginal Studies* 1: 81–96.

3. Tracking *Wurnan*: Transformations in the trade and exchange of resources in the northern Kimberley

Anthony Redmond

Trade: buy and sell, engage in…(in commodity, with person); have a transaction (with person for thing); carry merchandise (to place) [ME, F. MLG *trade* track, f. OS trada, f. tredan TREAD].

— *Concise Oxford Dictionary*

The recent intensification of the demands from a range of government agencies that Indigenous Australian landholders shift their focus from a previously valorized cultural identity-based attachment to land to an economic-development approach to those lands has drawn upon the long-prevailing perception of a sharp division between usufruct (a rights-based model) and landed cultural identities (an underlying title-based model) in traditional Aboriginal Australia. In this overly dichotomised schema, economic use rights occupy the unmarked position, reflecting the naturalisation of market-derived notions of the alienability of property while the marked position has been occupied by an exoticised notion of Indigenous people spiritually bound to country. This tendency to separate the cultural from the economic requires an exploration of some of the assumptions underpinning the supposed incommensurability of a modern economy and Aboriginal exchange networks.

In contrast with that dichotomisation between land rights/economy and land title/culture, this chapter explores transformations in the traditional *wurnan* trade network that overarches a number of socio-cultural regions in the Kimberley and beyond, operating at both small-scale interpersonal and larger-scale inter-group levels, channelling ritual and simple economic objects of desire through predetermined but flexible trading routes (Redmond 2001).

The conceptual and political polarities between economy and culture referred to above have manifested in slightly different forms over time, so that sometimes they have been framed as a distinction between an enduring mythic consciousness with its timeless traditions attributed to indigenes and an agent-driven history with a peculiar capacity for innovation attributed to the colonial powers—in short, between modernity's focus on time as opposed to an Aboriginal focus on place (Rumsey 1994).[1]

---

1 Some might also recall here the debates sparked by Tony Swain's *A Place for Strangers* (1993).

The same conceptual polarity has also been articulated in the anthropological distinction drawn between flexible economic bands, with their range of foraging grounds, vis-a-vis totemic clans, with their immoveable estate-based sacra and descent-based identities. This last distinction was, of course, fully elaborated by Les Hiatt in his 1962 critique of Radcliffe-Brown's long-prevailing model of the horde (1930–31), which had conflated the heterogeneous economic group possessing use rights in land with the more stable descent groups holding title to lands by dint of a sacralised ancestral identity.

Hiatt's necessary clarification of that issue subsequently spawned a tendency to over-sacralise Indigenous property rights so that cultural and economic property rights have often been construed as distinct. This division is reflected most clearly in the *Aboriginal Land Rights (Northern Territory) Act 1976* (Cwlth) (NT *ALRA*), which defined the traditional owners for any tract of country with a double aspect: as someone with 'primary spiritual responsibility' for Dreaming sites (defining such owners by means of genealogical legitimation), and as those who use that tract of country in the sense of hunting and foraging.

This splitting off of an Aboriginal high culture from the economy has been made ever more explicit in native title case law, in which the holistic beneficiary possession originally inscribed in the *Native Title Act 1993* (Cwlth) (*NTA*) has been reduced to a fragile and fragmented 'bundle of rights' resulting in a situation in which the right to trade in resources taken from a claim area has yet to be recognised by the courts.[2] Opponents of such a right have generally mounted an argument that ritual objects rather than utilitarian ones were the main items of exchange in Aboriginal Australia, despite the abundant evidence that both these kinds of goods and services were exchanged or 'sold'.

The polarisation of ceremonial exchange vis-a-vis highly objectivised barter or pure trade has been a central analytical tool of social anthropology at

---

2   *Northern Territory of Australia v Alyawarr, Kaytetye, Warumungu, Wakaya Native Title Claim Group* [2005] FCAFC 135 (29 July 2005). The claim group comprises seven landholding estate groups of traditional country south-east of Tennant Creek. The court held that in relation to the pastoral lease land, native title rights were not exclusive, but did include a range of rights; however, the right to trade resources is not included. A right to trade the resources of the land may be regarded as a right in relation to land; however, in this case, there was insufficient evidence to support the finding of a native title right to trade in the resources of the claim area: [152]–[157]; *Yarmirr v Northern Territory of Australia* (1998) 82 FCR 533; *Yanner v Eaton* [1999] HCA 53; (1999) 201 CLR 351 considered. 156: 'The Northern Territory argued that the right to trade in the resources of the land necessarily implies a native title right to exclusive possession thereof. It was submitted that his Honour's reference to *Yanner v* Eaton [1999] HCA 53; (1999) 201 CLR 351 and the absence of any right to own flora and fauna implied a view that the evidence was consistent with a native title right to take flora and fauna but not to own it. In any event, the evidence was said not to support any right to "trade" in the resources of the land as that term is generally understood...The Northern Territory argued that that evidence made no reference at all to any commercial or profit motives or any level of organised business operation.' 157: 'In his reasons for judgment the learned trial judge found that the use or exercise of the right to use and enjoy the resources of the claim area was well supported. Evidence had also been given by the applicants that they had asserted the right to use the natural resources of the claim area including water, trees, bush medicines, soakages, sacred sites and other things including ochre from various places in the claim area.'

least since Malinowski's ethnography of the Kula trading ring (1922), which established a functionalist template for explicating the production of social cohesion and political alliance in the acephalous hunter-gather and/or small-scale horticultural societies of the British colonial possessions in Africa and Oceania.

Malinowski described various types of exchanges ranging from the 'free gifts' flowing between spouses and between fathers and their children to the various types of 'equivalent' and 'non-equivalent' exchanges that he saw as being spread across a continuous field, with non-relational barter or trade at the far end of his gift/exchange spectrum (Malinowski 1922:177–91)—a position that Sahlins later termed 'negative reciprocity' (1972).

Mauss's seminal, comparative monograph, *The Gift* (1924), drew extensively upon Malinowski's ethnography and drafted a template for modern sociology to draw distinctions between the personalising, exchange-focused gift economies of small-scale societies and the depersonalising independent transactor market economies of modernity.

The cultural capacity for reciprocity between persons and small groups in gift economies to 'annul time' was equated with an alluring capacity to annul political power (Gell 1992:24). Annette Weiner's critique of 'axiomatic reciprocity' in studies of Melanesian societies (1992) argued that 'the anthropological confidence' in reciprocity as the motivation for social exchanges in non-state societies—far from being an appreciation of marked cultural and economic difference—derived from the central place accorded to a norm of reciprocity elaborated in a political philosophy that 'has its roots in the market beliefs of Locke, Stewart and Adam Smith. These in turn arose from ideas about authority and the sacred in the Middle Ages where norms of reciprocity were used to sanctify dominant political hierarchies, involving gifts of patronage and charity' (Weiner 1992:28).[3]

This author suggested that if reciprocity is presented as 'natural' to man's economic and religious life, the give and take of exchanges between men and between men and gods allowed hierarchical relationships to be represented as mutually beneficial to all (Weiner 1992). Weiner went on to show how Henry Maine's distinction between 'moveable' and 'immovable' property posited the category of 'immovable' (that is, inalienable) property as the 'greatest impediment to the free circulation of objects'—the ultimate goal of an emergent commodity economy. The cosmological authentication of immovable property produced in origin myths and fictive or real genealogies gave rise

---

3   See Norman Freeman's *A Short History of the Norman Conquest* (1880) for an exploration of the notion of reciprocity as the essence of feudal relations.

to high-status, 'transcendent' patrilineal possessions, such as inherited landed estates imbued with a quality of 'timelessness' derived from being repositories of gods and genealogies.

During her 1935–37 Kimberley fieldwork, Phyllis Kaberry quickly recognised the similarities between Malinowski's descriptions of the Kula and the regional institution of 'Wirnan', noting that cosmological beliefs about Galaroo, the Rainbow Serpent, permeated and authenticated this exchange network.

> A man may sicken because he has not played his part in a particular kind of exchange resembling somewhat the Kula of the Trobriands. His exchange partner compels him to dream of a pearl-shell, one of the articles of exchange, and said to have been given to a man by the rainbow serpent. (Kaberry 1936: 284)

Kaberry produced a sketch map (Map 3.1) that showed that the routes along which different classes of items were traded in different directions from west to east were 'shells…mandi (stones), and sacred objects'. From east to west run 'dilly bags; fighting sticks; bamboo; wax; nagas; milinyin (bamboo shafts)'.

At the same time, 'reciprocity' was identified as a central organising feature of Arnhem Land ('Murngin') sociality in Warner's monograph *A Black Civilization* (1958, original 1937). Drawing on a functionalist model from Malinowski (1922), Warner described the 'ritual and economic reciprocity' that formed the 'fundamental basis of this ceremonial exchange which produces a stability and balance in the social relations of the groups and individuals. It organizes the structure of the economic group by the exchange of ceremonial objects' (1958:96). This was seen to mirror the reciprocity in marriage exchanges, together forming the ultimate basis of the local social contract. Donald Thomson's (1949) monograph on this subject, however, eschewed strong distinctions between ritual and economic exchanges, noting that for north-east Arnhem Landers, the ceremonial exchange cycle 'is not in any sense barter although circulation of goods on a large scale results' (1949:77). Thomson's view was ultimately consistent with that of Malinowski, who had noted that, while they appeared at opposite ends of a spectrum, in the Kula 'it is impossible to draw any fixed line between trade, on the one hand, and exchange of gifts on the other' (1922:176).

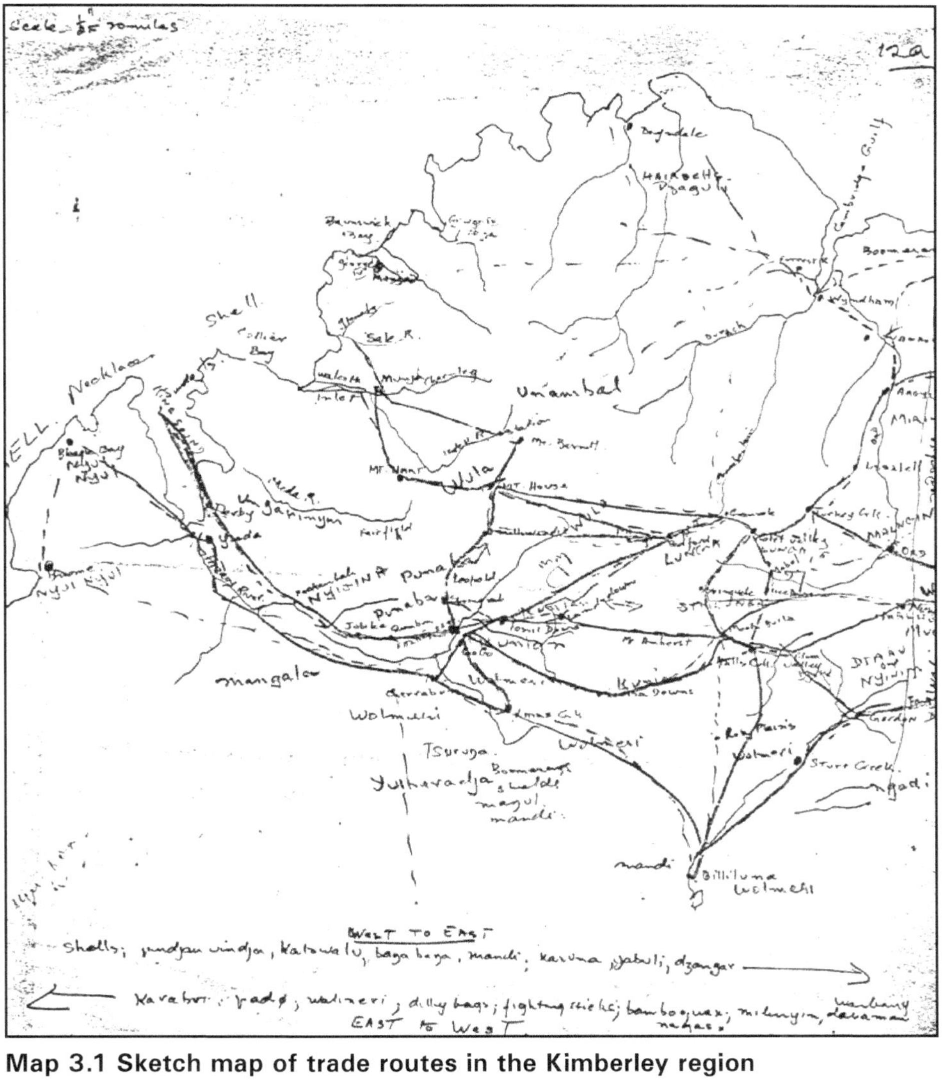

Map 3.1 Sketch map of trade routes in the Kimberley region

Source: Kaberry (1936).

Kimberley Ceremonial Exchanges and Trade

Traditional Kimberley Aboriginal ritual and economic life were clearly not experienced as dichotomous realms of social life. The transactions that occur between groups and individuals through the *wurnan* channels have always involved pragmatic, ephemeral economic objects such as meat and hunting implements as well as ritual sacred/secret objects. Frederick McCarthy noted that

> the making of gifts—foods, ornaments and weapons—is really part of the kinship system, forms a necessary adjunct to betrothal, marriage and initiation, and especially to the settling of grievances and quarrels; indeed it occurs at all large gatherings of natives…recent researches in north-eastern South Australia, north Western Australia, the Daly River district and elsewhere, have revealed that the economic customs and institutions dovetail into the kinship, ceremonial and legal aspects of social life. (McCarthy 1939:12)

McCarthy produced a map showing the north Kimberley trade routes and listing the objects exchanged through Ngarinyin country as 'stone axes, red ochre, stone spear points, bamboo spears' (McCarthy 1939:436). McCarthy noted that a single exchange object may have both pragmatic and ritual qualities compressed into it such as quartz spear-tips, which were used for the hunting of kangaroo as well as for revenge killings involving the dangerously magical properties of quartz. Another example of the compression of ritual/economic properties into an object is in gifts of chewing tobacco, which might contain ritual qualities from having been 'sung' by someone seeking to make the recipient a sexual partner. It is clear that other elements of the economics of everyday life (such as the increase ritual for the supply of available foods) are intimately bound up with ritual beliefs.

Tindale later recorded that objects as diverse as songs, ochres, shells, spear-tips, axes, second-hand clothes and scraps of tin and steel have made their way through the *wurnan* routes over the years (Tindale 1953:1015–17, 1033). As one senior Kimberley man told me: 'Man share 'em out, give me away everything *wurnan*, like selling clothes, present, all the spear, bush sugarbag, honey, that's what they do.'

Another noted:

> Sometimes, if I need ochre for my paintings that I sell or else for a ceremony, I can make a private *wurnan*. I get in touch with my *gumbali* [namesake] in Kununurra and he will talk to his mob to make sure that it's OK. Then we can do a private trade without going through all the

partners in between. Then when I see him next I can kill a kangaroo for him. Later on he might need something from me and he will let me know.

Another clear example of this ceremonial exchange for an only slightly delayed quotidian gift occurs in the yearly initiation ceremonies where clothes, cash and other presents are given to performers at the conclusion of the ceremonial cycle. Senior Ngarinyin man Paddy Neowarra told me how,

> after we go to other communities for ceremonies, we will come back later to receive presents from them during a 'smoke', after all the business is finished. Everybody can relax then. People give us clothes and food and blankets for bringing our ceremony to them. Maybe to Looma or Fitzroy Crossing or Kununurra. Ceremony and everyday things are mixed up together.

> This is how we trade one thing or another right across the Kimberley and down into the desert. All sorts of things, not just secret thing, but meat and sugar-bag, clothes and motorcars and money too. Or I might need a special type of wood for something I'm making or bamboo. All these sorts of things I can get through the *wurnan*.

This confluence between ritual and economic exchanges is particularly pronounced in gifts that are due to a man's in-laws. Peter Lucich, conducting fieldwork in Mowanjum and Kalumburu in 1963, found for instance that

> the system for giving gifts to a *waia* (father-in-law) was named *embadi*… made up of durable goods such as mirrors, tomahawks and clothes. Previously, they had included spears, spinifex wax, pearlshells and hair-belts. If a man shared food in the settlement he was expected to give portions to his wife's parents, his own parents, and his immediate neighbours, in that order. (Lucich 1967:196)

Akerman subsequently demonstrated the efflorescence of this trade during his fieldwork in the early 1980s.[4] Akerman's study of the *wurnan* showed that cash and food were amongst the objects that were traded and that by the mid-1970s the trade routes had been re-routed through the pastoral stations and missions where the majority of people lived (Akerman 1980).

Map 3.3 is a conflation of a number of different ways of looking at Ngarinyin country. The base map shows the moiety blocs, *mamalarrba* and *mornarrba*, overlaid upon a clan map in which the clan epicentre is represented by the

---

4   Andrew Strathern described this impact of prestigious new goods from the colonial commodity economy accelerating the existing cycles of trade and exchange in local Indigenous gift exchange economy as 'efflorescence' (Gregory 1982:115, 166).

small circles with numbers in the middle. Over the moiety shapes, I have drawn in the *wurnan* segments that Rumsey (1996) showed as links between many of the clans in the region. This produced the jagged series of lines, with directional arrows showing which clans made *wurnan* gifts in a major west to east branch of the exchange routes. Naturally, this jagged series of straight lines forms vectors only and does not represent the actual course over which *wurnan* would have been carried, which would have followed valleys and river courses. Thus, the tracks of the journeys would have responded much more closely to the contours of the country, also taking into account the position in which the *wurnan* gatekeeper would have been living at the time, and the locations within the clan countries of recognised *Barurru* (law grounds) for such exchanges, such as Monggowa, Nyaliga, Bijili, and so on. Nevertheless, even the straight lines linking clan epicentres tend towards a distinct patterning.

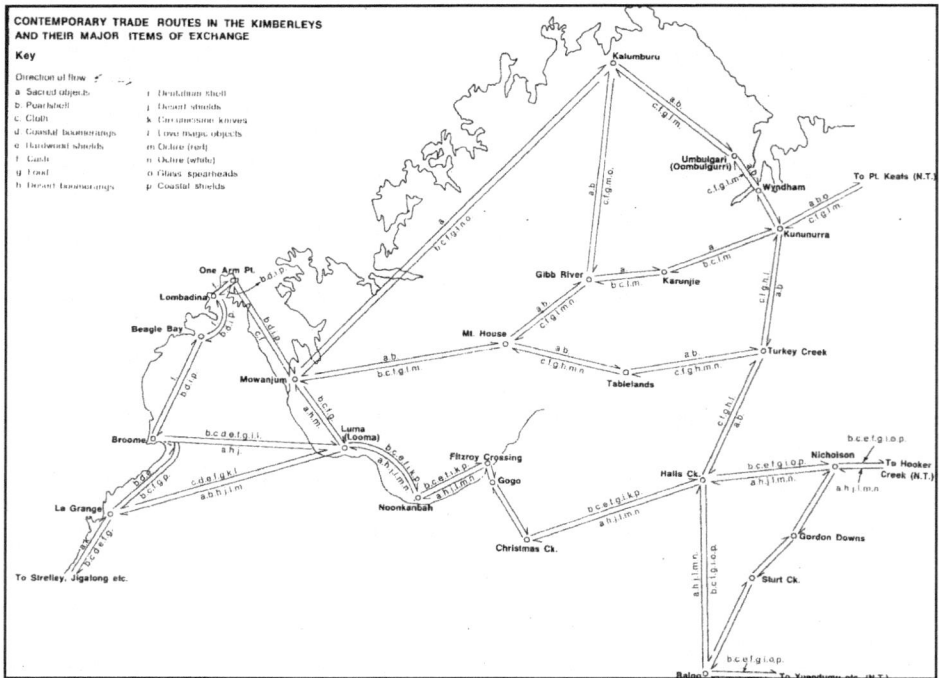

Map 3.2 Contemporary Trade Routes in the Kimberleys and their Major Items of Exchange

Source: Akerman (1980).

In the second stage of the process, I have then coloured the line segments to show what type of kin relationships exist between each of the particular clans that are linked by *wurnan* exchanges. The colour key on the map shows the relationship pertaining between the clans as *wurnan* partners, rather than an egocentric view of a person from one clan of all the other linked clans. Thus, at a clan level, each clan is assumed to be calling the other either the one relationship name or the two names that are available to the members of the adjacent generations of each clan. Thus, the green lines represent both a mother and a wife link for the members of the trading partners' clans, the orange lines both a mother-in-law and a mother's mother link, and the blue lines all the patrilineal links. The thin pink line, representing another branch of the *wurnan* running in the opposite direction (east to west), links clan countries for which I have not marked the nature of the kin relationships pertaining between them.

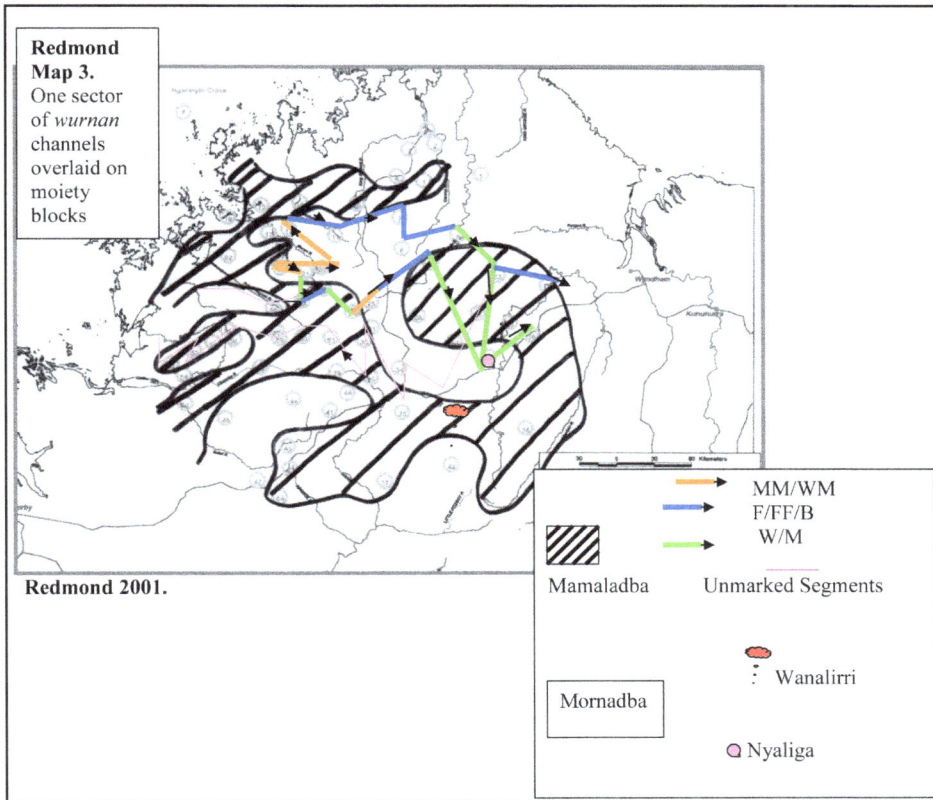

Redmond Map 3. One sector of *wurnan* channels overlaid on moiety blocks

Redmond 2001.

MM/WM
F/FF/B
W/M

Mamaladba — Unmarked Segments

Wanalirri

Mornadba

Nyaliga

Map 3.3 *Wurnan* channels overlaid on moiety blocks

Source: Redmond (2001).

It will be observed that the coloured lines linking clans—the *wurnan* segments—follow rather closely the contours of the moiety shapes. It will also be evident that each time there is a linking green line (the M and W links), there is a crossing of the moiety boundary. On the other hand, the orange (MM/WM) segments and the blue (F/FF/B) segments tend to mark out the boundary of the moiety shapes. I have included the location of the major *wanjina* gallery Wanalirri because it is from here that the distribution of *wanjina* across the entire region is said to have occurred and its position in a relatively narrow land bridge of *mamalarrba* country seems to be suggestive. I have also included the major *wurnan* site Nyaliga, located near Karunjie Station, to show its significant spatial positioning as a *nyornarrba* nodal point reaching into the heart of *mamalarrba*.

While maintaining their overall directionality, the *wurnan* channels can be re-routed to take account of the location of new communities. The law ground near the settlement where I lived played a crucial role in current exchange relations despite the settlement having existed in the general area only since the postwar period. As the holders of important ritual objects, a number of the senior residents formed a ritual partnership with another same-moiety man who acted as their 'manager' or 'player' in ceremonial activities. The status of being one who 'holds' objects, or country, was framed in terms of the nurturance attaching to the authority exercised in this ritual arena of men's sociality (see also Myers 1980a:119). This role places a responsibility on the participants to care for the country where the ritual objects are stored before they are passed along to their partners in neighbouring communities. As members of the Jun. gun moiety association of clans relating to each other as 'brothers, fathers and sons', the ritual relationships are underpinned by prior relationship between the clan countries that are jointly holding the objects of exchange (see also Blundell and Layton 1978). Significantly, although two of these senior men were said to be the holders of the objects, another man on whose clan country this ground lies was asserted to be the 'real boss'.

There is an integral connection between the relationship to countries that is forged through the initiation ceremonies and through ceremonial exchange networks. When initiates are sent to a far-flung community to 'go for law', ritual exchange objects are often sent back to the community to which the adolescents belong. While this exchange is delayed rather than direct, the exchange remains one way in which person and country are identified in the sense that a new social identity is created through initiation and the objects are provided as a kind of 'compensation' to the country and people who have 'lost a child'. This is certainly the case for one of these men's links, which emanated from his having taken over his older brother's role of initiator for a wide region of country. His services were thus in much demand and he was often engaged in negotiations with initiation bosses both outside and within the region.

In many of the settlements created after European settlement, such as the large encampment of Ngarinyin people that existed at Kimberley Downs until the 1980s, the camp itself was located adjacent to important *wurnan* trading locations. At Karunjie Station, the community was located at what was regarded by local people as a 'safe' distance from important *wurnan* storage places. The site for an emergent new community gained considerable local prestige from its proximity to a major *wurnan* intersection. It is at inter-group boundaries that the position of 'gatekeeper' (one who holds the 'seat' for a segment of the *wurnan*) is most important, since these individuals come to embody the social and cultural differences that are being both transcended and maintained through inter-group exchanges. Senior men with affinal ties to different cultural blocs acted as conduits with far-flung communities and commonly oriented their camps towards those places. The power of the *wurnan* to maintain social stability through 'ranking' individuals and communities in relation to each other is enforced by the sanction of expulsion from the *wurnan*, which effectively leaves a man 'outside the law' and thence socially and physically vulnerable. Someone who feels he has been 'left out of business' can also bring relationships between *wurnan* partners to crisis point by threatening to 'close the road' in his segment of the exchange route, thus bringing all exchanges to a halt since it is impermissible to deliberately bypass one sector of the exchange complex. Such closures can result in periods of stagnation in *wurnan* exchanges lasting several years, fuelled by the resentment of one man nursing a grievance of perceived neglect. Since these days the segments are actually linked by physical roads, the threat of a ceremonial 'road' closure has the possibility of inhibiting the movement of people between adjacent communities.

At least until the late 1990s, *wurnan* remained one of the strongest traditional social institutions operating across a wide area of the Kimberley in terms of inter-group communication and organised exchange. As such it carried enormous social prestige, which was enhanced by the secret/sacred nature of some of the exchanges that form its basis.[5]

Despite its capacity for flexibility, the *wurnan* system might become periodically ossified (though the process is perhaps already, in a local sense, 'ossified', the term *wurnan* being suggestively similar to *wurnorr*, a word meaning 'the bone of'—in this case, the social world). Stagnation results from a failure of participation by particular living people for one reason or another.

Many of the Ngarinyin myths about the founding of exchange relationships between groups and individuals in the Kimberley region have a strong focus upon vegetable foods, which became transformed into sacred objects and induced the necessity of organised sharing of resources. The feminine quality of the boards is underscored by the boards being known, in their most generic appellation, as *mayangarri*—a word glossed by Ngarinyin people as 'belonging to vegetable

---

5   One of the consequences of the prestige arising from the secret/sacred nature of the wurnan is that it has become a strongly identifying feature of Kimberley Aboriginal traditional political life vis-a-vis the colonial political structures that have been introduced over the past hundred years. Amongst these we must count the 'post-colonial' land councils and other forms of political organisation (such as the Aboriginal and Torres Strait Islander Commission) arising from the era in which self-determination was official Federal Government policy (1972–96). That policy has now been replaced with the much more conservative and market-oriented jargon of 'self-management'.

foods'. They are regarded as 'life-giving' and 'full of Wunggurr'—evidenced by their lustrous fat-smeared surfaces, which keep them 'living'. Older people believed that *'garnmanggu* [yam] and *jarrgun* [bush potato] all blang *wurnan* because everyone share that tucker'. Their association with *angga*—women's 'U'-shaped bark coolamons—as the holding body for the gathered vegetable foods highlights their capacity to symbolise the feminine power intrinsic to such foods. Nancy Munn came to a similar conclusion when she wrote that 'if we take the boards as being progeny of the women and as also containing the women's substance within them, then what the men take over is the objectified form of the "women-children"—that is, they take control of the immortal, objective aspect epitomized in the sacred boards' (1970:156).

One of the other major *wurnan* gifts was *Gulangi* black plum cakes, which were produced by washing, pounding and drying the fruit and then mixing this with 'sugarbag' (wild honey), the process and object being evocative of condensed female labour. This labour promotes the possibility of a convivial sociality, just as freshly baked bread and newly cooked damper from the coals now always elicit a gathering of young men and women around the fire.[6] In *wurnan* exchanges, a baler shell filled with honey was commonly presented to a partner with ribald comments concerning its female symbolism.

In the story of how men came to possess these sacred boards, the stolen objects are said to have originally belonged to women.[7] An old woman, Nyambuliji, had been blinded by *gorid*, a whirlwind, which allowed her husband, Wibalma, to take them from her and then to fashion his own. His wife's blindness conveniently allows Wibalma to continue to fashion his boards without women being able to view them—a practice that persists to this day.[8]

The moiety heroes, Wodoy and Jun.gun, subsequently steal the boards from Wibalma, escaping with the embodiments of his wife's sexuality and fertility.[9] The moiety heroes banded together to steal the boards because Wibalma had tried to store the boards and keep them for himself, refusing the sociality of others. After stealing the boards, the moiety heroes, Wodoy and Jun.gun, instituted the marriage system of exchanges of women between moieties by fighting over the stupidity of Jun.gun in trying to cook honey and planning to marry his own daughter (see also Blundell and Layton 1978).

---

6   Love noted that 'the camps of young men, who have no wives, will share in the vegetable food, which is specially the province of the women to provide, and the married men, too, will receive food from other women than their own wives' (1936:73).

7   This is a very common theme in regards to sacred objects (cf. Berndt 1952:16–17; Morphy 1991:86; Strehlow 1947:94; Taussig 1999:180).

8   In a Papunya story with similar thematics, the husband, rather than the wife, is blind (cited by Morton 1985:129).

9   Roheim noted of the ancestral Arrernte women who held sacred objects that 'an alknarintja woman means a woman who "turns her eyes away"' (1971:156).

In the foundational *wurnan* story, the plum cake is stolen by a female emu who escapes from the sphere of exchange in which the different clan animals are instituting the law for sharing. She absconds with this plum cake tucked under her wing only to be speared to death, finally becoming embodied in the dark hole of the Milky Way, the spears still visible in her body, forever grazing on the ground beneath the *gulangi* tree, which forms the Southern Cross (see also Morton 1985:120).

The relationships most marked by avoidance for Ngarinyin people are those between people who are defined as *rambarr*—mother-in-law and son-in-law to each other (that is, those who are linked by the transmission of female resources). *Wurnan* partners live in anticipation of receiving objects that both increase their charisma and enhance human fertility. This is achieved through expressive acts of giving, the expansion of the self into widening circles of relatedness.

The concealing containers in which *wurnan* gifts are given—from the honey-filled baler shell and the spear-tips wrapped in paperbark to the sweat-stained old shirt in which red ochre is passed on—all partake of a powerful female embodiment. The paperbark, *wulun* (*wulun nyindi* is an idiomatic reference to woman in Ngarinyin), wallets, *nguwarra*, are bound with red-ochre-stained string just as the bones of funerary packages are presented to the maternal relatives for cradling before second burial.

Wurnan and Karunjie Station

For many Kimberley Aborigines, much of the significance of Karunjie Station in the north-east Kimberley derives from the ways in which the Indigenous and settler cultures and economies have been inextricably interwoven throughout living memory. This station lease, originally taken by hard-bitten, repatriated World War I veterans and 'Afghan' (actually north Indian) cameleers, some of whom had also fought with the British Army in Afghanistan, was the location of one of the biggest exchange centres in the region, drawing in sometimes hundreds of participants to its *wurnan* ceremonies where bolts of red cloth from the Chinese stores in Wyndham port, as well as spear-tips, bamboo, shells and ochres, were traded. By the early 1920s it had also become a ration depot to induce some of those who were there for ceremony to stay for longer periods and to work at the station. Others were drawn into working on sandalwood finding and cutting, which the Afghan camel teams then carried overland to Wyndham port from where it was shipped to South-East Asia for joss-stick manufacture.

In my earlier paper with historian Fiona Skyring (Redmond and Skyring 2010), we analysed the effects of the emergent frontier economy of the interwar period in creating an efflorescence of *wurnan* trade, not dissimilar to that discerned by Kim Akerman in the late 1970s when wages, welfare cash, vehicles and a capacity for high mobility first became available to Aboriginal pastoral workers.

One of the consequences of the ritual prestige of the *wurnan* in the twenty-first century is that it has now become a strongly identifying symbol of continuing desires for an autonomous Aboriginal political life vis-a-vis the post-colonial political structures such as land councils and resource agencies introduced over the past 30 years. I perceive a strong desire amongst many Indigenous people to keep this distance and autonomy between *wurnan* relationships and the post-1980 corporatisation of Aboriginal political life. This means always staying a diffident step ahead of the creeping tide of acronyms and acrimonies of government agencies, which are now major political players in Kimberley economic life. The perceived dangers associated with *wurnan*'s ritual objects help to deter the complete absorption of the Indigenous economy into the mainstream economy and continue to allow a sociopolitical space for Kimberley people to set their own 'gold standards', prices and exchange rates within a semi-compartmentalised intra-Indigenous domain.

The Indigenous desire for this form of political autonomy, however, ought not cover the tracks of the obvious—namely, that the level of autonomy that is demanded by the post-welfare state is likely to be possible only if the Indigenous right to trade in the resources of native title claim areas is recognised by the courts as a right flowing from the inextricably bound nature of economic and ritual exchanges inherent to the underlying Aboriginal title to those lands.

References

Akerman, K. 1980. Material culture and trade in the Kimberleys today. In *Aborigines of the West: Their past and their present*. Perth: University of Western Australia Press.

Berndt, R. M. 1951. Ceremonial exchange in western Arnhem Land. *Southwestern Journal of Anthropology* 7 (2): 156–76.

Berndt, R. M. 1952. *Djanggawul*. London: Routledge and Kegan Paul.

Blundell, V. and Layton, R. 1978. Marriage, myth and models of exchange in the west Kimberleys. *Mankind* 11: 231–45.

Freeman, A. 1880. *A Short History of the Norman Conquest of England*. Oxford: Clarendon Press.

Gell, A. 1992. *The Anthropology of Time*. Cambridge: Cambridge University Press.

Gregory, C. 1982. *Gifts and Commodities*. London: Academic Press.

Hiatt, L. R. 1962. Local organization among the Australian Aborigines. *Oceania* 32 (4): 267–86.

Jebb, M. 2002. *Blood, Sweat and Welfare: A history of white bosses and Aboriginal pastoral workers*. Perth: University of Western Australia Press.

Kaberry, P. 1935–6, AIATSIS MS739/2 Item 14. Sketch Map of trade routes in the Kimberley region, Australian Institute of Aboriginal and Torres Strait Islander Studies, Canberra.

Love, J. R. B. 1936. *Stone Age Bushmen of Today: Life and adventure among a tribe of savages in north-western Australia*. London and Glasgow: Blackie & Son.

Lucich, P. 1967. The development of Omaha kinship terminologies in three Australian Aboriginal tribes of the Kimberley division, Western Australia. MSc in Anthropology thesis, University of Western Australia, Perth.

McCarthy, F. D. 1939. Trade in Aboriginal Australia, and trade relationships with Torres Strait, New Guinea and Malaya. *Oceania* 9 (4) (1939): 405–38; 10 (1) (1939): 80–104; 10 (2) (1939): 171–95.

Malinowski, B. 1922. *Argonauts of the Western Pacific*. London: Routledge and Kegan Paul.

Mauss, M. 1954. *The Gift*. London: Routledge.

Morphy, H. 1991. *Ancestral Connections: Art and an Aboriginal system of knowledge*. Chicago: University of Chicago Press.

Morton, J. 1985. Sustaining desire: a structuralist interpretation of myth and male cult in Central Australia. 2 vols. Unpublished PhD thesis, Australian National University, Canberra.

Munn, N. 1970. The transformation of subjects into objects in Walbiri and Pitjanatjara myth. In Ronald M. Berndt (ed.), *Australian Aboriginal Anthropology: Modern studies in the social anthropology of the Australian Aborigines*. Perth: University of Western Australia Press.

Myers F. 1980a. The Cultural Basis of politics in Pintupi Life. *Mankind* 12 (3): 197-214

Peterson, N. 1997. Demand sharing: reciprocity and the pressure for generosity among foragers. In F. Merlan, J. Morton and A. Rumsey (eds), *Scholar and Sceptic: Australian Aboriginal studies in honour of L. R. Hiatt*. Canberra: Aboriginal Studies Press.

Radcliffe-Brown, A. R. 1930–31. The social organisation of Australian tribes. Parts 1 & 2. *Oceania* 1: 34–63, 199–246.

Redmond, A. 2001. Rulug Wayirri: moving kin and country in the northern Kimberley. Unpublished PhD thesis, University of Sydney, Sydney.

Redmond, A. and Skyring, F. 2010. Exchange and appropriation: the *Wurnan* economy and Aboriginal land and labour at Karunjie Station, north-western Australia. In I. Keen (ed.), *Indigenous Participation in Australian Economies: Historical and anthropological perspectives*. Canberra: ANU E Press.

Roheim, G. 1971 [1945]. *Eternal Ones of the Dream*. New York: International Universities Press.

Rumsey, A. 1994. The Dreaming, human agency and inscriptive practice. *Oceania* 65: 116–31.

Rumsey, A. 1996. Aspects of native title and social identity in the Kimberleys and beyond. *Australian Aboriginal Studies* 1996 (1): 2–10.

Sahlins, M. 1972. *Stone-Age Economics*. New York: Aldine.

Schutz, A. 1967. *Collected Papers. Volumes 1 and 2*. The Hague: Nijhoff.

Strehlow, T. G. 1947. *Aranda Traditions*. Melbourne: Melbourne University Press.

Swain, T. 1993. *A Place for Strangers. Towards a history of Australian Aboriginal being*. Cambridge: Cambridge University Press.

Taussig, M. 1999. A joyous thing with maggots at the centre. In *Defacement: Public secrets and the labour of the negative*. Stanford, Calif.: Stanford University Press.

Thomas, N. 1991. *Entangled Objects: Exchange, material culture, and colonialism in the Pacific*. Cambridge, Mass.: Harvard University Press.

Thomson, D. F. 1949. *Economic Structure and the Ceremonial Exchange Cycle in Arnhem Land*. Melbourne: Melbourne University Press.

Tindale, N. 1953. Anthropological field notes on the UCLA–UA Anthropological Expedition, NW Australia. Unpublished, South Australian Museum, Adelaide.

Warner, W. Lloyd 1958. *A Black Civilization: A social study of an Australian tribe*. New York: Harper & Brothers.

Weiner, A. 1992. *Inalienable Possessions: The paradox of keeping-while-giving*. Berkeley: University of California Press.

4. Camels and the Transformation of Indigenous Economic Landscapes

Petronella Vaarzon-Morel

Introduction

Over the past hundred or more years camels (*Camelus dromedarius*)—at once symbols of mobility and of domestication—have figured prominently in Indigenous socioeconomic landscapes. As 'animal powered transport' (Kennedy 2005), they have played a pivotal role in the colonisation of desert Australia and in the development of the settler economy (Blainey 1966; Kennedy 2005). They have also had a part to play in the incorporation of Indigenous people into the encapsulating society. Due to the suitability of camels to the arid conditions of Central Australia, European explorers, Muslim cameleers, pastoralists, missionaries, doggers, police, anthropologists and miners, among others, used camels to variously penetrate, transport goods across, survey and expand the settler frontier. Often Indigenous people were involved in these ventures. Reflecting on the role of camels in Australia from a Western economic perspective, McKnight wrote that 'in no other extensive portion of the world, except where there was landward dispersal into adjacent and contiguous regions, have large numbers of exotic cameloids become sufficiently adapted to play a major role in economic development' (1969:130).

Yet, as McKnight notes, their contribution to development was 'short-run'. In the 1920s motor vehicles began to replace camels in the transport industry, and thousands of camels were progressively released to range free in the bush (Edwards et al. 2008; McKnight 1969). Gradually, camels were incorporated into the domestic economy of the Pitjantjatjara and some neighbouring groups in the eastern Western Desert. Commenting on this phenomenon in the 1960s, McKnight wrote that 'some natives of central Australia have, apparently with a minimum of cultural dislocation, assimilated the camel into their way of life' (1969:131; see also Rose 1965). Less than a decade later, however, Indigenous people were to gain access to cars and abandoned the use of camels for transport (Layton 1986:80; Peterson 2009). Since that period some Indigenous people have taken up new economic opportunities afforded by the growth of the feral camel population and camel tourism.

While there has been renewed interest in the role of Muslim cameleers in the settler economy (for example, Jones and Kenny 2007; Rajkowski 1987; Stevens 1989), surprisingly, with the exception of the sources mentioned earlier, information on Aboriginal people's interactions with camels is scant. Yet camels are bound up with transformations in Indigenous socioeconomic, moral and ecological landscapes in significant and complex ways. Moreover, these multi-layered linkages have ramifications for the economic utilisation and management of feral camels today. It is thus important to have a better understanding of Aboriginal relations to and with camels on the settler frontier than has been the case to date.

The purpose of this chapter is to trace the changing nature of Indigenous people's engagements with camels in Central Australian economies. My primary focus is the eastern Western Desert. Combining anthropological and historical perspectives, I draw on recent research (Edwards et al. 2008; Vaarzon-Morel 2008) as well as secondary and archival sources to show that the socioeconomic history of Indigenous people's engagements with camels is more varied and complex than has been documented to date. In doing so, I seek to problematise approaches that neglect or oversimplify the role played by introduced animals in Indigenous–settler relations in Australia.

Following a brief overview of relevant research, I examine Western Desert people's responses to camels during the early contact period. I then consider Pitjantjatjara and Yankunytjatjara people's use of camels during the transition to mission and pastoral stations, before discussing incipient engagements with the camel market economy during the 1980s and 1990s. Finally, I briefly address recent proposals to facilitate Indigenous economic involvement in the management of feral camels today. The chapter is exploratory in character and suggests further avenues for research.

History of Research

Inspired by Murphy and Steward's 1955 paper on cultural change among Mundurucu Indians in Brazil and Algonquians in Canada,[1] Gould et al. published a paper in 1972 comparing the history of the Western Desert Indigenous economy in Australia with that of Indians in the Great Basin of North America. They argue that, since contact, both of these hunting-and-gathering desert societies had 'followed a pattern of economic acculturation characterised by increasing dependence on European food and goods' (1972:265). In the case

---

1 The paper followed a line of anthropological inquiry into human interactions with fur-bearing animals and the relationship of these to territorial organisation, property and economy (see, for example, Leacock 1954, 1955; Nadasdy 2002; Snow 1968).

of Australia, they conclude that, unlike the Mundurucu and Algonquians, who, respectively, sold or bartered rubber and beaver pelts (1972:266), Western Desert people did not establish a viable relationship to the world economy because they lacked goods to sell or exchange (1972:265, 278). As part of their supporting evidence, they discuss 'Pitjantjatjara-speaking' (1972:266) people's reactions to introduced camels. Ignoring the earlier work of Rose (1965), they claim that these Aborigines simply hunted camels as they did native species. In their view, hunting camels involved nothing more than the 'application of new materials to traditional methods of exploiting available resources' and could not be considered a genuine adaptation (Gould et al. 1972: 265, 278).

In 1962 Fred Rose conducted research among Pitjantjatjara people at Angas Downs cattle station to the south of Alice Springs in the Northern Territory. He found that Pitjantjatjara people used camels extensively for their own transport. Employing a Marxist materialist perspective, he argued that the use of white flour and the utilisation of camels for transport had 'completely changed the relations of production between the sexes inside the family' (Rose 1965:99). Furthermore, he speculated that the use of camels had contributed to the demise of polygyny because men no longer required women to carry food, children and belongings. Unlike Gould et al. (1972), Rose regarded Pitjantjatjara society as dynamic and adaptive, but thought that the traditional economy was undermined by the appropriation of new techniques.

Shortly after Rose's book appeared, the geographer McKnight (1969) briefly addressed the topic of Indigenous people's use of camels in his landmark history of camels in Australia. On the basis of a survey of European pastoralists, he concluded that while Indigenous people primarily used camels for their own travel they also employed camels in other enterprises such as sandalwood gathering (in Western Australia) and tourism activities (for example, at Uluru). Camels, he said, were 'valuable chattels' that 'greatly enhanced their owner's mobility' (McKnight 1969:99). In fact, as I indicate later, from the Pitjantjatjara perspective, camels were not merely moveable possessions but actors with whom the Pitjantjatjara formed sentimental relationships. Sandall and Peterson captured some aspects of the Pitjantjatjara people's use of camels in their 1969 film, *Camels and the Pitjantjara*. The film documents the catching and domestication of a wild camel in the sandhills near Wallara Ranch north of Angas Downs. It then follows a group of people, who had independently hired camels from a Pitjantjatjara man known as Captain, as they travel with the camels from Areyonga to Papunya.[2] Layton (1986) also documented aspects of Indigenous people's use of camels. In doing so, he criticised Gould et al.

2   I thank Nicolas Peterson for this synopsis.

for failing to acknowledge that not only had people mastered camel husbandry techniques and used camels for their own purposes but they had also worked as camel guides for the anthropologist Mountford and others (Layton 1986:80).

Apart from these sources, however, information on Indigenous people's engagements with camels in the settler economy is fragmentary. The general impression given is that while Muslim cameleers played a crucial role in the development of the economy, Indigenous people's use of camels in the process was unimportant (see, for example, McKnight 1969). The historian Bulliet, for instance, claimed in *The Camel and the Wheel* that '[i]n Australia the Aborigines took to using camels very slowly and played a relatively small role in their history'. 'What the American Indians would have done with the animal', had it become established in America, he surmised, would be 'another matter entirely' (1990:254).

I now want to explore Pitjantjatjara and Yankunytjatjara people's interactions with the animal, focusing primarily on the period prior to the 1970s, when Indigenous people generally ceased using camels for transport. First, however, I situate Indigenous and settler use of camels in the context of the Western Desert environment. For the sake of brevity, in what follows when I refer to Pitjantjatjara people I also include Yankunytjatjara.

The Western Desert: A country for nomads

The Pitjantjatjara and their Environment

The Western Desert is characterised by low and unpredictable rainfall, with often extensive periods of drought. At the onset of European colonisation Aboriginal hunters and gatherers moved from place to place in search of water and food (Gould et al. 1972; Keen 2004). During summer people gathered at more reliable waterholes, then, following summer rains, people dispersed into small groups.[3] As people had no domesticated animals that could be used for transport, they travelled on foot (Keen 2004:84, 88). The availability of food varied according to rainfall and, to some extent, the season, and production was organised on the basis of a division of labour according to gender (see Keen 2004).

Reflecting the pressures of the environment, Western Desert local territorial organisation was flexible and people's kin networks were extensive and dispersed (Keen 2004; Peterson 1976; Strehlow 1965). People married partners from countries distant to their own, which meant that they were able to

---

3   See Keen (2004) for a detailed description of Pitjantjatjara economy and practices.

establish 'relations of production and access to land within a larger ecological region' (Myers 1986:71; see also Hamilton 1979:47). This was critical in a region where people could not subsist for long in one place. In relation to the Pintupi, Myers (1986:71) pointed out that 'mobility of individuals is a primary feature of the social structure'. Furthermore, he stated that it is important to recognise 'the spatial component of production in hunting and gathering societies, rather than envisioning the organisation of productive roles as reflecting only the division of labour by sex' (Myers 1986:71). These observations broadly apply to the Pitjantjatjara people in the eastern Western Desert. While their patterns of movement and exploitation of land changed following colonisation, mobility remained an important feature of their economy, with camels playing a significant role.

European Settlers

From a pastoral perspective, the eastern Western Desert and fringing area are marginal. Lack of water and fertile land and remoteness from the main transport routes meant that the region was not taken up for cattle stations until the railway was extended from Oodnadatta in South Australia to Alice Springs in 1929. The main economic enterprises that Europeans carried out in the area were sheep farming and dogging, which, as Rowse (1998) points out, were also both somewhat nomadic. The use of camels was pivotal to European developments in the region (Rose 1965). Camels are able to survive in arid conditions where horses and donkeys perish (Kennedy 2005). Not only can they go for a considerably longer period without access to surface water but they are also able to eat most of the native plant food that is available, including plants that will poison cattle and horses (Edwards et al. 2008). Moreover, pack camels are able to haul twice the weight of goods per day that horses are, and in draught work fewer camels are needed than horses to haul loads (Kennedy 2005:28).

Early Indigenous Encounters with Camels

Camels were not the first animals associated with Europeans to leave their imprint upon the Western Desert cultural landscape. Once the advantages of camels became known, however, many early explorers of Central Australia such as Warburton (1872–73), Gosse (1873), Giles (1875–76) and Lindsay (1885–86 and 1891–92) (see Jones and Kenny 2007:48; McKnight 1969:27–30; McLaren 1996) used camels to travel through the region, as did the stream of surveyors and prospectors who followed in their wake. In 1844 Cawthorne recorded the reaction of Aboriginal people in the Flinders Ranges to their first sighting of a camel. He noted: 'They saw a huge monster, to them it was an incomprehensible monster, it was at last concluded to be "white fellow's Emu'" (Cawthorne 1844, quoted in Foster 1991:59).[4] What, then, was the initial effect of camels on Western Desert people?

Western Desert stories of first encounters with camels and horses tell of the fear people felt at the sight of the strange animals and how, gradually, they came to grips with their bizarre form (see, for example, Richards et al. 2002:56–7, 71–5). After their initial shock, people sought the measure of the animals by observing how they moved through country and interacted with others. For example, Andy Tjilari, a Pitjantjatjara man, saw his first camels and a horse when a European came in search of dingo scalps. At the time Andy was a child camping with his family. He recalled: 'While we were camping there we saw them arriving and we ran away in fear thinking…"What is this that has arrived?" We were very frightened and ran away' (Tjilari 2009). After being given gifts of food, Andy 'followed them and became familiar with the camels and the horse. We were all the time talking to the horse as though it was human but we were unable to talk to it so that it would talk back to us. We were saying: "This horse is ignorant."'

Although many Western Desert people adopted the European term for 'camel', they also coined new names that referred to the animal's unique physical attributes and behaviour. For example, a Kukatja word for camel is *murtitikilpa*, which means literally 'knees bump together' (Valiquette 1993:123).[5] As the diaries of explorers and prospectors attest, camels had a profound impact on the water supplies of the local people, and the camel's capacity to drink enormous quantities of water at one sitting instilled apprehension in people. According to Hilliard (1976:57), by the 1880s Pitjantjatjara people knew that camels emptied waterholes, and people frequently avoided contact with European travelling parties or attacked them with spears (see also Basedow 2008:95). On occasion, local people were run down, captured and forced to lead the strangers to water (Gould 1969:45; Hilliard 1976). Lacking guns, and not having the advantages of height and speed afforded to a pursuer on camelback,[6] the Pitjantjatjara soon accommodated the strangers' presence. When Basedow travelled through the region in 1903, he noted that 'the deadly effect of firearms was generally known' (Basedow 2008:41). People's reactions to camels clearly varied, however, depending on the circumstances. For example, Basedow (2008) described people fleeing from camels and pestering them as they grazed. Yet he also wrote that the camel was an 'object of admiration and respect' and that it was 'the ambition

---

4 Interestingly, Aboriginal people's reactions to the camel—interpreting the unknown in terms of the known—resonate with those of the Romans when Julius Caesar first introduced the giraffe to Rome. In trying to understand the radical otherness of the giraffe, the Romans concluded that it resembled 'a mixture of camel and leopard' and they called it a 'camelopard' (Belozerskaya 2006:108), which is the origin of the scientific name used today: *Giraffa camelopardalis*.

5 I thank Peter Sutton for alerting me to this example as well as the Flinders Ranges example mentioned earlier.

6 See Kennedy (2005:71–6) for a discussion of the role of the horse in European settlement of Australia.

of the native youth to have the privilege of a short ride upon the hump of a camel, although he is quite unaccustomed to that kind of locomotion' (Basedow 2008:41–2).

The tracks camels made were also an object of fascination: while a single camel has a light footprint, a string of camels leaves a distinctive trail on the ground. Over time, as explorers and others followed camel pads in search of water, the trails became travel routes connecting the outside world with the people of the region. The early integration of the camel and its tracks into Pitjantjatjara artforms such as paintings in rock shelters, as observed by Mountford and others, illustrates that camels made a lasting impression on people and their country. Mountford recorded cave paintings with images of camels at Waliny (Cave Hill) during his camel trip to the Musgrave and Mann ranges in 1940. The camels are depicted in various poses, some with riders, some in strings and one with waterbags (Mountford 1976:67–9, 74). Intriguingly, a drawing made by an elderly Pitjantjatjara woman depicting the Seven Sisters Dreaming track at rockholes in the Musgrave Ranges also depicts the track of Mountford's camel string through the area (Mountford 1976:477, 480).[7]

Camels were not, however, merely a matter for inscription. Contemporary Indigenous oral histories of early encounters with stray camels describe the camel being killed for its meat and eaten. Killing a camel was not easy: unlike native animals, camels are extremely large and can be aggressive, particularly a bull camel in the mating season or one under attack. As a Ngaanyatjarra man explained, the method of killing required an adjustment to customary methods and involved a combination of spearing and clubbing: 'They speared it in the leg first. When it sat down they would come and hit it with a stick on the neck and the head—many times until it died. Then they would skin it, cut it and cook it' (D. Brooks, Personal communication, 24 August 2008).

Being a newcomer to the Western Desert cultural landscape, camels had no local Dreaming or associated food taboos.[8] Although, depending on context, particular cuts of meat may be shared with particular kin, the sheer abundance of meat on a camel means that it can sustain many people beyond the set of relatives normally taken into account in the customary distribution of smaller native game such as kangaroo. While there were few stray camels in the early part of the century (see Basedow 2008:106), they increased over time. This was particularly the case when they were replaced with motor vehicles and released

---

7   Kenny (2007:174) has pointed out the importance of attending to how Aborigines symbolically perceived European animals during the early contact period. This is a complex topic that I can only partly address in this chapter.

8   Interestingly, Altman (1982:280) found 'no taboo restrictions' on buffalo meat in north-central Arnhem Land. His informants attributed this to the fact that there was 'no business' associated with buffalo and to its large size.

into the bush. Once Indigenous people began using camels as pack animals, however, camels tended to be eaten only if people were exceptionally hungry or if a camel became hopelessly bogged in a claypan following rain. In addition to the flesh being consumed, other parts of the camel were also utilised. For example, the fat from the hump of the camel was mixed with bush plants such as *irmangka irmangka* (an *Eremophila*) to make a bush medicine for the treatment of aches, pains and coughs, and camel hair was spun into string to be used in ritual. As I discuss later, people are increasingly eating camels today.

Working with Camels

Contrary to Gould et al.'s claims (1972), Western Desert people did not simply hunt camels. From the beginning of European exploration until the extension of the railway, both Muslim cameleers (hereinafter referred to by the historically commonly used term 'Afghans') and Europeans used Indigenous people in camel work. Invariably, the work did not just involve camel handling, but also other services. Camel work included unloading, hobbling and searching for stray camels, as well as guiding people through country, locating water and acting as go-betweens and translators with local people. Station lessees, doggers, police, missionaries and anthropologists all employed Indigenous people as cameleers. While at first Indigenous people worked with camels owned by Afghans or Europeans, over time—especially from the 1930s onwards (McKnight 1969:27)—a small but significant number of men acquired their own camels, which they sometimes hired out for transport along with their own services as guides.

Some Indigenous cameleers were of mixed descent and had been recruited by Afghans and Europeans at settlements such as Oodnadatta and the Alice Springs Telegraph Station.[9] For example, Dick Gillen was 'camel boy' for Plowman and Partridge of the Australian Inland Mission between 1914 and 1919 (Grant 1989; Plowman 1933a, 1933b). In this role, he acted as camel handler and guide for the travelling padres who ministered to white settlers at mining fields, cattle stations and towns along the Overland Telegraph Line between Oodnadatta and Tennant Creek (Grant 1989).

It is difficult to estimate the numbers of Indigenous people engaged in camel work at any one time. Most activity occurred on the margin of European settlement, and the names of Indigenous people who worked with camels were often not recorded; explorers' journals and books written about the colonial period tend to refer to them simply as 'Aboriginal boys'. While cattle stations and missions did record employees' names, work such as camel shepherding

---

9   See also Ford (1975) and Kimber (1986).

was often subsumed under the generic terms 'stockwork' or 'labour'. The task of estimating numbers is also complicated by the fact that much camel work was multi-locale and sometimes resulted in the migration of a person to a distant region. I will now briefly consider the varieties of camel work in which people were engaged.

Learning from Afghans

Although I cannot develop the matter here, there was frequent social interaction between Indigenous people and Afghans along the telegraph line from Alice Springs to Oodnadatta. Jones and Kenny note that exchanges 'occurred at every level' and included material objects such as sugar, tea and *pituri*, as well as knowledge of country and, importantly, camel husbandry skills (2007:111). Intermarriage and sexual relations were also common (see, for example, Hercus 1981; Rajkowski 1995; Stevens 1989). As Simpson (2000) has shown, Afghan–Aboriginal interaction around camels also resulted in 'the spread of features which became markers of Aboriginal pidgins and creoles'.

By the 1930s some Indigenous people had taken up work with Afghan cameleers in the freight-hauling industry, using pack and draught camels. For example, John Kemp from Finke told me how his grandmother

> was working with Afghans, carting loads to Hermannsburg, Tempe Downs, starting off from Marree, Oodnadatta and Finke. Then my mother joined in—hard work. Follow the feed, water; long way between bores. I used to muster up the camels. We had five camels and they pulled a cart…I grew up with them. (Quoted in Vaarzon-Morel 2008)

To take another example, Pompey Douglas, who was affiliated with the Uluru area, learnt to drive camels for Afghans when his family moved to the railhead at Oodnadatta (Layton 1986:63). There, his father, Paddy Muruntu, worked as a 'camel boy', initially for Afghans then for Europeans. Interestingly, Paddy was an informant for anthropologist A. P. Elkin in Oodnadatta in 1930, and later, when Paddy returned to the Pitjantjatjara lands, for Tindale (Sutton and Vaarzon-Morel 2003:26). As I show elsewhere in this chapter, the mobility of Indigenous cameleers was not merely physical but also cultural, and the range of activities involved in 'camel work' included translation and other intercultural practices.[10]

---

10   I draw on Greenblatt (2009) in thinking about this issue.

Camels, Dogging and Other Use of Camels

As well as work with Afghan cameleers, Pitjantjatjara people's early use of camels developed in the context of dogging. In the period from 1908 to the 1930s, sheep runs were established to the south of Tempe Downs across to the Musgrave Ranges (Sutton and Vaarzon-Morel 2003:56). This drew Europeans to the area to kill dingoes, for which they collected a government bounty. Known as 'doggers', these men used camels when trading with local Aborigines, exchanging dingo scalps for flour, tea and sugar (Gee 2003:45; Hilliard 1976:81; Layton 1986:63, 69). Many had relationships with Pitjantjatjara women, who bore their children and worked with them in the dingo trade (Hilliard 1976:81). By the mid-1930s there were between 15 and 20 doggers trading with local people (Gee 2003:45). One dogger was Tommy Dodd, a man of Pitjantjatjara–Afghan descent who had driven camel teams from Oodnadatta to Alice Springs and was later cameleer and interpreter for patrol officers and anthropologists including Norman Tindale (Edwards n.d.).

Gee has noted that during this period the dogging trade was critical for local people, as a severe drought led to the decline of native fauna and other food resources on which people depended, including introduced species such as rabbits (2003:45; see also Finlayson 1935; Frith 1978). Finlayson commented at the time that the scalps were 'a sort of currency, filling the same place in the intercourse of the two peoples as the beaver skin formerly did in the territories of the Hudson Bay Company' (1935:116; see also Layton 1986:63–5, 78–9). As Gould et al. (1972) note, however, dingoes were not 'saleable' so, unlike furs, were not part of an international trade. Nor did dogging activities result in the profound social dislocation, warfare and displacement of populations occasioned by the fur trade (Wolf 1982:161). As Sutton has pointed out, there is little evidence of any full-scale, uniform 'tribal migration' involving Pitjantjatjara peoples during this era; rather, there were 'multiple small-scale movements of individuals and families' to the east, south and west (Sutton and Vaarzon-Morel 2003:52). Hilliard noted that for Pitjantjatjara people during this period 'working with the doggers as "camel boys" were means of obtaining the prized flour, tea and sugar' (1976:82). In a relatively short time, camels became the means for people to travel widely and access and transport large quantities of dingo scalps.

Concern over exploitation by doggers and the conditions of Pitjantjatjara and Yankunytjatjara people led the Presbyterian Church to buy Ernabella Station in 1936 and establish a mission (Gee 2003:47; Hilliard 1976). In this same period stations were taken up to the south of Alice Springs, with owners of stations such as Curtin Springs and Mount Connor using Yankunytjatjara and Pitjantjatjara guides and camels to locate water, help them establish their properties and shepherd sheep (Layton 1986:67; Rose 1965; Rowse 1998:62). The introduction of livestock to the area had a further impact on the resources on which the Indigenous subsistence economy was based (Layton 1986:61; see also Gee 2003) and contributed to increased movement to, and participation in, the cattle stations and missions (Layton 1986:59–60). Partly in an attempt to halt the flow of people to the settled areas, in 1940 the Hermannsburg Mission established the ration depot at Haasts Bluff and soon after another at Areyonga. Camels played a significant role in the domestic economy at this time.

During this period, many people pursued something of a hybrid economic existence, living off the land while supplementing their diet with food from Ernabella Mission and the depots. Rose (1965) noted that at Angas Downs in 1962 people used camels to travel between Areyonga, the Petermann Range, Ernabella Mission and cattle stations in the region. This is confirmed by my own research with the Pitjantjatjara and by McKnight, who observed that 'there is particularly frequent movement between such places as Maryvale [Titjikala] and Hermannsberg [sic], Areyonga and Ernabella, and Musgrave Park [Mimili] and Ernabella' (1969:100).

In this way people were able to maintain contact with their country (see also Kimber 2005), visit family, collect and trade dingo scalps and engage in seasonal stockwork as well as other irregular economic activities—for example, the sale of craft items to tourists, for which they received cash (Rose 1965). A few men were also employed as cameleers and trackers on police patrols (see, for example, Brown and Studdy-Clift 1990), and a select group in tourism. For instance, Tiger Tjalkalyiri and Mick Mitinkirri, who spent periods of time at Areyonga and occasionally undertook camel work for the Hermannsburg Mission, took European visitors on camel safaris (Scherer 1994; see also Henson 1992). In 1947 Tiger took Arthur Groom to Ayers Rock (Uluru) via Lake Amadeus (Groom 1977; Sutton and Vaarzon-Morel 2003).[11] A feature of long camel treks was the bond of friendship and respect that developed between the Indigenous cameleers and their companions in the intimate and shared space of the journey.

Camel Ownership

According to Rose (1965:25), the Pitjantjatjara's use of camels greatly increased after World War II when Europeans bought surplus army four-wheel-drive jeeps and sold or traded their camels to Pitjantjatjara people. In addition to the camels, saddles and conveyances (including old vehicle chassis) that were traded or found abandoned by Europeans were used for camel carting (Hamilton 1987; Rose 1965:25–6; Vaarzon-Morel 2008:101) (Figure 4.1). Rose has charted the decline in the price of a camel on the open market (1965:26), which facilitated

---

11   More famously, Albert Namatjira took Rex Battarbee and the Teague sisters on camel trips during which he observed their techniques of painting landscape (French 2002).

increased Indigenous ownership. In contrast, horses retained their value for Europeans and were rarely given or sold to Aborigines (1965:30). It tended to be married men with traditional seniority who owned camels (Edwards, Personal communication, 30 October 2009; Rose 1965:29–30). To give the reader an idea of the extent of camel ownership in the 1960s, Rose (1965:28–30) noted that of 18 'family units' who visited Angas Downs during his period of fieldwork in 1962, eight possessed camels, some of whom owned up to five.[12] McKnight estimated that in 1966 there were more than 297 'Aboriginal-owned camels' in the north-west SA and lower NT region and some in Western Australia (1969:100). Significantly, camels were sold and traded for dingo scalps and other items, not only between Europeans and Aborigines but also among Pitjantjatjara people (Harney 1988:135–6; Vaarzon-Morel 2008). Some Indigenous people today recall that owners of camels were perceived as being 'rich' (Vaarzon-Morel 2008), which indicates the significance of camels to the domestic economy of that time.

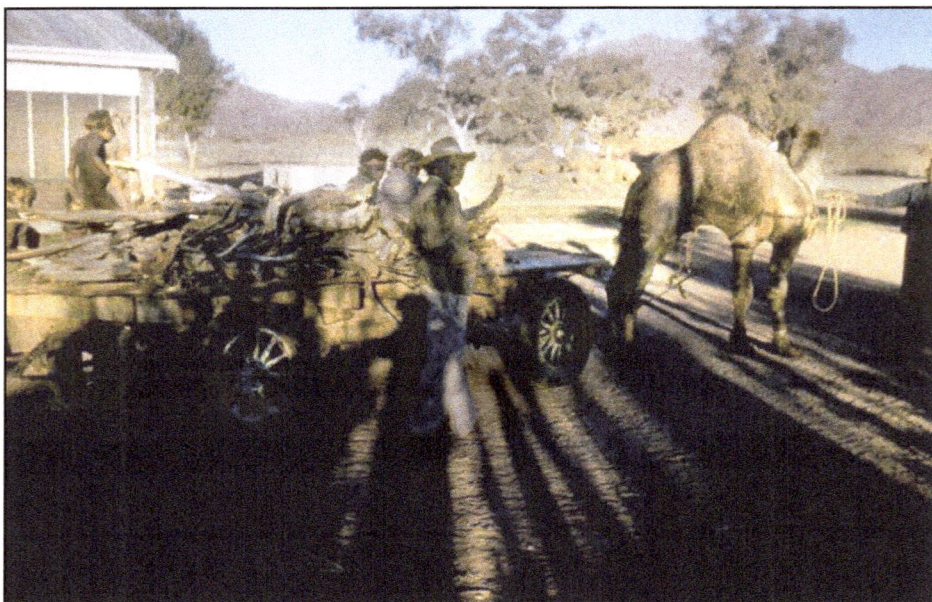

Figure 4.1 Charlie Ilyatjari uses an old camel wagon for his wood carting business, circa 1960

Image supplied by Bill Edwards.

---

12   Other non-camel groups were attached to these units.

Figure 4.2 Louis Wirultjukurnga and family with camels approximately 20 km north of Ernabella, 6 September 1960

Image supplied by Bill Edwards and copied from Ara Iritja archive.

Camels in the Mission Economy

When the Reverend Bill Edwards first arrived at Ernabella in 1958, he found that there were numerous camels belonging to Pitjantjatjara people (Figure 4.2). Following shearing in July, which was timed to end before the dingo pupping season, the mission closed the school and craft room, and most of the population returned to their traditional homelands on camels, donkeys and horses (see also Hilliard 1976:147, 150). They took goods purchased from the store with wages obtained through craft, construction and shepherding work and supplemented this food with traditional foods and foods exchanged with missionaries for dingo scalps. Before they left Ernabella, people would mend camel saddles and other equipment (Edwards, Personal communication, November 2009). Reverend Edwards recalled these country trips as follows: 'We arranged to meet them at given sites every couple of weeks and would drive out with supplies of flour, sugar, tea, baby foods, etc. to trade with them for the [dingo] scalps… The camels were the main load bearers for these trips.' (See Figure 4.3.) This pattern of activity came to an end by the late 1960s as people gained access to motorcars. By that time, however, a strong connection between the mission order, Christianity and camels had been established in people's minds. This connection was also entangled with earlier events, some of which I will now briefly explore.

Figure 4.3 Trading on the road at Yulpartji, 22 August 1958

Image supplied by Bill Edwards and copied from Ara Iritja archive.

Camels and the Christian Imagination

From 1928 to 1933, the missionary Ernest Kramer undertook camel safaris in Central Australia with the aim of spreading the gospel. On most journeys, he employed Arrernte man Mickey Dow Dow[13] as cameleer, guide and translator and sometimes a man called Barney (Metters and Schroeder 2008). The first of Kramer's trips was to the Musgrave and Mann ranges, and was sponsored by the Aborigines Friends Association, which sought a report on Indigenous living conditions. According to Kramer's biography, as the men travelled through the desert and encountered local people, they handed them boiled lollies, tea and sugar and played *Jesus Loves Me* on the gramophone. At night, using a 'magic lantern projector', Kramer showed slides of Christmas and the life of Christ (Metters and Schroeder 2008:81–2, 94). For many people, this was their first experience of Christmas and the event picturesquely established an association

---

13   Initially, Mickey worked with Spencer and Gillen and later as cameleer, guide, translator and informant for T. G. H. Strehlow and Olive Pink (Marcus 2001).

between camels, gifts and Christianity that was not merely symbolic but had material reality. In the next decades, this association was to be strengthened in various ways among the Pitjantjatjara and neighbouring groups.

Figure 4.4 Wise Men on a camel at Ernabella, circa 1960. Christmas pageants were presented in the creek bed with a donkey carrying Mary and 'Three Wise Men' leading camels as the Ernabella Choir sang carols in the background

Image supplied by Bill Edwards and copied from Ara Iritja archive.

In the 1950s and 1960s, for example, nativity plays were performed at Ernabella Mission with Pitjantjatjara enacting the parts of Mary, Joseph, the shepherds and the Three Wise Men. Camels, donkeys and sheep were also actors in the pageants (Figure 4.4). Hilliard described the impressive spectacle created during a moonrise 'over the horizon, as the Wise Men and the camels approached along a flame-lit path from the east' (1976:187). Although these events were relatively infrequent, they were nevertheless powerful rituals that helped shape people's emotional reactions to camels. Today many people still associate camels with the Three Wise Men and Jesus, and for this reason some are opposed to the killing of camels for meat or other purposes (Vaarzon-Morel 2008, 2010).

Camels and the Indigenous Landscape Post 1970s

By the 1970s the nature of Indigenous people's engagements with camels had changed dramatically: people no longer used camels for transport, and the introduction of welfare as well as other factors such as the need to keep children in school meant that mobility was no longer such an important factor in the Pitjantjatjara domestic economy.

Over the past 20 years, a few individuals and groups have participated in sporadic economic activities involving camels. These activities include harvesting camels for community consumption, the commercial harvesting of camels for pet meat and human consumption, tourism, ranger work and land-management work (Vaarzon-Morel 2008). For example, in about 1989 the late Charlie Ilyatjari and his family ran a tourist venture on his traditional country at Angatja Homeland in South Australia (see Vaarzon-Morel 2008).[14] To take another example, during the 1990s near Fregon in South Australia, a group of men supported by the State Government mustered and sold more than 50 camels (Vaarzon-Morel 2008:93–4). More recently at Docker River and Kintore, harvesting of camels was undertaken as a community youth group activity to help reduce substance abuse, to provide a free, healthy source of meat, and to maintain the integrity of country (Vaarzon-Morel 2008:28–9, 48).

Camels have long played a role in the Central Australian art economy. At Angas Downs camels were used to obtain wood for craft items such as woomeras and carved animals, which were sold to tourists en route to Uluru. While in those days the animals depicted in craft items were native species, today artists from the region incorporate images of the camel in their artworks. Bessie Liddle, a local Luritja woman who was married to the owner of Angas Downs, a man of Arrernte–European descent, is one such artist. As the subject matter of her paintings, she features people riding camels on picnics to Inindia waterhole, where men caught kangaroo and women gathered bush food. At Titjikala artists such as Johnny Young make wire sculptures of Pitjantjatjara cameleers and their camels, as well as of camel trains. Elsewhere artists make stuffed, baked, woven and block-printed camels using different materials. The artworks recall people's fond memories of early times with camels and the significant role they played in their lives. The recent proliferation of camel images in Indigenous art also reflects the tourist demand for desert exotica as well as the growing presence of camels in the landscape.

---

14   Significantly, Charlie Ilyatjari was one of the people who used camels for dogging at Ernabella. Bill Edwards told me (Personal communication, 30 October 2009) that in the 1960s Charlie attempted to set up a business as a wood carter, using an old camel wagon. His venture was unsuccessful because people argued that as he was '*waltja*', or close kin, he should give them wood. More prosaically, the wagon did not have good brakes and kept running into the camels' legs when he tried to stop.

Today, apart from a small number of camel calves kept as pets, there are comparatively few domesticated camels on Aboriginal land. Feral camel numbers, however, have increased dramatically. Currently, there are an estimated one million feral camels in Australia. With a rate of increase of 8 per cent per year, the population would double every nine years (Edwards et al. 2008). The majority of these camels are on Aboriginal land in the Northern Territory, South Australia and Western Australia. In areas of high density (more than 0.3 camels per square kilometre), camels are having a significant impact on the ecosystem; they are damaging vegetation, wetlands and sites of biological and cultural significance (Edwards et al. 2008, 2010) and transforming parts of the desert landscape.

In 2006 I conducted research on Indigenous perceptions of feral camels for the Desert Knowledge Cooperative Research Centre. In areas of high camel density such as much of the Pitjantjatjara region, there is increasing concern over the negative impacts of feral camels on water places, animals, plants and other natural and cultural resources (Edwards et al. 2008). People can no longer hunt and gather native species or otherwise engage with the country as they wish and they avoid areas where camels are known to be present. Fatalities involving motor vehicles and camels on remote roads are also increasing. Whereas once camels facilitated people's physical mobility, they now hinder it. Yet, although in general many people perceive a need to manage camel impacts, the majority of people are prepared to consider only limited management options (Vaarzon-Morel 2010). Significantly, as a result of Christian and personal historical associations, many people have sentimental attachments to camels that influence how they weigh up negative camel impacts in respect of management options and also their preparedness to eat camel meat (Vaarzon-Morel 2010). In general, the preferred camel management strategies are live removal, harvesting camels for meat and ranger activities. Where people's main livelihood is the management of country for biodiversity as well as cultural outcomes, many are, however, prepared to consider a wide range of management strategies, including shooting for waste (Vaarzon-Morel 2010). Yet whatever occurs, I argue that a better understanding of past Indigenous uses of camels is essential in order to contextualise present views.

Under the Caring for Country, Indigenous Protected Areas and other sponsored land-management programs, Indigenous participation in the management of feral camel impacts and the utilisation of camels is likely to expand in the near future. If this were to happen it would provide significant economic benefits to Indigenous people. At the time of writing, commercial harvesting of camels for sale locally and overseas has recommenced on Aboriginal land. While the viability of the potential international trade in live camels is still being assessed, with the majority of feral camels being on Aboriginal-owned land, this means that Indigenous communities are key players in what is a developing new camel economy. In the long run, it can be seen that Indigenous people have shown considerable ability to adapt to the introduction of camels to their landscape and that practices of using camels have been central to developing intra-cultural and economic relationships in the Western Desert.

Conclusion

To date, anthropological and historical studies of intercultural relations have tended to neglect or oversimplify the role of introduced animals in processes of intercultural formation and economic transformation. The conceptual framework I adopt here recognises the importance of understanding human, animal and environmental interrelationships in their historic specificity. In this chapter, I have reconsidered Indigenous people's engagements with camels in the eastern Western Desert and adjacent region. In doing so, I have shown that rather than simply hunting camels, Indigenous people used camels in a range of ways that contributed to and helped sustain both the domestic and the frontier economies. I have further demonstrated that Indigenous people's engagements with camels were and remain intrinsically bound up with transformations in Indigenous socioeconomic and ecological landscapes. Among other things, these complex connections have direct implications for social, intercultural and human/animal relations, as well as issues of ontology and power.

References

Altman, J. C. 1982. Hunting buffalo in north-central Arnhem Land: a case of rapid adaptation among Aborigines. *Oceania* 52 (4): 274–85.

Austin-Broos, D. and MacDonald, G. (eds) 2005. Culture, Economy and Governance in Central Australia. Proceedings of a Workshop of the Academy of Social Sciences in Australia, 30 November – 1 December 2004, Sydney.

Barker, H. M. 1995. *Camels and the Outback*. Carlisle, WA: Hesperian Press.

Basedow, H. 2008. *Notes on Some Native Tribes of Central Australia*. Virginia, NT: Compiled, edited and published by David M. Welch.

Belozerskaya, M. 2006. *The Medici Giraffe: And other tales of exotic animals and power*. New York: Little, Brown & Company.

Blainey, G. 1966. *The Tyranny of Distance: How distance shaped Australia's history*. Melbourne: Sun Books.

Brown, R. and Studdy-Clift, P. 1990. *Bush Justice*. Carlisle, WA: Hesperian Press.

Bulliet, R. W. 1990. *The Camel and the Wheel*. New York: Columbia University Press.

Edwards, B. n.d. Dodd, Tommy (1890?–1975). *Australian Dictionary of Biography. Online Edition*. Viewed 14 August 2009, <http://adbonline.anu.edu.au/ biogs/A140015b.htm>

Edwards, G. P., Zeng, B., Saalfeld, W. K. and Vaarzon-Morel, P. 2010. Evaluation of the impacts of feral camels. *The Rangeland Journal* 32 (1): 43–54.

Edwards, G. P., Zeng, B., Saalfeld, W. K., Vaarzon-Morel, P. and McGregor, M. (eds) 2008. *Managing the impacts of feral camels in Australia: a new way of doing business*. DKCRC Report 47, Desert Knowledge Cooperative Research Centre, Alice Springs, NT. <http://www.desertknowledgecrc.com.au/ resource/DKCRC-Report-47-Managing-the-impacts-of-feral-camels-in-Australia_A-new-way-of-doing-business.pdf>

Finlayson, H. H. 1935. *The Red Centre*. Sydney: Angus & Robertson.

Ford, B. M. 1975. Among the last of the camel men. *Northern Times*, 20 November 1975. Viewed 18 September 2011, <http://www.anu.edu.au/linguistics/ nash/ca/walker.html>

Foster, R. (ed.) 1991. *Sketch of the Aborigines of South Australia: References in the Cawthorne Papers*. Adelaide: Aboriginal Heritage Branch, South Australia.

French, A. 2002. *Seeing the Centre: The art of Albert Namatjira, 1902–1959*. Canberra: National Gallery of Australia.

Frith, H. J. 1978. Wildlife resources in central Australia. In B. S. Hetzel and H. J. Frith (eds), *Nutrition of Aborigines in Relation to the Ecosystem of Central Australia. Papers presented at a Symposium, CSIRO, 23–26 October 1976, Canberra*, pp. 87–93. Melbourne: Commonwealth Scientific and Industrial Research Organisation, Division of Land Resources Management, Central Australian Laboratory.

Gee, P. 2003. The European history of the Anangu Pitjantjatjara lands. In A. C. Robinson, P. B. Copley, P. D. Canty, L. M. Baker and B. J. Nesbitt (eds), *A Biological Survey of the Anangu Pitjantjatjara Lands South Australia 1991–2001*. Report for Department of Environment and Heritage, Adelaide. <http://www.environment.sa.gov.au/science/pdfs/biosurvey/anangu/ anangu_pt1.pdf>

Gould, R. A. 1969. *Yiwara: Foragers of the Australian desert*. New York: Scribner.

Gould, R. A., Fowler, D. and Fowler, C. S. 1972. Diggers and doggers: parallel failures in economic acculturation. *Southwestern Journal of Anthropology* 28 (3): 265–81.

Grant, A. 1989 [1981]. *Camel Train & Aeroplane: The story of Skipper Partridge*. Erskineville, NSW: Frontier Publishing.

Greenblatt, S. J. 2009. *Cultural Mobility*. Cambridge: Cambridge University Press.

Groom, A. 1977. *I Saw a Strange Land: Journeys in Central Australia*. Adelaide: Rigby.

Hamilton, A. 1979. Timeless transformations: women, men and history in the Western Australian desert. PhD thesis, University of Sydney, Sydney.

Hamilton, A. 1987. Coming and going: Aboriginal mobility in north-west South Australia, 1970–1971. *Records of the South Australian Museum* 20: 47–57.

Harney, W. E. 1988. *To Ayers Rock and Beyond*. Bayswater, Vic.: Ian Drakeford Publishing.

Henson, B. 1992. *A Straight-Out Man: F. W. Albrecht and Central Australian Aborigines*. Carlton, Vic.: Melbourne University Press.

Hercus, L. A. 1981. Afghan stories from the north-east of South Australia. *Aboriginal History* 5 (1): 38–70.

Hilliard, W. 1976. *The People in Between: The Pitjantjatjara people of Ernabella*. Adelaide: Seal Books/Rigby.

Jones, P. and Kenny, A. 2007. *Australia's Muslim Cameleers: Pioneers of the inland 1860–1930s*. Kent Town and Adelaide: Wakefield Press in association with South Australian Museum.

Keen, I. 2004. *Aboriginal Economy and Society: Australia at the threshold of colonisation*. Melbourne: Oxford University Press.

Kennedy, M. J. 2005 [1992]. *Hauling the Loads: A history of Australia's working horses and bullocks*. Rockhampton, Qld: Central Queensland University Press.

Kenny, R. 2007. *The Lamb Enters the Dreaming: Nathanael Pepper and the ruptured world*. Carlton North, Vic.: Scribe Publications.

Kimber, R. G. 1986. *Man from Arltunga: Walter Smith, Australian bushman*. Victoria Park, WA: Hesperian Press.

Kimber, R. G. 2005. 'Because it is our country': the Pintupi and their return to their country, 1970–1990. In M. Smith and P. Hesse (eds), *23°S: Archaeology and environmental history of the southern deserts*, pp. 345–56. Canberra: National Museum of Australia.

Layton, R. 1986. *Uluru: An Aboriginal history of Ayers Rock*. Canberra: Aboriginal Studies Press.

Leacock, E. 1954. The Montagnais 'hunting territory' and the fur trade. *American Anthropological Association Memoir* (78).

Leacock, E. 1955. Matrilocality in a simple hunting economy (Montagnais-Naskapi). *Southwestern Journal of Anthropology* 11: 31–47.

McKnight, T. L. 1969. *The Camel in Australia*. Melbourne: Melbourne University Press.

McLaren, G. 1996. *Beyond Leichhardt: Bushcraft and the exploration of Australia*. South Fremantle, WA: Fremantle Arts Centre Press.

Marcus, J. 2001. *The Indomitable Miss Pink: A life in anthropology*. Sydney: UNSW Press.

Metters, F. K. and Schroeder, E. 2008. *Outback Evangelist: The story of Ernest Kramer*. Norwood, SA: Peacock Publications.

Mountford, C. P. 1976. *Nomads of the Australian Desert*. Adelaide: Rigby.

Myers, F. 1986. *Pintupi Country, Pintupi Self*. Washington, DC, London and Canberra: Smithsonian Institution Press and Australian Institute of Aboriginal Studies.

Nadasdy, P. 2002. 'Property' and Aboriginal land claims in the Canadian subarctic: some theoretical considerations. *American Anthropologist* 104 (1): 247–61.

Peterson, N. 1976. The natural and cultural areas of Aboriginal Australia: a preliminary analysis of population groupings with adaptive significance. In N. Peterson (ed.), *Tribes and Boundaries in Australia*, pp. 50–71. Canberra and Atlantic Highlands, NJ: Australian Institute of Aboriginal Studies and Humanities Press.

Peterson, N. 2009. Camels and the Pitjantjara: filming the end of an era. Abstract. Indigenous Participation in Australian Economies Conference, National Museum of Australia, Canberra.

Plowman, R. B. 1933a. *The Man from Oodnadatta*. Third edn. Sydney: Angus & Robertson.

Plowman, R. B. 1933b. *Camel Pads*. Sydney: Angus & Robertson.

Povinelli, E. A. 1993. Labor's Lot: The power, history, and culture of Aboriginal action. Chicago: University of Chicago Press.

Rajkowski, P. 1987.*In the Tracks of the Camelmen: Outback Australia's most exotic pioneers*. North Ryde, NSW: Angus & Robertson.

Rajkowski, P. 1995. *Linden Girl: A story of outlawed lives*. Nedlands, WA: University of Western Australia Press.

Richards, E., Hudson, J. and Lowe, P. 2002. *Out of the Desert: Stories from the Walmajarri exodus*. Broome, WA: Magabala Books.

Rose, F. G. G. 1965. *The Wind of Change in Central Australia: The Aborigines at Angas Downs, 1962*. Berlin: Akadamie-Verlag.

Rowse, T. 1998. *White Flour, White Power: From rations to citizenship in Central Australia*. Cambridge: Cambridge University Press.

Sandall, R. (dir) 1969. *Camels and the Pitjantjara*. Canberra: Australian Institute of Aboriginal Studies. (Film. Duration: 45 minutes.)

Scherer, P. A. 1994. *Camel Treks in the Outback*. Tanunda, SA: P. A. Scherer.

Simpson, J. 2000. Camels as pidgin-carriers: Afghan cameleers as a vector for the spread of features of Australian Aboriginal pidgins and creoles. In J. Siegel (ed.), *Processes of Language Contact: Studies from Australia and the South Pacific*, pp. 195–244. Saint-Laurent, Quebec: Fides.

Snow, D. R. 1968. Wabanaki 'family hunting territories'. *American Anthropologist* 70 (6): 1143–51.

Stevens, C. 1989. *Tin Mosques and Ghantowns*: *A history of Afghan cameldrivers in Australia*. Melbourne: Oxford University Press.

Strehlow, T. G. H. 1965. Culture, social structure, and environment. In R. M. and C. H. Berndt (eds), *Aboriginal Man in Australia*, pp. 121–45. Sydney: Angus & Robertson.

Sutton, P. and Vaarzon-Morel, P. 2003. *Yulara Anthropology Report*. Word-processed, plus nine appendices and 16 maps. Alice Springs, NT: Central Land Council.

Tjilari, A. 2009. Seeing camels. Oral history text recorded and translated by W. Edwards, made available to P. Vaarzon-Morel, 30 October 2009.

Vaarzon-Morel, P. 2008. *Key stakeholder perceptions of feral camels: Aboriginal community survey*. DKCRC Report 49, Desert Knowledge Cooperative Research Centre, Alice Springs, NT. <http://www.desertknowledgecrc. com.au/resource/DKCRC-Report-49-Key-stakeholder-perceptions-of-feral-camels_Aboriginal-community-survey.pdf>

Vaarzon-Morel, P. 2010. Changes in Aboriginal perceptions of feral camels and of their impacts and management. *The Rangeland Journal* 32 (1): 73–85.

Valiquette, H. 1993. *A Basic Kukatja to English Dictionary*. Wirrimanu [Balgo], WA: Luurnpa Catholic School.

Wolf, E. R. 1982. *Europe and the People Without History*. Berkeley: University of California Press.

Acknowledgments

I thank Nicolas Peterson, Philip Jones and Alison French for generously participating in the panel 'Exotic relations: camels and the articulation of Indigenous and settler social and economic forms', which I organised for the conference Indigenous Participation in Australian Economies held at the National Museum of Australia. This chapter grew out of a paper I delivered as part of the panel. It benefited from comments by Nicolas Peterson, Ase Ottoson, Geoff Bagshaw, Margaret Bowman, Rev. Dr. W. H. (Bill) Edwards, Craig Elliott, David Nash, Noah Pleshet, Peter Sutton and James Wafer, and I thank them all.

I am particularly indebted to Rev. Dr. W. H. (Bill) Edwards who generously shared with me his memories, oral histories, and photographic images concerning Pitjantjatjara use of camels. Bill kindly copied the images from the Ara Irititja archive and provided descriptions of the photos.

Research for this chapter was supported in part by the Northern Territory through the NT History Grants Program of the Department of Natural Resources, Environment and the Arts.

5. 'Always Anangu—always enterprising'

Alan O'Connor

As a result of primary research in Arnhem Land, Altman developed a hybrid economy model for Indigenous Australians living in remote areas in which people move between the state, market and customary sectors (Altman 2005). He asserts that development policies for remote areas based on the state and the market have failed because of the existence of a customary sector and very different intercultural value systems. In addition, he suggests the commercial marginality of Aboriginal-owned land is the reason it was alienated, and as a result the potential to increase the market sector is very limited (Altman 2005).

In this chapter, I examine Anangu involvement in economic life until the mid-1970s with a particular focus on Ernabella and its homelands, and explore elements of the hybrid economy on the Anangu Pitjantjatjara Yankunytjatjara (APY) Lands. This work is part of my thesis, developed from a larger study of enterprise development on the lands resulting from an Australian Research Council grant in 2007 obtained by Banerjee and Tedmanson. The research was conducted through the University of South Australia. The research partners in this work were from the communities of Ernabella, Turkey Bore and the Anilalya Homelands as well as UnitingCare Wesley Adelaide.

Geography, Climate and Traditional Food Sources

The APY Lands are located in the far north-west of South Australia and make up 102 500 sq km or 10.4 per cent of the area of South Australia. Ernabella is the largest community on the lands (with a population that has varied about 450 for many years) and is approximately 440 km by road from both Alice Springs and Coober Pedy. The lands have a very hot, dry climate with short, cool to cold winters and a low and unreliable rainfall. As a result of the very hot summers (and the fact that this period also coincides with important ceremonies), travel to the lands by outsiders is minimal between December and February.

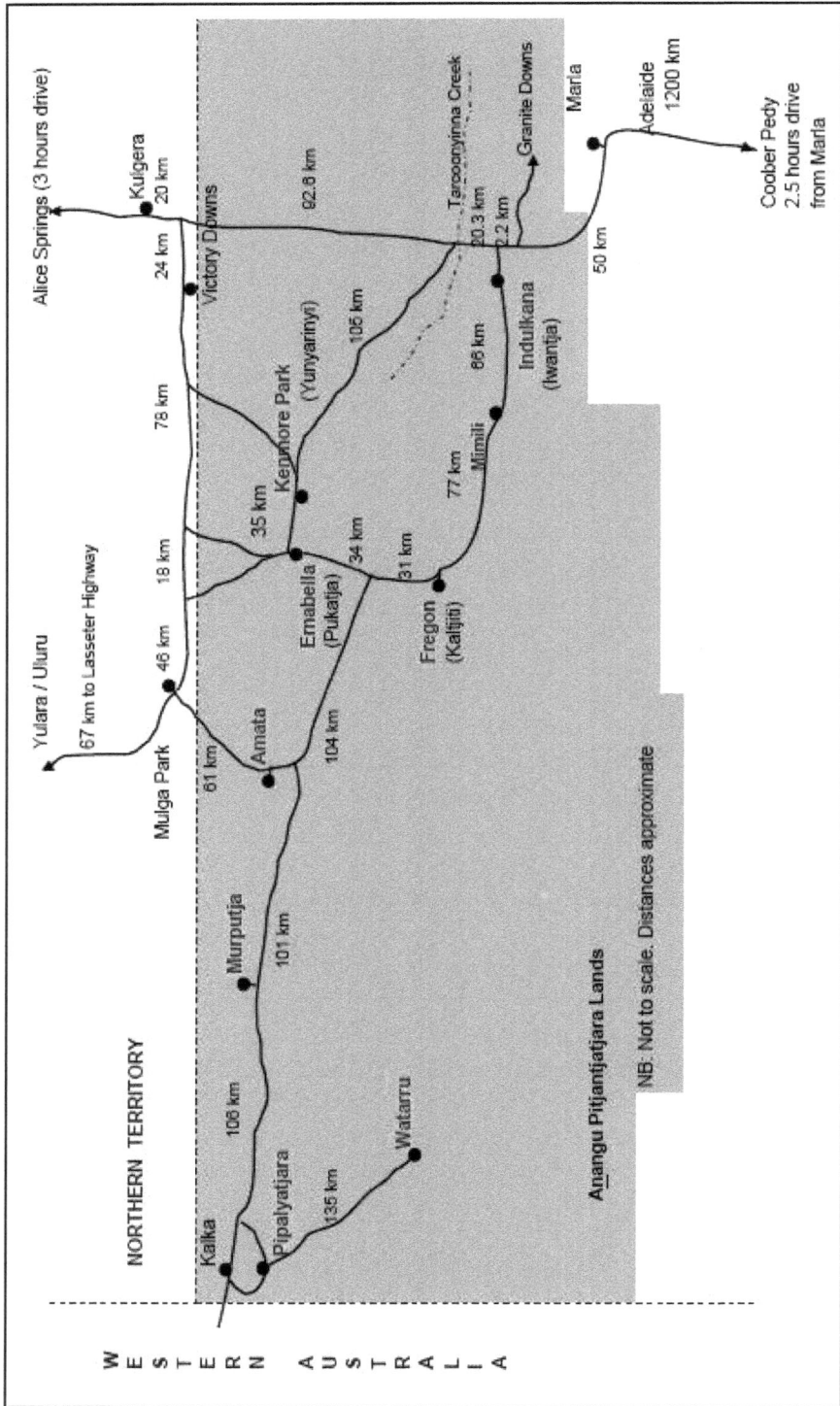

Map 5.1 The APY Lands

Source: Lea et al. (2008:5).

Evidence suggests that in the past small groups of Anangu regularly moved around the desert on large food-gathering and ceremonial circuits (Cocks 1978).

> Anangu were expert in finding *kuka* (food) in their harsh environment. Men were trained from their youth to become skilled hunters of *malu* (red kangaroo) and *kalaya* (emu). Women knew how to find smaller game, such as *watu* (wombat), *tjirilya* (echidna), goanna, lizard and snake. Women and children were adept foragers and gatherers of fruits, berries and seeds, often walking long distances to locate them. (Mattingley 2009)

There was a well-defined kinship system and rules for sharing food. Anangu were highly mobile and moved with the seasons to make the most of the available food sources. Any spare time was spent expanding social networks. In contrast with the mainly commercial and residential land use by mainstream society, Anangu worked the land for economic return by the controlled use of fire in different areas (Cocks 1978).

Finlayson (1935) observed that Anangu formed no permanent camps, and, except on ceremonial occasions and during droughts, they travelled in small groups of families of rarely more than 30 people. The movement of groups was based on a deep knowledge of the country and its resources. Movement was also determined by the totemic link that each group claimed to specific areas (Edwards 1992).

Trade and Exchange Systems

In the past there was an extensive network of trade routes along which valuable items were passed. Native tobacco 'finds its way down the desert route to the southern tribes and is exchanged for wombat's fur and red, white, or yellow ochre used for ceremonial purposes' (Berndt 1941:3). Stone spearheads, red ochre, pearl shell, manganese dioxide pigment and human-hair belts were other items traded:

> Women distributed items mainly within the camp and amongst certain close kin…Women also provided food to their unmarried male relatives in the bachelor's camp…Receiving meat in return…The unmarried men gave meat to their families in return for damper of wangunu seeds and for other vegetable foods, including fruits collected and prepared by women. (Keen 2004:341)

Redmond (Chapter Three, this volume) highlights that the ceremonial exchanges and trade in the Kimberley region have always involved pragmatic, ephemeral economic objects such as meat and hunting implements as well as ritual sacred/

secret objects (Redmond 2009:7). Redmond has mapped the *wurnan*[1] channels over which these exchanges occur to more clearly identify the direction of the trade.

Hunters supported themselves while on the move, but their main responsibility was to look after the rest of the group. Keen describes the nature of gift exchange that occurred 'as part of obligations between kin…when small residence groups met; and at large scale meetings for rituals. In addition people with special skills such as healers were also paid with food, tobacco or artefacts' (Keen 2004:357–8).

Last (1976) highlighted the crucial role played by a well-defined kinship system in a harsh environment. By the mid-1930s, Anangu were trading dingo scalps to doggers for flour, tea and sugar. These doggers were in turn receiving a government bounty of 7s 6d for each scalp (Mattingley and Hampton 1987).

First Contact

The earliest European entries into the region were the exploring expeditions of Ernest Giles and William Gosse (1873) and John Forrest (1874), searching for good pasture, stock routes and gold. As well as being a strategic watering point, the country around Ernabella, as Ernest Giles described it, was the most delightful that he had seen. Adventurers, prospectors and traders followed the early explorers; however, hopes for mineral wealth and fertile grazing areas for cattle soon faded. The water supply was too low and unreliable and neither gold nor other precious metals could be found in appreciable quantities (Gee 2003; Hilliard 1968).

In December 1920 the WA Government gazetted 56 600 sq km as Aboriginal Reserve and in 1921 the Commonwealth Government created the NT section. The public had lobbied the SA Government for several years to establish a similar reserve that excluded Europeans. These efforts were strengthened by the continuing news about living conditions in the north and reports of killings (Summers 2004). As a way of providing some protection for Anangu from the frequent intrusions by Europeans, an area was proclaimed as the North-West Aboriginal Reserve in 1921, and subsequently expanded in 1938 and 1949 (Summers 2004).

Reverend Downing, who worked in Alice Springs with the John Flynn Uniting Church with a special role for Aboriginal people in the 1960s, considered that it was probably the severe drought of 1928 that forced people to go to Ernabella prior to the establishment of the mission (Downing 1988). By 1929 the rail

---

1   *Wurnan* is similar to *wurnorr*, meaning 'the bone of'—in this case, the social world (Redmond 2009:15).

line had been extended to Alice Springs and proved an attraction to Anangu living to the west. 'The Yangkunytjatjara, who were the original occupiers of the Musgrave Ranges, moved towards the east and their territory was occupied by the Pitjantjatjara of the Mann Ranges' (W. D. Scott Proprietary Limited 1971:2.3–4). Ernabella Station lease was granted to Stanley Ferguson in 1933 under a scheme that rewarded whoever found good water.

Other factors considered to have caused people to leave their land were competition with pastoralists for water, early settlers wanting Aboriginal women, pressure applied to keep people away from Ayers Rock (as it was then; now Uluru) and the violence of some early settlers. The use and control of Aboriginal labour by pastoralists, the attraction of white man's food and hence the need to work and the establishment of missions such as Hermannsburg and Ernabella as safe havens were also significant (Downing 1988).

Mission Life, 1937 to 1973

As a result of the poor treatment of Anangu particularly by doggers, Dr Duguid from Adelaide visited their lands in the far north-west of South Australia in 1935 and played a key role in purchasing the Ernabella pastoral lease in 1937 to establish a mission and enable Anangu to have a buffer area to adapt to this new situation (Last 2002).

Anangu were encouraged to trade dingo scalps for food and other commodities, and the setting up of permanent waterholes enabled them to live near their homelands. This continued 'until the early 1970s when the sheep industry was discontinued, due to the lack of viability' (Last 2002:2–3).

Many Anangu were drawn to Ernabella from the Musgrave, Tomkinson and Everard ranges country and, less commonly, from the Petermann Range in the Northern Territory. Some of the destructive elements of missions and government settlements were missing, as the Ernabella Mission refused to gather or round up people and children were never taken from their parents (Hope 1983).

Ernabella's policies of minimal interference included teaching children in their own language, encouraging parents to hunt in the traditional manner rather than become dependent on the mission for food, not confining children in dormitories and not making children (or their parents) wear clothes (Kerin 2006). This does not mean that all elements of mission life were benign for the community. In common with other missions, here, Anangu were never paid award wages for the work they performed, they lived in very basic accommodation and were in effect 'colonised' by their increasing dependence on mission food and other services.

Young makes a compelling case for the significance of the dingo trade in developing a 'frontier economy' when 'it was far from a marginal activity but one that lasted for forty years' (Young 2008:17). The mission was able to see that '[g]oing out for dingo skins, west into the Reserve, stopped Anangu going to settled areas, justifying the Reserve's existence, and at the same time fulfilled the desire of Anangu to acquire European things' (Young 2008).

In terms of the Altman model, in the early years of the mission, Anangu were moving between the customary and market economies with the mission authorities gradually assuming the roles of the state in areas such as education, health services and rations.

The commercial craft industry began in 1948 following the visit of Mrs Bennett of Kalgoorlie who taught women to adapt their own spinning techniques to use wool and weave the yarn. The yarn was also used to make floor rugs in designs developed from the pastel drawings of schoolchildren (W. D. Scott Proprietary Limited 1971). Winifred Hilliard arrived in 1954 and spent many years working with community members to refine and expand their craftwork (Hilliard 1968).

Figure 5.1 Anangu display their craft work, Ara Irititja, 1960

Photo: J. Fletcher Collection.

The film *Men of the Mulga*, made by the Reverend Aitkin, while clearly designed to display the work of the mission in a favourable light, shows Anangu involved in a wide range of occupations including rug making, rounding up sheep, milking goats, collecting firewood by truck, growing vegetables, helping to build the Ernabella Church and transporting wool to the Finke railway siding. The film also depicts several examples of Anangu being trained by the European education and health professionals as to how best to deliver these services to their own community (Aitkin 1952).

The stories of shearing in the 1950s are recorded by authors such as Palypatja Tiger:

> We sheared every single day and sometimes until very late. In those days long ago, we worked hard and were excellent shearers, just as good as the white men. We sent the sheep away wiped clean and naked…As we sheared the sheep we taught the younger men saying 'Don't cut too hard or you might hurt the sheep'. (Tiger 2008:19, 25)

Figure 5.2 Shearing at Ernabella, Ara Irititja, circa 1960

Photo: Shirley Gudgeon (Hill) Collection.

Drought in the late 1950s and throughout the 1960s encouraged people to remain at Ernabella as food and water were easier to obtain. Edwards (1992) indicated that a number of groups of people living together away from their own land caused tension. This also placed pressure on resources such as firewood and water and created a demand for more work.

As time passed, Pitjantjatjara and Yankunytjatjara people were using more resources from the world of their non-Anangu neighbours to maintain their traditional lifestyle:

> Rifles made it easier to hunt kangaroos and rabbits and windmill rod, when fashioned into crow bars, made it easier to dig for honey ants, maku grubs and rabbits. In exchange for these items people traded dingo scalps and worked for short periods on various projects around Ernabella. Tarpaulins were very popular and were used as a waterproof covering over the top of the wiltja (shelter). As more goods were required, people worked for longer periods and became more involved in community projects. During the 1950s, people committed themselves to a twelve week work period after which they would return to traditional living. (Last 2002:3)

Money became part of the process only in the 1950s, and, by 1960, most people, except shepherds, received full pay for their work (Last 2002).

In 1999 Eickelkamp recorded the views of a number of Anangu women about their life at the mission in the 1950s:

> I used to live in a bush hut with my parents, and my father was making spears and spearthrowers while mother was spinning wool. She would then take the spun wool (to the craftroom or the mission) and get money for it to pay for food.

> The young girls washed wool by hand. It came from sheep that were shepherded by two couples at Young's Well, Kunma Piti, Balfour Well, Womikata and other places while their children were at school. Most of these old sheep camps are homelands now. The women made jam from a white fruit like a melon, and Topsy made quandong jam. Other women were cooking and making bread in the bakery. The mission had goats which were milked by Nura Rupert's parents every morning. Rations were taken out on the only car the mission had, the green 'Lucy truck'. (Curley, Brumby and Ward cited in Eickelkamp 1999:26–8)

At Ernabella, Anangu were encouraged to keep contact with their country. Edwards described the mission practice of helping people to go back to their homelands twice a year, at dingo pupping season and again at Christmas when mission activity came to a standstill. Trucks would take supplies to a number of important areas such as Kanpi, Pipalyatjara and the site of the later settlement of Fregon (Downing 1988:34).

Working with sheep at Ernabella played a major part in the transitional process between two cultures. Some Anangu living out at sheep camps would 'maintain cultural links with the land, while others would hunt or collect bush food which was supplemented with the rations they received each week in return for looking after the sheep' (Last 2002:3). Palypatja Tiger indicated that he still participated in hunting expeditions when not shearing. 'On Saturdays we would each go our separate ways hunting, returning in the evening with meat to share with our parents' (Tiger 2008:17).

These practices can all be seen as conducive to the development of a hybrid economy at Ernabella, with Anangu able to move freely between their customary roles, the market and the state. Employment for men existed but was frequently inadequate to meet the demand for work. 'The isolation of the Mission while helping in Pitjantjatjara transition was also a severe handicap as far as employment options go' (Hilliard 1968:147).

Gardening, especially vegetable gardening, was regarded as significant for the whole community and was a perennial source of employment for men. To assist with this work, every cottage had sufficient water for both household and garden needs. Men also participated in a range of work in the community (most of which has since disappeared):

> Men have been left to work on their own in fields such as well-sinking, erection of windmills, fencing and brickmaking. All of the cement bricks for the church and hospital were made by a team of native men and since then the men have made stabilised earth bricks both for use on mission buildings and for sale to neighbouring stations. The Industrial Training School has proved its value in the knowledge shown by the men both theoretically and practically. (Hilliard 1968:147)

Figure 5.3 Building the first house for Anangu, Ernabella, Ara Irititja, 1963

Photo: Fred Turvey.

By the early 1950s men received remuneration of shirts, trousers, soap, blankets and a small amount of money. Men not working would spend their time hunting and were also skilled at making artefacts for tourists (Hilliard 1968). Initially, there was work only for about 20 women—for example, domestic work in houses, schoolteaching, work in the hospital, a few cooks and shepherds. Early on, the women were taught knitting, to make raffia hats, spinning wool and weaving. The making of floor rugs on a hessian base was the main occupation, with designs chosen from schoolchildren's pastel drawings. The manufacture of kangaroo-skin moccasins, decorated with Ernabella designs on the insteps, proved successful. The skins used were purchased from the south because of tribal taboos (Hilliard 1968:177). The cooks were key workers for many years. In the days of community feeding when all workers had meals in a dining hall, a group of Anangu cooks prepared these meals (Hilliard 1968).

After incorporation in the 1970s, Town Management and Public Utilities funding financed the employment of Anangu involved in community-management projects. In addition, 'Housing Associations received finance to fund the building of houses. At Ernabella, the craft industry relied on the income from sales to employ highly skilled local artists and crafts people' (Last 2002:5). As the sheep industry became less viable, it was phased out in the early 1970s. Anangu relied less on living a traditional lifestyle until the homelands movement began later in the decade. As the economy changed, it became difficult to maintain the quality of life achieved in the 1950s and 1960s. 'The lack of finance made it difficult to fund a just and fair wage structure for Anangu' (Last 2002:5).

Busbridge considered that in the north-west of the State, resources were very limited and the land could not support many people. Busbridge indicated that the problem of Aboriginal employment on reserves was a result of a previous history of paternal protection whereby all responsibilities were met by the department—for example, concessions were given for house rent, medical treatment, electricity, fuel and subsidised foodstuffs (Busbridge 1966).

This supports the view of Brock, who argued that 'Aboriginal people were generally treated as a labour reserve which could be drawn on for seasonal and casual work. When not employed Aboriginal workers and their families were expected to return to segregated communities on pastoral stations or reserves' (Brock 1995:102).

Employment off the Mission

Anangu often worked on cattle stations in areas near the APY Lands during the mission period. Aboriginal workers voluntarily left the mission to participate in seasonal work in other areas with two main objectives: to bring additional finances back to boost the restricted funds available and to experience living conditions applicable to the general community in more settled areas (Busbridge 1966:98).

Chrysoprase mining in Western Australia (Wingelina) and Mount Davies was often assisted by Anangu workers who would live onsite for a week and fill 44-gallon (200 L) drums with the mineral for shipment to Hong Kong (W. Edwards, Personal communication, November 2009). Downing (1988) identifies the main motivation for Anangu as not the mining but to return to their country and care for it. A group of 18 young men, mostly from the mission, was recruited for station work at Snake Bay, Melville Island, in 1964 (Hilliard 1968:154).

Following a shortage of fruit pickers at Barmera, a trial was undertaken in 1965–66 whereby up to 25 Anangu men from Ernabella were engaged as fruit pickers. Edwards felt that the project could be considered a success because of a number of factors. There was a sympathetic liaison person in Barmera who helped the workers adjust, the men did not experience discrimination and they were helped by the fellowship in the church. In addition, the time of seven to eight weeks was not too long for them to miss their families (Edwards 1966). By 1971 this practice was expanded to include men from other communities. The only problem raised by fruit growers was that they wanted the crop picked as soon as possible, whereas the men from the mission were happy with their income and were not keen to work weekends (W. D. Scott Proprietary Limited 1971). Men from Ernabella also worked in Alice Springs as labourers, truck drivers and council employees (W. D. Scott Proprietary Limited 1971).

Employment after Mission Life

The Ernabella community was incorporated on 1 January 1974. Anangu, while still maintaining a considerable amount of their tribal lifestyle, had to adapt to many new situations. Ceremonial life continued strongly. Ginger Wikilyiri was keen to work on a vegetable garden, and, after receiving Commonwealth assistance, the garden began in 1972. Trickle irrigation was used, and poultry were introduced as well. Last considered that it was crucial that future garden projects should not be developed on a European economic model but be sensitive to the needs of local Anangu (Last 1976).

Figure 5.4 The vegetable garden at Ernabella, Ara Irititja, 1973

Photo: Alan Morris Collection.

Many of the fruit and vegetables grown came from the demand by the community. Last was also instrumental in the establishment of a reafforestation program with Anangu starting a nursery to grow trees for dust control, shade and control of erosion (Last 1976:109).

Ernabella bought a percussion water-drilling rig in 1960. It was operated by Anangu man Louis Wirultjukur, who drilled all the town and stock bores on Fregon as it was being established and kept up this work on the APY Lands up to the late 1970s (Last 2002:6).

In a rare plaudit from the mainstream press, the Adelaide *Advertiser* featured an article on enterprise development in Ernabella in 1978:

> Outsiders would do well to look at SA's remote Ernabella—its Pitjantjatjara people its community awareness and its fierce pride. The people of Ernabella…are working examples of community development. There are a variety of enterprises at Ernabella for individuals to work in. Many do so while others set up their own businesses. Peter Nyaningu is Ernabella's baker. For five years he has operated his own business in a small bakery behind the Ernabella store. When I visited him early one morning to ask about his work he was busy mixing dough to make 100 loaves—the average daily demand. (Ball 1978)

This business was funded by a $1600 loan from the Aboriginal Loans Commission.

The use of unemployment benefits on the APY Lands was seen as being in conflict with community employment. As a result, in 1977 the Ernabella community wrote to the Federal Minister for Aboriginal Affairs and raised with him their concerns of inadequate funding being provided for their community employment programs. By the late 1970s Anangu were employed across a wide range of community programs, mainly due to skills they had acquired from training on the job. According to Last, there was a clear policy to employ Anangu, as contractors were not geared to include Anangu in their work programs (Last 2002).

Figure 5.5 Water drilling near Ernabella, Ara Irititja, 1970

Photo: Bill Edwards Collection.

The Homelands Movement in the Ernabella Area

Those who wanted to escape the pressures of the larger communities but still remain within reach of their services moved in small family groups to satellite communities called homelands.[2] In the Ernabella area, bores once used for the sheep industry had been re-equipped, new bores had been sunk and

---

2   Homeland centres were 'small decentralised communities of close kin, established by the movement of Aboriginal people to land of social, cultural and economic significance to them' (Blanchard 1987:7).

families moved to these sites, which varied in distance from approximately 6 to 50 km from Ernabella. Perhaps the first proposal for a homelands/outstation movement came from Reverend Victor Coombs, then Secretary of the Australian Presbyterian Board of Missions, who suggested establishing outstations based around Ernabella:

> He proposed that the church administer this through Ernabella and that the outstations be kept small with small sheep and cattle projects and other employment possibilities. He emphasised the need to find sites with plenty of water and firewood...the South Australian Aboriginal Protection Board was decidedly cool on the idea. (Downing 1988:56)

In 1959 the Protection Board had put down bores in the Musgrave Ranges and decided to start their own station; this became the settlement of Musgrave Park, later known as Amata, about 145 km west of Ernabella. 'Fregon was started in 1961 as an outstation both to secure the land for the people and to help some of them move closer to their lands' (Downing 1988:56).

Another movement to develop homelands began at Ernabella in the late 1970s, with three established by the end of 1980. The first, Katjikatjitjarra, was 15 km north of Ernabella. It was begun by a few older men who took with them about a dozen pensioners and two younger couples with no children. Wamikata was then established with a small family group of about eight people. They planted grapevines early and carted water by hand to keep the plants alive. Ngarutjarra was established next as a place where alcoholic adults and petrol-sniffing children could be reunited with their law and their land. Even in the township itself people were planning separate groups of housing a little away from the main centre (Downing 1988:65).

Cane and Stanley (1985) recorded the sequence as Itjinpiri settled in about 1976, followed soon afterwards by Katjikatjitjara, Wintuwintutjara and Wamikata. Black Hill, David's Well, Tjatja and Ngarutjara were next, then more recently, Eagle Bore, Araluen, Umbaganda and New Well. Downing considered that a range of positive results was to be found in the outstation communities including a return to Aboriginal decision making and control and to a more Aboriginal lifestyle, a strengthening of family and family authority and a recovery both of an individual and a group identity and of useful roles and involvement in the work of the community. He also held the view that there had been 'an observable improvement in social and general health...a desire to control the kind of education which their children receive and to make sure that they are thoroughly educated in their own culture and the easing of pressures in the larger settlements' (Downing 1988:97).

More than 20 years after these observations, with some notable exceptions, most of the homelands around Ernabella (that is, the Anilalya homelands) are clearly struggling as the result of decisions by governments and organisational service-delivery policies and out-migration, with many of them currently unoccupied or used infrequently.

The Hybrid Economy Revisited

During the course of my fieldwork, I met many Anangu who had managed to maintain their connections with their land (via hunting or gathering bush tucker, visiting sacred sites, participating in ceremonies and attending funerals), received assistance from the state (most often in the form of CDEP or unemployment benefits) and participated in the market economy (for example, by selling artwork or artefacts, or pursuing employment either on the APY Lands or in nearby locations).

Austin-Broos (2009) considers that people need a diverse economy and life projects to prosper. She suggests that there is no hunter-gatherer economy in Central Australia (it is certainly difficult to argue about its decline in importance). Employment options are very restricted, with only marginal work left. She does not believe that the hybrid model is as relevant in Central Australia due to the limited number of jobs and the fact that it seems to foreclose on how local people want to live (it does not include education and literacy in English). Indeed, Young noted in her evidence to the House of Representatives Inquiry into the Aboriginal Homelands Movement in Australia that 'while there are estimates of up to 70% of food being derived from the land in Arnhem land, in Central Australia bush tucker may not provide more than 20% of food depending on variations in the kind of country' (Young 1987:133).

This is not the same as arguing that the customary economy has declined in importance in terms of the commitment of time. There are many older Anangu who spend a considerable number of their waking hours working out how they can access bush tucker, who has a vehicle that might be heading towards their country and how they can next visit their extended family members.

The economist Gregory (2004:125) has suggested that in other countries many members of poor, remote communities with few natural resources would leave and send money back home. This has not occurred to a major extent at Ernabella. As Gregory also points out, however, national policies have not created an environment in which unskilled Indigenous Australians can successfully out migrate. I suggest that Anangu are torn between their obligations and attachment to country and how best to ensure that future generations are able to remain on their land and prosper.

A sustainable Indigenous enterprise needs to take into account not only economic issues, such as revenue and profits, but also social and cultural factors such as ceremonial activity, family issues and subsistence activities. Remote Indigenous communities also face social problems of health, nutrition, substance abuse, unemployment, poor education and training, and lack of transport and communication. Whereas enterprises can provide additional sources of revenue, they also have the potential to generate positive social outcomes such as employment, community participation, access to fresh food (through market gardens) and the transfer of cultural knowledge to the next generation (through cultural tourism ventures and art).

Conclusion

Anangu have had significant involvement in the general economy from the beginnings of mission life until the establishment of a range of enterprises in the mid-1970s. They also managed to retain their contacts with their land and the customary economy during this period.

I suggest that Altman's hybrid model still has relevance on the APY Lands, taking into account the reservations of researchers such as Austin-Broos and Gregory. In an economic climate where large corporations are adjusting to the impact of the global financial crisis, small enterprises (and the contribution of entrepreneurs) are becoming even more important contributors to economic development.

The current dominance of the state economy and very limited nature of the market economy could be seen as having the potential to transition to a new phase. The work currently being undertaken in Ernabella and its homelands by community members and researchers in new enterprise development around cultural tourism and retail ventures, along with existing enterprises based on arts and crafts and the work on natural resource management, gives hope for future growth in the market economy and a means for some in the community to move to greater independence from the state than is currently the case.

References

Aitkin, Rev. H. (dir) 1952. *Men of the Mulga*. Presbyterian Church of Australia. (Colour film.)

Altman, J. 2005. Economic futures on Aboriginal land in remote and very remote Australia: hybrid economies and joint ventures. In D. Austin-Broos and G.

Macdonald (eds), *Aborigines, Culture and Economy: The past, present, and future of rural and remote Indigenous lives*, pp. 121–34. Sydney: University of Sydney Press.

Altman, J. 2007. Alleviating poverty in remote Indigenous Australia: the role of the hybrid economy. *Development Bulletin* 72 (March 2007).

Anangu Pitjantjatjara Yankunytjatjara web site. Viewed 15 October 2009, <http://www.anangu.com>

Ara Irititja for historic photos. <http://www.irititja.com/index.html>, assisted by John Dallwitz.

Austin-Broos, D. 2009. Workfare, welfare and the hybrid economy: the Western Arrernte in Central Australia. Indigenous Participation in Australian Economies Conference, National Museum of Australia, Canberra.

Ball, R. 1978. Pitjantjatjara pride. *The Advertiser*, [Adelaide], 26 June 1978.

Berndt, R.. 1941 Tribal migrations and myths centreing on Ooldea South Australia. *Oceania* 12 (1): 1-20.

Blanchard, C. 1987. *Return to Country: The Aboriginal homelands movement in Australia*. Report of the House of Representatives Standing Committee on Aboriginal Affairs. Canberra: Australian Government Publishing Service.

Brock, P. (ed.) 1995. Pastoral stations and reserves in South and Central Australia, 1850s–1950s. In *Aboriginal Workers*. Sydney: Australian Society for the Study of Labour History, University of Sydney.

Busbridge, D. L. 1966. Aboriginal employment problems in South Australia. In I. Sharp and C. Tatz (eds), *Aborigines in the Economy*. Brisbane: Jacaranda Press.

Cane, S. and Stanley O. 1985. *Land Use and Resources in Desert Homelands*. Darwin: North Australia Research Unit, Australian National University.

Cocks, C. (chairperson) 1978. *Pitjantjatjara Land Rights Working Party of South Australia*. Adelaide: Parliament of South Australia.

Downing, J. 1988. *Ngurra Walytja: Country of my spirit*. Darwin: North Australia Research Unit, Australian National University.

Edwards, W. 1966. Report on the Ernabella labour export project. In I. Sharp and C. Tatz (eds), *Aborigines in the Economy*. Brisbane: Jacaranda Press.

Edwards, W. 1983. *Pitjantjatjara Land Rights. Aborigines, land and land rights*. Canberra: Australian Institute of Aboriginal Studies.

Edwards, W. 1992. Patterns of Aboriginal residence in the north-west of South Australia. *Journal of the Anthropological Society of South Australia* (30 December).

Eickelkamp, U. 1999. *The Women from Ernabella and their Art.* Canberra: Aboriginal Studies Press.

Finlayson, H. 1935. *The Red Centre: Man and beast in the heart of Australia.* Sydney: Angus & Robertson.

Gee, P. 2003. The European history of the Anangu Pitjantjatjara Lands. In A. Robinson, P. Copley, P. Canty, L. Baker and B. Nesbitt (eds), *A Biological Survey of the Anangu Pitjantjatjara Lands, South Australia, 1991–2001.* Adelaide: Department for Environment and Heritage.

Gregory, R. 2004. Between a rock and a hard place: economic policy and the employment outlook for Indigenous Australians. In *Culture, Economy and Governance in Aboriginal Australia Conference.* Sydney: University of Sydney Press.

Hilliard, W. 1968. *The People in Between: The Pitjantjatjara people of Ernabella.* New York: Funk & Wagnalls.

Hope, D. 1983. Dreams contested: a political account of relations between South Australia's Pitjantjatjara and the Government, 1961–1981, PhD thesis.

Keen, I. 2004. *Aboriginal Economy and Society: Australia at the threshold of colonisation.* Melbourne: Oxford University Press.

Kerin, R. 2006. Natives allowed to remain naked: an unorthodox approach to medical work at Ernabella Mission. *Health and History* 8 (1): 20.

Last, M. 1976. *The Ernabella Community and its Development. The nutrition of Aborigines in relation to the ecosystem of Central Australia.* Canberra: CSIRO.

Last, M. W. 2002. *Community Employment on the Anangu Pitjantjatjara Lands,* Anangu Pitjantjatjara Yankunytjatjara web site. Viewed 23 October 2009, <http://www.anangu.com>

Lea, T., Tootell, N., Wolgemouth, J., Halkon, C. and Douglas, J. 2008. *Excellence or Exit: Ensuring Anangu futures through education.* Darwin: School of Social Policy and Research, Charles Darwin University.

Marshall, A. 2001. Ngapartji-Ngapartji: ecologies of performance in Central Australia. PhD thesis, School of Social Ecology and Lifelong Learning, University of Western Sydney, Sydney.

Mattingley, C. 2009. *Maralinga: The Anangu story*. Sydney: Allen & Unwin.

Mattingley, C. and Hampton, K. (eds) 1987. *Survival in Our Own Land: Aboriginal experiences in South Australia since 1836*. Adelaide: Wakefield Press.

Peterson, N. 2004. What can the pre-colonial and frontier economies tell us about engagement with the real economy? Indigenous life projects and the conditions for development. In *Culture, Economy and Governance in Aboriginal Australia Conference*. Sydney: University of Sydney Press.

Redmond, A. 2009. Tracking *wurnan*: transformations in the trade and exchange of resources in the northern Kimberley. Indigenous Participation in Australian Economies Conference, National Museum of Australia, Canberra.

Summers, J. 2004. The future of Indigenous policy on remote communities. Australasian Political Studies Association Conference, Adelaide.

Tiger, P. (ed.) 2008. *Iriti Tjiipi Ejiramilanytja Anapalala*. Adelaide: Department of Education and Children's Services.

Toyne, P. and Vachon, D. 1984. *Growing up the Country: The Pitjantjatjara struggle for their land*. Melbourne: McPhee Gribble/Penguin Books.

W. D. Scott Proprietary Limited 1971. *An assessment of the Social and Economic Opportunities Open to the Aborigines of the North West Reserve Region*. Report for Office of Aboriginal Affairs.

Young, D. 2008. *Dingo Scalping and the Frontier Economy in the North West of South Australia*. I. Keen (ed.). Canberra: ANU E Press.

Young, E. 1987. Transcript of evidence to Blanchard, C. *Return to Country: The Aboriginal homelands movement in Australia*. Report of the House of Representatives Standing Committee on Aboriginal Affairs. Canberra: Australian Government Publishing Service.

Labour History and Stolen Wages

6. 'The Art of Cutting Stone': Aboriginal convict labour in nineteenth-century New South Wales and Van Diemen's Land

Kristyn Harman

The nation's understandings of its convict founders underwent a profound transformation in the late 1980s. Previously viewed as 'hardened and professional criminals' or 'prostitutes', convict men and women were no longer simply seen as 'prisoners undergoing punishment' but were reconfigured as 'a well-organised, efficient labour force' (Nichols 1988:viii; Nichols and Shergold 1988:3). Rewriting the convict period as a narrative about forced migrants and the labour they provided enabled the penal settlements, in the words of the then Prime Minister Bob Hawke, to 'become an integral part of the economic history of an immigrant society, rather than an unsavoury aberration that preceded free settlement' (Nichols 1988:viii). This timely re-imagining of the nation's past coincided with Australia's celebrations of its bicentenary in 1988.

Historians, taking what Ann Curthoys later termed an 'imperial approach', re-contextualised convict labourers within the networks of forced migration characteristic of the nineteenth century (2002:146). Research across imperial and colonial networks revealed the diversity of the convict population (Curthoys 2002:146). It became evident that rather than solely comprising white people, Australia's penal settlements had also been populated by numerous people of colour transported to the Australian penal settlements from places as diverse as the Cape Colony, Corfu, Bermuda, India, New Zealand and China (Nichols and Shergold 1988:32, 36; see also Duffield 1985, 1986, 1987, 1999a, 1999b; Duly 1979:39; Malherbe 1980, 1985, 2001, 2002a, 2002b; Pybus 2006). While the newly emerging transnational histories of transportation shed light on the nascent multiculturalism apparent in the Australian penal colonies, one small yet highly significant cohort of convicts continued to be overlooked.

Between 1805 and the 1860s, at least 60 Aboriginal men from New South Wales were transported as convicts. Exiled to some of the harshest penal stations such as Norfolk Island and Port Arthur in Van Diemen's Land, these men laboured alongside convicts from all over the British world. Others laboured on the penal islands at Port Jackson, or worked alongside other convicts, including Maori from New Zealand and Khoi from the Cape Colony, at the probation station on Maria Island off the east coast of Van Diemen's Land.

Aboriginal convicts were generally taken captive within the first decade or so of colonial contact in their respective districts of New South Wales as conflict was intensifying over competing land-use practices. Those captured were considered to have committed an offence against the person or property of a colonist or in some cases against the person of another Aborigine. In the early decades of the colonial incursion, this resulted in several Aboriginal men being exiled to penal stations at the behest of the Governor. What set these men apart from others similarly exiled was that their punishments were intended to be exemplary. Procuring their labour was a secondary consideration. For example, when banishing Duall to Van Diemen's Land in 1816 for having committed 'various atrocious Acts of Robbery, Depredation, and Barbarity on the Property and Persons of His Majesty's loyal Subjects residing in the Interior', Governor, Lachlan Macquarie, hoped this would deter other Aboriginal people from committing similar 'flagrant and sanguinary acts' (*Sydney Gazette*, 3 August 1816:1). The same rationale underpinned the transportation of Aboriginal men over the decades that followed.

The efficient management of convict labour was a key concern of the colonial authorities. Convict labourers were sometimes organised into work gangs but at other times work was allocated on an individual basis. Aboriginal convict labour was organised in the same way, with these men allocated to work gangs to labour alongside other convicts or assigned to individual positions. Determining the best match between convict workers and the available jobs was a crucial step in achieving efficiencies, yet this process could be subverted by men and women who were unwilling to reveal their particular skills to the colonial authorities. They could then market their specialities privately outside the set hours of labour that they were required to perform within the convict system, and thus earn a useful private income. Conversely, new convicts could claim skills they did not possess in the hope of securing a more favourable position within the system. Either way, in a domestic market characterised by labour shortages, possessing scarce skills gave convicts negotiating power despite their situation of forced servitude (Robbins 2000:147, 148).

Because the emerging colonial economy differed markedly from Aboriginal economies, Aboriginal convicts generally possessed few marketable skills and were thus most often relegated to the rank of 'labourer'. This annotation is written across virtually every extant convict record pertaining to these men in the space reserved for 'occupation';[1] however, one notable exception applied. Aboriginal trackers were utilised to recapture escaped convicts, with those outside the convict system paid for their work with goods such as 'maize and

---

1   See, for example, CON37/2, p. 588, Archives Office of Tasmania [hereinafter AOT]; CON 37/3, p. 625, AOT; and Convict Indent for 'Warrigle Jemmy', 47/453 4/2779.3, State Records of New South Wales [hereinafter SRNSW], Sydney.

blankets' (Bigge 1822:117). Other enticements to work as trackers were offered to Aboriginal men already held captive within the convict system, as will become evident in relation to Musquito.

An imperial perception of the utility of deploying Aboriginal trackers in the Australian penal colonies was neatly encapsulated in the 1817 report of John Thomas Bigge (1822:117), the Commissioner dispatched by the British Government to New South Wales to report on the state of the colony:

> By the extraordinary strength of sight that they possess, improved by their daily exercise of it in pursuit of kangaroos and opossums, they can trace to a great distance, with wonderful accuracy, the impressions of the human foot. Nor are they afraid of meeting the fugitive in the woods, when sent in their pursuit, without the soldiers; by their skill in throwing their long and pointed wooden darts they wound and disable them, strip them of their clothes, and bring them back as prisoners, by unknown roads and paths, to the Coal River.

The favourable impression Bigge formed as to the utility of Aboriginal trackers in retrieving convict absconders led to Aboriginal people being employed as trackers for convict establishments at Bathurst, Wellington Valley, Port Macquarie and Moreton Bay (Roberts n.d.:1). Aboriginal convicts were also deployed as trackers, with extant records confirming their use in Van Diemen's Land.

Before the Supreme Court of New South Wales was established in Sydney in 1824, several Aboriginal men from the Hawkesbury and Cowpastures respectively were transported at the behest of the colonial Governor. They represent the first incidences of labour being extracted from Aboriginal people within the colonial convict system. The earliest extant records pertain to two men known to colonists as Musquito and Bull Dog, both of whom provide an illustrative example of Aboriginal men forced to labour amongst the lowest ranks of convict society. Musquito's skills as a tracker, however, coupled with changes in the ways in which convict labour was being managed, later saw him occupy a more favourable position within the convict system.

Musquito and Bull Dog were involved in actions to repel the colonial incursion at the Hawkesbury River before being taken into custody and later shipped to Norfolk Island. The Governor of New South Wales, Philip King, wrote to the Acting Commandant at Norfolk Island on 8 August 1805, telling him:

> The two Natives Bull Dog and Musquito…are sent to Norfolk Island where they are to be kept, and if they can be brought to Labour will earn their Food—but as they must not be let to starve for want of subsistence—they are to be victualled from the Stores.[2]

After arriving at the penal station on 5 September 1805, they were put to work as assistants to the convict charcoal burners and continued in this position for the next seven years (Nobbs 1988:192, 198). This job was amongst the lowest that could be allocated to convicts, but was nevertheless important to the daily functioning of the penal station, as charcoal was essential to the process of infusing iron with carbon (Maxwell-Stewart 2008).

According to former convict charcoal burner William Derrincourt, he was provided with two barrow men to assist him in his job (Derrincourt 1975:78). The charcoal burner and his assistants worked to ensure that the wood being reduced to charcoal did not burn too quickly, as this would ruin the process. The men were required to gather tree limbs and form them into a pyramid shape, which was then covered in wet sand. Once the wood was set alight, constant monitoring was required. Any smoke issuing from the top of the structure indicated to the men that they needed to add more sods and wet sand to it to slow the burning process sufficiently for it to result in the desired charcoal (Maxwell-Stewart 2008:30, 31).

By December 1810, the number of convict charcoal burners resident at Norfolk Island had decreased from five to only one (Nobbs 1988:125). This diminishing number reflected the declining general population of convicts on the island—a phenomenon resulting from a decision dating back to 1806 to close the penal establishment there as it was being kept up 'at very great expense'.[3] Bull Dog's fate following the closure of Norfolk Island is uncertain. The archival record is more complete in relation to Musquito, who was transferred to Van Diemen's Land in 1813. During this period, convicts were routinely being assigned to private individuals and put to work as their servants. As was the case for many other convicts, Musquito was assigned sequentially to several different settlers as their convict servant, working as a stock-keeper in return for a roof over his head and 'rations and cloathes equal to that issued from the [government] stores'.[4] While in Van Diemen's Land, Musquito was required to work as a tracker. He was so effective against the bushrangers who continued to plague the island colony that he was later described as 'an admirable bloodhound' (Bonwick 1969:93).

---

2   King to John Piper, 8 August 1805, New South Wales' Colonial Secretary's Office Correspondence, Reel 6040, p. 41, AOT.

3   Right Honourable William Windham to Governor William Bligh, 30 December 1806, *Historical Records of Australia* [hereinafter HRA], Series I, Volume VI, p. 70.

4   King to Portland, 28 September 1800, Enclosure No. 5, 'General Orders', *HRA*, Series I, Volume II, p. 624.

Surviving correspondence indicates that Musquito was to have been repatriated to Sydney, possibly as a reward for his services as a tracker; however, this never transpired. Instead, he went on to have an illustrious career as a leader of a group of Tasmanian Aborigines dubbed 'the tame mob'. Ultimately, their acts of resistance against Vandemonian settlers resulted in several of their number being tried and executed, including Musquito, who was hanged on a scaffold 'erected within the Gaol-walls, but in view of the town' of Hobart on 25 February 1825 (*Hobart Town Gazette*, 25 February 1825:2).

It has been suggested that Musquito was assisted in his work as a tracker by another Aboriginal convict, a Dharawal man from the Cowpastures known to settlers as Duall (Wise 1983:3).[5] He was transported to Van Diemen's Land in 1816 at the behest of Governor Macquarie, who instructed the Commandant at Port Dalrymple that the 'Black Native' Duall was 'to be kept at Hard Labour and to be fed in the same manner as the other Convicts'.[6] Despite extensive research, I am yet to locate any primary sources that demonstrate Duall worked as a black tracker. Nevertheless, his situation is of particular relevance because Macquarie's rationale for having Duall transported has survived and (as indicated above) sheds light on the sort of thinking that underpinned such decisions during the early colonial era.

Duall was taken captive during the punitive expedition ordered out by Macquarie during 1816 following a series of altercations between Aboriginal people and colonists in the districts of Airds, Appin and Bringelly to the west of Sydney. Despite close friendships with notable settlers such as Hamilton Hume and Charles Throsby, Duall was labelled a 'hostile native' after being implicated in the retaliatory killing of some settlers several years earlier. Macquarie's strategy in dealing with Duall was embedded in a policy of exclusion.[7] Duall was removed not only from colonial society at the Cowpastures, but also from his tribe. The punishment was meant to be exemplary, as explained in the *Sydney Gazette* when Duall's banishment was announced:

> The banishment of the native *Dewal*…may possibly produce a greater dread in the minds of his predatory associates than if he had been killed when in the act of plunder. The doubt of what may be his fate, when absent, is likely to excite a dread which may render them less liable to a similar treatment. (*Sydney Gazette*, [Supplement], 3 August 1816:2)

---

5 Duall belonged to what settlers termed the 'Cowpastures' tribe—a collective that some anthropologists have concluded spoke the Dharawal language. See Liston (1988:49).

6 Macquarie to Brevet-Major James Stewart, 31 July 1816, *HRA*, Series III, Volume II, p. 471.

7 Lachlan Macquarie, 'List of hostile natives', New South Wales Colonial Secretary's Office Correspondence, Reel 6005, p. 44, AOT.

Fear and intimidation excited through the apparently inexplicable absence of Duall's body were meant to ensure that his kinsmen desisted from attacking colonists and their property. Clearly, there were also economic consequences. As Aboriginal people traditionally lived in small groups, depriving a group of a young man such as Duall reduced its capacity to hunt and to defend itself.

As it happens, Duall was eventually repatriated to the Cowpastures in January 1819, as he was required to work as a translator for an exploratory expedition led by Throsby to find a direct route from the Cowpastures to Bathurst. In recognition of his exemplary service to the expeditioners, Duall received some blankets and a brass breastplate.[8] He was therefore also repatriated to the subject position of 'friendly native' that he had occupied prior to the outbreak of hostilities at the Cowpastures and went on to work with other expeditionary parties.

From the inception of the law courts in New South Wales in the 1820s, Aboriginal men began appearing before the colonial judiciary on charges ranging from murder and wounding with intent to kill to robbery and the theft of sheep. Other men, too, appeared on such charges. What distinguished the actions of Aboriginal defendants from those of other prisoners, though, was that many of these acts were explicit attempts to drive the colonial intruders from their lands. For example, in January 1843 a large party of Aborigines attacked C. Doyle's station in the Mooney district. They killed a stockman, destroyed the huts, removed the horses, drove off the entire herd of cattle and took six months' supplies from the station. Doyle's workers were in no doubt as to Aboriginal motivations as they were 'coming opposite to the hut and daring the men to go out, saying they had killed all the horses, and would kill or drive all the white fellows off the Mooney, M'Intyre, and Barwin Rivers'.[9]

Despite various arguments put forward in the colonial law courts by solicitors like George Nichols, who argued before Chief Justice, Francis Forbes, in the Supreme Court of New South Wales that conflict between settlers and Aborigines near the Williams River had amounted to 'open warfare', in the absence of any official declaration of war, Aboriginal men were classed as criminals.[10] Complicating the matter further, because Aborigines were considered to be British subjects, it was thought that they could not be at war with other British subjects. Aboriginal men were therefore put on trial as British subjects with the only concession to their obvious disadvantage under the newly imposed colonial legal system being the provision of a court interpreter. As Justice Alfred Stephen told the

---

8   Throsby, 'Journal of a tour to Bathurst through the Cow Pastures', Reel 6038, p. 89, AOT.
9   'Namoi River', Extract of a letter from Mr B. Doyle, of the Namoi, to his father, C. M. Doyle, Esq., 19 January 1843, *Maitland Mercury*, 28 January 1843, p. 2.
10   *R v Jackey 1834* in Kercher (n.d.) (<http://www.law.mq.edu.au/scnsw/Cases1834/html/r_v_jackey__1834.htm>).

Maitland Circuit Court in 1843, 'the same measure of justice, and in the same scales' applied to all alike 'whatever the offender's colour' (*Maitland Mercury*, 16 September 1843:2).

During the late 1820s, some Aboriginal prisoners appeared before the colonial judiciary but tended to be discharged (sometimes to the Benevolent Asylum) for want of an official interpreter. Very few of these men were transported.[11] From the 1830s onwards, particularly following the hangings of six white men and one man described as a 'mulatto' after the Myall Creek Massacre, increasing numbers of Aboriginal defendants received guilty verdicts in the colonial law courts.[12] Some were sentenced directly to transportation, while others were transported following the commutation of their death sentences by the Executive Council.

In the middle decades of the nineteenth century, the colonial rationale for incorporating Aboriginal men into the convict system became more nuanced. The emphasis on imposing exemplary punishments remained, but was tempered with the idea that captivity provided an excellent opportunity to try to Christianise and civilise Aboriginal convicts. This shift is amply illustrated by the outcome of a series of trials held in Sydney after a period of frontier warfare north of the settlement in the early 1830s. These trials involved 18 Aboriginal defendants who represented about 10 per cent of the combined Aboriginal force that waged war against colonists in the Brisbane Water district.[13]

One of the Aboriginal defendants, known as Mickey, was hanged; however, most of the remaining prisoners were sentenced to transportation. Governor, Richard Bourke, tried to arrange for these Aboriginal convicts to be sent to Van Diemen's Land. On 14 February 1835, he wrote to the Lieutenant Governor and told him that 'they are more than half civilized and will make decent herdsmen'. Bourke might have been inspired to suggest this after observing Khoi working with their cattle at the Cape Colony.[14]

---

11   For example, the blanket-clad Binge Mhulto who was described in *The Australian* as being 'in a state of near nature' was remanded in custody for want of a suitable interpreter. As staging a trial seemed to involve insurmountable difficulties, it was recommended that he simply be sent into exile. See *R v Binge Mhulto 1828* in Kercher (n.d.) (<http://www.law.mq.edu.au/scnsw/Cases1827-28/html/r_v_binge_mhulto__1828.htm>). For the release of Aboriginal prisoners to the Benevolent Asylum, see Plomley (1987:582).

12   For the trials held in the aftermath of the Myall Creek Massacre, see *R v Kilmeister (No. 1) 1838* (<http://www.law.mq.edu.au/scnsw/Cases1838-39/html/r_v_kilmeister__no_1__1838.htm>) and *R v Kilmeister and Others (No. 2) 1838* (<http://www.law.mq.edu.au/scnsw/Cases1838-39/html/r_v_kilmeister__no_2__1838.htm>) in Kercher (n.d.).

13   See *R v Monkey and Others 1835* (<http://www.law.mq.edu.au/scnsw/cases1835-36/html/r_v_monkey__1835.htm>); *R v Mickey and Muscle 1835* (<http://www.law.mq.edu.au/scnsw/cases1835-36/html/r_v_mickey_and_muscle__1835.htm>); *R v Long Dick, Jack Jones, Abraham, and Gibber Paddy 1835* (<http://www.law.mq.edu.au/scnsw/cases1835-36/html/r_v_long_dick__1835.htm>) in ibid. See also Justice Burton, Notes of Criminal Cases, 2/2420, Volume 19, pp. 4, 6, SRNSW.

14   Governor Richard Bourke to Lieutenant Governor George Arthur, 14 February 1835, in *Arthur Papers*.

Rumours abounded that the Aboriginal prisoners would be bound for Van Diemen's Land. This proposal attracted public opprobrium, with *The Australian* newspaper printing: 'It has been supposed by some persons, but we have reason to believe without foundation, that these poor wretches are to be worked in irons—or at least subjected to some form of "prison discipline"; the idea is too monstrous for belief' (*The Australian*, 17 February 1835:2).

In any case, the colonial authorities in Van Diemen's Land strongly opposed receiving a group of Aboriginal convicts. They had, after all, only recently resolved what they saw as their own 'Aboriginal problem' by exiling the remnant Aboriginal population to an island in Bass Strait. This did not, however, preclude individual Aboriginal convicts being transported to Van Diemen's Land well into the 1840s where they were put to hard labour (Harman 2008).

Given the Vandemonian position, Bourke arranged to transport the Brisbane Water men—Lego'me, Toby, Whip-em-up, Currinbong Jemmy, Tom Jones, Little Freeman, Monkey, Little Dick and Charley Muscle—to Goat Island at Port Jackson. He engaged a Wesleyan Methodist catechist, George Langhorne, on a salary of £100 per annum to instruct the men. Langhorne was to teach them 'elements of the Christian Religion' as well as the English language.[15] In colonial New South Wales, the penal station became the site par excellence for the state in its endeavours to produce the civilised native. The suspension of any legal rights that Aboriginal captives had notionally been entitled to claim as free British subjects meant, as Satadru Sen (2000:89) explained in a different colonial context, that 'the state's power to coerce, to manipulate, and to experiment was relatively unimpeded by its own constructed limits'.

The Government's treatment of these Aboriginal convicts was once again denounced in the columns of *The Australian* newspaper: 'To teach religion and literature to these poor wretches is absurd—the one it is impossible that they should understand—the other cannot be accomplished without putting a force upon the inclinations of the adults, to which they would never submit' (*The Australian*, 6 March 1835:2).

Despite the misgivings expressed in *The Australian*, Bourke intended for the men to be worked in irons for two years on Goat Island and housed in the prison hulk *Phoenix* that lay at anchor nearby.[16] By day, the Aboriginal convicts were taken off the hulk to be put to work on Goat Island cutting stone 'under charge

---

15 Bourke to Secretary of State, *HRA*, Series I, Volume XVII, p. 718. It is unclear why Bourke mentioned eight Aboriginal convicts when there were nine intended for Van Diemen's Land. Possibly one of the men had already died in custody prior to the rest of the cohort being sent to Goat Island.
16 George Langhorne to the Colonial Secretary, 30 August 1835, Reel 2204, Bundle 4/2322.2, SRNSW.

of one of their own kindred' (*The Australian*, 1 May 1835:3). Sandstone was required for the construction of a powder magazine on the island where more than 200 convicted men were put to hard labour.

Aboriginal men certainly had some insight into the colonisers' urge to civilise them and the role that jail played. An exchange between William Speed at the Brisbane Water district and his Aboriginal employee Charley later cited by Charles Swancott illustrates this point: 'Old Conkleberry Charlie, was in the bad books with the boss one day, who told him to "run away Charlie, you're only a bloody Myall". Charlie got very indignant and corrected [him] "Me no Myall, Boss, me been breakum stone along Wyndham gaol"' (Swancott 1953–61:Part 4, p. 67).

Swancott (1953–61:Part 4, p. 67) rounded off this anecdote with the exclamation 'He'd been civilized!' This phrase neatly encapsulates Charlie's understanding of the purpose of the jail's disciplinary regime and the outcome sought in relation to Aboriginal inmates.

Their harsh existence took its toll on the Aboriginal convicts. During their first year of captivity, several died. The missionary Langhorne speculated that one of these men was 'perhaps among the first...of the New Holland Tribes gathered in to the Kingdom of God'.[17] Aboriginal convicts generally exhibited a high mortality rate in colonial custody, being 10 times more likely to die than non-Aboriginal male convicts transported to Van Diemen's Land in the early 1840s.

The Port Macquarie missionary Launcelot Threlkeld took a keen interest in the Goat Island experiment. He visited the island to assess the progress of the surviving Aboriginal convicts. Threlkeld later reported that 'under the superintendence of Mr Langhorne they were improving fast in their English reading'.[18] Langhorne told him that 'on asking the Blacks who made all things, one of them immediately to his surprise replied, God! and on being further questioned as to his source of knowledge he replied it was at Lake Macquarie'.[19] This clearly gratified Threlkeld.

In November 1836, with their sentences about to expire, the surviving Aboriginal convicts were transferred to Threlkeld's mission at Lake Macquarie.[20] Threlkeld showed the prisoners a large hut put aside for their use. He planned to build a small fishing boat for them.[21] In return for their catch, the men could get rations of flour, tea, sugar and clothing, but were prohibited from buying alcohol or tobacco. They were also not to leave the mission without a pass.

---

17 George Langhorne to the Colonial Secretary, 30 August 1835, Reel 2204, Bundle 4/2322.2, SRNSW.
18 Threlkeld, Fifth Report, in Gunson (1974:122).
19 Threlkeld to Parker, 15 November 1836, in ibid., p. 132.
20 Threlkeld, Fifth Report, in ibid., p. 122.
21 Threlkeld, Sixth Report, in ibid., p. 133.

Threlkeld noted that 'to all this they appeared cordially to agree', providing him and Langhorne with 'much gratification on the prospect of carrying into effect a plan long contemplated'.[22]

The missionaries' gratification was short lived. Their Aboriginal charges escaped during the night, leaving their clothes behind. Threlkeld's assessment of the outcome of this experiment in Christianising and civilising Aborigines in captivity is illuminating:

> The mere mechanical external operation of human instruction, is too transitory in its effects to calculate upon, as was clearly exemplified in the Aborigines confined at Goat Island, who whilst under coercive instruction, rapidly advanced in their respective attainments of reading, writing and arithmetic, repeating prayers, singing hymns, and the art of cutting stone, in which they exhibited much skill; but when removed from under restraint, proved to Man, that coercive religious instruction is of no moral avail, however much we may deceive ourselves with specious appearances of success during compulsory education.[23]

The missionary later heard that the men had returned to the Brisbane Water district. Whether they agreed with Conkleberry Charlie's view that breaking stones in jail meant they were no longer 'myalls' is not recorded, but when some of the former prisoners were asked to engage in stone-cutting in return for payment they refused on the grounds that it had been their punishment (Swancott 1953–61:Part 4, p. 67).

Over time, Indigenous peoples adopted, and adapted, some of the methods introduced by colonists. When such changes were entirely their own initiative, these innovations did not always meet with the colonists' approval. Such was the case in the circumstances leading to the transportation of Yanem Goona.

Between 1838 and 1840, the lands adjacent to the Grampians in the Port Phillip District of New South Wales occupied by neighbouring peoples of Djab Wurrung and Jardwadjali were subject to what Ian Clark (1990:94) has termed a 'squatting invasion'. The white intrusion resulted in violence, with between 30 and 40 men of the Konongwootong gundidj section of Jardwadjali killed by the Whyte brothers in March 1840 (Clark 1990:239). Both Djab Wurrung and Jardwadjali engaged in what was later described by a settler who lived in the area between 1841 and 1842 as 'guerrilla warfare'. Nearby Mount Arapiles—a natural fortress—provided an ideal base from which to launch their attacks.[24]

---

22   Threlkeld to M'Leay, 17 November 1836, in ibid., pp. 258–9.
23   Threlkeld, Eighth Report, in ibid., p. 144.
24   Hall to La Trobe, 6 September 1853, in Bride (1898:222).

Economic sabotage was one of the principal means of resisting white encroachment onto Aboriginal lands. As had been the case elsewhere in New South Wales, here, the Indigenes deprived the squatters of large numbers of their stock and flocks. In this particular locale, however, reports began to emerge as early as 1840 that highlighted the ways in which local Aboriginal peoples were adopting new practices, particularly in relation to animal management. Blending their traditional practices with methods adapted from observing squatters at work, Djab wurrung were found to have constructed an extremely well-built bush fence to enclose the numerous sheep they had taken from Trawalla, a station owned by Kirkland and Hamilton. In a similar way to which a kangaroo would have been dealt with, they also broke the legs of the sheep to prevent them from straying, thus keeping the animals in close proximity for when they might be required for food (Clark 1990:34).

Henry Dana and his contingent of Native Police discovered one such bush yard when they were deployed to track a flock taken from a station in the Wimmera. Dana later described how, during the ensuing melee between the Native Police and 'natives', 'the Ringleader of the party was cut down after a long resistance... and made a prisoner of; he is badly wounded'.[25] The 'ringleader' referred to by Dana was Yanem Goona, also known as Yanengoneh ('spring from the earth') or Old Man Billy Billy.[26]

Yanem Goona—described as being 'almost grey with age'—was lodged in Melbourne Gaol to await trial (*Geelong Advertiser*, 7 August 1845:3). Eventually, he was charged in the Court of the Resident Judge on 17 October 1845 with 'having on the 10th of July last, stolen fifty wethers, fifty ewes, and fifty lambs, the property of Mr. Bailey and another, of Colkennett, in the District of Port Phillip' (*Melbourne Courier*, 17 October 1845:2). At the conclusion of the trial, Justice Roger Therry controversially found 'that if this black was a member of the community where the sheep were found altho he had no hand in the actual stealing or killing, yet as a member of that community was equally guilty' (Clark 1990:244). The prisoner was sentenced to 10 years' transportation to Van Diemen's Land.[27]

After arriving in Van Diemen's Land on 29 December 1845, Yanem Goona was required to serve three years of probation and was sent to join a convict gang stationed at Norfolk Island. Less than two years later, an ailing Yanem Goona was transported back to Van Diemen's Land where he arrived on 18 August 1847. After spending the night in the prisoners' barracks in Hobart, he was forwarded to Saltwater River, near Port Arthur, to complete the remainder of his

25 Dana to La Trobe, July 1845, 45/1379 4/2741, SRNSW.
26 For the English interpretation of Yanem Goona's name, see Rose to La Trobe, in Bride (1898:148).
27 Robinson, Saturday, 18 October 1845, in Clark (1998:336).

three years' probation.[28] This was the site of one of Van Diemen's Land's convict-worked coalmines, which was established following the discovery of coal on the Tasman Peninsula in 1833 (Tuffin 2008:43).

By the 1840s, four shafts had been sunk at the Coal Mines at Saltwater River and more than 120 prisoners laboured there under trained miners and the watchful eye of their guards (Tuffin 2008:44). The work involved in bringing out the coal was dirty and exhausting. The former convict Derrincourt (1975:57) described how when working at the Coal Mines he and his workmates were 'tired, dirty, and as black as any devils through crawling in slush and mud, made up of wet coal dust'. Derrincourt (1975:53, 54) explained that at the bottom of the mineshafts, men in groups of three, nicknamed 'Devon donkeys', were required to be harnessed to, and haul, trucks of water:

> They were, because of the lowness of the drive, almost on all fours, holding on and dragging with their hands on the rails. Some of them had boots, and some of them, who were not yet due for 'slops,' had none. They were puffing and blowing, and reeking and steaming from their exertions. The poor donkeys were forced to make every effort to get their work over by a certain time. The sooner this was done the sooner they were allowed on top; while, on the other hand, if any should lag, he and his companions would have to wait down without food while the next two shifts were being hauled up.

The harshness of this existence took its toll on the already unwell Yanem Goona. Little more than a year after being sent to the Coal Mines at Saltwater River, he died in the nearby hospital for convict invalids at Impression Bay on Tasman Peninsula.

Aboriginal convicts filled a wide range of occupations as convict labourers working alongside other convicts. They were identified as 'labourers', and their work as charcoal burners, stock-keepers, coalmine workers, sandstone cutters and land clearers took its toll on their health. Despite utilising transportation as a means towards quelling Aboriginal resistance in New South Wales, there is no evidence to suggest that the colonial authorities achieved this objective through sending Indigenous men into exile to labour as convicts. There is also no evidence to suggest that utilising the convict system as a means through which to educate some of the Aboriginal convicts about Christianity and to inculcate the Protestant work ethic was at all effective. To the contrary, some of the very few to survive custodial sentences dismissed convict labour as having formed part of their punishment rather than having equipped them with new skills with which to exploit the labour market.

---

28   CON37/2, p. 588, AOT.

References

Primary Sources

Arthur Papers. Volume 8: Correspondence with Sir R. Bourke, 1831–6, Reel 3, A2168. Hobart: Law Library, University of Tasmania.

Bigge, J. 1822. *Report of the Commissioner of Inquiry into the State of the Colony of New South Wales. Volume I*. London: Ordered by the House of Commons to be printed.

Bride, T. (ed.) 1898. *Letters from Victorian Pioneers: Being a series of papers on the early occupation of the colony, the Aborigines, etc., addressed by Victorian pioneers to His Excellency Charles Joseph La Trobe, Esq., Lieutenant-Governor of the Colony of Victoria*. Melbourne: R. S. Brain, Government Printer for the Trustees of the Public Library.

Burton, J. Notes of Criminal Cases, 2/2420, Volume 19. Sydney: State Records of New South Wales.

Clark, I. (ed.) 1998. *The Journals of George Augustus Robinson, Chief Protector, Port Phillip Aboriginal Protectorate. Volume Four: 1 January 1844 – 24 October 1845*. Oxford: Heritage Matters, Clarendon.

Colonial Secretary's Inward Correspondence. Volume 4/2741. Sydney: State Records of New South Wales.

Conduct Registers of Male Convicts Arriving on Non-Convict Ships or Locally Convicted, CON 37. Hobart: Archives Office of Tasmania.

Convict Indent for Warrigal Jemmy, 47/453 4/2779.3. Sydney: State Records of New South Wales.

Gunson, N. (ed.) 1974. *Australian Reminiscences & Papers of L. E. Threlkeld: Missionary to the Aborigines 1824–1859.Volumes I and II*. Canberra: Australian Institute of Aboriginal Studies.

Kercher, B. (ed.) n.d. *Decisions of the Superior Courts of New South Wales, 1788–1899*. Sydney: Division of Law, Macquarie University.

Miscellaneous Correspondence. New South Wales' Colonial Secretary's Office Correspondence, Reel 2204, Bundle 4/2322.2. Sydney: State Records of New South Wales.

New South Wales' Colonial Secretary's Office Correspondence, Reels 6005, 6038, 6040, (Australian Joint Copying Project). Hobart: Archives Office of Tasmania.

Secondary Sources

Bonwick, J. 1969 [1870]. *The Last of the Tasmanians, or the Black War of Van Diemen's Land*. Reprint. Adelaide: Libraries Board of South Australia.

Clark, I. 1990. *Aboriginal Languages and Clans: An historical atlas of western and central Victoria, 1800–1900*. Melbourne: Department of Geography and Environmental Science, Monash University.

Curthoys, A. 2002. Does Australian history have a future? *Australian Historical Studies* 118: 140–52.

Derrincourt, W. 1975 [1899]. *Old Convict Days*. Louis Becke (ed.). Reprint. Harmondsworth, UK: Penguin.

Duffield, I. 1985. Martin Beck and Afro-blacks in colonial Australia. *Journal of Australian Studies* (16): 3–20.

Duffield, I. 1986. From slave colonies to penal colonies: the West Indian convict transportees to Australia. *Slavery and Abolition* 7 (1): 25–45.

Duffield, I. 1987. The life and death of 'Black' John Goff: aspects of the black contribution to resistance patterns during the transportation era in eastern Australia. *Australian Journal of Politics and History* 1 (33): 30–44.

Duffield, I. 1999a. Billy Blue: power, popular culture and mimicry in early Sydney. *Journal of Popular Culture* 33 (1): 7–22.

Duffield, I. 1999b. Daylight on convict lived experience: the history of a pious negro servant. *Tasmanian Historical Studies* 6 (2): 29–62.

Duly, L. 1979. 'Hottentots to Hobart and Sydney': the Cape Supreme Court's use of transportation 1828–38. *Australian Journal of Politics and History* 25 (1): 39–50.

Harman, K. 2008. Aboriginal convicts: race, law, and transportation in colonial New South Wales. PhD thesis, University of Tasmania, Hobart.

Liston, C. 1988. The Dharawal and Gandangara in colonial Campbelltown, New South Wales, 1788–1830. *Aboriginal History* 12 (1): 49–62.

Malherbe, V. 1980. David Stuurman: 'Last chief of the Hottentots'. *African Studies* 39 (1): 47–64.

Malherbe, V. 1985. Khoikhoi and the question of convict transportation from the Cape Colony, 1820–1842. *South African Historical Journal* [*Suid Afrikaanse Historiese Joernaal*] (17): 19–39.

Malherbe, V. 2001. South African Bushmen to Australia? Some soldier convicts investigated. *Journal of Australian Colonial History* 3 (1): 100–24.

Malherbe, V. 2002a. How the Khoekhoen were drawn into Dutch and British defensive systems to c1809. *Military History Journal* 12 (3): 94–9.

Malherbe, V. 2002b. The Khoekhoe soldier at the Cape of Good Hope. Part two: life and times in the Cape Regiment, c1806 to 1870. *Military History Journal* 12 (4): 148–54.

Maxwell-Stewart, H. 2008. *Closing Hell's Gates: The death of a convict station*. Crows Nest, NSW: Allen & Unwin.

Nicholas, S. 1988. Foreword. In S. Nicholas (ed.), *Convict Workers: Reinterpreting Australia's past*. Cambridge: Cambridge University Press.

Nichols, S. and Shergold, P. 1988. Unshackling the past. In S. Nicholas (ed.), *Convict Workers: Reinterpreting Australia's past*. Cambridge: Cambridge University Press.

Nobbs, R. 1988. *Norfolk Island and its First Settlement, 1788–1814*. North Sydney: Library of Australian History.

Plomley, N. 1987. *Weep in Silence: A history of the Flinders Island Aboriginal settlement*. Hobart: Blubber Head Press.

Pybus, C. 2006. *Black Founders: The unknown story of Australia's first black settlers*. Sydney: UNSW Press.

Robbins, W. 2000. The lumber yards: a case study in the management of convict labour 1788–1832. *Labour History* (79): 147–8.

Roberts, D. n.d. Aborigines, commandants and convicts: the Newcastle penal settlement. *Awaba*. University of Newcastle. Viewed 3 June 2006, <http://www.newcastle.edu.au/centre/awaba/awaba/group/amrhd/awaba/history/convicts.html>

Sen, S. 2000. *Disciplining Punishment: Colonialism and convict society in the Andaman Islands*. Oxford: Oxford University Press.

Swancott, C. 1953–61. *The Brisbane Water Story. Parts 1 to 4*. Booker Bay, NSW: Brisbane Water Historical Society.

Tuffin, R. 2008. 'Where the vicissitudes of day and night are not known': convict coal mining in Van Diemen's Land, 1822–1848. *Enterprise & Livelihood in the Tasmanian Past, Tasmanian Historical Studies* 13 (2008): 35–61.

Wise, C. 1983. Black rebel Musquito. In Eric Fry (ed.), *Rebels & Radicals*. North Sydney: Allen & Unwin.

7. Indigenous Workers on Methodist Missions in Arnhem Land: A skilled labour force lost

Gwenda Baker

Indigenous workers on Methodist missions in Arnhem Land were not only vital to mission development and survival; over time, they became an increasingly skilled, competent and reliable workforce. By the end of the mission era, Indigenous participation in the economy of these missions led to an increased skill base amongst the majority of workers. Indigenous workers who remember life on the missions see the end of 'mission time' as the beginning of the end of full employment and participation in a 'real economy' and the hopes of Indigenous control over a new social order (Baker 2005, 2010). They were to be a skilled labour force lost.

Indigenous leaders talk about Indigenous achievements in 'mission time' in the face of current problems, including a generation of young people who have grown up without the example of a fully engaged Yolngu workforce. Reverend Dr Djiniyini Gondarra (2009) in his submission to the NT Government talks about the future of these children:

> When we look around our communities today, we see all the work being done by dominant culture people…Our children want to know why they need to go to school when there is no role for them in our community. Our parents wonder what role or future our children have…it is very sad.

Leaders are seeking narratives and photographic evidence to support the stories they tell to their children and grandchildren. They also need these narratives to speak to a wider audience, telling of their fears for their children and the necessity for Indigenous labour to be the main workforce in their communities.

The stories Yolngu tell about their work on Methodist missions emphasise that mission establishment and development were *joint* enterprises between Indigenous participants and missionaries in Arnhem Land (Baker 2005). The Yolngu have repositioned the role of the early leaders in the creation of the missions in an attempt to take charge of narratives of mission development (Baker 2005). They tell stories of their fathers and grandfathers forming contracts with the missionaries and working together to establish the towns.

One of these stories from a Wangurri clan leader tells about how his father participated in the founding of the mission on Elcho Island. Badanga was his father; Makarrwalla was Badanga's brother. They both travelled to Elcho Island from Milingimbi with the first missionary, Reverend Harold Shepherdson, to establish a new mission (Baker 2005). The story was told to me at Galiwin'ku, Elcho Island, in 1998:

> The mission began when…Yolngu moved over to Elcho…They came to establish a town for themselves with the missionaries…There were smokes, food; jobs that got men to come here…Badanga and Makarrwalla went out and told the others about the town…They learnt about clothes, how to grow gardens, work hard to earn something in the future.

Rudder (1993:302) was told a similar story by the father of Djiniyini Gondarra, Golumala clan leader Willi Walalipa, who also travelled to Elcho Island on this first trip.

I lived on Methodist missions in Arnhem Land in the period 1968–71, and I witnessed the rapid growth of industries and the development of a skilled Indigenous labour force. My research reinforces my view that Indigenous people who pioneered mission development strove to develop working skills within the mission system. A close examination of government and mission documents reveals that a large number of industries were closed down and the workforce was drastically reduced by government action in the creation of award wage positions at the end of the mission era. The later uptake of social service benefits exacerbated the problems of creating a new Indigenous economy.

Indigenous writers identify these problems in stories of the decline of the Indigenous workforce in other areas. Pearson (2009:157–9) suggests that during the period of mission influence in the Cape York area the Indigenous economy, although operating at the lower end of the labour market, was a real economy. People had to work in order to be paid. There was a combination of work on the mission and off the mission. Pearson sees the introduction of the 'welfare economy' at the end of the mission era as the most destructive reason for the collapse of the Indigenous economy and the widespread social dislocation that followed. The 'welfare economy' was not a 'real economy' in that it required no social involvement or work to be paid. The nexus between work and reward was broken.

Trudgen (2000) addresses the long-term effects of white intervention in one of the areas of the operation of the Methodist missions in north-east Arnhem Land. In his book and in workshops run by Trudgen and Yolngu presenters for the Aboriginal Research and Development Services (ARDS), continuing problems of lack of communication and understanding of Yolngu ways are explored. There is a focus on the negative outcomes of white contact—the reduction in the power of leaders, the loss of power over Indigenous lives—and the effects of the drop in Indigenous employment opportunities and the introduction of a new, far more lethal 'welfare economy' of dependence and despair.

While acknowledging the damage of colonial incursion into their territory and the resultant disruption to their social and religious lives, Yolngu leaders also identify levels of local leadership, active learning situations, and gains and achievements during the mission era. In the mid-1950s, Indigenous builder Stephen Bunbaitjun and his team built a new school on Elcho Island. (Bunbaitjun is an old spelling of the name, as used by Stephen on his paintings. There are two new spellings of his name in current usage at Galiwin'ku: Bunbatjun and Bunbatju.) By the mid-1960s, Bunbaitjun had moved his group to Howard Island near Elcho Island, where he planned and built houses on his outstation (see Baker 2005:Figure 7.1). He sold his own bark paintings and watercolour paintings, mats and baskets made by the women and logs floated over to Elcho Island to help finance his building program. Reverend Peter O'Connor (2004), Mission Superintendent at Goulburn Island from 1967 to 1972, reported that by the 1970s Indigenous carpenters were skilled enough to build their own houses. The Goulburn Island mission tendered for and built a staff house on the nearby government settlement at Maningrida using Indigenous builders.

Figure 7.1 Stephen Bunbaitjun: Builder, Howard Island

Photo: Ivan Baker.

Missionary accounts about the effectiveness of the Indigenous workforce vary, but by the 1970s on Elcho Island and Goulburn Island the workforce was increasingly competent and many workers could and did work independently of mission supervision. At Elcho Island, Indigenous workers went out and cut and collected timber on the mainland and the islands with small gangs of men who worked unsupervised for several days at a time (Figure 7.2). Building was a priority and experienced workers could plan, set out and build houses with their own gangs and under minimal supervision.

Figure 7.2 Unloading logs

Photo: Ivan Baker.

In an interview with Paul Myers (2010), Doug Miller, manager of Roebuck Plains, talked about helping to make Indigenous youths 'work ready', reinventing the place of the Indigenous stockman. The proponents of these worthwhile projects appear to be unaware that at the end of the mission era there was an Indigenous workforce that was more than 'work ready': it was a workforce that operated at a high level of competence and contributed greatly to the development, wellbeing and maintenance of new European-style towns. At the end of the mission era the Government took over the towns, dismantled the fledgling industries, rejected proposals for Indigenous-run enterprises and shrank an Aboriginal workforce that was building their own houses and buildings for community use and providing the workforce for the majority of town enterprises.

From Barter to Training Wages

The Methodist Church established missions along the coast of Arnhem Land on Goulburn Island in 1916, on Milingimbi in 1923, at Yirrkala in 1935 and on Elcho Island in 1942 (Map 7.1). Missionaries were setting up towns and developing infrastructure in remote areas with inadequate financing from church and government sources. It was crucial to the mission venture for missionaries to elicit help from the Indigenous people either as unpaid or as paid workers. To do this, they sought and gained the cooperation of the Indigenous people who moved to the mission sites.

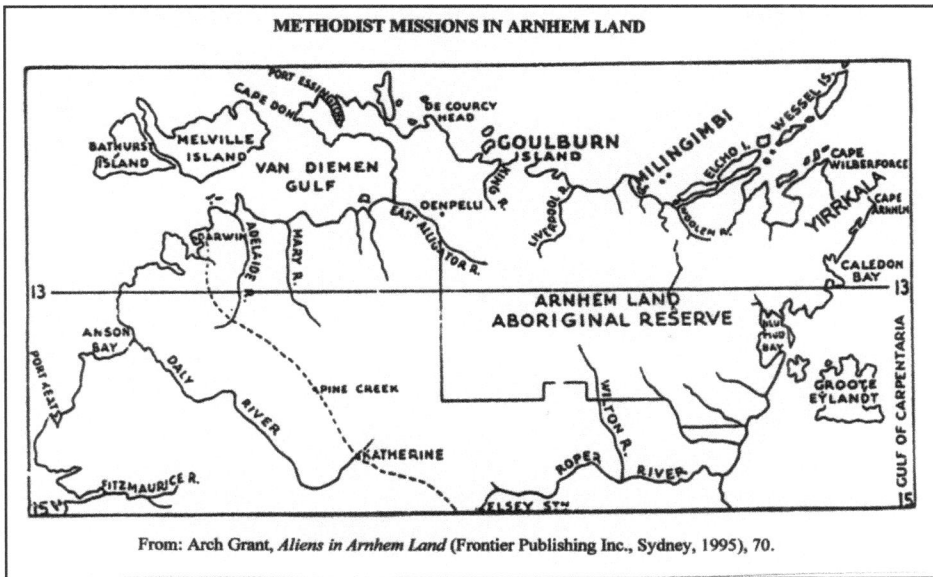

From: Arch Grant, *Aliens in Arnhem Land* (Frontier Publishing Inc., Sydney, 1995), 70.

Map 7.1 Methodist missions in Arnhem Land

Source: Grant (1995:70).

Foundation Methodist missionary Ella Shepherdson (1981) wrote of the cooperation and contribution of Yolngu workers in mission development. In the only comprehensive account of the Methodist missions in Arnhem Land, Maisie MacKenzie (1976) evaluates the workload and enterprise of the missionaries above the contribution of the Indigenous population. The support of the local population is noted, and individuals praised for their contributions.

A barter economy operated in early transactions on and off Methodist missions for up to 20 years. Aborigines accepted food as payment for their labour and crocodile skins were exchanged for axes, flour, tobacco, cloth and tools. Ella Shepherdson (1981:36) explains: 'In those days there was no money available to pay people for work done on the [air] strips, only food and hand tools were supplied.' There were advantages for Aborigines who could remain off the mission while developing new skills and exchanging goods. For the missionaries, it was a way of existing without proper monetary support.

The change from barter trading to a cash economy came as a result of demands from Indigenous workers. Contact with the outside world intensified during the war years. Patrol officer Gordon Sweeney (1951) recorded the change, noting that 'Arnhem Land natives…are becoming more money conscious'. In 1950 at Elcho Island he had witnessed the arrival of a message stick from 'a group of natives' living in the Buckingham Bay area: 'Marks made on one half of the letter stick signified the two groups who were waiting and small circles on the other half signified money which they desired in payment.' He reported that when missionary Harold Shepherdson made the next trip to Buckingham Bay an exchange of money for skins took place (Sweeney 1951:6). He paid £16 to the 'head boys', who distributed the money to the other workers:

> The trade goods were then unpacked from the aeroplane—flour, sugar, jam, tobacco, soap, matches, razor blades, combs, mirrors, billy cans, towels, shorts and skirts were spread out and the men came forward and made their purchases; following the men came their wives, who had also shared in the returns.

The 1950s brought changes to mission funding that would enable the mission societies to pay Indigenous workers. Paul Hasluck became Minister for Territories with Aboriginal Affairs as his responsibility. At the first Native Welfare Conference in 1951, he promoted a greater priority for government funding for Aborigines. From 1952 the new Welfare Branch reorganised mission funding, and biennial mission/administrative conferences dealt with policy issues including finance. With the new emphasis on the Aborigine as an individual and with increased demands for welfare and training, the Church renewed its claim for increased funding.[1]

The *Wards' Employment Ordinance* of 1953 undertook to provide more protection for Aboriginal workers (classified in the legislation as 'wards'). The Employment Advisory Board was to be established with only one Aboriginal representative and that had to be a non-ward. Provisions were set down for training, employment and assistance to wards. The director decided the suitability of wards for training and the type of training they would receive. Employers could be given permission under licence to employ wards as apprentices. General employers of wards were also licensed. Welfare officers could inspect the workplaces of wards and licences could be cancelled. Part of the ward's

---

1   Letter from C. F. Gribble, Chairman, Methodist Overseas Mission [hereinafter MOM], to the Administrator, 17 September 1952, CRS F1/0, 1952/645, National Archives Australia (Northern Territory) [hereinafter NAA (NT)].

wage could go into a trust fund administered by the director. The Ordinance specified that on missions, trading posts could be established to 'enable wards to buy, sell or barter articles'.

In its practical application, the *Wards' Employment Ordinance* of 1953 was to provide little assistance to Aboriginal workers on missions and reserves. Peterson (1998:107) argues that the legislation that determined that Aborigines were wards whilst on missions and reserves actually led to a situation where Aboriginal workers were confined and therefore disadvantaged. The Ordinance did not come into effect until the Aboriginal Register had been completed in 1959. In 1960 missions and government settlements applied for exemption from the provisions of the Ordinance on the grounds that they were not employers in the strictest sense but providers of social welfare and training.[2] In 1962 the Commonwealth Government accepted the missions' proposal.[3] In 1962 an amendment to the *Commonwealth Electoral Act* enfranchised all Aboriginal adults with the resultant anomaly that Aborigines were officially citizens without the right to equal wages.

By 1963 changes to the *Wards' Employment Ordinance* made the Crown (and therefore government settlements) subject to the provisions of the Ordinance, and the missions could no longer claim special exemption. The Department of Territories advised the minister that it was a 'matter of natural justice' for Aboriginal workers on missions to 'have the same opportunities and scope for training and advancement as other Aboriginal workers in the Territory'.[4] It noted that

> Aboriginals employed on missions constitute roughly 1/3 of the aboriginal labour force in the Northern Territory and as long as their conditions are not up to the standards of Aborigines employed in outside industry and on Government settlements, their employment is a potential source of discontent among the Aboriginal people themselves and a potential target for the political critics of policy.[5]

The *Social Welfare Ordinance* of 1964 removed restrictions under the 1957 Ordinance except the power of the NT administration to control wages and access to reserves.

Criticism of government policy came from diverse groups such as the Communist Party, the Australian Board of Missions and the Federal Council for the

---

2 Application Wards' Employment Ordinance, Department of Territories, Paper on Memorandum 61/605 [12 June 1963], CRS E460/51, 74/718, NAA (NT).
3 Letter, Secretary, Department of Territories, C. R. Lambert, to Administrator of the Northern Territory [19 February 1962], CRS E460/51, 74/718, NAA (NT).
4 Paper on Memorandum 61/605 [12 June 1963], CRS E460/51, 74/718, NAA (NT).
5 Ibid.

Advancement of Aboriginal and Torres Straight Islanders, which argued for equal wages for Aborigines on the basis of their status as Australian citizens recently given the right to vote. In 1966 the Conciliation and Arbitration Commission agreed to delete the clauses in the *Social Welfare Ordinance* that had excluded Aboriginal workers from the Cattle Station (Northern Territory) Award. They would be given full pay but the date for full implementation was deferred until December 1968. This put pressure on mission societies to match the wage expectations of Aboriginal workers on missions. In 1968 the annual Northern District Synod petitioned the Social Welfare Branch over the disparity between mission wages and the proposed new wages for Aboriginal workers on pastoral properties. The missions would be unable 'to make substantial wage increases establishing equality' and the synod requested that the Social Welfare Branch 'increase subsidies for industries and community services on Mission stations'.[6]

From 1951 until the introduction of the government-funded Training Wages Scheme in 1969, the Church Synod set rates of pay. In 1954 the government subsidy for each missionary worker (male and female) was £750.[7] From this subsidy the mission paid a sliding scale of wages to married male missionaries, single male missionaries and single female missionaries.[8] MacKenzie (1976) recorded that the rest of the subsidy money was used to finance more mission employees and to pay Indigenous workers.

Contract labour allowed for a variety of payment schedules: piece work and hourly rates of pay; in later years there were more weekly rates of pay. While it suited the mission to have some permanent employees, the flexibility of contract work allowed for more Indigenous participants in the workforce. From the mid-1950s, the mixture of contract and weekly schedules appears in the mission wage schedules. The jobs available to Indigenous men included painting and woodwork, sawmilling, carpentry, electrical work, mechanical work, agriculture, hygiene, boat crews and teaching. Indigenous women were employed as house girls, as seamstresses and cooks, with teaching and nursing as the most prestigious occupations.

An apprenticeship scheme approved at the 1962 Synod proposed a five-year training program for fitters and turners, motor mechanics, electricians, carpenters and joiners, boat builders and cabinet-makers.[9] By the mid-1960s, following a significant increase in government subsidies, apprenticeship schemes were set

---

6   Synod Report [1968], 52, 37.1.14, Northern Territory Archives Service [hereinafter NTAS].
7   Welfare Branch Correspondence [1948–62], Financial Assistance to Missions in the Northern Territory, 40, 9.14.1, NTAS. Letter from Acting Director of Native Affairs, R. K. McCaffery, to Rev. G. Symons, Chairman North Australia District, MOM, Darwin [10 March 1954].
8   Board Minutes [1951–53], 343, MOM.
9   Synod Report [1961–62], 52, 37.1.5, NTAS.

up on the missions. In a personal interview I conducted with Ruth Bray (1992), she talked about how most apprenticing of Aboriginal workers was done in an ad-hoc manner, using the available missionaries to school their workers. By the late 1960s, many workers had completed nursing and teaching training courses in Darwin after basic training on the missions.

Older Aboriginal men and women who remember life on the missions now comment on how they were paid low wages or no wages, or how they were given small amounts of food in lieu of wages for their labour. In an interview I conducted in 2006 with Daisy Dhulwatji (1) and Mangalalil (1), they talked about working as children for little money or for sugar as a reward. When wages were paid, missions estimated the value of rations and housing, power and water, which were supplied to Indigenous workers living on the missions, and this amount was deducted from their wages. From 1965, wages were paid in cash only, with no rations.

To make a comparison between wages for Indigenous mission workers and wages for other Australian workers, I have used male wage rates, as female Indigenous wages are not as highly represented in mission wage schedules. As with female mission workers, female Indigenous wages were less than male wages. The male wage rates for Indigenous mission workers is taken from the highest-paid jobs employing the greatest number of people: carpenters, painters, sawmillers, boat builders, mechanics, drivers, teaching assistants, agricultural/pastoral workers (Table 7.1).[10]

Table 7.1 Indigenous Male Mission Wages as a Percentage of the Commonwealth Male Basic Wage

Year	Percentage of basic wage
1951	17
1961	19
1964	47
1966	42
1968	49
1969	78

From Training Wages to Award Wages

The first stage of award-wage implementation came with the 1969 Employment Training Scheme for Aborigines. The 'Training Allowance Scheme' designed

---

10   ABS (1960–65, 1962, 1966–73, 1968, 1970); 52, 37.1.3, NTAS; CRS F1: 54/80 and CRS E460: 75/544, NAA (NT).

specifically for Aborigines on settlements was introduced a month later. The movement from a 'managed consumption' model to cash wages and social service payments exposed a divide between old and new missionaries. To older missionaries, the expansion of the moneyed economy would bring temptation and little satisfaction. Ella Shepherdson (1981:108) commented that 'a sudden influx of money did not bring happiness'. To younger staff, 'training wages' were pitifully low and the type of work perpetuated on the missions was demeaning. The difference between wages and conditions on and off the missions was becoming more transparent to those Aboriginal workers who had received training and worked in other locations for better wages. Reverend Brad Harris expressed these concerns in a series of letters to the Chairman of the Northern District, Reverend Gordon Symons:

> The training allowance arrangements still fail to provide a sufficient living income, still fail to provide workers at management level, and still fail to provide enough work. Many...know very well that they are cheap labour doing work white people don't do. This is especially true where workers have had long experience or even training for a job... they are painfully aware that what they got as a driver, carpenter, plant operator or even labourer in Darwin or elsewhere in the Territory has no relation to what they get at Milingimbi.[11]

From 1 December 1973, award wages were introduced for Aborigines on missions and settlements.[12] 'Training' positions and 'unproductive' jobs would be abolished, including many positions occupied by women. Married women would not be eligible for unemployment benefits.[13] The department calculated that the workforce would reduce by one-third under the awards scheme, although in fact, as Peterson (1998:108) reported, it would be a two-thirds reduction.[14] The missions had warned that this would be the possible outcome of the savage cut of jobs deemed to be 'unviable' under the Commonwealth Government's appraisal of mission-based work.

Award-wage implementation was already in progress when meetings with Aboriginal communities began. In 1974 an inter-departmental committee was

---

11   Letter from Rev. E. Bradley Harris to Rev. Gordon Symons [13 July 1972], Milingimbi Correspondence [1960–73], 40, 8.1.1, NTAS.

12   Introduction Award Wages to Aboriginal Communities in the Northern Territory, Copy 68, Decision 1534 [5 November 1973], Submission to Minister for Aboriginal Affairs Mr J. L. Cavanagh, CRS E460/51:74/695, NAA (NT).

13   Report on Meeting of Inter-Departmental Committee on Abolition of the Training Allowance Scheme in the Northern Territory, Canberra, [29 March 1974], CRS E460/51:74/542, NAA (NT).

14   Termination of Training Allowances and Introduction of Award Wages, Telex from ABAUS Darwin to ABAUS Canberra [23 May 1974], CRS E460/51: 74/1199, NAA (NT).

formed to look at the possibility of alternative schemes of payment and the social distribution of money. Project consultative teams set up to visit communities were advised:

> In many Aboriginal communities the impact of an award wage economy similar to that in urban Australia, together with unemployment benefits, could be unnecessarily disruptive of traditional life styles. In some areas, award wage structures will be appropriate and acceptable to the community, but in a community within its own understanding of its goals. The principle function of the teams should be to present and stimulate community consideration of alternative methods.[15]

The Government apparently did not regard Aborigines as citizens in the same economy, or sharing the values of other Australian citizens.

Town councils petitioned the Government to take heed of their concerns. Milingimbi Town Council urged the Government to recognise the conditions that had historically placed Aboriginal people living on missions in a unique position:

> Aboriginal people want an opportunity to earn wages within their community. The government should be made aware of the stress and hardship, which would prevail if employment is lacking. Aboriginal people now firmly accept the money system and it is quite impractical for them to break away from it and return fully or in part to a tribal economy.[16]

The council saw problems if 'non-productive' jobs such as those of administrative workers, service staff and adult literacy were not funded and if more award-wage positions were not approved. The council complained about delays in government financial assistance for Aboriginal companies to run work-based enterprises on the stations, the loss of community members forced to seek work elsewhere, the plight of less than skilled workers, and the possibilities for social disruption from the loss of waged positions and unfunded economic enterprises resulting in a 'substantial move towards unemployment benefits'.

The House of Representatives Standing Committee on Aboriginal Affairs, which visited Yirrkala in 1974, stated that award wages would mean that 'those employed will be properly reimbursed for their labours and fewer people will be engaged on meaningless and demeaning tasks'. The payment of unemployment

---

15   Report on Meeting of Inter-Departmental Committee [29 March 1974] 104, CRS E460/51: 74/542, NAA (NT).

16   Review of Training Allowances and Progression to Award Level Wages, Letter from Milingimbi Council to Mr Shurmer, Department of Aboriginal Affairs [hereinafter DAA], Darwin [1 March 1974], CRS E460/51: 74/1838, NAA (NT).

benefits would, however, 'aggravate an already serious drinking problem' and make it 'difficult to introduce alternative employment schemes'. The committee suggested extending the 'phasing in period' indefinitely.[17] The committee appeared to be suggesting that 'meaningless work' would continue without 'proper reimbursement' indefinitely.

On the Maningrida government settlement in western Arnhem Land, CEO, Reverend Peter O'Connor (2004), former Mission Superintendent at nearby Goulburn Island, reprised the mission model of contract work:

> Officials questioned why we never had anyone on the dole...Our way was simply that every person on our workforce worked on an hourly basis and attended for as many hours as they wished. In this way we spread our employment budget over a much larger group of people, as the average employee wished to work only twenty hours a week. Our way proved to be more desirable and rewarding than to arrange working for the dole as was applied in later years.

The future of work, funding and wages could not be resolved in the short period allotted for consultation. Mission negotiations resulted in the creation of additional award-wage positions, additional money for a continuation of training allowances and an extension in the timetable for the transition to award wages.[18] By November 1974, both training allowance payments and special interim grants had been terminated.[19]

Aftermath

The period of transition, at the end of mission time, is now seen by the community leaders as a government takeover, not the assumption of Indigenous control. At the end of the mission era, the Government shut the existing industries without replacing them. Artist Peter Datjin Burarrwanga (2006) was working as a fisherman at the time. He talked about the shutdown of the large-scale fishing enterprise, which exported half their catch to Darwin, when the Government revoked their fishing licence. 'They ran out of licence, fishing licence...When they stopped the fisherman: get the boat back, get the net back, everything back. They took the big boat back, the fishing boat...when the government took this township from

---

17   House of Representatives Standing Committee on Aboriginal Affairs, Letter to Minister J. L. Cavanagh [20 March 1974], CRS E460/51: 74/1838, NAA (NT).

18   Copy 68, Submission to Mr J. L. Cavanagh, CRS E460/51: 74/695, NAA (NT); Abolition of Training Allowances, from B. G. Dexter to the Minister, DAA No. 1478 68/389, NT [6 June 1974], CRS E460/51: 74/542, NAA (NT).

19   New Employment Arrangements in Settlement and Mission Communities, Letter, I. Pitman to Regional Officer, DAA Alice Springs [1 November 1974], CRS E460/51: 74/695, NAA (NT).

the mission.' The transition from fledgling training schemes to a proper industry-based system was never realised. White workers now fill most jobs with no sense of Aboriginal ownership in the work of the towns.

The transition from mission governance introduced a period of instability and a general decline in work practices. Reverend Dr Djiniyini Gondarra (2009) commented on how the people built their own houses during the time of the mission and the effect of changes to the work environment after the mission. His assessment of the collapse of the Indigenous economy after the mission era includes a story about how the Indigenous builders disappeared:

> Here's one story about housing. We were building our houses on a contract basis until it was decided by the then Aboriginal Development Commission (ADC) that we were not building enough houses each year. ADC was concerned about their construction statistics, so the ADC started letting contracts to outside builders. People in the community saw that the outsiders were building pre-cut houses much faster than our own people so they began to question the skills and speed of our own people. Within a year, our Yolngu builders and tradesmen had put down their tools and said, 'Well if the Government wants to shame us in front of our people, then they can build all the houses'. These men walked away in shame even though the cost of their completed houses was under that of the Balanda [white] contractors. The Balanda had won again. When we look around our communities today, we see all the work being done by dominant culture people.

The change from a close working relationship with the missionaries to working with transient government workers contributed to this outcome. The Government did not understand the principles and concerns of Indigenous workers; and Indigenous leaders were now nominally in charge of a system that they did not have full control over.

Ian Keen noted in a conference response (Keen 2009) that in the mid-1970s, at the time when the regime was changing, there was a general lack of interest in work amongst the Yolngu at Milingimbi. This is reflected in a letter from missionary A. Baker in 1973 to Djawa, Town Council President at Milingimbi. It illustrates the kind of operational problems associated with the hand over to Aboriginal control:

> Tomorrow the barge will come in and on that barge is food and other things for the people of Milingimbi. AS YET I DON'T KNOW WHO IS GOING TO UNLOAD THE GEAR BECAUSE THE PEOPLE THAT SHOULD DO IT, THE WORKS TEAM, DO NOT SEEM VERY INTERESTED IN IT, PERHAPS THE MOST IMPORTANT PART OF THEIR WORK. I cannot

unload the barge by myself and will not try. All of the Balanda could unload it but will not because in this time of self-determination Aboriginal people make decisions AND do the work coming from those decisions.[20]

Indigenous leaders also associate the government takeover of the missions and the decline in work practices as part of the control mechanisms of the welfare economy. Reverend Dr Djiniyini Gondarra (2009) speaks of the various white invasions of their land:

Yolngu have always lived with this land. In recent times an invasion took place in this country…Since that time many foreigners have come to north-east Arnhem Land; with missions and welfare, with the police, with the mines. Each time we have lost more of our spirit and our identity.

Gondarra looks back to the achievements of the mission era and the way in which the Yolngu worked to build new communities:

Yolngu are strong people though and even after all these things and changes, we worked hard and rebuilt our communities in the Balanda way so that in the 1970s we were: building all our own housing; doing all our own road works; carrying out most of the office work; involved to a high level in…essential services; involved in…provision of health and education.

There was a sense of empowerment through employment and a real sense of ownership in the towns. It would seem that the current situation of low Indigenous employment and the lack of control over the running of the towns as they are now constituted in Arnhem Land has intensified and shaped this memory.

Recent Federal Government intervention policies and practices and the removal of community councils as administrative bodies are seen as more attacks on Indigenous control over local affairs. On Elcho Island, the Galiwin'ku Community Council is no longer the organising body for the town. The newly constituted East Arnhem Land Shire Council includes local representatives, but its administrative jurisdiction is much larger. The establishment of Community Advisory Committees, which report to the people and to the shire council, mitigates but does not remove a feeling of lack of control over local activities.

---

20 Town Council and Public Meetings, Baker, A. (1973) to Djawa, Town Council President at Milingimbi [5 December 1973], 40, 11.39.3, NTAS.

Conclusion

Indigenous leaders now tell the story of 'mission time' as a period of exceptional Indigenous enterprise and involvement. Indigenous labour was both essential and effective in the process of mission development, and as the missions grew and training improved, the skill level of Aboriginal workers increased. By the end of the mission era there was high Aboriginal employment and involvement in the work of the community. In its haste to achieve wage parity with other Australian workers by moving to an award-wages scheme, the Government abandoned training schemes, emerging industries and flexible work arrangements. It was unable to address the problems of the unusual circumstances of an isolated, artificially constructed workforce or contemplate flexibility on the question of appropriate work and wage structures. Indigenous workers rightly questioned the likely outcomes of the new government model, but their input into the plans for their future went unheeded. They were a skilled labour force lost.

References

Aboriginal Ordinance Northern Territory of Australia Wards' Employment Ordinance No. 24 of 1953.

Aboriginal Ordinance Northern Territory of Australia No. 2 of 1957.

Aboriginal Ordinance Northern Territory of Australia Wards' Employment Ordinance No. 6 of 1959.

Aboriginal Ordinance Northern Territory of Australia Wards' Employment Ordinance No. 2 of 1961.

Aboriginal Ordinance Northern Territory of Australia Wards' Employment Ordinance No. 2 of 1963.

Australian Bureau of Statistics (ABS) 1960–65, 1966–73. *Northern Territory, Statistical Summary* 1–6. Canberra: Australian Bureau of Statistics.

Australian Bureau of Statistics (ABS) 1962. *Year Book of Australia*. No. 48 of 1962. Canberra: Australian Bureau of Statistics.

Australian Bureau of Statistics (ABS) 1968. *Year Book of Australia*. No. 54 of 1968. Canberra: Australian Bureau of Statistics.

Australian Bureau of Statistics (ABS) 1970. *Year Book of Australia*. No. 56 of 1970. Canberra: Australian Bureau of Statistics.

Baker, G. 2005. Crossing boundaries: negotiated space and the construction of narratives of missionary incursion. *Journal of Northern Territory History* 16: 17–28.

Baker, G. 2010. We just cry for our country: 'the boycott' and the Goulburn Islanders. *Australian Historical Studies* 41 (3): 302–18.

Bray, R. 1992. Life on the missions. Interview with Gwenda Baker, 31 July 1992, Melbourne.

Burarrwanga, P. D. 2006. Remembering 'mission time'. Interview with Gwenda Baker, 5 June 2006, Galiwin'ku, NT.

Dhulwatji, D. (1) and Mangalalil (1) 2006. Remembering 'mission time'. Interview with Gwenda Baker, 1 June 2006, Galiwin'ku, NT. Nancy Manurr Dhurrkay (interpreter).

Gondarra, D. 2009. Submission to Territory 2030. <http://www.ards.com.au>

Grant, A. 1995. *Aliens in Arnhem Land*. Sydney: Frontier Publishing.

Keen, I. 2009. Respondent to paper by Baker, G., 'From barter to award wages: Aboriginal labour on Methodist missions in Arnhem Land'. Indigenous Participation in Australian Economies Conference, National Museum of Australia, Canberra, 9–10 November 2009. <http://www.nma.gov.au/audio/search/all/query:gwenda+baker>

MacKenzie, M. 1976. *Mission to Arnhem Land*. Adelaide: Rigby.

Methodist Church of Australasia n.d. Methodist Overseas Mission [MOM]. MOM 343, Mitchell Library, Sydney.

Myers, P. 2010. New wave. *The Weekend Australian*, 30–31 January: 12–15.

National Archives Australia (Northern Territory) Darwin: CRS E460/51: 74/542; CRS E460/51: 74/544; CRS E460/51: 74/695; CRS E460/51: 74/718; CRS E460/51: 74/1838; CRS F1 54/80 MOM–Elcho Island [1950–55]; CRS F1/0 1952/645 MOM Funding [1951–53].

Native Welfare in Australia. Report on the 1951 and 1952 Native Welfare Conference.

Northern Territory Archives Service, Darwin: 40 Milingimbi Township; 40 8.1.1; 40 9.14.1; 40 11.39.3; 52 37.1.1 Synod Reports [1946, 1947, 1948, 1949, 1951, 1952, 1952]; 52 37.1.2 Synod Reports [1953, 1954, 1955, 1956, 1957, 1958, 1959]; 52 37.1.3 Synod Report [1959–60]; 52 37.1.4 Synod Report [1960–61]; 52 37.1.5 Synod Report [1961–62]; 52 37.1.6 Synod Report [1962–63]; 52 37.1.7 Synod Report [1964]; 52 37.1.8 Synod Report [1965]; 52 37.1.9 Synod Report [1966]; 52 37.1.11 Synod Report [1967]; 52 37.1.12 Synod Report [1967]; 52 37.1.14 Synod Report [1968]; 52 37.1.15 Synod Report [1968–69]; 52 37.1.17 Synod Report [1969–70].

O'Connor, P. 2004. Unpublished memoirs. Brisbane.

Pearson, N. 2009. *Up From the Mission*. Melbourne: Black Inc.

Peterson, N. 1998. Welfare colonialism and citizenship: politics, economics and agency. In N. Peterson and W. Sanders (eds), *Citizenship and Indigenous Australians: Changing conceptions and possibilities*, pp. 101–17. Cambridge: Cambridge University Press.

Rudder, J. 1993. Yolngu cosmology: an unchanging cosmos incorporating a rapidly changing world? Unpublished PhD thesis, Australian National University, Canberra.

Shepherdson, E. 1981. *Half a Century in Arnhem Land*. Adelaide: One Tree Hill.

Social Welfare Ordinance No. 31 of 1964.

Sweeney, G. 1951. An experiment in a mission trading outpost. *The Missionary Review* 59 (7).

Trudgen, R. 2000. *Why Warriors Lie Down and Die: Towards an understanding of why the Aboriginal people of Arnhem Land face the greatest crisis in health and education since European contact*. Darwin: Aboriginal Resource and Development Services Incorporated.

8. Low Wages, Low Rents, and Pension Cheques: The introduction of equal wages in the Kimberley, 1968–1969

Fiona Skyring

The introduction of equal wages for Kimberley Aboriginal pastoral station workers[1] during the northern wet season of 1968–69 has been characterised as a disaster—the cause of mass evictions and unemployment in Western Australia's far north. Former stockmen such as John Watson and Eric Lawford, who recorded their accounts in the publication *Raparapa*, remembered the devastating impact of being kicked off the stations. The evictions were particularly destructive because the stations were on the traditional country of most of the Aboriginal people who lived and worked there. Significantly, although they remembered the period as catastrophic, none of these Kimberley Aboriginal men said they did not want proper wages (Marshall 1998). Peter Yu, former Executive Director of the Kimberley Land Council, wrote that the equal wages decision 'broke the back of the feudal relationship between station managers and Aboriginal families. Pastoralists began to force Aboriginal people from the stations which precipitated a refugee crisis of enormous proportions' (Yu 1994:19).

Historian Bill Bunbury argued that the implementation of the equal wages decision was badly planned and had ruinous consequences. It ultimately meant loss of work, skills and land for the Aboriginal people the decision was supposed to benefit (Bunbury 2002). But while no-one in these contemporary analyses has argued that Aboriginal station workers should have continued to be paid the pittance they received for their labour before 1968, there was the inference in Bunbury's account that equal wages were bad for Aboriginal workers. This idea was openly discussed in 1968, and station employers and some State Government officials argued that money in the hands of Aboriginal people was a dangerous thing. Station owners at the time cited Aboriginal people's alleged inability to manage money as one of the excuses to keep the wages

---

1 Throughout this chapter I use the word 'Aboriginal' and not 'Indigenous'. In the work I have done for the Aboriginal Legal Service of Western Australia Incorporated (ALSWA), the Executive Committee has always preferred that option. The members of the Executive Committee are elected from Aboriginal communities across the State, and 'Aboriginal' is the term they use when not identifying more specifically with their traditional country, such as Noongar or Bardi. When I was asked to research and write ALSWA's submissions to the Senate Legal and Constitutional Affairs Committee Inquiry into Stolen Wages in 2006, the Executive Committee asked me to adopt the word 'Aboriginal' even though the terms of reference for the inquiry referred to 'Indigenous' people and wages. See ALSWA (2006a:10). I am grateful to ALSWA for their permission to quote from the research materials I used for the submissions I prepared for the Senate Committee Inquiry.

of their Aboriginal employees negligible or non-existent, even though it was Aboriginal labour that sustained the regional economy. In today's context of the Federal Government's authoritarian micro-management of Aboriginal people's abysmally low incomes—with echoes of the notion that Aboriginal people are not capable of managing their own money—the background to the introduction of equal wages for Aboriginal workers is worth revisiting. The event is also important for analyses of the northern Australian economy generally. In relation to non-Aboriginal workers, the argument that employers could not afford to pay their workers a minimum wage would be considered risible.

There are some enduring misconceptions about the history of the northern Australian economy and in particular about the impact of the introduction of equal wages for Aboriginal workers. Thalia Anthony, in her work about Aboriginal pastoral workers in the Northern Territory, referred to the introduction of equal wages there in 1966 as an event 'shrouded in myths'. Equal wages for Aboriginal station workers were 'just one factor in a range of transformations', including the increased use of helicopter mustering and a worldwide recession that changed the workforce profile of the northern cattle industry. Along with these changes was a new direction in government policy that made it increasingly difficult for station owners to argue that because they supported the elderly dependants of Aboriginal workers they could deny or reduce wages to their Aboriginal workers accordingly. This was a spurious argument anyway, since most of these so-called dependants worked in some capacity around the station (Anthony 2006).

As in the Northern Territory, in the Kimberley the introduction of equal wages was not the sole cause of social disaster. There were other economic factors that contributed to the impact of the award decision. Some of these economic factors, I argue, were specific to Western Australia and have received little attention in historical analyses of the trauma that unfolded in the far north of Western Australia in 1969. The social and economic collapse in Western Australia's far north does not make sense without including stolen wages and stolen pension moneys as crucial factors in that collapse.

In the Kimberley, the economic contribution made by Aboriginal people to the pastoral industry was just one of three types of subsidy that sustained the economy. It was the end—in the mid to late 1960s—to this tripartite subsidy that had such a profound impact on that economy, and shattering social consequences for the Aboriginal people who comprised the majority of the pastoral workforce in the Kimberley. Another type of subsidy was that pastoral lease rents were kept extremely low by the State Government until the late 1960s, when rent levels increased dramatically. In 1969 pastoral lease rents paid by Kimberley station owners were trebled, and increased again by between two and four times in 1979. A further type of subsidy that supported the

Kimberley regional economy were Commonwealth pension cheques intended for Aboriginal people. It seemed that after government policy changes in 1965 and 1966 it became increasingly difficult for station owners to misappropriate old-age pension payments for Aboriginal people as many of them had done in previous years. Elderly station residents who had represented a source of Commonwealth Government money for the stations were no longer an economic advantage to station owners. The withdrawal of this unacknowledged yet substantial stream of station income was, I argue, an important factor in the mass evictions that coincided with the introduction of equal wages for Aboriginal workers. An increase in Aboriginal wages was only part of the history of the era of devastation for Kimberley Aboriginal people.

The very low labour cost of the Aboriginal pastoral workforce—imposed through a racially discriminatory legislative and administrative regime—was one type of subsidy that enabled station owners to remain economically viable. Unpaid or underpaid Aboriginal workers underpinned station profitability. Thalia Anthony has reached similar conclusions in relation to the operation of the cattle industry in the Northern Territory (Anthony 2007:5–6). Anthony has written extensively about the feudal nature of the Northern Territory's pastoral industry (Anthony 2004, 2007). In the Kimberley, prior to 1950, most Aboriginal station workers were paid no wages at all, and were given food, clothing and tobacco rations in return for their labour (ALSWA 2006b:7). Various commentators have for a long time identified the feudal basis of the relationship between Aboriginal workers and station owners in the northern pastoral industry, and it was also referred to as a system of slavery. In 1910 the Australian Workers' Union (AWU) condemned it as 'a demoralising system of employing native labour in Western Australia', and sent their 'emphatic' protests to the newly elected Labor Prime Minister, Andrew Fisher.[2] AWU delegates in 1910 argued that 'the condition imposed on the natives in Western Australia is a blot on our boasted civilisation—worse than on the cotton fields of America before the Civil War', and they sought publicity for the abuses as a way of promoting reform. They condemned the WA Government because 'a system of the most abject slavery was allowed to exist through official indisposition' (*The Worker*, 2 February 1910).

The AWU delegates were right. In 1925 Chief Protector A. O. Neville wrote that many Aboriginal workers in Western Australia existed 'under a system of semi-slavery'.[3] This did not trouble the Chief Protector at all, and through to the equal wages decision in 1967 the State Government administered a

2 General Secretary of AWU to Prime Minister Fisher, 14 February 1910, item A63, A1910/4980, 'Employment of native labour in WA', National Archives of Australia (NAA), Canberra.
3 A. O. Neville to Hon. Minister for the North West, 3 October 1925, in 'Payment of wages to natives', item 1933/0451, State Records Office of Western Australia (SROWA), Consignment (Cons.) 993.

system of low-cost bonded Aboriginal labour throughout the pastoral regions of the State, with penalties for Aboriginal workers who sought to leave or to challenge the boss. Even after 1963, when most of the punitive aspects of so-called 'protective' legislation had been repealed, the records show that the Native Welfare Department in the Kimberley acted like an employment agency for station managers, sending Aboriginal workers when asked.

John Watson, former Chairman of the Kimberley Land Council, described it this way:

> From the early days Aboriginal people were forced to work on the stations. The police issued the station managers with permits to work the Aboriginal people and to take charge of their welfare. That happened right across the Kimberley. All the stations came to depend upon cheap Aboriginal labour. The Aboriginal people knew they were being exploited but they didn't have any choice. Then, during the 'fifties and 'sixties Aboriginal stockmen started pushing for better wages. They didn't realize the drastic effect it would have on their lives.

> When the equal wages decision was handed down by the Courts twenty-odd years ago, the Aboriginal people were forced off the stations. Hundreds of people were forced to leave the stations they'd grown up on, and to live under appalling conditions in town reserves. Those station managers just came out and said, 'We can't afford to pay you the basic wage, and we can't afford to keep feeding you. The Welfare mob have a lot of money for you to live on in the town. So pack up your camp and start walking'. (Marshall 1998:208)

For the former Kimberley stockmen who published their recollections, the introduction of equal wages was remembered as devastating. Senior Walmajarri man Eric Lawford recalled that the Emanuel family, who owned Christmas Creek Station, decided they would pay only a few stockmen and that everyone else had to leave the station. Out of a community of 300 or 400 people, Lawford estimated, most were forced off the station into the temporary camp at Fitzroy Crossing. 'That's how they split this community up!' Lawford said (Marshall 1998:23–6). John Watson, who by his own description was 'born into the pastoral industry' and spent much of his adult life working as a stockman, recalled 'drinking rights came in at the same time as the equal wages' (Marshall 1998:209). An increase in alcohol consumption followed when the prohibition on Kimberley Aboriginal people buying or consuming alcohol was removed. Between 1970 and 1971, they, along with Aboriginal people in the Goldfields, were among the last groups of Aboriginal people to have been targeted by these prohibition clauses under the *Native Welfare Act*.[4] Increased drinking by people in the reserve camps, unemployment and widespread homelessness all happened at roughly the same time for Kimberley Aboriginal people. These changes conflated as one catastrophe.

Across the Kimberley, Aboriginal people were evicted from the stations and congregated in squalid refugee camps at Fitzroy Crossing, Halls Creek, Broome and Derby. When managers from Christmas Creek Station south-west of Fitzroy Crossing removed the Aboriginal workforce and their families from the station and left them on the banks of the Fitzroy River in January 1969, that started what was soon to become a refugee population of more than 200 people. They had very little food, no money except some women's and children's bankbook balances averaging $3, and only a few pit latrines for the entire camp. Many families did not even have tents for shelter and trachoma was endemic amongst the children. More Aboriginal workers and their families were evicted from or walked off stations in the Fitzroy Valley and congregated at the camp, which by 1971 had increased to between 600 and 700 people (Eggington and Skyring 2006:xxi–xx). And that was just in Fitzroy Crossing. The State Government's officers in the Native Welfare Department wrote reports on the 'displaced persons' in equally impoverished and overcrowded makeshift camps at Derby, Broome and Halls Creek. At Halls Creek there were 600 people camped there over the wet season and even though some of the men worked out of town as contractors, there was an acute shortage of housing in town for their families.[5]

The equal wages decision was portrayed in Bunbury's book *It's Not the Money It's the Land* as one imposed from afar with no thought for the social consequences or communication with the people directly affected—the station owners and the Aboriginal station residents. While some stations retained their employees on the lesser 'slow worker' rate allowed in the new award, the impact on other stations was a drastic decline in the station population as only the younger skilled workers and their immediate families were allowed to stay. Bunbury wrote with sympathy for both station owners and Aboriginal people, and referred to the 'long standing relationship—not an equal one but a relationship nonetheless' that was broken with the introduction of award wages. He said that in talking with people about the event, it was remembered with 'mutual regret rather than blame' (Bunbury 2002:12).

The Kimberley stockmen in *Raparapa* did not express any nostalgia for their former bosses in the same way that the station owners in Bill Bunbury's account fondly recalled their Aboriginal employees. Rather, these former stockmen

---

4   Minister for Native Welfare, E. M. Lewis, 18 September 1970, in 'Native Citizenship Rights General Correspondence', item 1964/0249, SROWA, Accession (Acc.) 1733.
5   Report from K. Johnson, 27 June 1969, in 'Pastoral Industry Award 1968—Welfare of Unemployed natives ex. Pastoral stations', item 1969/0116, SROWA, Acc. 1733.

recalled with pride their skill at all kinds of station work, from fencing and building windmills to mustering. They also remembered how they trained the white men sent to manage them. Kimberley native title holders told much the same story in the Karajarri, Rubibi and Neowarra native title trials in the Federal Court. As a young stockman, senior Yawuru man Paddy Roe worked on Roebuck Plains Station, which is in Yawuru country. He remembered that working on the station was a 'hard life' but also a 'good life' because they had few worries. Steve Possum, a senior Karajarri man, said that he really liked stock work and had good memories of life on Thangoo Station and on Frazier Downs, a station in Karajarri country. Even though he considered himself to be the 'right-hand man' to the station manager at Frazier Downs, Steve Possum used the word 'slave' to describe how they worked for no money (ALSWA 2006b:17–18). Women did station work as well. As a young woman, senior Karajarri woman Edna Hopiga helped to build fences at Frazier Downs, where her brother was the boss for that job. Gordon Smith worked as a stockman in Ngarinyin country, which was his traditional country. In response to a question during the Neowarra native title trial about the kind of pay he received, Smith replied: 'Nothing. I was just working for my pride, that's all' (ALSWA 2006b:18).

Until the equal wages decision, Aboriginal pastoral workers were specifically excluded from being paid the wage rates stipulated in the Federal Pastoral Industry Award, which was very similar to, though not the same award as, the Cattle Station Industry (Northern Territory) Award. In 1968 the Federal Pastoral Award for a station hand working 44 hours a week was between $38.90 and $41 per week, less $9.41 for food and accommodation (*West Australian*, 27 February 1969). Most Aboriginal men working on stations in the Kimberley at that time were paid between $6 and $20 per week, with stockmen receiving the highest wages and 'yardmen' and older workers on the lowest rates. These payments represented between 19 per cent and 63 per cent of the award, minus the cost of food and accommodation. Many of these older workers in the late 1960s had been skilled and valuable station employees in their younger days when they were paid no wages at all. Aboriginal women who worked on the stations in 1968—many of them as domestic servants in the homestead—were paid between $3 and $10 per week (ALSWA 2006b:22–3). Some stockmen referred to in the records as 'half caste' received the same wages as white stockmen, but through to the late 1960s most Aboriginal men, women and teenagers working on stations in the Kimberley did so for little money. In September 1967, the Commonwealth Conciliation and Arbitration Commission decided to remove the racially discriminatory clause from the federal award (the decision in relation to the NT award had been made in 1966), and equal wages for Aboriginal pastoral workers were phased in from December 1968 during the wet season in the Kimberley (Chesterman 2001:207–12).

In 1944 when the AWU first took up the case to amend the Federal Pastoral Award and remove the racially discriminatory clauses, their respondents were the graziers' associations of New South Wales and Western Australia, and others.[6] The Kimberley station owners who talked with Bill Bunbury gave the impression that they were innocent bystanders to the decision to pay equal wages to Aboriginal pastoral workers (Bunbury 2002). But this is not correct. Station owners fought collectively against the introduction of decent wages for Aboriginal workers over decades, starting with the first challenge in the Conciliation and Arbitration Commission in 1944. In 1950 station owners opposed the first attempts by the WA Government to introduce minimum wages for Aboriginal workers in the north-west. The station owners who criticised the introduction of the award in 1968–69 were the same people who had earlier opposed attempts to introduce a wage system for Aboriginal workers. In 1971, West Kimberley Shire President Rowell was reported as saying that the introduction of award wages had done 'much harm' and that 'most Aborigines had not been ready to handle the situation' (*West Australian*, 3 June 1971). In 1950 Rowell was one of the well-known west Kimberley station owners— including the Blythes, J. Forrest, the Duracks and the Roses—who attended a meeting in Perth where he and fellow pastoralists argued against paying their Aboriginal employees anything. At the 1950 meeting they reluctantly agreed with the Commissioner of Native Affairs to pay Aboriginal stockmen £1 per month, and 'yardmen' and women employees 10 shillings (10 s) per month.[7] These minimum rates for Aboriginal workers were slightly below what the State Government had proposed (between £1 and £3 per month for stockmen) and way below award rates for white workers. Nevertheless, station owners complained that 'misinformed' public opinion was forcing them to pay wages. They also wrote this:

> The consensus of opinion of the meeting was that the present system whereby working natives, their dependents and pensioners, were provided with all the necessities of life, virtually from the cradle to the grave, was the one best suited to the present stage of development of the natives in the area, and one moreover calculated to avoid the evils inevitably associated with the circulation of money, among the native people not generally educated to its value.[8]

That money was a source of harm for Aboriginal people is a theme that is repeated throughout the history of labour in Western Australia. It was regularly stated by employers and by government officials as an argument for restricting

---

6 Judgment, 1 September 1944, *The Graziers' Association of NSW and Ors v the Australian Workers Union*, in 'Federal Pastoral Award—Employment of Natives', item 1946/1010, SROWA, Acc. 1733.

7 Circular, 13 March 1950, from Pastoralists' Association of Western Australia, in ibid.

8 Ibid.

cash payments to Aboriginal workers (ALSWA 2006b:7–8). Yet this invented inability of Aboriginal people to fully participate in the mainstream economy belied the very real contribution they made to that economy. The low-wage system for Aboriginal pastoral workers provided a massive subsidy for station owners. The top award rate for an adult male station worker in 1951 was £10 8s with 'keep', which was food and accommodation provided by the employer.[9] Compared with these wages, most skilled Aboriginal stockmen were paid about 3 per cent, or less than one-twentieth, of the award. In 1951 station owners in the Kimberley were saving more than £520 a year in labour costs on every skilled Aboriginal male worker, except for the few head stockmen who were paid close to award wages. The net value of pastoral production for the year 1949–50 was £26 million, and Native Affairs Commissioner, Stanley Middleton, argued that Aboriginal pastoral workers had made a substantial contribution towards this total.[10] Even if the station owners were providing food rations to a number of elderly dependants of each adult male worker—which was the main argument they used to justify low or non-existent wages—the value of these rations per week would have come nowhere near the difference between 5s and £10 8s. The difference in these amounts was £10 3s, and equivalent to more than three times the weekly old-age pension in 1950 (Department of Social Security Research and Statistics Branch 2006:115).

The wage differential was not quite as extreme when equal wages were phased in for Aboriginal workers in 1968–69, and then most Aboriginal men were earning between 19 per cent and 63 per cent of the award rate. Even with this slightly lesser difference, it was a saving of at least $12 per adult male worker per week. This represented an annual subsidy for station owners of at least $624 for each Aboriginal stockman. With a total of 931 Aboriginal men employed on Kimberley stations in 1968, the annual labour cost saving for station owners in the region was close to $581 000, and this is a conservative estimate based on wage rates for Aboriginal male workers being 63 per cent of the award wage. This did not include the cost savings on the 628 Aboriginal women who were recorded as being employed (Altman and Nieuwenhuysen 1979:66, for numbers of Aboriginal employees). Non-payment and underpayment of wages to Aboriginal workers represented, over the decades to 1969, an enormous labour cost subsidy for station owners. As a Native Affairs patrol officer commented of two Kimberley stations in 1949:

> Both places are enjoying extremely cheap labour—both know it, but are wondering how much longer these dreamlike conditions are to continue. That they are all alive to impending changes is very evident—

---

9   Circular, 6 November 1951, from Pastoralists' Association of Western Australia, in ibid.
10   S. G. Middelton, 25 August 1952, in 'Native Policy in Western Australia', item 1945/0803, SROWA, Acc. 1733.

partly in their demeanour and partly in their desire to talk about the natives—a sure sign of nervousness—and to put forward their own ideas...Arguments against the payment of wages to native workers are rarely heard now, but the question has progressed to the stage of how much they should be paid and the mechanics of paying. This is a definite advance in public opinion in the short period of from 4 to 5 months ago.[11]

Although no Kimberley Aboriginal pastoral workers were involved in the AWU's case in the Conciliation and Arbitration Commission, there had been industrial action in the Kimberley prior to 1967. In 1951 the Aboriginal workforce at Thangoo, south of Broome, walked off the station because management refused to pay them £4 per week plus rations (still less than half of the award rate). In the mid-1960s at Mount Hart Station in the central Kimberley, Aboriginal workers staged several walk-offs in protest against ill treatment by the manager, Jack Webber, and because he refused to pay their wages. In one instance in 1966, Webber followed a group of men with a rifle and 'persuaded' them to return with him in the truck. Once back at the station, Webber placed a horse's bridle on one of the Aboriginal men as punishment for leaving the station. Aboriginal workers and their families did not return to Mount Hart until the manager was replaced in 1967 (ALSWA 2006b:19–20). The pressure for decent wages intensified in the 1960s—much of that pressure coming from Aboriginal workers themselves. As John Watson said, they knew they were being exploited.

Another form of subsidy for Kimberley station owners that was also under threat by the 1960s was the extremely cheap pastoral lease rents throughout the region. In 1948 the reappraisal of Kimberley pastoral lease rents identified them as substantially undervalued, based on estimates of stock carrying capacity. The WA Surveyor General concluded that rents should be increased fourfold but this was not possible under the *Land Act*, and the Surveyor General recommended legislative changes to enable the increased rents to be imposed.[12] Government reports from the 1950s onwards were generally critical of the standard of land management on Kimberley stations. The irreversible environmental damage caused by uncontrolled grazing, no fences and inadequate station improvements, and the corresponding steady decline in herd quality, meant that the vast pastoral areas of the north were not as economically productive as they should have been.[13] The old-style cattlemen—and these included the financially marginal resident owners and the more numerous absentee landlords—were regarded by government policy makers as an impediment to development of the north. The State Government had invested in better roads and transport

---

11   Patrol report, West Kimberley, 2–9 September 1949, in 'Wages. Scale for natives in the Kimberley District. Implementation of', item 1949/0034, Cons. 993, SROWA.

12   W. Fyfe, Surveyor General, 17 June 1952, in 'Reappraisement of pastoral lease Kimberley Division 1948', item 1950/1987, Cons 6231, SROWA.

13   Reports by G. A. Buchanan, February 1951, and W. W. Henwood, Inspector, November 1950, in ibid.

infrastructure in the Kimberley in the decades after World War II, but there had been little corresponding capital investment from the pastoral leaseholders themselves. Pastoral Inspector Bill Henwood was particularly critical of what he called 'absentee owners', mostly based in Perth, who refused to invest in improvements and often stymied resident managers' attempts to run the stations to acceptable standards.[14]

In a report for the Commonwealth Bureau of Agricultural Economics in 1952, the author, J. H. Kelly, found that there was only one station in the Kimberley that he considered to have adequate station improvements. His central argument—substantiated by statistical research—was that the underdevelopment of the beef industry in the north was because of poor pastoral land management and inadequate herd control. Kelly also condemned the majority of station owners in the Northern Territory and the Kimberley for the deplorable conditions under which their Aboriginal employees lived and worked. He identified the neglect of Aboriginal people as a central problem in the lack of development of the beef industry in northern Australia (Australian Bureau of Agricultural Economics 1952).

By the late 1960s the WA Government was becoming less willing to tolerate substandard land and herd management by station owners in the Kimberley. In 1969 the WA Pastoral Appraisement Board considered that extremely low pastoral lease rents promoted inefficient land use, and should be reviewed 'in the light of modern day practice and economics'. The Kimberley pastoral leases returned about $40 000 in terms of rentals to the State Government, and this represented only about 1 per cent of the actual gross returns to pastoral stations of livestock sold. The Pastoral Appraisement Board thought it was fair that rents should increase so that the total rent was 2.5 per cent of gross returns, and the board recommended this to the minister (Pastoral Appraisement Board 1969). The Pastoral Appraisement Board's proposal represented an increase of about 600 per cent in annual pastoral lease rents, but the board suggested it was 'more prudent' to limit this increase to 400 per cent. In the end, the State Government decided to limit the pastoral lease rent increase for Kimberley stations to 300 per cent, effective 1 July 1969. Pastoral lease rents were again increased in the Kimberley division in 1979 by between two and four times the 1969 annual rental, with some stations paying substantially larger increases than others. The Pastoralists' and Graziers' Association argued with the State Government against these increases (Pastoral Appraisement Board 1979). By 1969 the days of negligible land costs for Kimberley station owners were over.

The third form of subsidy for the Kimberley pastoral industry started in 1960 with the removal of racially discriminatory clauses in Commonwealth legislation governing the payment of old-age pensions and maternity allowances.

---

14   W. W. Henwood, Inspector, November 1950, in ibid.

The amendments meant that for the first time many Aboriginal people living on pastoral stations across Western Australia became eligible to receive these Commonwealth benefits. A Native Welfare officer in Derby described it as 'a flood of money' into the Kimberley economy (Jebb 2002:260). On the eve of the legislative changes, a memo was distributed to all Native Welfare Department field officers detailing the administrative arrangements for distribution of Commonwealth benefits. It listed the amounts of 'pocket money' that would be paid in cash to each pension recipient, with the remainder held by the various mission authorities and station owners for 'maintenance' of the pensioners and improvements in their accommodation. Missions and station owners or managers were appointed warrantees so they could receive the cheques, and those pensioners resident on pastoral stations would each receive 10s in cash, which was 10 per cent of the weekly pension payment of £5 in 1960.[15]

By the mid-1960s both State and Commonwealth Government officials at the most senior levels knew that abuses were widespread, and that many stations kept most of the Commonwealth benefits intended for Aboriginal people. A senior Native Welfare officer commented of the station owners that '[t]hey are all making a quid out of the pensioners'.[16] The Department of Social Services appointed Special Magistrate Davies to investigate the allegations of misappropriation, and he conducted reviews of stations across the Kimberley in 1965 and 1966. Decimal currency was introduced in Australia in February 1966, so Magistrate Davies' investigation included results in pounds, shillings and pence and in decimal currency figures. He found that several stations were charging hugely inflated prices for food rations provided to pensioners, and on one station this charge was more than the value of the pension itself. Commonwealth cheques were going to station owners in Perth and Melbourne, with no accounting for the amounts supposedly spent on food and clothing for the pensioners. The owner of one Kimberley station, who actually lived in Melbourne, was charging hugely inflated prices for food rations provided to the nine pensioners on the station, and Magistrate Davies doubted that these pensioners received the full food ration anyway. At another station there were no built dwellings to house the pensioners and the owner charged each pensioner £6 0s 5d for substandard food rations, which was more than the full value of their £6 pension payment. Magistrate Davies considered that one prominent station-owning family acted like 'a law unto themselves' and set the example for other Kimberley stations to use Aboriginal pensioners' money however they liked. They charged pensioners £4 15s per week for food, and the accommodation the station owners provided

---

15 Commissioner of Native Welfare, Circular memo, 24 December 1959, in 'Old Age and Invalid pensions for natives—general file', item 1939/1104, Cons. 993, SROWA. (A copy of this is in Supplementary information to submissions from ALSWA November 2006 at Submission 30C: <http://www.aph.gov.au/senate/committee/legcon_ctte/completed_inquiries/2004-07/stolen_wages/submissions/sub30C.pdf>)
16 K. Johnson, 8 August 1966, in 'Social Services. Pensions—general', item NDG 33/3/1a, Cons. 3412, SROWA.

was described by Davies as 'disgustingly filthy'. The station owners claimed that a shed had cost £700 to build, and that same amount had been transferred from the pensioners' account to the station account. The use of pensioners' money to build sheds to house them was a policy openly encouraged by both the State and the Federal Governments, but pensioners did not share in the ownership of these station improvements paid for with their money (ALSWA 2007:1–14).

The amounts of money paid to the stations as Commonwealth benefits intended for Aboriginal people were substantial. One Kimberley station collected a total of $30 268 in Commonwealth benefits between 1960 and 1966, and the pensioners on this station were not given any cash pocket money but were given biscuits and lollies instead, freighted from Perth. Another station collected £9 900 in pension cheques between January 1962 and April 1964, and never paid pensioners anything. A manager on one east Kimberley station withdrew all the money from the pensioners' account and took it with her when she cleared out. No-one was ever prosecuted for these identified instances of misappropriation and theft, and despite complaints by the Department of Social Services it seemed that their only practical response to the perpetration of such abuses was to cancel pension payments entirely on some stations (ALSWA 2007:1–14).

In mid-1965 the Director of Social Services in Western Australia wrote to his boss, the Director General in Canberra:

> It seems that some warrantees regard the pension as a form of station subsidy and consider that they are entitled to restrict the value of the benefits flowing to the pensioners for various reasons. One being that wages paid to native station workers will not show adversely by comparison.
>
> The effect is that instead of Commonwealth pension moneys benefiting the pensioners only, they are undeservedly and unnecessarily benefiting the station to the extent to which value is withheld from the pensioner.[17]

The fact that many skilled Aboriginal workers were being paid the same as, or sometimes less than, the value of the old-age pension—a subsistence welfare payment—was a further pressure for award wages. Station owners resisted that pressure in a number of ways, one of which was to keep most of the Commonwealth pension cheques for themselves so the disparity would not be so obvious. More research needs to be done on the rise and demise of the Aboriginal pension money bonanza for Kimberley station owners, but it appeared from the departmental response that the more flagrant abuses by warrantees declined after Davies' investigations in 1965 and 1966.

---

17   Director Humphreys, 2 July 1965, in ibid.

So there were three types of substantial economic subsidies pastoral leaseholders received: from the Aboriginal workforce in the form of unpaid or underpaid labour; from the State Government as cheap rent way out of proportion to the value of their leases; and from elderly Aboriginal people in the form of Commonwealth social services benefits. Cheap Aboriginal labour, cheap rent and, from 1960, Commonwealth social services benefits intended for Aboriginal people sustained the pastoral economy in the Kimberley. In the space of a few years from the mid-1960s into the early 1970s, this tripartite subsidy was withdrawn under pressure from Aboriginal people themselves and from governments tired of supporting an inefficient and embarrassingly feudal industry. The introduction of award wages and of realistic lease rentals had both been a long time coming and pastoral leaseholders were well aware of these developments, since they had actively resisted both reforms since the 1940s and 1950s. A few station owners responded to criticism of their poor land management and inadequate station improvements and changed their practices, but most did not. With a few exceptions, most station owners ignored increasing demands over decades for them to improve housing and living conditions for their Aboriginal employees in lieu of direct wage increases. With the social security cheque bonanza, several station owners were genuine in passing on the value of those payments to their elderly former employees, but the investigations in 1965 and 1966 showed that too many station owners abused the system for their own benefit. The end of opportunity for such abuses was also something these station owners must have foreseen.

The Christmas Creek managers who kicked the station workers and their families off the station and left them on the banks of the Fitzroy River in January 1969 were not just responding to the equal wages decision. This was not the result of actions by heartless city folk in a cold, distant courtroom, but the outcome of a combination of changes that had been a long time in the making and with which Kimberley people were very familiar. When the tripartite subsidy of low labour costs, cheap lease rents and Commonwealth benefits intended for Aboriginal people was removed from the equation, the local economy declined dramatically. The people who suffered the most in this economic collapse were the Aboriginal people whose labour had built the pastoral industry and whose pension cheques had boosted station accounts in the 1960s. Many of the people in the reserve camps across the Kimberley had in their own lifetime gone from no wage to low wage to unemployment benefits.

The chronic poverty of Aboriginal communities in the Kimberley that effectively began as refugee camps in the late 1960s and early 1970s did not start with the introduction of equal wages and the sudden move to welfare dependency. Aboriginal workers and their families had always lived in poverty on the stations. Government reports had for decades identified this poverty as an impediment to regional development, and Aboriginal people themselves protested against their enforced low wages and poor living conditions. But the difference in 1969 in places like Fitzroy Crossing and Halls Creek was that Aboriginal workers and their families were homeless and unemployed as well as poor.

The history of the northern pastoral economy and the central role that Aboriginal people played in the development of that economy, both as workers and as recipients of Commonwealth pension benefits, deserves more research. The introduction of equal wages was only part of the history of the station exodus that had such traumatic outcomes for Aboriginal people in the Kimberley. When the tripartite subsidy that upheld the northern pastoral economy was removed, there was little to sustain it and the regional economy collapsed. Jon Altman, in an introduction to his co-edited book (Altman, 2010), addresses the dominant development paradigm that has become the standard, and completely ineffective, response to the poverty and dysfunction of much of remote Aboriginal Australia. In the light of Altman's analysis of the contemporary situation and his conclusion that policy responses so far have been a destructive failure, the question worth asking is whether the northern regional economy was ever a normal modern economy in the first place. It had long been identified as feudal or based on slavery. In the postwar 'golden era' of the pastoral industry in the Kimberley, a closer interrogation of its history showed that it functioned only with subsidies that were huge and largely unacknowledged and, in later years, illicit. Without acknowledging the enormity of the value of Aboriginal people's underpaid or unpaid wages and their stolen pension cheques, contemporary policy responses miss a central point. Aboriginal poverty and the economic dysfunction of many remote Aboriginal communities did not start with welfare dependency in 1969; they were created through dispossession of Aboriginal land and of the value of Aboriginal labour across generations (Eggington and Skyring 2006: xxi). These are the origins of intergenerational poverty. And while government policy responses to remote poverty continue to fail, the Aboriginal people from whom the most has been taken to sustain the northern economy—their land, the value of their labour and for a number of years their pension cheques—continue to be the ones who lose the most.

References

Aboriginal Legal Service of Western Australia Incorporated (ALSWA) 2006a. Submission from ALSWA, July 2006, to the Senate Legal and Constitutional Affairs Committee Inquiry into Stolen Wages. Submission no. 30, <http://www.aph.gov.au/senate/committee/legcon_ctte/completed_inquiries/2004-07/stolen_wages/submissions/sub30.pdf>

Aboriginal Legal Service of Western Australia Incorporated (ALSWA) 2006b. Further submission from ALSWA, October 2006, to the Senate Legal and Constitutional Affairs Committee Inquiry into Stolen Wages. Submission no. 30B, <http://www.aph.gov.au/senate/committee/legcon_ctte/completed_ inquiries/2004-07/stolen_wages/submissions/sub30b.pdf>

Aboriginal Legal Service of Western Australia Incorporated (ALSWA) 2007. Correspondence received from the Aboriginal Legal Service of Western Australia dated 26 March 2007, re Senate Legal and Constitutional Affairs Committee, Inquiry into Stolen Wages, including Attachment 1, Parts 1 and 2. Additional information received, <http://www.aph.gov.au/senate/ committee/legcon_ctte/completed_inquiries/2004-07/stolen_wages/ submissions/sublist.htm>

Altman, J. 2010. What future for remote Indigenous Australia? Economic hybridity and the neoliberal turn. In J. Altman and M. Hinkson (eds), *Culture Crisis: Aboriginal politics in Aboriginal Australia*. Sydney: UNSW Press.

Altman, J. and Nieuwenhuysen, J. 1979. *The Economic Status of Australian Aborigines*. Cambridge: Cambridge University Press.

Anthony, T. 2004. Labour relations on northern cattle stations: feudal exploitation and accommodation. *Drawing Board: An Australian Review of Public Affairs* 4 (3): 118–36.

Anthony, T. 2006. Equal pay: an anniversary shrouded in myths. Australian Policy Online, 22 August 2006. <http://www.apo.org.au/webboard/results. chtml?filename_num=95297>

Anthony, T. 2007. Crime and transgression on northern cattle stations. In I. MacFarlane and M. Hannah (eds), Transgressions: Critical Australian Indigenous *histories*. Canberra: ANU E Press. <http://epress.anu.edu.au/ transgressions_citation.html>; <http://epress.anu.edu.au/aborig_history/ transgressions/pdf/ch03.pdf>

Australian Bureau of Agricultural Economics 1952. *Report on the Beef Cattle Industry in Northern Australia, by J. H. Kelly*. Canberra: Australian Bureau of Agricultural Economics.

Bunbury, B. 2002. *It's Not the Money It's the Land: Aboriginal stockmen and the equal wages case—talking history with Bill Bunbury*. North Fremantle, WA: Fremantle Arts Centre Press.

Chesterman, J. 2001. Defending Australia's reputation: how Indigenous Australians won civil rights. Part two. *Australian Historical Studies* (117) (October): 201–21.

Department of Social Security Research and Statistics Branch 2006 [1983]. *Developments in social security: a compendium of legislative changes since 1908*. Department of Social Security Research Paper No. 20, Commonwealth of Australia, Canberra.

Eggington, D. and Skyring, F. 2006. Preface. In S. R. Silburn, S. R., Zubrick, J. A. De Maio, C. Shepherd, J. A. Griffin, F. G. Mitrou, R. B. Dalby, C. Hayward and G. Pearson (eds), *The Western Australian Aboriginal Child Health Survey: Strengthening the capacity of Aboriginal children, families and communities*. Perth: Curtin University of Technology and Telethon Institute for Child Health Research.

Jebb, M. A. 2002. *Blood, Sweat and Welfare: A history of white bosses and Aboriginal pastoral workers*. Perth: University of Western Australia Press.

Marshall, P. (ed.) 1989. *Raparapa Kularr Martuwarra: All right, now we go 'side the river, along that sundown way—stories from Fitzroy River drovers*. Broome, WA: Magabala Books.

National Archives of Australia (NAA) Item A63, A1910/4980, 'Employment of native labour in WA', NAA, Canberra.

Pastoral Appraisement Board 1969. *Report of Pastoral Appraisement Board on Reappraisement of Pastoral Leases, Kimberley Division, 1969*. Perth: Department of Lands and Surveys.

Pastoral Appraisement Board 1979. *Report of the Pastoral Appraisement Board on the Reappraisement of Pastoral Leases, Kimberley Division, 1979*. Perth: Department of Lands and Surveys.

State Records Office of Western Australia (SROWA), Item 1933/ 0451, 'Payment of wages to natives', Cons 993.

SROWA Item 1939/1104, 'Old Age and Invalid pensions for natives – general file', Native Welfare Department archival file. A copy of this is in *Supplementary information to submissions from ALSWA November 2006*, on the Senate Committee website at <http://www.aph.gov.au/senate/committee/legcon_ctte/completed_inquiries/2004-07/stolen_wages/submissions/sub30C.pdf>

SROWA, Item 1945/0803, 'Native Policy in Western Australia', Acc 1733.

SROWA 1946/1010, 'Federal Pastoral Award - Employment of Natives', Acc. 1733.

SROWA Item 1949/0034, 'Wages. Scale for natives in the Kimberley District. Implementation of', Cons. 993.

SROWA, Item 1950/1987, 'Reappraisement of pastoral lease Kimberley Division 1948', Cons 6231.

SROWA, Item 1964/ 0249, 'Native Citizenship Rights General Correspondence', Acc. 1733.

SROWA, Item NDG 33/3/1a, 'Social Services. Pensions – general', Cons. 3412.

SROWA, 1969/0116 , 'Pastoral Industry Award 1968 - Welfare of Unemployed natives ex. Pastoral stations', Acc. 1733.

Yu, P., 1994, Aboriginal Peoples, Federalism and Self-Determination. In *Social Alternatives,* Vol. 13, No. 1, April 1994, pp. 19-21.

9. Aboriginal Workers, Aboriginal Poverty

Ros Kidd

If I were a young Aboriginal woman living in Queensland between the 1920s and the late 1960s, there would be a one in two chance that my life was totally controlled by the Government. I would have no rights about where I lived, where and when I worked, my own future or the futures of my children. I would probably be removed to a government settlement where I would be separated from my mother and siblings from the age of five and confined in a dormitory, taught only basic English and arithmetic, and trained as a domestic servant. At thirteen or fourteen, I would be given some clothes and sent to a town or a remote cattle station to start my life of work. Many young boys were also sent to work on the stations, along with men and women trapped in a 51-week labour cycle.

The 'Protection' Regime in Queensland

The Queensland Government established this system of enforced labour in 1897 under *The Aboriginals Protection and Restriction of the Sale of Opium Act*. Under this law, and subsequent legislation until 1971, the Government granted itself powers to control the lives of anyone of Aboriginal descent, in order to protect them from physical, sexual and employment abuses. It set up a network of protectors—in most cases, the lead police officer in each district—whose surveillance during most of the twentieth century generated detailed files on all aspects of people's private lives. Critical police reports triggered government approval to deport individuals and families to distant missions or government-run settlements—often a life sentence. Aboriginal people were not told of the reason for such 'removals'; there was no due process and no right of appeal (Copland 2005). I have elsewhere detailed the abundant primary evidence of the appalling conditions endured by families confined on the grossly under-funded missions and settlements (Kidd 1997, 2002). This chapter will reveal whose interests were best served during the Government's long-running contract employment scheme.

It is a common misconception that settlements in Queensland were closed institutions, tightly excluding Aboriginal people from the wider community. In truth, the Government had no intention of supporting thousands of people on the reserves;[1] nor could it afford—economically or electorally—to exclude such a vast, cheap, malleable workforce from the State's development. The 1897 Act introduced the euphemism 'work agreements' that no Aboriginal man, woman or child could refuse without punishment (Aboriginal child labour was still prevalent in the late 1950s).[2]

Contrary to the longstanding 'whitewashing' of Aboriginal labour from our economic history, these workers have been absolutely crucial to our development as a nation. By the mid-1880s, more than 1000 Aborigines were already in permanent work in Queensland, mostly in rural areas where white labour was scarce. A government survey in 1899 listed more than 2000 permanent workers south of the Tropic of Capricorn. By 1907, there were more than 3000 contracted Aboriginal workers across the State, nudging 4000 in the pastoral industry alone by 1920, rising to 4500 in the early 1930s and 5000 in the mid-1960s.[3]

Queensland was not alone in its 'protection' interventions and employment controls. Each State government, and the Commonwealth Government in the Northern Territory from 1911 to 1928, carefully crafted laws controlling Aboriginal lives and labour, and surveillance systems to force individuals to abide by them (Kidd 2007). If you were a person of Aboriginal descent, these governments could dictate where and when you worked, the type and conditions of that work, what you may be paid and if you could spend it. In Queensland, until 1968 in rural areas and until 1979 on government settlements, Aboriginal legislation overrode the raft of industrial protections enjoyed by every other Australian worker.

Labour Conditions

Official files amassed by the Queensland Government reveal how it executed its self-appointed mandate to 'protect' the employment interests of the Aboriginal people it controlled. The files show that for 20 years there were no limits on how many hours were worked, how hard was the labour, how bad was the treatment or the provision of food and living quarters. Minimum conditions were gazetted in 1919 (*Queensland Government Gazette*, 6 June 1919), but in the absence of any inspections widespread abuses continued. In 1921 the Chief Protector admitted shelter for many Aboriginal workers was 'worse than they would provide for their pet horse, motor-car or prize cattle'; in 1936 a group of families on one station had to live in the open with no protection from rain or wind; in the 1940s it was reported that most employers in the Gulf area thought

---

1 *Queensland Parliamentary Debates*, 1901, p. 1139.
2 Queensland State Archives [hereinafter QSA], TR1227:258 23.1.57.
3 COL/A140 99/3618, QSA; employment numbers from departmental annual reports.

'anything is good enough for a nigger'; in 1959 one group of workers lived in an open shed without any bedding, light or table, and was paid only tobacco and matches each week. All these things the Government knew, because they are on files received and indexed at head office. Only in 1956, after the system had run for 60 years, did the Government instruct industrial inspectors to include Aboriginal employees in their tours of rural areas. Even then, as the records show, abuses continued: sexual assaults, wet living quarters, rough handling, beatings with chains, lack of water and cooking facilities, and widespread hookworm and ill health, especially among children. Clearly, the Government betrayed its mandate to protect Aboriginal wards from physical and labour exploitation.

Wage Rates

Acting as employment broker through its agents, the police protectors, the Government also had a duty to negotiate wages commensurate with the skill levels and market demand for Aboriginal workers, who were chiefly sent to outlying areas where white labour was scarce. The Government charted the value of this contracted workforce through regular surveys of local protectors. In the first years of the past century, the Government knew Aboriginal workers were often regarded as more reliable than and superior stockriders and bushmen to their white counterparts, yet it set their wage at about 3 per cent of the white rate. In the early 1930s when white rural labour was described as 'often useless' and Aboriginal labour as 'indispensable', 4500 Aboriginal workers were sold at about 40 per cent of the pastoral award rate.[4] In 1949 Aboriginal wages were as low as 31 per cent of the award rate, and only 59 per cent in 1956, when an employment inspection confirmed the pastoral industry was entirely dependent on Aboriginal workers, particularly in remote areas where white stockmen were rare. The inspector said the entrenched mentality was to pay 'as little as possible for Aboriginal workers', while 'white men of markedly less ability and industry receive higher wages and better living conditions than Aboriginals who are better workmen'.[5] By the mid-1960s, the 5000 Aboriginal workers were paid only 70 per cent of the award rate. The Queensland Government defied the 1966 'equal pay' judgment of the Commonwealth Conciliation and Arbitration Commission directing Aboriginal pastoral workers be paid the same rates as their white counterparts, by simply categorising its controlled Aboriginal workforce as 'trainees', and continuing to sell them at a discount, although most had decades of skill and experience.[6] Only after 1972 were Aboriginal pastoral

---

4   Comparing rates under successive Aboriginal regulations with the contemporary pastoral award.
5   Box 16 22, October 1956, SRS 505-1, QSA.
6   28 May 1965, SRS 505-1 1A/29, QSA.

workers free from conscripted employment. For the first time, elderly family members and wives who had been compelled to work for free on the stations could refuse such exploitation.

The Government's own records thus confirm that the prime motivator for the Aboriginal labour market was the needs of rural industries: the supply of as many men and women as required *for a price that the market claimed it could bear*. Send them out to the remote areas that white workers shunned, arrest them and return them if they abscond; do not look too closely at hours and conditions. But that was only half the story. The other half was the rank financial exploitation of this captive workforce. There is no doubt that generations of Aboriginal people were mired in poverty despite decades of contracted work. The files reveal that while they were trapped in poverty, the Government grew fat on their earnings.

Savings and Trust Funds

For the whole of its 70-year contracted labour system, the Government gave employers the right to pay into workers' hands between 30 and 80 per cent of their wage. But the Government never bothered to secure this payment despite warnings from both protectors and auditors that workers were routinely cheated of this 'pocket money'. An internal inquiry in 1932[7] concluded it could be 'reasonably assumed' that workers did not get this money. In a 1943 survey of pocket money payments, protectors said the whole system was a farce and a direct profit to employers; in 1956 protectors described the system as useless, futile and out of control, with workers 'entirely at the mercy' of employers who simply doctored the books. In the mid-1960s, auditors again condemned the Government's continued lack of control of pocket money payments.[8] Records show that in the 60 years to 1968, successive governments knew the Aboriginal workers it controlled were being cheated of potentially 50 per cent of their wage. They knew these systemically impoverished workers were effectively subsidising the State's pastoral interests.

What of the portion paid directly to police protectors, ostensibly to 'protect' Aboriginal earnings from European cunning and Aboriginal incapacity? The Government knew from the start that its agents, the police protectors, were often incompetent and fraudsters, yet it continued this system. As early as 1904, and again in the 1920s, it introduced a thumb-print system to reduce rampant fraud. It did not work. A public service inquiry in 1922 revealed absolutely no

---

7   Report on the Inspection of the Office of the Chief Protector of Aboriginals, 9 November 1932, A/58856, QSA.
8   Audit Report 1964–65, TR254 1B/69, QSA.

supervision of the 8000 rural savings accounts, and said police practices were so unreliable workers should be allowed to appeal dealings on their accounts.[9] The 1932 inquiry found that 'the opportunity for fraud existed to a greater degree than with any other Governmental accounts'. The Chief Protector again admitted there were no real controls over official dealings on private accounts, and again refused to allow workers to check dealings on their accounts.

When the Government did centralise the bulk of the rural savings accounts in Brisbane in 1933, in order, it said, to minimise police fraud,[10] it promptly locked about 80 per cent of these savings—more than $12 million today[11]—in investments, and kept the interest bonus for itself. Until the late 1960s, only about 20 per cent of their savings were available at any one time for Aboriginal workers. The files are full of rejections for those who asked for a few dollars of their own money.

In 1904 a trust fund was set up to hold monies owing to, or saved by, missing or deceased workers for distribution to their families; a second trust fund was set up in 1919 by simply taxing all Aboriginal savings for an unemployment relief fund. Internal investigations show both trust funds were consistently raided for government costs. In the decade from 1925, covering the Depression years, the Government simply transferred to itself more than $930 000 (in today's money) from Aboriginal savings accounts and more than $3.5 million from the two trust funds[12]—money that has never been repaid. Vast sums from the Commonwealth child endowment paid to Aboriginal mothers after 1941 were also transferred into state revenue, by paying only a fraction to settlement mothers and by reducing grants to the missions by the amount of incoming endowment. From 1960, invalid, aged and widows' pensions were 'diverted to revenue',[13] bringing an annual bonanza of more than $500 000 (in today's money) in 1960, rising to almost $750 000 by 1964. Meanwhile, the people whose lives were supposed to be improved by the pensions struggled and died in poverty. When Aboriginal people in Queensland finally got control of their lives and their finances in the early 1970s, many found to their horror that their new bankbooks showed pitiful balances despite decades of work and financial privation. Those who queried head office were told that the records were too inconclusive and so many files lost or destroyed that it is impossible to confirm claims of missing money.

---

9   Report on the Office of the Chief Protector of Aboriginals, 15 March 1923, A/69452, QSA.
10   14 November 1933, TR1227:129, QSA.
11   All amounts converted to approximate equivalent today using the retail price index.
12   6 November 1935, A/58856, QSA.
13   17 March 1959, SRS 505-1, Box 91, QSA.

Fighting for Justice

As Aboriginal workers and their families become aware of the wealth of evidence of government financial mismanagement across generations, there is increased action for justice. Government responses have been characterised by denial, miserly compensation and non-disclosure of file evidence.

Underpaid Wages

At a 1996 Human Rights Commission hearing into the charge by seven Palm Islanders that the Queensland Government's entrenched underpayment of community wages was illegal after passage of the 1975 *Racial Discrimination Act*, the Government said I could be sued for damages if I presented evidence from its own files to the commission. This evidence convinced the commission to conclude that the Government had 'intentionally, deliberately and knowingly' underpaid six of the seven claimants, and it recommended compensation of $7000 each.[14] The Borbidge Coalition Government initially dismissed the findings, paying the $7000 only after action was launched in the Federal Court, and only after demanding claimants sign an indemnity against further legal action. Yet the Government knew those claimants were due amounts varying between $8500 and $21 000.

When the Beattie Labor Government extended the $7000 compensation in 1999 to all community employees illegally underpaid from 1975,[15] we now know it had already settled 22 actions out of court, one for $4000 (about one-quarter of the debt showed on government records), and 21 for $7000 (where official estimates of underpayment ranged between $13 000 and $27 000). The Government again demanded it be indemnified against future legal action, knowing that most claimants had never seen the official records detailing what they might really be owed. Fewer than half the potential claimants took the $7000, costing the Government almost $40 million—less than one-quarter of the profit it had made from the underpayment of community workers in the decade from 1975. Two workers who each sued the Government for $100 000 for their underpaid wages (*The Courier-Mail*, 28 November 2002) settled in 2004. In 2006 several hundred workers on two former Lutheran communities won their case on appeal, and were paid based on their wage records; many received more than $20 000; one was paid four times that much.

---

14   HREOC Decision No. H95/74-80, H96/88, 24 September 1996, Human Rights and Equal Opportunity Commission.
15   *Queensland Parliamentary Debates*, 26 May 1999.

Stolen Wages

In May 2002, Premier Peter Beattie admitted there were 4000 potential litigants waiting to sue the Government for the stolen wages[16]—that is, the wages, savings, child endowment, pensions and inheritances lost during 70 years of government mismanagement. He offered compensation of $55.6 million, which he said was 'generous', despite admitting my own research indicated about $500 million is in question. This offer was a maximum $4000 per person; thousands of deceased account holders were simply disqualified; and again claimants had to sign away their legal rights. Facing a barrage of public condemnation and a poor uptake of only $20 million, in August 2008, the Bligh Labor Government reopened the scheme and increased the maximum payouts to $7000 (*The Courier-Mail*, 18 August 2008). In November 2010, it declared its intention to tip the $20 million still unclaimed into the notoriously misused Aboriginal Welfare Fund for distribution as education scholarships, in blatant contempt of its own survey in which more than 90 per cent of respondents demanded the whole stolen wages allocation be distributed among eligible claimants as promised by the Premier in May 2002 (*National Indigenous Times*, 11 December 2008).

A National Scandal

Exploitation of Aboriginal labour, wages, savings and entitlements was not peculiar to Queensland. All State governments, and the Commonwealth Government in the Northern Territory, ran contract labour systems and banking controls. In 2004 I wanted to generate a national report with detailed submissions from local experts, but this gradually shrank to my compiling a summary gleaned from other research work, and was published by Australians for Native Title and Reconciliation (ANTaR) in 2007 as *Hard Labour, Stolen Wages* (available free online from their web site).[17] In 2006 I met Democrats Senator Andrew Bartlett at a stolen wages strategy meeting and he suggested a senate inquiry should look into the issue nationally. After months of persistent lobbying by Bartlett, the inquiry was launched in 2007, attracting submissions from around Australia, which confirmed the terrible losses suffered by those whose lives and livelihoods were controlled by various governments. Initially, the Queensland Government scorned the inquiry, hastily appearing only on the last day. The evidence is damning; it is all on the Senate's web site.[18]

---

16   *Queensland Parliamentary Debates*, 16 May 2002.
17   <http://www.antar.org.au/sites/default/files/stolenwages.pdf>
18   <http://www.aph.gov.au/senate/committee/legcon_ctte/completed_inquiries/2004-07/stolen_wages/submissions/sublist.htm>

Predictably, all governments are in denial. I believe the WA Government has made a preliminary investigation of its records relating to the management of private Aboriginal monies, including endowment and pensions, but it has refused to disclose this information to the individuals and families concerned. The NSW Government has initiated a reparations scheme to repay money shown to be outstanding to particular individuals. This scheme takes no account of wages and entitlements lost through decades of mismanagement. The Victorian Government committed only a few days to its official investigation of its financial records. These governments—and those who to date have refused to address their role in this national scandal—are claiming that 'lost' records are a bulwark against legal accountability.

International Precedent?

Given there is overwhelming evidence of negligence and mismanagement by successive Queensland governments, I have long been convinced that it is the Government that should be in the dock and on the defence, not an individual trying to provide cast-iron evidence of fraud on his or her account—evidence that the Government might have withheld, lost or destroyed. I am inspired by the case of Elouise Cobell,[19] an enterprising woman of the Blackfeet tribe of Montana, who brought action against the US Government in 1996 on behalf of thousands of individual Native American men and women who were cheated of royalties for oil, mineral and other leases during more than a century of government mismanagement of their accounts. Government claims that individual entitlements cannot be proven because so many records have been lost and destroyed over time were, as the judge pointed out, primary evidence of the breach of their fundamental trust duty to keep proper records.

In 1999 the US courts found in favour of the Cobell claim, which comprises half a million living and *deceased* claimants; one government estimate suggested US$40 billion was at stake. The Bush Administration refused to accede to court demands to negotiate a settlement. In December 2009, the Obama Administration provided US$3.4 billion to finalise this massive class action.

There is a major hurdle for such a case in Australia. In the United States, the courts had already declared that, in its stewardship of the enterprises on Indian reserves (as they were referred to) and management of individual bank accounts, the Federal Government was a legal trustee of those Indian interests with full legal obligations. In Australia, as the many supportive lawyers in our battle informed me, our courts see things differently. In their view, the people are

---

19   The detailed history of this case can be found on <http://www.narf.org> and <http://www.indiantrust.org>

the ones who empowered the governments to implement their wide-ranging 'protection' schemes, and it is not the role of the courts to interfere with how governments carried out this mandate. The lawyers suggest our courts might not find our governments are legal trustees of Aboriginal interests. Cases mounted for members of the Stolen Generations bear this out.

But I firmly believe that a stolen wages case, based on the wealth of incriminating *financial* evidence on government files, will prove different. It is much harder to argue 'benign intent' in illegally using private savings than in removing children from their families. To convince the legal profession and the courts, I wrote *Trustees on Trial* (Kidd 2006), analysing national and international cases relating to trust law and fiduciary duties, and applying those legal prohibitions and responsibilities to the negligent and exploitative conduct of successive Queensland administrations. Let me mention a few of the legal duties of a trustee: a trustee must protect the trust property, must keep proper records of accounts and provide full information to any beneficiary requesting it, and must not profit from, or have personal interests that conflict with, the trust. You can see the connections. For any trustee, loss of records is not a defence; it is a fundamental breach of trust duties.

In September 2009, the Queensland Council of Unions launched court action for breach of trust on behalf of Conrad Yeatman, whose labour and wages were controlled by government mandate from the age of fourteen. In December the Government lodged its defence. It claims it has no responsibility for the missing wages and savings of the Aboriginal and Islander people it controlled for most of the twentieth century. The Government states that it all happened too long ago and records have been destroyed.[20]

In my view, the Government's blatant denial of the evidence on public record shows contempt for fundamental human rights. Throughout the twentieth century, governments lied to the Australian public about their flawed guardianship of thousands of Aboriginal families; this was no benign paternalism. Governments mishandled the money of the poorest people in Australia who were forced to be utterly dependent on their integrity. Government stonewalling continues this rank injustice; their contemptuous disregard for historical accountability continues the whitewashing from our national history of the mammoth part played by Aboriginal workers, and feeds the pernicious insinuation that Aboriginal poverty today is an outcome of a cultural aversion to work. How different would their lives have been—and those of their descendants today—if these highly valued essential workers had not been cheated of their wages. Why should they not be compensated for this institutionalised loss?

---

20   <http://www.qcu.asn.au/newsletter_dec_09.pdf>

If I were an Aboriginal woman who had been trapped in this system, I would be hoping that my day in court would not only bring me justice and reparations but also inscribe on the public mind the vital labour input of Aboriginal people in the generation of our national wealth, and constant participation in the national economy.

Postscript

In March 2012 the WA government offered an ex gratia payment of $2000 to surviving residents of government settlements born before 1958 who can provide evidence of withheld entitlements, estimating that fewer than 1500 people may be eligible.

References

Copland, M. 2005. Calculating lives: the numbers and narratives of forced removals in Queensland 1859–1972. PhD thesis, Griffith University, Gold Coast, Qld.

Kidd, R. 1997. *The Way We Civilise*. St Lucia: University of Queensland Press.

Kidd, R. 2002. *Black Lives, Government Lies*. Sydney: UNSW Press.

Kidd, R. 2006. *Trustees on Trial. Recovering the stolen wages*. Canberra: Aboriginal Studies Press.

10. Indigenous Peoples and Stolen Wages in Victoria, 1869–1957

Andrew Gunstone

Introduction

Throughout much of the nineteenth and twentieth centuries, Commonwealth, State and Territory governments and their agencies largely controlled Indigenous people's wages, savings and social security benefits. Many Indigenous workers either received no wages or were underpaid for years and decades of employment. The savings and social security benefits of many Indigenous people were paid into trust accounts, which were regularly mismanaged, often fraudulently, and were generally inaccessible to Indigenous people. Commonwealth and State governments excluded Indigenous people from accessing many social security benefits, such as maternity allowances, child endowment and old-age pensions. These and other such acts are referred to today as the 'stolen wages' practices.

In this chapter, I analyse a number of stolen wages practices that occurred in the nineteenth and twentieth centuries in Victoria. These practices were the failure to pay any or adequate wages to Indigenous people, the lack of accountability and poor governance in the administration of Indigenous affairs and the enforcement of harsh employment controls on Indigenous people. I explore these practices in relation to a particular period of Indigenous affairs administration in Victoria—that of the Board for the Protection of the Aborigines (BPA) (1869–1957). The BPA era was the longest and most influential period of Indigenous affairs administration in Victorian history. In particular, I analyse the Victorian Government's legislation, regulations and inquiries of this period that relate to Indigenous wages and employment. Although I focus on the BPA period in this chapter, it is important to note that practices of stolen wages occurred prior to 1869, in the early days of non-Indigenous people living in Victoria, and also after 1957, during the administrative periods of the Aborigines Welfare Board (AWB: 1957–67) and the Ministry for Aboriginal Affairs (1968–75) (for more analysis on these and the BPA periods, see Broome 1995, 2005; Gunstone and Heckenberg 2009; Kidd 2007).

The Board for the Protection of the Aborigines

The *Aborigines Protection Act 1869* (Vic.) enabled governments to exert substantial control over the lives of Indigenous peoples. It allowed for regulations to be implemented across a range of areas, including employment contracts and certificates for Indigenous people, the wages of Indigenous people and the housing and education of Indigenous children (*Aborigines Protection Act 1869*, pp. 111–12). It created the BPA, which operated from 1869 to 1957 and exerted strong and discriminatory controls over most aspects of the lives of Indigenous people, including employment and wages (*Aborigines Protection Act 1869*, p. 112; Broome 1995:136). For example, in 1909, the BPA informed the Manager of Coranderrk reserve that 'it is not desirable that they [Indigenous people] be kept in idleness, nor should the Board be required to pay the natives for every hour worked by them' (BPA 1909–11:15). The 1869 Act also defined Indigenous people as 'every aboriginal native of Australia and every aboriginal half-caste or child of a half-caste, such half-caste or child habitually associating and living with aboriginals' (*Aborigines Protection Act 1869*, p. 113).

The *Regulations and Orders made under the Act 1871* (Vic.) granted substantial powers to the BPA. The BPA and employers could negotiate contracts over employing Indigenous people, looking at issues such as the nature and duration of employment, wages and rations (*Regulations and Orders made under the Act 1871*, p. 338). Interestingly, there is no mention in these regulations that the BPA or employers needed to consult with Indigenous workers regarding the contracts. The BPA could order Indigenous wages to be paid indirectly to a third party, such as a 'local guardian' (who was an 'authorised agent of the Board'). The third party and the BPA could determine where the wages should be directed (*Regulations and Orders made under the Act 1871*, p. 338). The BPA had these last two powers until 1931 (Wampan Wages 2006b:2). The BPA could issue work certificates to Indigenous people (*Regulations and Orders made under the Act 1871*, p. 338). Employers and Indigenous workers could be fined or imprisoned without a valid work certificate (*Aborigines Protection Act 1869*, pp. 112–13; Kidd 2007:118). The BPA could sell goods produced by Indigenous people on reserves and 'out of the net proceeds of the sale pay to the aboriginals who have labored on the reserves such sums as the Board may deem right' (*Regulations and Orders made under the Act 1871*, p. 338). Finally, the BPA could remove 'neglected' or 'unprotected' children from their families (*Regulations and Orders made under the Act 1871*, p. 338). This was the first of numerous regulations that enabled governments and their agencies to exert substantial controls over Indigenous children (Haebich 2000:149).

Over the next decade, further legislation was enacted concerning the control of Indigenous children. *The Neglected and Criminal Children's Amendment Act*

1874 (Vic.) allowed the following for Indigenous and non-Indigenous children: children deemed 'neglected' could be detained until sixteen years of age; detained children could be 'boarded out' or apprenticed; any wages owed to children could be recovered by any person appointed by the Chief Secretary; and amounts could be deducted from a child's wages for any expenses caused by their 'ill-behaviour or misconduct' (*The Neglected and Criminal Children's Amendment Act 1874*, pp. 2–3). The *Regulations made under the Act 1880* (Vic.) enabled reserve managers to order Indigenous children on reserves to be removed from their families and to 'reside, and take their meals, and sleep' in separate buildings (*Regulations made under the Act 1880*, p. 1912).

The Royal Commission on the Aborigines was conducted in Victoria in 1877. It was to 'inquire into the present condition of the Aborigines of this colony, and to advise as to the best means of caring for and dealing with them in the future' (BPA 1877:vii). The Royal Commission advocated government control over Indigenous people. It argued Indigenous people living on reserves had better lives than those living off reserves, and governments should be able to control all Indigenous people (BPA 1877:vii–xiii). The Royal Commission also supported government control over Indigenous employment. It argued for the continuation of the practice of apprenticing out Indigenous children, and for Indigenous people living on reserves to have any wages they earned paid through the manager of the reserve by their employer (BPA 1877:xii, xiv).

During the 1870s and 1880s, reserves were built all over Victoria through the widespread employment of Indigenous people, undertaking jobs such as clearing, building, fencing and farming on the reserves (Kidd 2007:121). This employment was often a requirement for Indigenous people to receive rations (Broome 2005:141–2; Critchett 1998:93). On many reserves, however, Indigenous people often received little or no pay for this employment (Broome 2005:148). At Framlingham, Indigenous people working between 1869 and 1877, and for periods after 1877, received no wages (Barwick 1981:178–82). At Coranderrk, while Indigenous workers received wages for growing hops from 1874 as a result of their protests, they received just one-third of the non-Indigenous rate, were often paid late, the proceeds from the selling of the hops were 'appropriated [by the BPA] for general expenses', and Indigenous workers employed in other work, such as collecting firewood, received no wages (BPA 1882; Broome 2006:43.7–43.8; Kidd 2007:121). At Lake Condah, following protests, the practice of paying Indigenous workers in rations ceased in 1887 and the workers were instead paid a 'nominal wage' (Kidd 2007:121). At Ramahyuck, Lake Tyers and Ebenezer, Indigenous workers also 'forced [the payment of] wages…although not at the rate of white workers or [generally] what they might receive outside' (Broome 2005:142).

Also during this time, many Indigenous people worked for private employers off the reserves in occupations such as harvesting, shearing and stockwork. In some instances, the wages of Indigenous workers were less than (often about half) the wages of non-Indigenous workers (Broome 2005:148). In other instances, Indigenous and non-Indigenous workers received generally the same wages (Broome 2005:189). This occurred in the 1870s and 1880s at Framlingham, until the mid-1870s at Coranderrk, in the 1870s at a farm in Eastwood and in the late nineteenth century at the Snowy River (Attwood 2003:12; Barwick 1981:179; Broome 1995:137; Campbell and Vanderwal 1999:84). Indigenous people who worked off the reserves also could have some control over their wages (Broome 2005:150); however, the poor financial records of many private employers means that there is considerable uncertainty regarding the actual degree of control Indigenous workers had over their employment and wages with private employers (Kidd 2007:121). There are examples of Indigenous people not having control over private employment. For instance, Indigenous people at Lake Condah in the 1880s were not granted work certificates, which prevented them from being able to work for private employers off the reserve (Critchett 1998:151–2; Kidd 2007:121). Kidd (2007:121–2) argues that

> this suggests some stations acted as employment agents and might have negotiated wage rates and perhaps partly controlled access to savings, as in other states…[and also] it is likely that part or all of the wages of adults employed under Board work certificates were controlled by the Board.

In order to minimise expenditure on Indigenous affairs, the BPA argued in 1884 that all 'half-caste' Indigenous people should be exiled from reserves and located within the wider community (BPA 1956–57:5; CAR 1965:3; PROV 2005:85). This assimilationist approach remained government policy for decades. In 1965, the Council for Aboriginal Rights (CAR), an organisation that fought for Indigenous rights, argued that 'assimilation of part-Aborigines has been the official policy of past Victorian governments since 1884' (CAR 1965:3).

The *Aborigines Protection Act 1886* (Vic.) addressed this view of the BPA. It repealed the definition of Indigenous people stated in the *Aborigines Protection Act 1869* (Vic.) and in its place defined Indigenous people as including: '(1.) Every aboriginal native of Victoria ["full-bloods"] [and] (2.) Every half-caste…habitually associating and living with an aboriginal…[and who has] completed the thirty-fourth year of his or her age' (*Aborigines Protection Act 1886*, pp. 283–4).

The redefining of Indigenous people by the *Aborigines Protection Act 1886* had a substantial impact upon Indigenous people. The Act defined most Indigenous people who were under the age of thirty-four as not Indigenous. Haebich (2000:162, 164–5) argued that this 'policy of forced assimilation or ethnocide' was a 'significant shift in Aboriginal policy in Victoria' and 'was the first statute to legislate for the differential treatment of "full-blood" and "half-caste"'. The *Aborigines Protection Act 1886* dictated that only 'full-bloods' and 'half-castes' under thirty-four who held a licence granted by the BPA could reside on reserves, while those who were unlicensed had to relocate into the wider community (Broome 1995:139; Haebich 2000:162, 165–7). These licences stopped being issued in 1937 due to 'the clerical work involved' (BPA 1956–57:12). The *Aborigines Protection Act 1886* resulted in 'almost half the estimated 600 residents of the state's stations and missions, representing some forty families and including 160 children', being forcibly removed from reserves (Haebich 2000:166). Further, Barwick (1981:187) stated that 'the eligible residents who "harboured" them—even if they were unemployed or ill—risked the loss of their own rations' (see also Broome 1995:190). Indigenous people forced off reserves 'could apply for rations, clothing and blankets for [up to] seven years to assist their transition into the wider society'; however, they still faced extreme hardship, including unemployment, due to racial discrimination and competition from non-Indigenous workers, the ending of rations in 1893 and the 1890s economic depression, which saw 30 per cent unemployment in the wider community and no government welfare (Broome 1995:139–40; Kidd 2007:118). Also, Indigenous people—often unemployed—'were ordered off as "trespassers"' when they tried to return to the reserves (Barwick 1981:187).

The Neglected Children's Act 1887 (Vic.) included several sections relating to the employment and wages of children. These sections included: enabling authorities to 'sue for and recover any wages or earnings' owed to wards; ensuring all monies controlled by authorities as the 'guardian' be directed to the 'State Wards' Fund'; paying an amount 'not exceeding Five pounds per cent., from the moneys paid to the credit of the State Wards' Fund' into consolidated revenue; enabling expenses incurred by authorities 'for or on account of any person of whose estate he is guardian…[to] be payable out of the moneys received on account of such estate'; acknowledging 'if any ward of the Department for Neglected Children is guilty of any misbehaviour [which is not defined in the Act], of which the Minister shall be the sole judge' then 'the Minister may order the whole or any part of any moneys to which such ward is entitled' be removed to address the 'misbehaviour'; granting the minister the discretion to withhold monies from such wards until they have been in 'good conduct' for a year; and enabling regulations to be made concerning the 'collection and investment…of any earnings of any ward of the Department for Neglected Children' (*The Neglected Children's Act 1887*, pp. 126–8, 138–40). These sections were repeated in subsequent Victorian legislation (*The Neglected Children's Act 1890*, pp. 384–6, 396–8).

The *Aborigines Act 1890* (Vic.) further imposed controls over Indigenous people regarding employment. It contained several sections—in almost identical wording to that in the *Aborigines Protection Act 1869* (Vic.)—that allowed regulations to be made in several areas concerning Indigenous people, including employment contracts and certificates, wages and the housing and employment of children (*Aborigines Act 1890*, p. 12).

The *Regulations relating to Half-Castes 1890* (Vic.) enacted several regulations concerning Indigenous wages and employment. They allowed for Indigenous children over fourteen years of age to be apprenticed out for any trade (*Regulations relating to Half-Castes 1890*, p. 1788). They also required employers to send to the BPA 'one-half of the wages of every half-caste child licensed to service and of every apprentice' that would be 'paid to such child at the end of his or her service or apprenticeship' (*Regulations relating to Half-Castes 1890*, p. 1788). Wampan Wages (2006a:5) argued, however, that there are no recorded instances of these withheld wages being paid to Indigenous children.

As with the 1871 Regulations, the *Aborigines Act 1890 Regulations, 1890* (Vic.) enabled the BPA to enter into contracts with employers concerning Indigenous workers, pay the wages of Indigenous workers to third parties, determine where the wages of Indigenous workers were directed, issue work certificates to Indigenous people and remove any Indigenous child who was 'neglected' or 'unprotected' to a reserve or an industrial or reformatory school (*Aborigines Act 1890 Regulations 1890*, pp. 3720–1; Broome 1995:139–41; Haebich 2000:165).

The *Aborigines Act 1890 Alteration of Regulations 1899* (Vic.) broadened the BPA's long-held power to remove 'neglected' and 'unprotected' Indigenous children to include all Indigenous children (*Aborigines Act 1890 Alteration of Regulations 1899*, p. 4383). The BPA maintained this capacity to remove any Indigenous child until its dissolution in 1957, and 'removals' of Indigenous children 'to institutions, and then onto white families or employers, continued until 1967' (Broome 2005:193; CAR 1965:3).

Throughout the early to mid-twentieth century, a lack of accountability and poor governance occurred in two key areas of Indigenous affairs administration in Victoria. These issues are likely to have significantly and detrimentally impacted upon the capacity of the BPA to appropriately manage the wages and trust funds (see below) of Indigenous peoples.

First, the financial administration of the reserves was largely inadequate. In 1904, the Victorian Auditor-General notified the BPA of the lack of auditing of a number of Indigenous reserves and requested that these reserves be audited (BPA 1904–56:7 October 1904). Although the BPA allowed the Audit Office to examine the financial administration of the Lake Condah, Lake Tyers and Lake

Wellington reserves, the Auditor-General criticised the books and accounts of these reserves and argued that 'no audit could be made' of these reserves (BPA 1904–56:21 December 1905). In 1905, a financial report of Lake Condah reserve stated that 'as no bank books were produced I cannot certify to balances. It appeared to me that the Cash Books had been recently written up' (BPA 1904–56:19 December 1905). In 1906, the Audit Office audited several reserves and made a number of critical comments to the BPA concerning these audits. Regarding Ramahyuck, the Auditor-General stated that 'the stock book was, however, wrong', 'the Manager's stock and that of the Station are mixed', 'I do not know whether there is any understanding between your Board and the manager as to what [Indigenous] labor he is entitled to', 'the duty of the Manager to your Board and his private interests clash[es]' and 'there is no possible check on him [the Manager]' (BPA 1904–56:27 February 1906). Regarding Coranderrk, the Auditor-General stated that 'there was no cash book', although its process of forwarding all cash to the Secretary 'is preferable to the system of paying [all cash] into a bank account in the name of the manager as is done at the other Stations I have visited' (BPA 1904–56:7 March 1906). Regarding Lake Condah, the Auditor-General stated that 'it was impossible in consequence of the method of bookkeeping to reconcile the books with the cash on hand', and there was a 'faulty system of accounts' (BPA 1904–56:24 May 1906). Many of these issues continued for decades, with several audit reports conducted in the 1930s also stating concerns with the financial administration of reserves, such as cash books, store records and trust accounts (BPA 1904–56:58–9, 65–6).

Second, there was inadequate accountability of the BPA itself to the Victorian Parliament for almost all of the BPA's existence in the twentieth century. In 1912, the BPA ceased producing annual reports to the Parliament for several decades, with the exception of three reports in the 1920s (Broome 1995:142, 2005:206). After its 1925 report, the BPA failed to produce another report for more than 20 years (Barwick 1981:193). This lack of reports ensured that the BPA's 'management at Lake Tyers remained closed to Victorian eyes' (Broome 1995:142). In addition, for many years the BPA 'was rarely convened and executive control remained with the Under Secretary and a clerk' (Barwick 1981:193). Broome and Manning (2006:117) argued that, 'by the 1940s, Victoria's Aboriginal Protection Board, then over seventy years old, was moribund. It did not meet or report to parliament; its management of Aboriginal affairs, such as it was, was handled by a few public servants' (see also BPA 1956–57:13–14; Broome 1995:150–1). In 1947, despite the BPA being reconstituted, with new members, including an Indigenous member, it was 'convened only once or twice a year' until its dissolution in 1957, and 'two officers of the Chief Secretary's Department continued to control policy' (Barwick 1981:202). In 1955, even the BPA itself criticised 'the infrequency of meetings' as ensuring that the BPA 'has completely lost touch with administrative matters' (BPA 1929–63:67).

The *Aborigines Act 1910* (Vic.) extended the BPA's control to all Indigenous people, including 'half-castes' (*Aborigines Act 1910*, p. 1). This acknowledged the reality that 'the Protection Board was forced to support distressed "half-castes"' (Broome 1995:140). Haebich (2000:167), however, argued that the BPA 'insisted on helping only those families who moved to its station at Lake Tyers'.

The *Aborigines Act Regulations 1916* (Vic.) enforced strict controls over Indigenous peoples living on reserves, including over their employment and wages. The Regulations were similar to previous regulations and included: enforcing employment contracts and certificates; empowering the BPA to sell goods made on reserves and determine the wages to be paid to Indigenous workers who produced those goods; enabling the reserve manager to force Indigenous residents to 'do a reasonable amount of work' and to decide the employment and wages for Indigenous residents; controlling access to the reserve, which was critical in enabling Indigenous people to work off the reserve; and empowering the BPA to hold one-half of the wages paid to Indigenous apprentices until the end of their apprenticeship (*Aborigines Act Regulations 1916*, pp. 3547–8, 3550, 3552; Broome 2005:203; NAA and PROV 2008:3). Further, the Regulations forced all 'quadroon, octoroon, and half-caste lads' off the reserves and stipulated that they would 'not again be allowed upon a station or reserve, except for a brief visit [not exceeding 10 days] to relatives, at the discretion of Managers of stations' (*Aborigines Act Regulations 1916*, p. 3553). These regulations continued until 1957 (CAR 1965:3). Those Indigenous people who were forced off the reserves and required to 'assimilate into townships' experienced many difficulties, including rejection by the broader society, employment discrimination, ineligibility for government support and isolation from families and communities (NAA and PROV 2008:3–4, 13).

In 1917, the BPA implemented a 'Concentration Plan' (NAA and PROV 2008) that focused on closing all Victorian reserves, with the exception of the reserve at Lake Tyers, where the BPA aimed to 'concentrate all [Indigenous people] down to half-caste standard' (Barwick 1981:191; see also BPA and AWB 1918–63:26; NAA and PROV 2008:13). Consequently, only those Indigenous people living at Lake Tyers would be eligible for BPA support (Barwick 1981:191; PROV 2005:86). By 1923, the reserve at Lake Tyers was the only staffed reserve in Victoria, although some, mainly elderly, Indigenous residents remained at the reserves at Coranderrk and Framlingham (Broome 1995:142; Kidd 2007:119).

The Indigenous residents of Lake Tyers reserve experienced poor-quality rations, minimal, if any, wages, controls over all aspects of their lives and appalling levels of ill health and housing (Broome 2005:231; Haebich 2000:167; NAA and PROV 2008:4–5). Those Indigenous residents who left Lake Tyers to work off the reserve who did not first obtain a pass could be barred from receiving rations or fined (Harris 1988:8; see also *Aborigines Act 1915 Additional Regulation No.*

34 [A] 1927; BPA 1896–1907:125A). These conditions—such as poor rations, low, if any, wages and a fining system—continued for many decades, with some of these conditions not ceasing until 1966 (BPA and AWB 1949–58:45; HREOC 1997:59).

The 1925 *Report on the Lake Tyers Aboriginal Station*, commissioned by the BPA, discussed the employment of Indigenous residents at Lake Tyers. The report recommended that as 'there are few people actually working' because 'the Aboriginals can make money too easy elsewhere [such as selling goods, like boomerangs, to tourists]', 'tourists be requested to buy nothing direct from the Aboriginals' and instead could purchase goods from the reserve (BPA 1925:10, 15). The report also recommended that Indigenous 'inmates of the Station be prevented from working elsewhere when required for this work [agriculture] on the Station', be 'paid piecework at the ruling rate for the district (less cost of rations etc)' and 'the crop be sold and placed to the credit of the Station' (BPA 1925:25).

Those Indigenous people who lived in the wider Victorian community also found many aspects of their lives very difficult, including minimal, irregular and underpaid work, discrimination from non-Indigenous people, including employers, generally no welfare support, terrible standards of ill health and housing and negligible support from the BPA (Barwick 1981:194; Broome 1995:143–4; The Senate 2006:26).

The *Children's Welfare Act 1928* (Vic.) controlled children's wages in a similar manner to the *Neglected Children's Act 1915* (Vic.) (*Children's Welfare Act 1928*, pp. 381–2, 392–3). Further, the 1928 Act enabled regulations to be enacted concerning 'the collection and investment and deposit of any earnings of any ward of the Children's Welfare Department' (*Children's Welfare Act 1928*, p. 394).

The *Aborigines Act 1928* (Vic.) allowed for a range of regulations to be passed regarding Indigenous affairs, including the employment and wages of Indigenous people (*Aborigines Act 1928*, p. 2). In 1931, under the *Aborigines Act 1928 Regulations 1931* (Vic.), managers continued to be able to control Indigenous employment and wages on reserves. All 'able-bodied' Indigenous residents were 'required to do a reasonable amount of work, as directed by the manager, and… be renumerated at a rate to be arranged by the manager and approved by the Board', with those Indigenous residents who refused to work threatened with the withholding of their and their families rations and with being removed from the reserve (*Aborigines Act 1928 Regulations 1931*, p. 1558). The Regulations allowed for the creation of trust funds, in the names of Indigenous workers, which contained amounts deducted by the BPA from the wages of these workers, and stated that these trust funds would be expended under the direction of the BPA (*Aborigines Act 1928 Regulations 1931*, p. 1558). The Regulations also empowered the BPA to sell any goods produced by Indigenous labour on reserves and place all monies received into a trust fund called the Aborigines Board Produce Fund, from which the BPA 'may from time to time from this fund pay to the aborigines who have laboured on reserves such sums as it may determine, having regard to the kind and amount of labour performed by each' (*Aborigines Act 1928 Regulations 1931*, p. 1558; for further information on the Aborigines Board Produce Fund, see BPA 1860–1956:53–5).

Over the next two decades, the Aborigines Board Produce Fund made substantial profits. These profits were £398 3s 4d (1931–35), £2208 19s 5d (1935–40), £2966 7s 1d (1940–45) and £477 13s (1945–50) (BPA 1860–1956:53). The BPA could 'carry forward any surplus from one financial year to the next' (Felton 1960:53). In 1950, the fund lost the income from leasing Lake Condah and Coranderrk reserves when these areas were granted to returned non-Indigenous soldiers (BPA 1860–1956:55). As a result, the fund incurred a loss of £4112 6s 6d between 1950 and 1955 (BPA 1860–1956:53). Despite this, the fund was £3684 5s 10d in credit at the end of 1955 (BPA 1860–1956:53, 1929–63:67; for amounts up to 1957, see BPA 1879–1957). The fund was abolished in 1957, with £3485 11s 11d in credit transferred to a newly established trust fund: the Aborigines Welfare Fund (BPA and AWB 1921–66:127–8).

The impact of World War II enabled a limited increase in employment opportunities for Indigenous people working off the reserves, including 'well paid share-farming' (Barwick 1981:200); however, these opportunities ceased at the end of the war. A 1946 BPA conference argued that 'the necessity of paying award rates' significantly restricted Indigenous employment (BPA conference, cited in Barwick 1981:202). Further, the Indigenous residents of Lake Tyers were usually the only Indigenous people in Victoria who received rations (Barwick 1981:203). This was a consequence of the continuation of the Victorian Government policy that stated that most Indigenous people of mixed descent were 'legally white, had "full civil rights" and could secure adequate aid from the resources available to ordinary citizens'—a policy that lasted until the end of the BPA era (Barwick 1981:202).

The *Child Welfare Act 1954* (Vic.) ensured that governments and their agencies would continue to control the wages of children. The Act empowered the Director of the Children's Welfare Department to compel an employer of a young employee 'under the guardianship of the Director' to pay a portion of the wage to the department and for these monies to be spent on their benefit 'as the Director thinks fit' (*Child Welfare Act 1954*, p. 160). These powers were also contained in the *Child Welfare Act 1958* (Vic.) (pp. 492–3) and the *Social Welfare Act 1960* (Vic.) (p. 211).

The 1957 *Report upon the Operation of the Aborigines Act 1928* (also known as the *McLean Report*) analysed the administration of Indigenous people in Victoria (BPA 1956–57; Broome 2005:312–16; Manning 2002:159–76). The report has been criticised for failing to adequately consult with Indigenous people (Manning 2002:171, 173–4). The report made a number of findings and recommendations that significantly influenced Indigenous affairs administration in Victoria. It found that racial prejudice from the wider Victorian community adversely impacted upon Indigenous employment, which in turn negatively impacted upon Indigenous living conditions (BPA 1956–57:11, 15; Broome 1995:149; PROV 2005:88). It also found that at Lake Tyers reserve, in addition to rations, 'the standard working week is of 34 hours, and the "wages" paid range from £1 10s to £3 per fortnight' (BPA 1956–57:12). In contrast, the report found that Indigenous people who worked off Lake Tyers reserve could earn £5 or £6 per day (BPA 1956–57:13). The report recommended the Government pass legislation that broadened the definition of Aboriginality to include 'any person having an admixture of Australian aboriginal blood' (BPA 1956–57:20). It recommended further legislation be passed that would enable regulations to be enacted regarding 'funds in the possession or control of the Board' and 'prescribing conditions of employment, other than payment, of aborigines' (BPA 1956–57:21). The report recommended that a new administrative structure be created to replace the BPA (BPA 1956–57:16, 19–20; PROV 2005:88). The report also recommended that legislation did not need to be developed concerning the removal of Indigenous children, as the *Child Welfare Act 1954* (Vic.) addressed this issue (BPA 1956–57:19; Haebich 2000:500).

The *Aborigines Act 1957* (Vic.) addressed the majority of the report's recommendations and created 'a new era of bureaucratic interventionism' (Broome 1995:150; Manning 2002:173; see also AWB 1957–59:1–31; BPA 1957:1–109). The Act created the Aborigines Welfare Board, defined an Indigenous person more broadly to include 'not only full-blooded aboriginal natives of Australia but also any person of aboriginal descent', defined the function of the Aborigines Welfare Board as being to 'promote the moral intellectual and physical welfare of aborigines…with a view to their assimilation into the general community', enabled regulations to be introduced regarding 'conditions of employment (including housing) of aborigines in any area', except for those conditions concerning industrial awards or determinations on employment, and dissolved the BPA (*Aborigines Act 1957*, pp. 489, 491, 493). The Act also created another Indigenous trust fund, the Aborigines Welfare Fund, closed the Aborigines Board Produce Fund and transferred all funds from the Aborigines Board Produce Fund to the new fund (*Aborigines Act 1957*, pp. 492, 494; see also Rylah 1956–57:346).

Conclusion

In this chapter, I explore a range of practices relating to stolen wages in Victoria during the BPA era (1869–1957). The practices discussed in the chapter involved the underpayment or non-payment of wages to Indigenous people, the employment controls imposed upon Indigenous people, the creation of Indigenous trust funds and the lack of accountability and poor governance of Indigenous affairs administration. These practices are analysed through examining government legislation, regulations and inquiries concerning Indigenous wages and employment.

These practices of stolen wages in Victoria that occurred during this period also largely happened throughout the majority of Victoria's history—from the earliest days of non-Indigenous people living in Victoria in the 1830s to the handover of Indigenous affairs administration to the Commonwealth Government in 1975.

The legacy of these stolen wages practices continues to significantly impact upon Indigenous people today, both in Victoria and throughout Australia. The abysmal historical and contemporary socioeconomic disadvantage suffered by Indigenous people in numerous areas—including health, income, housing and education—has been substantially influenced by stolen wages practices. Over the past decade, Indigenous people have been campaigning for the Commonwealth and State governments to genuinely address the impact of the stolen wages practices and provide compensation for the wages, savings and social security benefits that were never paid to so many Indigenous peoples. The appalling historical governance of Indigenous affairs agencies, however, seriously limits the capacity of activists and researchers to accurately determine the levels of compensation owed to Indigenous peoples. Further, State governments have so far generally been intransigent in genuinely providing reparative justice for those numerous Indigenous peoples affected by the stolen wages practices.

References

Attwood, B. 2003. *Rights for Aborigines*. Crows Nest, NSW: Allen & Unwin.

Aborigines Welfare Board (AWB) 1957–59. Acts and Regulations 1957–1959, Regulations [including drafts], Box 1, B357/2, National Archives of Australia, Canberra.

Barwick, D. 1981. Equity for Aborigines? The Framlingham case. In P. Troy (ed.), *A Just Society: Essays on equity in Australia*. Sydney: George Allen & Unwin.

Board for the Protection of the Aborigines (BPA) 1860–1956. Accountancy Files, Comparative Expenditure [Aborigines Board Produce Fund], B412/2, National Archives of Australia, Melbourne.

Board for the Protection of the Aborigines (BPA) 1877. Royal Commission on the Aborigines, B353/WHOLE SERIES, National Archives of Australia, Melbourne.

Board for the Protection of the Aborigines (BPA) 1879–1957. Census & Statistics, B313/247, National Archives of Australia, Melbourne.

Board for the Protection of the Aborigines (BPA) 1882. Report of the Board of Enquiry into Coranderrk Aboriginal Station, B352/BOX 1, National Archives of Australia, Melbourne.

Board for the Protection of the Aborigines (BPA) 1896–1907. Minutes of meetings of the Board, B314/5, National Archives of Australia, Melbourne.

Board for the Protection of the Aborigines (BPA) 1904–56. Accountancy Files Audit, B412/3, National Archives of Australia, Melbourne.

Board for the Protection of the Aborigines (BPA) 1909–11. Outward Correspondence, January 1909 – March 1911, No. 10, B329/8, National Archives of Australia, Melbourne.

Board for the Protection of the Aborigines (BPA) 1925. Report on the Lake Tyers Aboriginal Station, 19 August 1925, MS12913, Box 8, State Library of Victoria, Melbourne.

Board for the Protection of the Aborigines (BPA) 1929–63. Correspondence Re Acts and Regulations, 1929–1955, B313/3, National Archives of Australia, Melbourne.

Board for the Protection of the Aborigines (BPA) 1956–57. McLean Inquiry—1957 report: Aborigines Act [regulations; orders], B408/10, National Archives of Australia, Melbourne.

Board for the Protection of the Aborigines (BPA) 1957. Correspondence re Acts & Regulations, B313/4, National Archives of Australia, Melbourne.

Board for the Protection of the Aborigines and Aborigines Welfare Board (BPA and AWB) 1918–63. Board meetings [business sheets and minutes], B335/5, National Archives of Australia, Melbourne.

Board for the Protection of the Aborigines and Aborigines Welfare Board (BPA and AWB) 1921–66. Aborigines Board Produce Fund [from 1957, Aborigines Welfare Fund]—Collector's cash book, B2058/1, National Archives of Australia, Melbourne.

Board for the Protection of the Aborigines and Aborigines Welfare Board (BPA and AWB) 1949–58. General comments by manager (L. Rule and others) [Lake Tyers], B356/78, National Archives of Australia, Melbourne.

Broome, R. 1995. Victoria. In A. McGrath (ed.), *Contested Ground: Australian Aborigines under the British Crown*. St Leonards, NSW: Allen & Unwin.

Broome, R. 2005. *Aboriginal Victorians: A history since 1800*. Crows Nest, NSW: Allen & Unwin.

Broome, R. 2006. 'There were vegetables every year Mr Green was here': right behaviours and the struggle for autonomy at Coranderrk Aboriginal reserve. *History Australia* 3 (2).

Broome, R. and Manning, C. 2006. *A Man of all Tribes: The life of Alick Jackomos*. Canberra: Aboriginal Studies Press.

Campbell, A. and Vanderwal, R. (eds) 1999. *John Bulmer's Recollections of Victoria Aboriginal Life 1855–1908*. Melbourne: Museum Victoria.

Council for Aboriginal Rights (CAR) 1965. The Victorian Aborigines: the past, and its effect on the present minority. Decisions to be made for the future, Pauline Pickford, 1965, MS12913, Box 7/2, State Library of Victoria, Melbourne.

Critchett, J. 1998. *Untold Stories: Memories and lives of Victorian Kooris*. Carlton South, Vic.: Melbourne University Press.

Felton, P. E. 1960. *Methods Adopted by the Aborigines Welfare Board in Victoria. Proceedings of Conference on Welfare Policies for Australian Aborigines, 1960*. Armidale, NSW: Adult Education Department, University of New England.

Gunstone, A. and Heckenberg, S. 2009. *'The Government Owes a Lot of Money to Our People': A history of Indigenous stolen wages in Victoria*. Melbourne: Australian Scholarly Publishing.

Haebich, A. 2000. *Broken Circles: Fragmenting Indigenous families 1800–2000*. Fremantle, WA: Fremantle Arts Centre Press.

Harris, M. 1988. A 'new deal' for Victorian Aborigines 1957–1968. Unpublished Master of Arts thesis, Monash University, Melbourne.

Human Rights and Equal Opportunity Commission (HREOC) 1997. *National Inquiry into the Separation of Aboriginal Children from their Families.* Canberra: Human Rights and Equal Opportunity Commission.

Kidd, R. 2007. *Hard Labour, Stolen Wages: National report on stolen wages.* Dulwich Hill, NSW: Australians for Native Title and Reconciliation.

Manning, C. 2002. The McLean Report: legitimising Victoria's new assimilationism. *Aboriginal History* 26: 159–76.

National Archives of Australia and Public Records Office Victoria (NAA and PROV) 2008. *Footprints: The journey of Lucy and Percy Pepper.* North Melbourne: National Archives of Australia and Public Records Office Victoria.

Public Records Office Victoria (PROV) 2005. *Finding Your Story: A resource manual to the records of the Stolen Generations in Victoria.* North Melbourne: Public Records Office Victoria.

Rylah, A. 1956–57. Parliamentary Debates, Hansard Legislative Council and Legislative Assembly, No. 5, Aborigines Bill, 4/5/1957, MS12913, Box 28/3, State Library of Victoria, Melbourne.

The Senate 2006. *Unfinished Business: Indigenous stolen wages.* Canberra: Standing Committee on Legal and Constitutional Affairs.

Wampan Wages Victorian Stolen Wages Working Group (Wampan Wages) 2006a. Submission to Standing Committee on Legal and Constitutional Affairs, Melbourne.

Wampan Wages Victorian Stolen Wages Working Group (Wampan Wages) 2006b. Submission to Standing Committee on Legal and Constitutional Affairs, Questions on Notice, Melbourne.

Indigenous Enterprises and Employment Schemes

11. Between Locals: Interpersonal histories and the 1970s Papunya art movement

Peter Thorley and Andy Greenslade

Acrylic paintings from Australia's Western Desert have risen to prominence internationally since their humble origins at Papunya, NT, in 1971. Papunya holds a special place in the history of contemporary Indigenous art as the first acrylic painting community. For roughly a decade, however, from the time paintings were first produced, Papunya remained little known and the paintings went largely unrecognised both within Australia and overseas. The first decade of the movement has attracted much recent interest from scholars and observers of the art movement (for example, Benjamin and Wieslogel 2009; Berrell 2009). In its initial phase of development, the market was far smaller and more geographically restricted than today. There was no real secondary market as there is now with a multitude of dealers, auction houses and internet suppliers. Buyers were not investors and the paintings could be bought for prices very much below what they bring in the present market. During this period, there were relatively few players, which allows the early history of Papunya panting to be viewed from the perspective of key individuals and their shared experiences. These experiences are tied up in the buying and selling of the paintings and the behind-the-scenes negotiations that take place around each painting's production and acquisition.

Western Desert paintings today are generally bought by an anonymous buyer who has never met the artist. The paintings are understood and marketed in different ways—as souvenirs, primitive art or as contemporary fine artworks—but when they are bought through a commercial vendor there is little if any direct engagement between artists and buyers. Buyers are sometimes provided with documentation that identifies the artist, the title and a synopsis of the painting's content. As a result, people who otherwise have no relationship with the painter are able to gain an insight into the artist's connection to country, even though the deeper ritual significance of the painting might not have been revealed in the information given. While the sale of artworks can help to raise cultural awareness of the painting community, the way paintings are distributed through an elaborate network of intermediaries and marketed to the fine-art world as an act of individual creation tends to distance buyers from the role of the market and the collaborative process by which the paintings came into being. This, it can be argued, actively disengages those who purchase Indigenous art from the everyday experience of the artists.

Market dynamics are critical to a broader understanding of the history of Papunya painting. From the outset, the types of paintings produced, the choice of palette and the size of the artworks have been tailored to market tastes. The provisioning of materials with which to paint, the documentation of the artist's story and the negotiation of the amount to be paid to the artist are all events in the life of a painting before it reaches the market. The market depends on these collaborations between individuals. There is both intimacy and agency between the players involved. There are stories of power and trust and of dependent relationships and close friendships. Each painting has potential to shed light on these formative events yet the stories remain, for the most part, hidden. As a social history museum, the National Museum of Australia (NMA) seeks to collect and display objects that embody individual lives and the social processes in which they are enmeshed. From the moment they come into being, objects accumulate stories associated with their production and their participation in the everyday lives of people. There is often a genuine desire on the part of buyers of Aboriginal art to empathise with the painters and their communities but the social practices that underlie the painting's construction remain largely invisible to the intended audience.

In this chapter, we want to show the potential of what we are calling 'interpersonal histories' not only for elucidating art-market dynamics but also as a means of documenting the history of individual paintings and of the painting movement itself. Here we attempt to show how, particularly in the early years, artists were active in establishing and maintaining valued relationships through which they were able to exchange paintings for cash and other desirable items. The sale of paintings cemented relationships with whitefellas, who became, in a sense, owned. The relationships were investments and were quarantined from others, as we later illustrate.

Our emphasis on inter-subjectivity sits well with the National Museum of Australia's approach to history through personal stories and life experiences that run throughout the museum's galleries. The act of acquisition is a key moment in the history of an object and the National Museum recognises this in how it defines its collections by treating each acquisition as a separate collection even if they have a similar provenance. As objects pass through long and increasingly complex chains, we often lose sight of these formative moments. Indigenous collections represent a special kind of challenge. The National Museum of Australia has inherited a large collection of Aboriginal objects, many of which are products of a nineteenth-century view of material culture that emphasises classification and description of types. Objects were collected and displayed to illustrate discrete cultural types rather than as products of intercultural contact and exchange. Artefacts were often collected without accompanying information about the artist or the circumstances behind their acquisition. Even so, colonial relationships are very much embedded in the objects themselves. Before the development of outlets for the sale of Aboriginal arts and crafts, all artefacts were the products of direct exchanges between producers and consumers. The acknowledgment of the inter-relatedness of object history has seen the significance of many nineteenth-century collections—once rejected as having little information of value—now re-evaluated as social history. In contrast with collectors of the past, however, buyers of Indigenous art today rarely have the opportunity to meet the artist or develop any sort of relationship, and in this way the purchase of objects becomes a mediated contact or substitute for an actual experience. In a similar way, people who come to the museum are able to have an encounter with Indigenous culture through its collections. Museum displays bring audiences face to face with real objects in a physical and embodied space—an experience that can be contrasted with a digital encounter. Yet both experiences have the potential to be intensely depersonalising. Consequently, one of the challenges for museums—in a world where communication is increasingly mediated—is incorporating a sense of the personal and interpersonal into their collections and exhibitions. In developing collections of early Papunya painting material, the NMA has been actively seeking works that illustrate these kinds of stories.

Artefact Exchanges in Central Australia

A market for Aboriginal products in Central Australia developed after the completion of the railway from Oodnadatta to Alice Springs in 1929. The trade was built initially around wood-carvings, with the watercolour painting movement emerging at Hermannsburg in the late 1930s, both of which had an influence on the 1970s Papunya painting movement.

Papunya was established as a welfare settlement in the late 1950s. When Geoff Bardon arrived there in 1971, there already were established artists and carvers who were familiar with the market and the sale of artefacts to local non-Indigenous residents of the settlements and towns and also to passers-by. As a result of Bardon's collaboration though, a new product emerged.

By the 1980s, acrylic paintings had replaced wooden artefacts as the primary source of income for Aboriginal artists in Papunya. In 1986 when one of us (PT) came to work in Kintore, a Pintupi settlement that was set up as an outstation from Papunya, Papunya Tula kept a tight rein on the production and sale of canvases, and discouraged local non-Indigenous residents from buying directly from artists. Paintings were outside the price range of most local buyers and in four years in the community PT bought only a single painting. This was bought through the company and was a painting PT had seen on a trip to Kiwirrkura and liked, rather than a work by a close personal friend. On the other hand, a number of close friends from Kintore were often keen to sell wooden artefacts, and PT ended up with a collection of these that he did not particularly set out to acquire; in a way, Pintupi made him a collector. This local economy based on wooden artefacts was also a significant income spinner for women artists, who at that time were not represented by Papunya Tula.

During the 1970s, before Kintore existed as a community, the art market was still finding its feet. Papunya Tula operated within the Papunya community but there was a higher turnover of staff within the company. Paintings were sold for slightly higher prices than wooden artefacts. Artists in Papunya were producing large quantities of paintings that were difficult to sell in the Aboriginal Arts Board shop in Alice Springs and many were stockpiled by the Arts Board and offered for donation to museums and art galleries, who at that time were unconvinced of their value (Bob Edwards, Personal communication, November 2009). While Papunya Tula and the Aboriginal Arts Board bought and commissioned canvases, another economy operated at Papunya, between locals, where artists sold to non-Indigenous residents with whom they worked and interacted on a daily basis. This was in addition to the tourist market, when people brought works into town to sell, or painted while they were there and sold them to whoever would buy. Sales of this type would generate direct encounters, though generally these were brief. Although not wanting to dismiss the significance of tourist sales or the Aboriginal Art Board purchases, we want to focus on exchanges 'between locals', as we have put it. In this chapter, we illustrate an example of local exchange between Kaapa Tjampitjinpa, an important artist in the early history of the painting movement, and a non-Indigenous buyer, Gwen Daniels, who worked in Papunya from 1976 to 1977.

Kaapa Tjampitjinpa and the Papunya Art Movement

Kaapa Tjamptijinpa's role as an artist and innovator was central to the birth and early development of the painting movement that started at Papunya in 1971. Geoffrey Bardon says of Kaapa Tjampitjinpa that 'the Papunya [art] movement was built around his classic artistry and his compulsive will to paint' (Bardon 1991). In some ways, the history or progression of Kaapa's work can also be seen to mirror the development of the movement itself. Kaapa was a wood-carver and watercolour artist before the painting movement began and was one of the first to transfer ritual designs onto boards with paint after Bardon's arrival at Papunya in 1971. The NMA's collection includes *Goanna Dreaming at Mirkantji*—one of the first works to be exhibited publicly. A carving of a goanna and a watercolour painting are among the works held by the museum that illustrate his early participation in the market. The NMA also holds a selection of paintings by Kaapa from the 'Big Canvas' period when the acrylic movement relied heavily on Commonwealth support through the Aboriginal Arts Board. This makes the NMA's collection of 14 works by Kaapa from various periods in a range of media especially important and interesting. Of the 14 works in the collection, however, only one painting, *Kalipimpa Rain*, produced by Kaapa in 1976–77, has a clearly documented interpersonal history attached (Figure 11.1). This chapter now describes the circumstances around the creation of this painting and its place in the local economy of Papunya in the 1970s. The painting was bought by Gwen Daniels, and the following account is based on a 2009 interview with Gwen and her husband, Owen, who were both in their eighties.

Figure 11.1 *Kalipimpa Rain* (more commonly known as *Kalipinypa*) by Kaapa Mbitjana Tjampitjinpa, painted in 1976–77

Photo: Jason McCarthy, NMA.

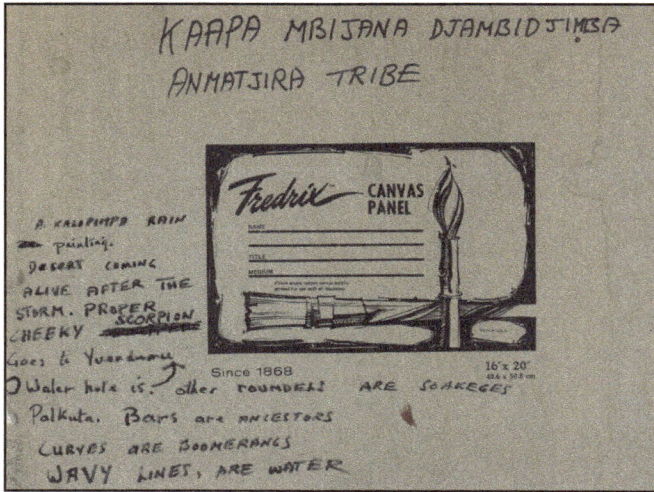

Figure 11.2 Reverse of *Kalipimpa Rain* by Kaapa Mbitjana Tjampitjinpa

Photo: Jason McCarthy, NMA.

Figure 11.3 Kaapa painting in the backyard of Gwen and Owen Daniels at Papunya, 1976–77

Photo: courtesy Gwen Daniels.

**Figure 11.4 Untitled painting by Kaapa Mbitjana Tjampitjinpa, 1984.
The purchase of this work, by Director, Don McMichael, was the first time
a Papunya painting was acquired by the National Museum of Australia**

Photo: Jason McCarthy, NMA.

Gwen and Owen Daniels went to Papunya in one of those serendipitous combinations of events that some take as meaning they were 'meant' to get there. Owen had suffered a number of heart attacks and expected that he had very little time left. They decided to use what time they did have travelling around the country, visiting outback communities, especially Aboriginal communities. During their travels, Owen's health returned to such a degree that they decided they would re-enter the workforce. Having spent a year travelling, Owen thought a job offered by the YMCA (the Y) looked appealing and he applied. He was accepted for the position of Recreation Officer for one of the Tiwi Island settlements. Owen's role was to provide options and activities for the youth of the community that could be an alternative to the growing use of alcohol.

Shortly before their departure north, they were contacted by the 'Y' to tell them that, although employed for the Tiwi Islands, they were in fact to ready themselves for a term at Papunya, where someone else had decided at short notice not to take up a position.

They arrived at Papunya to find no facilities for them, other than a house in less than perfect condition. Owen and Gwen, ever resourceful, fixed the house, then set about finding and repairing a building in which to base the recreational activities.

Gwen was given some part-time work at the women's centre, presumably for no other reason than because she was a woman. She had no training or expertise in production of fibre or the fabric work in which the women were working. Nor was her speciality in aesthetics.

At the women's centre, however, she met Kaapa. He often tried to gain entry to the centre, perhaps to access the resources for craft of one sort or another. Gwen found that if she spent time chatting with him outside on the steps, Kaapa would be satisfied and stop trying to get inside. The women inside found this rather amusing and instantly teased Kaapa as Gwen's 'boyfriend'—perhaps due to Kaapa's well-recognised succession of wives.

Gwen's lack of expertise in the art and craft arenas had implications in the transactions that would take place between herself and Kaapa. She would become a collector of his work and a supporter of the wider Papunya movement, though her intention had not been to gather so many examples of his paintings. What she did have that was of value, however, was faith in him and in their growing relationship. She found, as many before had also found, that Kaapa had a magnetic personality. When I was trying to explore this with her, Gwen could tell me only that he charmed her and everyone who came into contact with him. His nature shone out beyond all the other men at Papunya at the time. She also recognised that he could be a bit of a rogue, but that his character had a redeeming quality that kept Gwen and Owen true to him.

Gwen had time on her hands and she and Kaapa gradually developed a relationship of mutual advantage. Gwen recounts the moment she began to understand part of the nature of that relationship—though not as obviously as another colleague of ours who overheard her 'mother' angrily telling an interloper to 'clear off, this is MY whitefella'. She understood that an unspoken, formal relationship with him now existed that fitted both of their needs.

Johnny Warangkula (another of the original group of Papunya artists) had come to Gwen asking if she would buy some of his paintings only to end up in a fight with Kaapa, who was asserting his own right to have Gwen exclusively as 'his'. She became aware that part of her role with Kaapa was as his 'broker', his ready source of purchasing power and his sponsor. He was able to use her to shield himself against other white residents of the community, who from time to time would want him to paint for them but also wanted to bargain about the fee to be paid for his work. This effectively placed him at a remove from his patrons and placed him in a master-craftsman role, with his interests mediated by a third party.

In return, Gwen was afforded a place in the community: she was accepted in some more formal role within the structure of Papunya and she was also expected to fulfil the duties of that role. She gained some understanding of his work and some insight into 'why' and 'what' he painted. And she faithfully recorded the things that Kaapa spoke of in relation to specific paintings. She also received his friendship, which she valued highly.

This period coincided with a low-level presence of Papunya Tula at Papunya. In Gwen's understanding, to all intents and purposes, Papunya Tula did not seem to be operating. There was no-one representing the white organisational arm of the company; she saw no-one coming in to buy work apart from the occasional traveller; and no materials were being provided for the men to paint. Apart from Gwen helping Kaapa fill in his forms to keep him in government money, there was little that Kaapa could do to raise additional income in the community. And so Gwen would buy from the store in Alice Springs whatever materials she could that matched Kaapa's requirements. Often they would have fallen short of later Papunya fine-art standards, but at this period, she bought what she could—and this included the Frederix board on which *Kalipimpa Rain* has been made.

Gwen and Owen loved Kaapa and they were happy to give Kaapa the $30–50 he asked for his paintings, without questioning the figure. They trusted the value that Kaapa said he placed on them. From AG's conversations with the couple, they did not seem to relish the paintings aesthetically as much as the experience that underpinned the painting and the transaction between themselves and Kaapa. They also seemed to value the opportunity to give him assistance. As confirmation of this, many of the paintings Gwen acquired are still owned by her family, despite the need to put a few pieces to auction to supply an income for family necessities.

Kaapa, in return, sold to them what he called 'proper good one story'. When supplying paintings through his 'broker', however, for other people whom he held in lesser regard or with whom he did not have an ongoing relationship, he might be very happy to sell them the other sort of painting—the ones that he termed 'proper shit one'. Those might be produced for a more general, tourist market.

Gwen and Owen gave him physical care, too. They were happy to keep their freezer well stocked from the local abattoir for Kaapa and were ready to provide him with a variety of clothes, which Kaapa was well known to enjoy.

There was, however, clearly a line that Kaapa once crossed and which still gave Gwen enormous cause for laughter as she recounted the act that counted as 'a bridge too far' in Owen's mind. Kaapa was going to town, so they had found amongst some clothing a friend had sent them a black suit, white shirt and tie for Kaapa. They had bought him a new black hat from the store and Owen had donated a pair of Italian-made shoes. They also loaned the use of their bathroom for Kaapa to clean himself up and get dressed in his new outfit. What Owen had not intended to share with Kaapa was his last sharp razor blade, but when Kaapa emerged resplendent from the bathroom, sporting a pencil-thin moustache, Owen knew that the blade was no more.

Kaapa showed consummate knowledge and use of economic controls and mechanisms that ensured he was involved in sophisticated commerce. The arrangement he made with Gwen, and to a lesser degree with Owen, supplied him with a ready supplementary income and all the material benefits and controls offered by a contemporary art centre.

Kaapa took up residence in their backyard for use as his painting studio. It afforded him space and comfort in which to concentrate on his art production. There was grass to sit on; there was shade; there was a ready source of food; there were no children or dogs to provide those additional accretions that many paintings bear; and there was a supply of materials and a specific, reliable customer. And fortunately for the NMA, there was someone at hand to hear the story of the painting and to record it, to appreciate it and to care for it until its place in this collection was assured.

That the relationship was more than mere economics was proved some 12 or 13 years following Gwen and Owen's eventual move to the Tiwi Islands. In 1989, when Kaapa died, his family requested that the news of his death was sent to them. And the joy with which Gwen and Owen recall the man also indicates a lasting regard for him and an emotional connection between them all.

Conclusions

The Daniels' time at Papunya coincided with a time when Papunya was little known and art connoisseurs overlooked most of the paintings produced there. The painters, Papunya Tula and the Aboriginal Arts Board were all actively promoting their product in different ways but the market continued to languish throughout the 1970s. Small-scale transactions between artists and non-Indigenous employees living in communities helped to sustain the artists through the difficult times. With its elevation to fine art and its commercial success in the international arena, Papunya painting came to take on new meanings and paintings came to be displayed and reproduced in a wide range of contexts, in which their meanings shifted in subtle and often telling ways. The further removed from their original contexts the paintings were, both in time and in distance, the greater the potential for paintings to be inscribed with other meanings and values. One of the ways we can begin to redress this shift is to focus on works that show something of the local context in which they originated and acknowledge the act of acquisition as a key moment in an object's history. The relationships that grew around the painting movement were all important to its long-term survival. The Western Desert artists invested in social capital to achieve their own ends and to maintain a range of channels through which they were able to access the wider economy. The success of the Indigenous arts industry is testimony to the artists' ability to deliver desired outcomes for their communities. The artists and their descendants take great pride in these achievements, which are highlighted in local accounts of the history of the painting movement.

References

Bardon, G. 1991. *Papunya Tula: Art of the Western Desert*. Australia: Penguin.

Bardon, G. 2004. *Papunya: A place made after a story*. Melbourne: Miegunyah Press.

Benjamin, R. and Wieslogel, A. (eds) 2009. *Icons of the Desert: Early Aboriginal paintings from Papunya*. New York: Cornell University Press.

Berrell, N. 2009. Inroads offshore: the international exhibition program of the Aboriginal Arts Board, 1973–1980. *Recollections* 4 (1).

12. An Economy of Shells: A brief history of La Perouse Aboriginal women's shell-work and its markets, 1880–2010

Maria Nugent

Shell-work of the kind made by Aboriginal women at La Perouse in Sydney and in other communities along the NSW coast is not to everyone's taste. Indeed, it has long been described as kitsch or tacky, in part because for much of the twentieth century it was made and sold as a souvenir (Pakula 2007). Some of the most popular shell-work forms are heart-shaped, lidded trinket boxes and ornamental baby shoes (Figure 12.1), as well as the now highly collectible small-scale Sydney Harbour bridges (Figure 12.2). In some respects, La Perouse shell-work sits uneasily alongside other three-dimensional art and craft objects currently made by Aboriginal women in different parts of the country, such as the shell necklaces made by Lola Greeno and others in Tasmania that draw inspiration from pre-contact forms of female body decoration (Kleinert and Neale 2000:496, 698), or the coiled baskets and other fibre work that were recently celebrated in the national touring exhibition *ReCoil* (West 2007). Unlike these other contemporary art and craft objects, shell-work does not have a clear or certain lineage to 'traditional', pre-contact forms (McKenzie and Stephen 1987:179; although see Vanni 2000:402 for an argument about continuous practices); and there is not the same level of consensus about its aesthetic and artistic qualities among curators, taste-makers, collectors and scholars.

In some cases, La Perouse shell-work has recently become collectible precisely because it is considered kitsch, unusual or quirky (Hart 2003:14–16). For example, in four pieces made by (the late) Lola Ryan between 2000 and 2003, now held by the National Gallery of Australia (NGA), the artist has experimented with applying glitter between the shells in place of the shell-grit that earlier Aboriginal shell-workers typically used; dyed small white shells in bright, lurid colours, such as pink and green, for accent; and favoured fluorescent faux fur as backing instead of the traditional velvet, corduroy or satin (Figure 12.3). As Ryan notes: 'I always like to add a little glitter, that's my mark' (2003:13). These idiosyncratic developments in shell-work design are sometimes the result of collaborations between individual shell-workers and art collectors and curators. In the case of the pieces held by the NGA, the art collector Peter Fay had commissioned them from Lola Ryan for his celebrated collection of eclectic 'outsider art', and had worked collaboratively with her in producing them (Ryan 2003:13).

Figure 12.1 Shell-work baby slippers, maker unknown, La Perouse, New South Wales, 1952

Source: Powerhouse Museum, Sydney. Photo: Kristen Clarke.

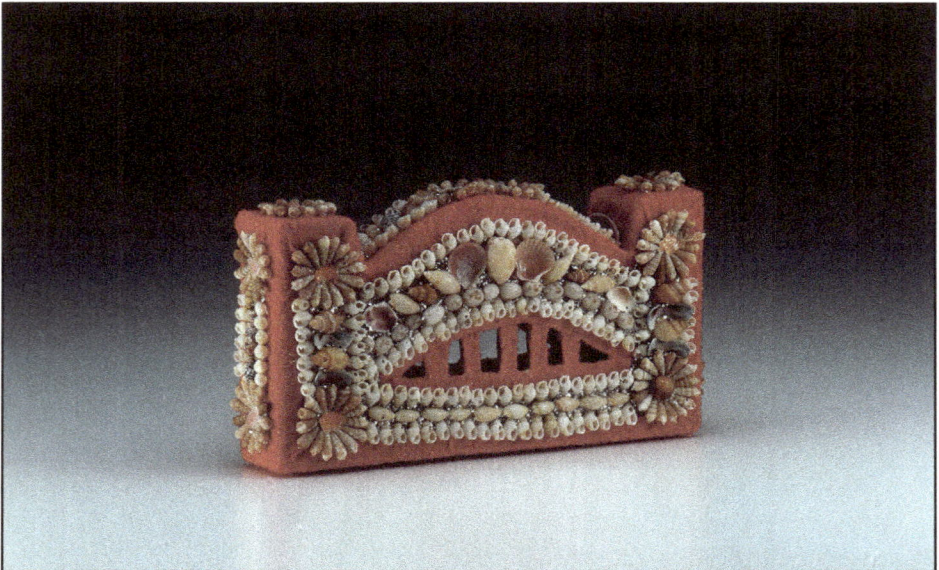

Figure 12.2 Shell-work Sydney Harbour Bridge, made by Mavis Longbottom and Lola Ryan, La Perouse, New South Wales, Australia, 1986

Source: Powerhouse Museum, Sydney.

Figure 12.3 Harbour Bridge, made by Lola Ryan, Dharawal/Eora people, La Perouse, New South Wales, Australia, 2000

Source: National Gallery of Australia, Canberra, Gift of Peter Fay 2005.

Not all contemporary pieces of La Perouse shell-work are quite as flamboyant as this. But much of it—particularly if made by one of the few remaining, long-practising shell-workers—has now become highly sought after and has, to some extent, acquired the status of art. As in the case of Lola Ryan's shelled harbour bridges in the NGA, this process has been helped along by art collectors and curators who have included La Perouse Aboriginal women's shell-work in exhibitions of contemporary 'urban' Aboriginal art, acquired it for public and private art collections and entered it into art competitions (Allas 2006:24–6). As though an endorsement of their collective efforts, in 2005 a blue-velvet, shell-encrusted model Sydney Harbour Bridge made by Esme Timbery won the inaugural Parliament of New South Wales Indigenous Art Award (Parliament of New South Wales 2005). Commenting upon this event, Aboriginal art curator Tess Allas claimed that 'no longer were [shell-works] mere souvenirs for tourism consumption…[They are] regarded as art objects worthy of discussion and collection' (Allas 2006:25).

The complex, and somewhat fraught, relationship between so-called 'tourist art' and 'high art' has been explored thoroughly in histories of Indigenous art in Australia and elsewhere (Finlayson 1990; Graeburn 1976; Morphy 1991; Myers 2002; Phillips 1998; Phillips and Steiner 1999), and it is not my concern to rehearse those arguments here. My more particular interest is in the accrual of new stories about Aboriginal women's shell-work as part of the process by which it is being ascribed anew as art, and especially the ways in which some recent accounts discount its previous value, including its economic value, to the women who made it. The North American art historian and curator Ruth B. Phillips has noted the ways in which the exclusion of tourist art from contemporary scholarly consideration and connoisseurship—disqualified apparently because of its hybrid, inauthentic quality—belies, and threatens to erase, its historical significance. She argues that it is important to study precisely for the evidence the objects themselves provide of 'aboriginal peoples' negotiation of Western artistic and economic systems' (Phillips 1995:99). Other scholars, such as Howard Morphy in Australia, have shown that the relationship between the tourist market and the fine-art market is not quite as distinct or discrete as is often suggested (Morphy 1991:10–38). These contexts are overlapping rather than opposed.

And so, I want to suggest that the situation in which Aboriginal women's shell-work now finds itself cannot be explained quite so simply or as straightforwardly by narratives that emphasise progress and development. A history of Aboriginal women's shell-work production from the late nineteenth century to the present clearly demonstrates that emergent narratives about shell-work's supposed liberation from the tourist market to the art world threatens to obscure more than it promises to reveal. Emphasising the aesthetics of these objects overshadows their earlier, more quotidian qualities, including their economic value to the women who made them. The new celebratory accounts of shell-work's development from tacky souvenir to art object rely upon staging a break between past and present: no longer mere souvenirs for tourist consumption; now artworks worthy of collection and discussion. But even a brief historical survey of shell-work and its markets shows that such a break is largely unsustainable.

This chapter traces some of the markets in which shell-work was sold prior to being embraced by the contemporary Aboriginal art market in Sydney (and other metropolitan centres) at the turn of the twentieth century. The period covered spans about 130 years. A long historical view that takes account of marketplaces, production methods, designs and forms reveals less a picture of discontinuity and disjuncture between what shell-work *was* and what it *is* now; rather, what emerges is some striking continuity over time. Throughout the history of its production by Aboriginal women, new, and sometimes surprising, markets regularly opened up for these commodities. Considered historically, then, the most recent putative transformation of shell-work into art object can be interpreted as yet one more instance of Aboriginal women's shell-work entering a new marketplace, appealing to a different cohort of consumers and acquiring additional meanings as it does so. Moreover, the ability of the few remaining active producers of shell-work to respond to this latest, unexpected assessment of its value and desirability as collectible art object should not be underestimated. That, too, has historical depth, as I hope to show.

As their shell-work circulated in a variety of marketplaces, Aboriginal women demonstrated an ability and acuity to negotiate 'changes in taste and market' (Phillips and Steiner 1999:9). Ruth B. Phillips and Christopher B. Steiner have argued that the capacity of Indigenous art and craft producers to react to market pressures has not always been recognised adequately in the scholarly literature. While this is no longer a criticism that can be easily levelled at studies of indigenous tourist art in many parts of the world, it remains true of historical studies of Aboriginal women's commodity production in nineteenth and twentieth-century Australia, particularly in the intensely settled south-east. This is borne out by the small, albeit growing, literature on shell-work. More emphasis tends to be given to the ability of Aboriginal women to maintain traditions and preserve knowledge (see Nash 2010; Vanni 2000) and less given to their responsiveness to the fashions and fancies of consumers. This is so despite evidence that across the many decades Aboriginal women have made shell-work, it was regularly modified to cater to the tastes of existing buyers or to appeal to new ones.

The relative absence of attention given to the market context might be due to the fact that most studies of Aboriginal women's shell-work production— or their production of similar kinds of craft objects such as feather flowers— in south-eastern Australia have emerged either from community or from art-historical studies. In those studies, themes of culture and identity are given more emphasis than economics. Indeed, in general terms, the economic value to Aboriginal women of making decorative objects expressly to sell has been little considered in Australian historical scholarship, including that of labour history. In the latter, most attention has been given to the services (rather than the commodities) that Aboriginal women provided in a colonial economy, such as domestic labour or sex (Curthoys and Moore 1995:20–9).

There are some notable exceptions (although few recent ones). Diane Barwick's work on the history of the Coranderrk settlement outside Melbourne is exemplary for revealing that the rush baskets and rugs that Aboriginal women (and some infirm old men) made for sale between the 1860s and 1880s were a vital source of income for the entire community—in some years, more profitable than men's participation in seasonal employment (Barwick 1974).

Barwick argued that not only was women's commodity production crucial to the settlement's viability in its early phase, but it also contributed to changes in gender relations. She argued that 'a major reason for the male station residents' increased willingness to treat their womenfolk as equals was their new economic importance' (Barwick 1974:54). Moreover, she suggested that this source of income influenced Aboriginal women's consumption patterns, allowing Aboriginal women to purchase 'luxuries' as well as necessities. Art historian Sylvia Kleinert is likewise attentive to the economic value of Aboriginal women's craft production in the early twentieth century in her study of Aboriginal art in south-east Australia (Kleinert 1994). Although her central concern is with art as a means of expression of Aboriginal identity in a colonised context, Kleinert also highlights the ways in which some Aboriginal women were able to use craft production—particularly of objects that white women desired, such as feather flowers and string purses made from water-rat skins—to enable them to live relatively autonomously, if precariously, in fringe camps on the edges of rural towns in Victoria (Kleinert 1994:155–8).

From the archival material available, which is mainly government reports, newspaper articles and missionary records, it is impossible to compile precise quantitative information about shell-work's contribution to the livelihoods of Aboriginal women and their families and communities. Only occasionally are the amounts of money made from the sale of shell-work mentioned. More common are assertions about its contribution to Aboriginal people's subsistence. For example, in a series of letters to the editor in the *Sydney Morning Herald* between 1902 and 1906, when the NSW Aborigines Protection Board threatened on repeated occasions to relocate the Aboriginal settlement at La Perouse to a more isolated site, the importance of the shell-work trade was repeatedly cited as a reason against the proposed move. Supporters of the La Perouse Aborigines argued that they should be permitted to remain where they were because their location allowed them to participate in a cash economy created by tourists and other visitors, which gave them a degree of economic independence and autonomy. 'For half a century', one letter noted, 'the natives have been allowed to occupy a small piece of land on the northern shore of Botany Bay, where they have established comfortable little homes, and are now able to make a few shillings by the sale of their shell work to visitors' (*Sydney Morning Herald*, 17 November 1906:17; see also *Sydney Morning Herald*, 9 November 1906:10). The writer noted anecdotally that 'I know of instances where expensive medicines, and other necessities, have been obtained by the proceeds of this work that would have been absolutely impossible otherwise' (*Sydney Morning Herald*, 17 November 1906:17). Another noted that 'not a small amount of money is obtained from the sale of shellwork' (*Sydney Morning Herald*, 13 November 1902:8), but does not quantify that claim.

While these public statements about shell-work emphasise the economic significance of the trade (and many more like them can be found), it should be noted that there is a plethora of statements preserved in the archival records, as well as within recorded oral histories of shell-workers, that suggest its contribution to Aboriginal women's livelihoods was at other times marginal at best (Nash 2010). Reconciling these conflicting assessments, and determining their respective historical specificity, requires further research. In the meantime, my approach in this chapter is to examine the markets through which these objects circulated at different times. Many markets are mentioned, some briefly, some in more detail, in archival material, particularly missionary records and newspaper reports. In taking this approach, I am influenced by Arjun Appadurai's observation that things have a social life. This 'conceit', as he calls it, helps to focus attention on the ways in which commodities circulated 'in different *regimes of value* in space and time' (Appadurai 2005:4, emphasis in original) as they moved in and out of markets—local, metropolitan, domestic and international.

The chapter is divided into three sections, each focusing on a distinct market. The first considers early reports that Aboriginal women originally sold their wares in Sydney streets and suburbs. In it, I speculate about the consumers of these commodities. In the second section, I discuss the influence of missionaries based at La Perouse in expanding the markets available to Aboriginal women shell-workers, which included both domestic and international ones. The final section considers the development and consolidation of a local market for these objects as visitors to La Perouse increased. I suggest this provided the conditions for the gradual transformation of shell-work into souvenirs for tourist consumption, which dominated the trade between the 1930s and 1960s. By shadowing shell-work as it moves in and out of these various marketplaces, something is revealed of its economic as well as its cultural, social and aesthetic values across time and place, even as its material form remained constantly recognisable.

Street Selling

By the opening years of the 1880s, certainly, and probably during the 1870s, if not before, the marketplaces for Aboriginal women's shell-work were the city's public streets and the suburbs' private homes. Reporting to the recently appointed NSW Protector of Aborigines in early 1883, the local policeman, Senior Constable Byrne, whose beat covered La Perouse on Botany Bay, stated that the Aboriginal women and girls living there contributed to the livelihood of their families 'by making shell baskets, which they sell in Sydney and the suburbs' (NSW Legislative Council 1883:315). It is one line in a longer report, but nonetheless contains a couple of illuminating details about the shell-work business.

First, it mentions that the objects made at this time were shell baskets. While there are no known surviving examples of shell-work made by La Perouse Aboriginal women from this period, shell baskets are described in many Victorian women's craft pattern books and magazines published about this time as well as in later histories of women's arts and crafts (Cochrane 1992; Isaacs 1987; Toy 1988). Shell baskets are essentially decorative items, perhaps used nominally for holding trinkets or as letter holders, so fit into the category that Ruth B. Phillips, historian of Canadian aboriginal women's art and craft production, refers to as 'tidies' (Phillips 1998:205–8). The Victorian era, she argues, was obsessed with orderliness and neatness, and so was the age of decorative containers.

Second, the policeman's report explains that the outlets for Aboriginal women's shell baskets were the city, where they were presumably sold by hawking them in the streets, and the suburbs, where they were probably sold door-to-door. In the middle to late nineteenth century, Aboriginal people living in and around Sydney survived mainly as mendicants, as Ann Curthoys (1982:32–3) has shown. This was the period, before the establishment of the office of the NSW Aborigines' Protector, in which there was an almost complete absence of organised social support for Aboriginal people, either from the state or from missionaries. In this context, the production and sale or exchange of commodities, such as shell baskets, which appealed to some Sydney residents, constituted a small component of Aboriginal women's precarious means of livelihood.

The policeman's report does not shed any light on who bought these shell baskets, and evidence is sparse on that matter. Nonetheless, some speculations can be made. Women's art and craft magazines from the period regularly included patterns for shell baskets and other ornamental objects (McKenzie and Stephen 1987:179). Jennifer Isaacs in her study of Australian women's domestic and decorative arts notes that it was a popular form of ornamental decoration (Isaacs 1987:166), and a few decorative pieces survive in museum and private collections (Logan 1998:66). Some early photographs of the interiors of Sydney houses reveal shelled items on display, although none that can be identified as having been made by Aboriginal women because their wares were likely to have been indistinguishable from similar objects made by non-Aboriginal women in the same period. Moreover, Isaacs notes that shelled objects, particularly small boxes, were sold commercially in this period, usually in coastal holiday places (Isaacs 1987:167). That there was a local shell-work industry in this period is further confirmed by reports that ornamental shell-work was being included in colonial industrial exhibitions, and claims that this contributed to greater demand for it. According to one report published in 1882:

> [I]n one of the colonies…the manufacture of ornamental shellwork formed part of its industry, and chiefly of the female industry. This manufacture was carried on to a very limited extent. An industrial exhibition was opened, and prizes were given, amongst other things for the best specimens of this ornamental shellwork…The result was very satisfactory. Orders came in to a very considerable extent from England and elsewhere, and created a great deal of sensation…and remunerative prices followed upon the increased demand—a demand which, I am sure, busied the hands, and I feel confident, lightened the hearts of many a struggling widow and her children. (*Mercury*, [Hobart], 27 June 1882:3)

Given this, it seems likely that the buyers for shell-work—whether made by Aboriginal women or other producers—were not fashionable Victorian women alone.

Nineteenth-century Sydney was a maritime city, and crews on mercantile ships are another plausible market for shelled objects. In suggesting this, Aboriginal women's shell-work warrants comparison with objects known as 'sailors' valentines' (see Fondas 2002). These were decorative shell mosaics, made of two hexagonal frames hinged together to form a box, which were made by local women in port towns in the Caribbean in the nineteenth century and earlier to sell to crews on visiting ships (Toller 1969:16–18). As Peter Cochrane notes, nineteenth-century Sydney was 'a little port city', with enterprise and activity centred on the wharves (Cochrane 2006:27). Grace Karskens paints a similar picture of Sydney, but one in which Aboriginal people are more visible. She describes Aboriginal men following the comings and goings of ships, working on the wharves or joining crews (Karskens 2009:425–32). The Aboriginal women and girls reported as making shelled objects in the 1880s were familiar with the wharves, especially around Circular Quay. At least some whom the policeman mentioned in his report had lived in the boatsheds there, before being forcibly relocated to La Perouse only a year or so earlier (Nugent 2005:46–7). This gives some sustenance to the idea that they had access to trade, formal or informal, operating around the wharves and boat sheds.

Missionary Markets

Throughout the closing decade of the nineteenth century and the opening one of the twentieth, the city and suburbs remained a prime marketplace for shell-work, and one in which Aboriginal people sold it to buyers directly. This is known to have been the case because when a new policy to make Aboriginal people pay fares on city trams was introduced in 1903, there was some outcry, with one opponent of the scheme writing that '[t]he Aboriginal people at La Perouse are in many cases, but half fed and clothed and they are to be still further impoverished by demanding from their already limited incomes (procured in some instances by selling shell-work, etc., in the city) fares for tram tickets' (*New South Wales Aborigines Advocate*, 30 June 1903:2–3).

The growing inaccessibility of the city's streets to Aboriginal people—a by-product of government efforts to spatially segregate Aborigines from white society (Goodall 1996:88–9; Nugent 2005:53–7)—allegedly threatened the shell-work business, but the emergence of missionary markets in this period provided some compensation.

Missionaries are a strong presence in the history of the Aboriginal shell-work business. It has been suggested that missionaries and church workers, particularly those who had spent time in the Pacific where shell-work production was common, were responsible for introducing the practice to Aboriginal women in a bid to assist them to become economically independent and industrious (McKenzie and Stephen 1987:179). For instance, in her work on Aboriginal shell-workers Jane and Olive Simms, Ann Stephen argues that '[t]he Methodist missionaries [at La Perouse] had formerly worked in Fiji and appear to have seen the potential for adapting South Pacific shellwork locally' (Stephen 1995). As an explanation of the *origins* of shell-work production among Aboriginal women at La Perouse, it is difficult to endorse this interpretation. The historical records suggest that they were already making shelled objects, such as shell baskets, before missionaries with experience in South Pacific mission fields took up permanent residence at the La Perouse settlement in the early 1890s (Telfer 1939). What is clear, though, is that missionaries were responsible for fostering and encouraging the practice, for providing contexts and conditions for its continuation, and, most importantly, for facilitating access to new markets for it.

In the opening years of the twentieth century, missionary and church outlets began to complement some of the existing markets for shell-work made by Aboriginal women. In addition to becoming part of a gift-giving economy that involved Aboriginal people and missionaries enacting and expressing relationships of obligation and reciprocity, Aboriginal women's shell-work was regularly included in missionary exhibitions, sometimes only for display, but often for sale. Within these contexts, the delicate shelled objects were presented as material evidence of the fruits of the missionaries' labour in encouraging Aboriginal women's assimilation. For instance, in 1903, the same year that the introduction of tram fares jeopardised its sale in Sydney's streets, Aboriginal women's shell-work was included in a display of 'the handiwork of the Aborigines in NSW' in a mission loan exhibition (probably the Church Missionary Society's

Loan Exhibition) held over a week at the Sydney Town Hall. This display—carefully choreographed—presented a melange of the material culture of 'traditional' ways of life (such as a 'native gunyah' and wooden implements such as boomerangs and spears) and contemporary manufactures (such as shell baskets) that had been produced under missionary tutelage (*New South Wales Aborigines Advocate*, 30 June 1903:3). The display, like all such mission displays, was as much about promoting the work of the missionary organisation active in Aboriginal settlements in New South Wales in this period, as it was about exhibiting objects made by Aboriginal men, women and children. A report on the exhibition tellingly captured this ambiguity, noting that the Aborigines' mission was grateful 'for the privilege of bringing under the notice of the public the work of our people' (*New South Wales Aborigines Advocate*, 30 June 1903:3).

In this same early twentieth-century period, missionaries also provided access to markets much further afield. In 1910, for instance, it was reported that La Perouse shell-work was included in an exhibition of Australian manufactures as part of the Girls Realm Guild Bazaar held in the Royal Opera House at Covent Garden in London (*Sydney Morning Herald*, 12 January 1910:5). According to one report, 'the Lady Rachel Byng and the Hon. Mrs. Schomberg Byng, were large purchasers, the latter buying the beautiful New Zealand cot blankets, and shell-work from Sydney, made by Queen Emma at the Aboriginal Camp at La Perouse' (*Australian Aborigines Advocate*, 28 February 1910:4). In this instance, as in many others, the shell-work made by Aboriginal women was included as part of a display of women's work, which also included items made by the white missionary women. The same report praises the 'beautifully designed post cards of Miss M. Oldfield, and the Water Colours of Miss Fry', two church-workers who lived at La Perouse and other Aboriginal settlements in New South Wales (*Australian Aborigines Advocate*, 28 February 1910:4). This is a quite singular account because it names not only the makers of things, but also the buyers, providing a rare glimpse of at least some consumers of these commodities. In this case, they are sisters-in-law from a prominent English church family, supporters of the Girls Realm Guild (Brewis 2009:765) and connoisseurs of women's domestic arts and crafts. Lady Rachel Byng, for instance, for a time owned an embroidery shop in London.

While Emma Timbery's shell-work was being bought in London, back in Sydney the same year (1910) other shell-work made by Aboriginal women at La Perouse and other parts of New South Wales was on display at the annual Royal Agricultural Show (RAS). There it was included as part of what was known as the Aboriginal Exhibit, which could be found in the Industrial Pavilion, although, as one newspaper article pointed out, 'in a quiet corner of it' (*Australian Star*, April 1910). In addition to shell-work, the exhibit included 'mats, and articles made by children attending schools on…mission stations' (*Australian Aborigines*

Advocate, 31 March 1910:1), as well as 'dilly-bags netted from various materials' (*Australian Star*, April 1910). Proceeds from the stall were reportedly £30 in total, but it is not clear how this money was distributed to the producers of the items sold. The report in the mission magazine simply noted that 'these exhibits being sold entirely for the benefit of the native people' (*Australian Aborigines Advocate*, 30 April 1910:6).

As was the case for the exhibition in London, at the RAS, it is clear from reports that Aboriginal women's shell-work was competing with shell-work made by non-Aboriginal people. Describing the La Perouse shell-work displayed at the Aborigines Exhibit, one journalist noted that 'by happy chance there is a stall quite near this one on which the shell work of English workers challenge[s] those of the black men [sic]' (*Australian Star*, 1910). Using the comparison to underscore his argument that the value of Aboriginal-made shell-work was the evidence it provided of the capacity for 'progress' of the makers of it, the writer claimed that the English-made examples are 'more advanced, for the shells are made up in the most perfect imitation of flowers. But the work of the aborigines is clear evidence of an attempt to cultivate the arts with some imagination, imitation and a sense of beauty—all of which go towards creating the highest culture' (*Australian Star*, 1910).

It was on aesthetic terms such as this that La Perouse shell-work was increasingly judged in this period, especially when it appeared alongside shell-work made by non-Aboriginal people. The following year, La Perouse women's shell-work (and bead-work) was once more on sale at a Girls Realm Guild bazaar, this time at the Sydney Town Hall (*Sydney Morning Herald*, 27 April 1911:7), and again it provided the basis upon which claims about the potential for education and improvement of Aboriginal women and girls were made publicly.

Local Traffic

In ways that overlapped and articulated with markets both near and far, there was always a demand for Aboriginal women's shell-work at La Perouse itself. Some of that trade came from the steady stream of visitors to the Aboriginal mission. According to one, perhaps exaggerated, report: 'Hundreds of people patronize the trams weekly in order to visit the little mission church, and see the results of the works amongst the people' (*Sydney Morning Herald*, 9 November 1906:10). Those numbers swelled for one week each year (initially in November, afterwards in January), when the mission held its annual convention. Aboriginal women took advantage of the situation by setting up shell-work stalls around the convention site, where they reportedly did 'a brisk trade' (*Australian Aborigines Advocate*, 30 November 1908:4).

In this same period, Aboriginal women's shell-work began to circulate in a local tourist market. That market had been growing as La Perouse on Sydney's periphery emerged as a metropolitan tourist site, tied to the city by the tram network (Nugent 2005:70–3). While shell-work's souvenir status is often emphasised in potted histories, relatively little attention is given to the ways in which Aboriginal women adapted their existing practices to cater more explicitly to a tourist market. Initially, the souvenir trade was dominated by Aboriginal men, who turned 'traditional' wooden objects into tourist objects by decorating them with iconography that would appeal to tourists and by performing the use of them (see McKenzie and Stephen 1987:179–81; Nugent 2005:79–83; Vanni 2000:400–2). Only gradually did Aboriginal women's shell-work come to be identified as a souvenir like the decorated boomerangs. That transformation happened by Aboriginal women making shelled objects in ways that borrowed from the iconography that Aboriginal men used on the wooden souvenirs that they made. For instance, while Aboriginal women continued to produce heart-shaped boxes, which reportedly remained the most popular line (Longbottom and Ryan 1986), decorative shelled objects in the shapes of maps of Australia and Sydney Harbour bridges, which were designs used to adorn tourist boomerangs, began to be produced (Figure 12.4). This development begins to occur from about the late 1920s and early 1930s onwards.

It seems that Aboriginal women were assisted by their male relatives in this process of turning shell-work into souvenirs. According to two sisters who were active shell-workers in the 1940s and 1950s: 'We had a father who was very clever at drawing things and you know, he used to do all the patterns for us' (Longbottom and Ryan 1986). This is suggestive of the ways in which the production of shell-work gradually came to take place within the context of Aboriginal families, with Aboriginal men and Aboriginal women as well as children working together. This mode of production contrasts with the earlier period, in which Aboriginal women and white women worked together to make shelled objects as feminine, domestic crafts rather than as souvenirs. Indeed, I want to suggest that critical to this development in the social life of shell-work, both in its production and in its sale, was the rise of individual Aboriginal family-owned souvenir businesses, such as the one operated by Joe Timbery and his family, which is a topic requiring further investigation and analysis. Moreover, whereas missionaries had previously occupied the role of 'agents', buyers increasingly assumed this function in getting shell-work into circulation, working on behalf of metropolitan department stores. As Gloria Ardler noted: 'My dad and mum and aunty had a little business going with their shellwork and boomerangs. They sold them to David Jones and sent work to Melbourne and even overseas' (Ardler 1988:39). Just as commonly, shop owners in the city bought stock directly from the makers (Longbottom and Ryan 1986).

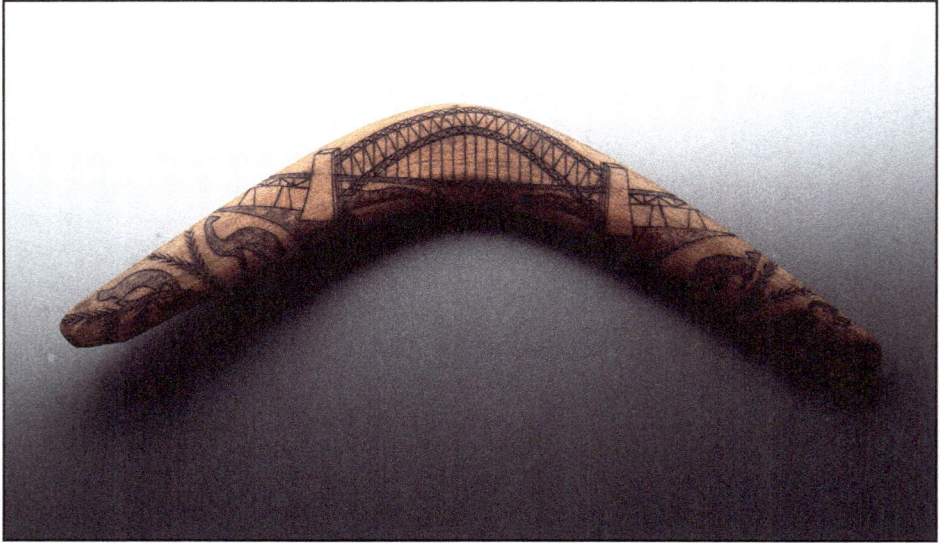

Figure 12.4 Boomerang, La Perouse Aboriginal community, New South Wales, Australia, circa 1935

Source: Powerhouse Museum, Sydney.

Conclusion

While it is not possible to measure with much precision the amount of income the shell-work trade provided to Aboriginal women, even the briefest of surveys of the markets through which shell-work has circulated over the past 130 or so years reveals that this commodity has been an enduring, if precarious, source of cash. Throughout this long period, Aboriginal women at La Perouse somehow managed to find a market for their handiwork on the city's streets and in the suburbs' houses, in metropolitan missionary exhibitions, in international charity fetes and in the industrial pavilion of local agricultural shows. It seems they had little trouble turning their skills to modifying their wares to cater to a tourist market emerging and expanding in their own backyard at La Perouse. These various markets for the same commodity overlapped. But it was as a souvenir that shell-work continued to be produced from the 1930s until the 1960s and 1970s, as the tourist trade became more important than earlier markets for it. Given this historical context, the recent marketing, production and circulation of Aboriginal women's shell-works-as-artworks appear less like a break with the past and more like a continuation of it. Art galleries, art collectors and art curators have joined the ranks of those who have, over the past 130 or so years, sought to acquire pieces. From the very outset, Aboriginal women produced shell-work as a commodity, and that has not changed as it has been taken up by the art world. Throughout this history, practising shell-workers negotiated the various markets available to them, even as the objects they made stubbornly retained something of the quality of a Victorian-era, feminine, decorative craft.

References

Allas, T. 2006. Esme Timbery. *Art Monthly Australia* (187) (March): 24–6.

Appadurai, A. 2005 [1986]. Introduction: commodities and the politics of value. In A. Appadurai (ed.), *The Social Life of Things: Commodities in cultural perspective*, pp. 3–63. Cambridge: Cambridge University Press.

Ardler, G. 1988. My grandmother and her family. In *La Perouse: The place, the people and the sea*. Canberra: Aboriginal Studies Press.

Barwick, D. E. 1974. And the lubras are ladies now. In F. Gale (ed.), *Woman's Role in Aboriginal Society*, pp. 54–7. Second edn. Canberra: Australian Institute of Aboriginal Studies.

Brewis, G. 2009. From working parties to social work: middle-class girls' education and social service 1890–1914. *History of Education* 38 (6): 761–77.

Cochrane, G. 1992. *The Crafts Movement in Australia: A history*. Sydney: UNSW Press.

Cochrane, P. 2006. *Colonial Ambition: Foundations of Australian democracy*. Melbourne: Melbourne University Press.

Curthoys, A. 1982. Good Christians and useful workers: Aborigines, church and state in NSW 1870–1833. In *What Rough Beast? The state and social order in Australian history*, pp. 31–56. Sydney: Allen & Unwin in association with Australian Society for the Study of Labour History.

Curthoys, A. and Moore, C. 1995. Working for the white people: an historiographic essay on Aboriginal and Torres Strait Islander labour. In A. McGrath and K. Saunders with J. Huggins (eds), *Aboriginal Workers*, pp. 20–9. Sydney: Australian Society for the Study of Labour.

Finlayson, J. 1990. Tourist art versus fine art. In J. Altman and L. Taylor (eds), *Marketing Aboriginal Art in the 1990s*, pp. 55–64. Canberra: Aboriginal Studies Press.

Fondas, J. 2002. *Sailors' Valentines: Their journey through time*. New York: Rizzoli.

Goodall, H. 1996. *Invasion to Embassy: Land in Aboriginal politics in New South Wales, 1770–1972*. Sydney: Allen & Unwin.

Graeburn, N. (ed.) 1976. *Ethnic and Tourist Arts: Cultural expressions from the fourth world*. Berkeley: University of California Press.

Hart, D. 2003. Home sweet home: an artist-collector's passion. In *Home Sweet Home: Works from the Peter Fay collection*, pp. 9–32. Canberra: National Gallery of Australia.

Isaacs, J. 1987. *The Gentle Arts: 200 years of Australian women's domestic and decorative arts*. Sydney: Lansdowne.

Karskens, G. 2009. *The Colony: A history of early Sydney*. Sydney: Allen & Unwin.

Kleinert, S. 1994. 'Jacky Jacky was a smart young fella': a study of art and Aboriginality in south east Australia 1900–1980. PhD thesis, Australian National University, Canberra.

Kleinert, S. and Neale, M. (eds) 2000. *The Oxford Companion to Aboriginal Art and Culture*. Melbourne: Oxford University Press.

Logan, J. 1998. *Everyday Art: Australian folk art*. Canberra: National Gallery of Australia.

Longbottom, M. and Ryan, L. 1986. Oral history interview, 26 November, Powerhouse Museum collection, Sydney.

McKenzie, P. and Stephen, A. 1987. La Perouse: an urban Aboriginal community. In M. Kelly (ed.), *Sydney: City of suburbs*, pp. 172–91. Kensington, NSW: UNSW Press in association with the Sydney History Group.

Morphy, H. 1991. *Ancestral Connections: Art and an Aboriginal system of knowledge*. Chicago: University of Chicago Press.

Myers, F. 2002. *Painting Culture: The making of an Aboriginal high art*. Durham, NC: Duke University Press.

Nash, D. 2010. From shell work to shell art: Koori women creating knowledge and value on the South Coast of NSW. *craft + design enquiry* 2 [not paginated].

New South Wales Legislative Council 1883. Report of the Protector of Aborigines, to 31 December 1882, Senior-Constable Byrne to Protector of Aborigines, 17 January 1883. *Journal of the New South Wales Legislative Council* 34, part 2.

Nugent, M. 2005. *Botany Bay: Where histories meet*. Sydney: Allen & Unwin.

Pakula, K. 2007. Shell bridge: the gap between kitsch and art. *Sydney Morning Herald*, 6 April.

Parliament of New South Wales 2005. *Parliament of New South Wales Indigenous Art Prize 2005*. Campbelltown, NSW: Campbelltown Arts Centre.

Phillips, R. B. 1995. Why not tourist art? Significant silences in Native American museum representations. In G. Prakash (ed.), *After Colonialism: Imperial histories and postcolonial displacements*, pp. 98–125. Princeton, NJ: Princeton University Press.

Phillips, R. B. 1998. *Trading Identities: The souvenir in Native North American art from the northeast, 1700–1900*. Seattle and Montreal: University of Washington Press/McGill-Queen's University Press.

Phillips, R. B. and Steiner, C. B. (eds) 1999. Art, authenticity and the baggage of cultural encounter. In *Unpacking Culture: Art and commodity in colonial and postcolonial worlds*, pp. 3–19. Berkeley: University of California Press.

Ryan, L. 2003. Shellwork: from bridges to maps. In *Steppin' Out and Speakin' Up*, pp. 11–21. Millers Point, NSW: Older Women's Network New South Wales.

Stephen, A. 1995. Jane and Olive Simms. *Dictionary of Australian Artists Online*. Viewed 22 December 2009, <http://www.daao.org.au/bio/emma-timbery/>

Telfer, E. J. 1939. *Amongst Australian Aborigines: Forty years of mission work— the story of the United Aborigines Mission*. Melbourne: Fraser and Morphett.

Toller, J. 1969. *The Regency and Victorian Crafts, or The Genteel Female—her arts and pursuits*. London: Ward Lock Limited.

Toy, A. 1988. *Hearth and Home: Women's decorative arts and crafts 1800–1930*. Sydney: Historic Houses Trust of New South Wales.

Vanni, I. 2000. Bridging the gap: the production of tourist objects at La Perouse. In S. Kleinert and M. Neale (eds), *The Oxford Companion to Aboriginal Art and Culture*, pp. 400–2. Melbourne: Oxford University Press.

West, M. 2007. Strings through the heart. In *ReCoil: Change and exchange in coiled fibre art*, pp. 13–27. Darwin: Artback Northern Territory Arts Touring.

13. Policy Mismatch and Indigenous Art Centres: The tension between economic independence and community development

Gretchen Marie Stolte

The concept of 'one size fits all' is an alluring one. It implies that no matter what an object's physical shape, there is a universal 'fit' that will suit. There is no big or small, no high or low; the one-size-fits-all model eliminates the need for the accommodation of difference. It is thus no surprise that the one-size-fits-all model would be the ultimate aphrodisiac for policymakers working in Indigenous affairs. This of course leads to real problems because, as many know, the one-size-fits-all model might work well within the average but poorly within the extremes. This chapter looks at a small section of a recent Australian Government report that focuses on a single model for Aboriginal and Torres Strait Islander art centres, and critiques that model as something counterproductive and ultimately destructive for the health of the communities involved in arts production.

The Report

In August 2006, the Senate Standing Committee on Environment, Communications, Information Technology and the Arts (hereinafter the Report) began an inquiry into and report on the Indigenous visual arts and craft sector. The purpose of this inquiry was to establish

1. the current size and scale of Australia's Indigenous visual arts and crafts sector;

2. the economic, social and cultural benefits of the sector;

3. the overall financial, cultural and artistic sustainability of the sector;

4. the current and likely future priority infrastructure needs of the sector;

5. opportunities for strategies and mechanisms that the sector could adopt to improve its practices, capacity and sustainability, including to deal with unscrupulous or unethical conduct;

6. opportunities for existing government support programs for Indigenous visual art and crafts to be more effectively targeted to improve the sector's capacity and future sustainability; and

7. future opportunities for further growth of Australia's Indigenous visual arts and craft sector, including through further developing international markets. (SSCECITA 2007a:1)

As illustrated in the number of references, the concept of sustainability was an important one for the committee. As will become evident, however, implied within ideas of sustainability are issues of economic independence from government funding. This implication is made apparent in the Report's association of success with the amount of funding an art centre receives from the Government: an art centre is successful if it is financially independent from Commonwealth funding and, therefore, unsuccessful if it is receiving such funding. The committee then mentioned two (of the 110) art centres that achieved such 'success'.

On Wednesday, 21 February 2007, the Senate Report held a hearing in Alice Springs, NT, to hear from stakeholders within the Indigenous arts and craft sector. When talking with the Manager of Papunya Tula, Paul Sweeney, Chairman Eggleston stated:

> I love the fact that you are not getting any government money...At the same time, you are doing that community development work, and I acknowledge very clearly that the art centres do that community development work. It is not just an art area; it is a community development area as well. But you seem to be doing the same and you are doing it all without a cent of government money. Why isn't your model the right model for everyone? (SSCECITA 2007b:10)

Sweeney's response was understandably vague, stating that his experience was limited to Papunya Tula only and that he could not speak for other art centres (SSCECITA 2007b:10). Eggleston's assumption that 'you seem to be doing the same' reflects his lack of knowledge of local art histories that created the Central Desert art movement and Papunya Tula's success, but also exemplifies how the Chairman equated Papunya Tula's on-the-ground involvement with other art centres. Is the Papunya Tula model the right model for everyone? Can there be a single, one-size-fits-all model for Indigenous art centres so the flow of government money is no longer needed or required? Should that even be the goal? It is necessary to outline some of the definitions, functions and roles of art centres in order to highlight the diversity as well as the challenges facing these institutions. Before doing so, I would first like to set the framework through which it is most beneficial to view an art centre.

Defining an Aboriginal Art Centre Cross-Culturally

Howard Morphy writes that anthropology by definition is a 'form of cross-cultural discourse [that] establishes equivalences through the creation of cross-cultural categories' (Morphy 2008b:8, 9). Some examples of cross-cultural categories include religion, kinship, marriage, land rights and artistic practices. The challenge of a cross-cultural definition is to 'allow what was and is different…to remain despite its placement within a more inclusive category' (Morphy 2008b:3). Morphy warns against taking the concept too far, writing that some categories are more limited than others and universalisms must 'always be open to question' (Morphy 2008b:7). I argue that art centres need to be treated as a cross-cultural category—to recognise what was and is different—and that the Senate Report does little to develop such distinctions. This lack of critical awareness is evident throughout the Report, as what is different about an Indigenous art centre is subsumed into broad definitions regarding general business practices.

Seeing art centres as cross-cultural categories is to go beyond an art centre as an arm of the arts industry. A cross-cultural art centre category allows for art centres to also go beyond being simple service providers. Although certainly not true for all art centres operating in Australia, some art centres have become the cultural hub of a community where the continuation of language, traditions and ceremonies is renewed, reinvented and put on display.

The cross-cultural category of 'art centre' is not a universal one and must be understood in both a Western framework and an Indigenous one. Associating the success of an art centre with its level of government funding is tantamount to defining success in such a narrow framework as to ignore the numerous activities in which an art centre engages. So what is an Indigenous art centre?

Indigenous art centres are defined in many different ways. The Senate Report defines an art centre as 'an Indigenous owned and operated entity, generally located on an Indigenous community' (SSCECITA 2007a:27). The Australia Council for the Arts (2007) defines a community art centre as a creator of 'bridges of understanding, regeneration and opportunity', but definitions of an Indigenous art centre can also vary according to their functions and obligations. In *The Art & Craft Centre Story*, Felicity Wright defines an art centre as 'any organization operating in remote Australia that is owned and controlled by Aboriginal people, where the principal activity is facilitating the production and marketing of arts and crafts' (1999:7). Wright's definition focuses on the commercial aspect of an art centre, but the rest of her report does much to describe the socio-cultural aspects as well. The Association of Northern, Kimberley and Arnhem Aboriginal Artists (ANKAAA) defines an art centre's roles as a protector of cultural property, as a resource for materials and as a general arts and culture facilitator. Finally, most definitions of art centres emphasise that art centres are located on country where opportunities for Indigenous people are limited.

DesArt, the Association of Central Australian Aboriginal Art & Art Centres, outlines the seven roles of an art centre: as a place for cultural maintenance, as a place of emotional and personal renewal, as a place of work and earning income, as a distributor to markets, as an avenue for strengthening the community, as a place of learning and as a place of respite and care (SSCECITA 2007a:30). DesArt is also quick to point out the many other services provided beyond art production and marketing. The social benefits include: a safe place to meet and talk, a place for help in filling out government forms, accessing the Internet, finding a ride to another community, and allowing space in which youths can engage in cultural activities (SSCECITA 2007a:30). Another key benefit and service provided is cultural maintenance for which art centres are a 'significant contributor in sustaining a cohesive and socially healthy community' (SSCECITA 2007a:32). A recent conversation I had with one of the leaders of the art centre in New Mapoon, located on the Cape York Peninsula in Queensland, stressed not only the economic benefits of being able to sell their artwork but also the benefit of publicly displaying the artefacts and works that have taken on community-wide cultural significance (New Mapoon Art Centre, Personal communication, 29 June 2010). In places such as New Mapoon, artworks become a source of community pride and are displayed and cared for in order to maintain a strong cultural identity.

As might be becoming clear, art centres do more than just art production—or they at least can do more, if given the space to do so. Given the diversity of Aboriginal communities across remote Australia, one cannot define an art centre based on a single definition. The Department of Communications, Information Technology and the Arts (DCITA) recognises this reality. DCITA states that 'some art centres operate as highly successful enterprises while others have more of a community arts development focus' (SSCECITA 2007a:33); in other words, some art centres are more industry based while others are more service based. The juxtaposition of a 'highly successful enterprise' with and even against the 'community arts development focus' is an important one. Within DCITA's statement exists the crux of the problem in desiring a single art centre model. Which one of the art centres is the one to be modelled after? This is especially problematic in the arts industry where fads and trends can dictate success as much as hard work and sound business practice. If art centres can be defined in so many different ways, how feasible is it to develop a single business model?

With a strong idea of the variety of different functions and objectives art centres occupy in general, it is beneficial to compare two art centre models in order to appreciate how complicated the desire for a single model can be. I have chosen Papunya Tula Artists (PTA) and Maningrida Arts & Culture (MAC) as the two models to compare based on their differences in structure and their similarities in success. This comparison illustrates how their different levels of and approaches to their engagement with their prospective communities will form the basis of a discussion on how focusing on 'economic independence' is problematic at best. More importantly, this comparison only uses information taken directly from the Report and its submissions as an example of how the Senate sees differences between art centres versus how that information was put to them. Afterwards, I will put forward some considerations the Report did not include and, in this way, hope to draw out how the Report conceptualises an art centre in its search for a one-size-fits-all model.

Two Models: PTA and MAC

Papunya Tula Artists (PTA) is an arts organisation owned and operated by Aboriginal artists comprising Luritja and Pintupi language groups (PTA 2007:1). PTA supports 160 artists in three communities—Papunya, Kintore and Kiwirrkura—and, at the time of the Report,functioned with nine full-time and two part-time staff and a fleet of four Toyota Troop-Carriers. The company is self-funded and has been without government support for more than 10 years. The aim of the PTA is 'to promote individual artists, provide economic development for the communities to which they belong, and assist in the maintenance of a rich cultural heritage' (PTA 2007:1). PTA's community involvement work includes helping to raise more than $900 000 for a swimming pool in the Kintore community and, from 2000 to 2007, donating more than $1 million towards a remote renal dialysis unit and associated programs (PTA 2007:2).

PTA's approach to its artists is fundamental to its success. The Troop-Carriers are used to deliver canvas and art materials to the communities where the artists execute their work on country (SSCECITA 2007c:8–9). PTA states that it is committed to its artists and admits to 'being very fortunate in that there is a great deal of natural talent in the area where we work' where 'basically, it comes back to a very good product which compares well on the market' (SSCECITA 2007c:8).

In comparison, Maningrida Arts & Culture (MAC) is located in central Arnhem Land and is one of the oldest Aboriginal art centres in Australia, supporting 790 artists in more than 34 outstations (SSCECITA 2007b:42; MAC 2007:1). MAC has a 'total acquisition policy', which means that the art centre buys all works presented to its doors. As stated in their submission to the Senate Report, this practice 'creates certainty and security for artists, ensures that their work is treated with respect, encourages the career of young and emerging artists and provides an income to ageing artists who are no longer producing their best work' (MAC 2007:1).

Figure 13.1 Maningrida Art Centre, 2005

Photo: By the author.

MAC has 10 full-time staff, with the National Arts and Crafts Industry Support (NACIS) program funding the salaried positions, and with six Aboriginal staff under the Community Development Employment Projects (CDEP) scheme (MAC 2007:2). During the financial year 2005–06, MAC's turnover was $1.7 million, with $1.1 million given directly back to the artists (SSCECITA 2007b:42). In addition to buying and selling art, MAC engages in many cultural maintenance activities such as: the production of dictionaries and musical recordings, preserving community archives, supporting researchers and students, and more than 20 exhibitions across Australia and the world (MAC 2007:2). MAC is also one of the largest employers of Aboriginal people within its region (MAC 2007:1).

Two Models: The comparison

If economic independence from government funding is the most desired trait in an art centre, why is PTA not the model for all art centres? In summing up the committee's view on the success of art centres, it is clear PTA was held up as one of the models for success. The Report states that, along with the Jirrawun Arts Corporation, 'these organisations currently require no government support, while delivering significant benefits to their communities' (SSCECITA 2007a:47). The committee recommended that an understanding of these organisations will help 'identify potential pathways for success of Indigenous arts business' (SSCECITA 2007a:47). Moreover:

> The committee is aware that there is a range of views about how art centres should do business, but it appears clear that one of the secrets to Papunya Tula's commercial success has been its *aggressive and disciplined approach* to the market, a well as its careful nurturing of long-term relationships with artists. (SSCECITA 2007a:48, emphasis added)

What should become apparent, however, are the major differences between MAC's engagement with its community and PTA's engagement. How does an 'aggressive and disciplined approach' translate into community development and involvement? Where does New Mapoon's desire for a cultural space come into play? If one were to compare dollars donated or large-scale projects funded, PTA would be the ideal model; the Report demonstrates quite clearly the amount of money PTA donates back into the communities. Furthermore, MAC's 'total acquisition policy' is not without its drawbacks. Sometimes, MAC acquires material that is hard to turn around and sell. For example, there can be an over-abundance of fibre work and beaded jewellery. So what are the benefits of a MAC model?

First, PTA's funding and financial successes are based on circumstances that border on the serendipitous. Papunya Tula, as Sweeney as stated, does have extraordinary talent—or at least extraordinarily *marketable* talent. The 2007 show at the National Museum of Australia (NMA) *Papunya Tula: Out of the desert* showcased this (NMA 2007b). NMA states that 'Central and Western Desert artists at Papunya, in Australia's Northern Territory, created a body of work that transformed understandings of Aboriginal art' (NMA 2007b). This type of internationally acclaimed cultural transformation does not happen more than once if it happens at all. As Peter Thorley and Andy Greensdale have demonstrated in their chapter (Chapter 11, this volume) on the importance of the interpersonal in creating a viable art market, there are many mitigating circumstances to an art centre's success.

Building models on circumstances such as those at Papunya is really to look at a unique situation—one that cannot be expected to be replicated. Thinking otherwise is to ignore the unique historical underpinnings of Aboriginal art's success. It is to ignore local art histories and the great variation of Indigenous art theories and practices. As Howard Morphy writes regarding the success of Yirrkala bark paintings, there was a tenuous thread that connected the events and collectors that produced a viable art market in Yirrkala (Morphy 2008b:58). Acknowledging art centres as a cross-cultural category includes recognising those local art histories and complexities, which give rise to the many different Aboriginal art centre models that exist in Australia and also the different levels of success.

Finally, the community work of PTA is not the same as the community work of other art centres such as MAC. Papunya Tula Artists Proprietary Limited is a corporation, not a community art centre. PTA might be involved in community development, but, swimming pools and medical equipment aside, it is not the same type of community involvement in which MAC engages. It is not just a matter of scale, priorities or resources. It is all of those things. The cultural archiving, the support of researchers and students, the production of dictionaries and the recordings of music are a few examples of the level of the cultural maintenance and community involvement of MAC. Above all, PTA supports and sponsors 160 artists whereas MAC supports almost 800 artists. Maningrida's total acquisition policy involves more Aboriginal people in the arts development program and stretches the centre's resources across a broader region. If MAC were forced to be more 'economically responsible', one of the first changes would have to be to their acquisition policy. This means less people involved in the arts, less communication of cultural knowledge and less stability for Aboriginal communities. In addition, being more critical of acquisition does not guarantee greater financial success, only the decrease of involvement of Aboriginal artists in the market.

Importantly, let me make it clear that I am not proposing one model over another. PTA and MAC have different arenas of success and different priorities. One is not better than another. It is because of this difference—the difference of all Indigenous art centres across Australia—that it is problematic to choose one art centre model over another. If a choice has to be made, it should be for the model that works for that community.

As Wright acknowledges in her report's summary, 'Aboriginal community art and craft centres are not conventional businesses. They operate in communities where educational, enterprise, and employment opportunities are extremely limited, and they fulfil important sociocultural and training functions in addition to their commercial activities' (Wright and Morphy 1999:5). These socio-cultural functions would be jeopardised if art centres such as MAC were modelled on art centres such as PTA—being more 'aggressive and disciplined' over other priorities MAC and its communities have chosen or might choose to pursue. Wright notes the objectives of art centres are not fixed and are an amalgam of cultural and commercial enterprises (Wright and Morphy 1999:6). This is one of the reasons that recognising an art centre as a cross-cultural entity and not strictly a Western institution simply located on Aboriginal land is so important.

Further, the Report does not address many of the messy issues that exist within the arts industry. For example, what are the contractual agreements between artists and art centres? Are there exclusivity clauses that bar artists from exhibiting elsewhere and thus potentially reduce outside sources of income? Can anyone located on country have access to art centre materials and resources? Do you *have* to live on country? How are the businesses structured, and how are the administration systems set up? Who is on the board, who can be on the board and how much power do those people have to change existing structures and systems? How much creativity are the artists allowed or are the canvas sizes and paint colours dictated by unseen managers? The Australian Indigenous art sector is a highly politicised and volatile arena and yet none of those aspects made it into the Report with regards to how art centres are run or structured. The search for a one-size-fits-all model was a sanitised and misdirected endeavour at best.

Conclusion

The Report acknowledges that 'art centres have two key cultural roles: they facilitate the *maintenance* of Indigenous culture within the community, as well as facilitating the *transmission* of that culture to the world beyond the community' (SSCECITA 2007a:30, original emphasis). In addition, the 'maintenance of cultural practice is also recognised by the [art centre's] community as a significant contributor in sustaining a cohesive and socially healthy community' (SSCECITA 2007a:32). Despite recognising the importance of the relationship an art centre has with its host community beyond art production, the three major recommendations the Report makes with regards to funding do not. Turning to these recommendations, they are as follows.

Recommendation 5

4.77 The committee supports the roles of DEWR [Department of Employment and Workplace Relations] and Indigenous Business Australia [IBA] programs in assisting where appropriate the transition to economic independence for art centres, and recommends that these initiatives be further promoted by DEWR and IBA and utilised by art centres.

Recommendation 6

4.78 The committee recommends that the Commonwealth further expand funding under the existing NACIS scheme and consider revising its guidelines to confine its use to non-infrastructure projects.

Recommendation 7

4.79 The committee recommends that the Commonwealth consult with stakeholders in the industry, particularly DesArt and ANKAAA, on reforms to NACIS funding criteria, so that funding decisions are guided in part by the aim of ensuring operation of art centres in accordance with best practice principles. These standards may include (but not be confined to):

- staffing requirements that meet the operational needs of art centres, and ensure flexibility to accommodate any particular requirements of such centres;
- governance and reporting systems; and
- training commitments, including financial, management and art education components.
(SSCECITA 2007a:50–1)

First and foremost is the recommendation to provide help to move art centres towards economic independence. The underlying assumption here is that it is only a matter of time before an art centre is economically independent, and it is simply a matter of proper education and infrastructure before that happens. Second, the recommendation asks for consideration in help in funding for 'non-infrastructure' projects and/or the flexibility to 'accommodate any particular requirements'. Are these the terms that are to be defined as those schemes that aide in cultural continuity and social cohesion? In the end, it seems that the recommendations, as extensions of the Report's understanding of this sector, do little to encourage general community involvement or support practices for cultural continuity and exchange as those concepts are subsumed under 'best-practice principles'. This is highly disappointing as the Report does make a good effort at illustrating the many different ways an art centre can be defined and their subsequent roles.

This chapter aimed to critically engage with the 2007 Senate Report into the Indigenous art sector and question the need for a single art centre model while arguing that art centres need to be understood within a cross-cultural category. Such recognition would not only require keeping the nuanced definitions regarding what an art centre is, what it should do and its priorities but would also expand the inquiry into the complex business structures and problems that exist. Morphy states that 'the distinctive art styles associated with different community art centres are in part the product of local art histories: people working together in a community and creating works that express their contemporary regional identity' (2008b:11). Seeing art centres as a cross-cultural category—needing to be defined as neither wholly Indigenous nor wholly mainstream—is important with regards to an arts policy and subsequent funding decisions. This is in part because there are so many different art centres, reflecting their different communities. Horribly absent from this report are the voices of the Indigenous artists who participate in and enjoy the benefits of art centres. Where are the on-the-ground stories? I have had the opportunity to ask some artists about their engagements with art centres and the reasoning focuses on cultural maintenance first and economic benefits last. Where is this understanding, this voice, in the Senate Report? It is in finding this voice that Morphy's cross-cultural category is an appealing model for researching the Indigenous arts sector because it demands perspectives from both Indigenous and non-Indigenous participants.

This volume is about Indigenous participation in the Australian economy. To make a business economically independent and sustainable (and this is no small feat), Papunya Tula's 'aggressive and disciplined' approach is admittedly necessary. Given the huge amount of community involvement most art centres engage in though, any aggressive and disciplined approach would jeopardise the art centre's ability to function in a healthy socio-cultural capacity. Art centres are engaged with so much more than just art 'production' and yet are continually under government pressure to be self-funded. In investing in art centres, the Government must take into account what the art centre does and does not do in policy's expectations of economic independence. Funding must take into consideration levels of community involvement in which the Commonwealth is not participating or present but which are extremely important to Indigenous participants. Aboriginal and Torres Strait Islander community art centres must not be viewed through the same lens as a mainstream business located in downtown Sydney. Art centres are so much more than just businesses and that needs to be recognised. In this case, one size does not fit all.

References

Altman, J. 2003. *Developing an Indigenous arts strategy for the Northern Territory: issues for papers in consultations*. CAEPR Working Paper No. 22/2003, Centre for Aboriginal Economic Policy Research, Australian National University, Canberra. Viewed 10 April 2008, <http://www.aph.gov.au/senate/committee/ecita_ctte/completed_inquiries/2004-07/indigenous_arts/submissions/sub11a.pdf>

Altman, J. 2007. Submission to the Inquiry into Australia's Indigenous Visual Arts and Craft Sector. Submission 11. Viewed 10 April 2008, <http://www.aph.gov.au/senate/committee/ecita_ctte/completed_inquiries/2004-07/indigenous_arts/submissions/sub11.pdf>

Association of Northern, Kimberley and Arnhem Aboriginal Artists (ANKAAA) 2007. Submission to the Inquiry into Australia's Indigenous Visual Arts and Craft Sector. Submission 63. Viewed 10 April 2008, <http://www.aph.gov.au/senate/committee/ecita_ctte/completed_inquiries/2004-07/indigenous_arts/submissions/sub63.pdf>

Australia Council for the Arts 2007. *The Arts: Community arts*. Viewed 5 June 2008, <http://www.australiacouncil.gov.au/the_arts/community_arts>

Maningrida Arts & Culture (MAC) 2007. Submission to the Inquiry into Australia's Indigenous Visual Arts and Craft Sector. Submission 51. Viewed 10 April 2008, <http://www.aph.gov.au/senate/committee/ecita_ctte/completed_inquiries/2004-07/indigenous_arts/submissions/sub51.pdf>

Morphy, H. 2008a. Acting in a community—art and social cohesion in Indigenous Australia. *Humanities Research* XV (2).

Morphy, H. 2008b. *Becoming Art: Exploring cross-cultural categories*. Sydney: UNSW Press.

National Gallery of Australia 2007. *Annual Report 2006–07*. Canberra: National Gallery of Australia. Viewed 3 June 2008, <http://www.nga.gov.au/AboutUs/Reports/AR07>

National Museum of Australia (NMA) 2007a. *Annual Report 2006–2007*. Canberra: National Museum of Australia. Viewed 3 June 2008, <http://www.nma.gov.au/shared/libraries/attachments/annual_report/annual_report_2006_2007/annual_report_2006_2007_parts_3_to_5/files/21134/NMA_Annual_Report_06-07_parts_3_4_5_electronic_optimised.pdf>

National Museum of Australia (NMA) 2007b. *Papunya Tula: Out of the desert*. Canberra: National Museum of Australia. Viewed 9 June 2008, <http://www.nma.gov.au/exhibitions/papunya_painting/>

North Sydney Community Centre 2006. *History of North Sydney Community Centre*. Viewed 4 June 2008, last updated 26 September 2006, <http://www.northsydneycentre.com.au/history-of-north-sydney-community-centre.php#Artists>

Papunya Tula Artists Proprietary Limited (PTA) 2007. Submission to the Inquiry into Australia's Indigenous Visual Arts and Craft Sector. Submission 14. Viewed 1 June 2008, <http://www.aph.gov.au/senate/committee/ecita_ctte/completed_inquiries/2004-07/indigenous_arts/submissions/sub14.pdf>

Senate Standing Committee on Environment, Communications, Information Technology and the Arts (SSCECITA) 2007a. *Indigenous Art—Securing the future: Australia's Indigenous visual arts and craft sector*. Canberra: Standing Committee on Environment, Communications, Information Technology and the Arts.

Senate Standing Committee on Environment, Communications, Information Technology and the Arts (SSCECITA) 2007b. Inquiry into Australia's Indigenous Visual Arts and Craft Sector: Public hearing transcript—Darwin, 20/02/07. Viewed 10 April 2008, <http://www.aph.gov.au/hansard/senate/commttee/S9977.pdf>

Senate Standing Committee on Environment, Communications, Information Technology and the Arts (SSCECITA) 2007c. Inquiry into Australia's Indigenous Visual Arts and Craft Sector: Public hearing transcript—Alice Springs, 21/02/07. Viewed 10 April 2008, <http://www.aph.gov.au/hansard/senate/commttee/S9978.pdf>

Wright, F. 1999. *The Art & Craft Centre Story*. *Volume one: Report*. Canberra: Aboriginal and Torres Strait Islander Commission.

Wright, F. and Morphy, F. (eds) 1999. *The Art & Craft Centre Story*. *Volume two: Summary and recommendations*. Canberra: Aboriginal and Torres Strait Islander Commission.

14. On Generating Culturally Sustainable Enterprises and Demand-Responsive Services in Remote Aboriginal Settings: A case study from north-west Queensland

Paul Memmott

The catalyst for this chapter[1] was the continuation of poor national outcomes in Aboriginal employment and quality of lifestyle, despite 35 years of sustained government service delivery. The persistence of Aboriginal identities and cultures, albeit in transformed states, is a dominant continuity despite the pulses and shifts of policies. Nevertheless, debate has recently embraced whether Aboriginal people can participate in the market economy and yet still retain traditional culture (Sarra 2009), and whether retention of traditional culture has contributed inadvertently to community dysfunction (Altman 2009; Sutton 2009).

For those many Aboriginal groups who do not wish to leave their traditional homelands and communities, one consistent challenge for their leaders and trusted advisors is to generate remote Aboriginal economies that are embraced by Aboriginal people. A second challenge is to ground these economies in Aboriginal culture and social capital, so as to assist in the veracity and persistence of the latter; and third, to seek a 'fit' between financially viable enterprise and voluntary economic behaviour in the local market conditions such that people are motivated to participate in such economies. In this chapter, I contend that such motivation can come from the fulfilment of demand-responsive service provision in remote communities, and that achieving such a symbiotic service delivery in remote communities that are marginal to mainstream economic markets is necessary to ensure viable health, quality of lifestyle, social cohesion and wellbeing. Service delivery encompasses the provision of such things as food, cars, music, religion, governance, housing, water, health treatment, recreational infrastructure and many other tangible and intangible commodities. Service delivery needs to be designed and cross-linked to satisfy both perceived needs and consumption styles or choices. In itself, consumption also needs to be considered and analysed as a form of self-definition and of cultural identification and process.

---

1   This chapter is based on a longer monograph that was written as a contribution to the Desert Knowledge Cooperative Research Centre (DKCRC) during 2007–09, and specifically to its Core Project 5 (CP5) on 'Desert Services that Work, Demand Responsible Approaches to Desert Settlements'. This is in turn based on earlier work by the author (PMA 2007).

In this chapter, I explore a case study of remote Aboriginal cultural and socioeconomic empowerment situated within the fields of both mainstream economy and service delivery. The Myuma Group is comprised of three interlinked Aboriginal corporations centred on the upper Georgina River in far western Queensland, which were established by the local traditional owners, the Indjalandji-Dhidhanu people. The Myuma Group first established a principal work camp on the outskirts of Camooweal (a township near the Queensland–Northern Territory border), then a second work camp at a remote limestone quarry, and an office in Mount Isa. From these three bases, they administer a combination of enterprises, training, service delivery and cultural heritage activities.[2]

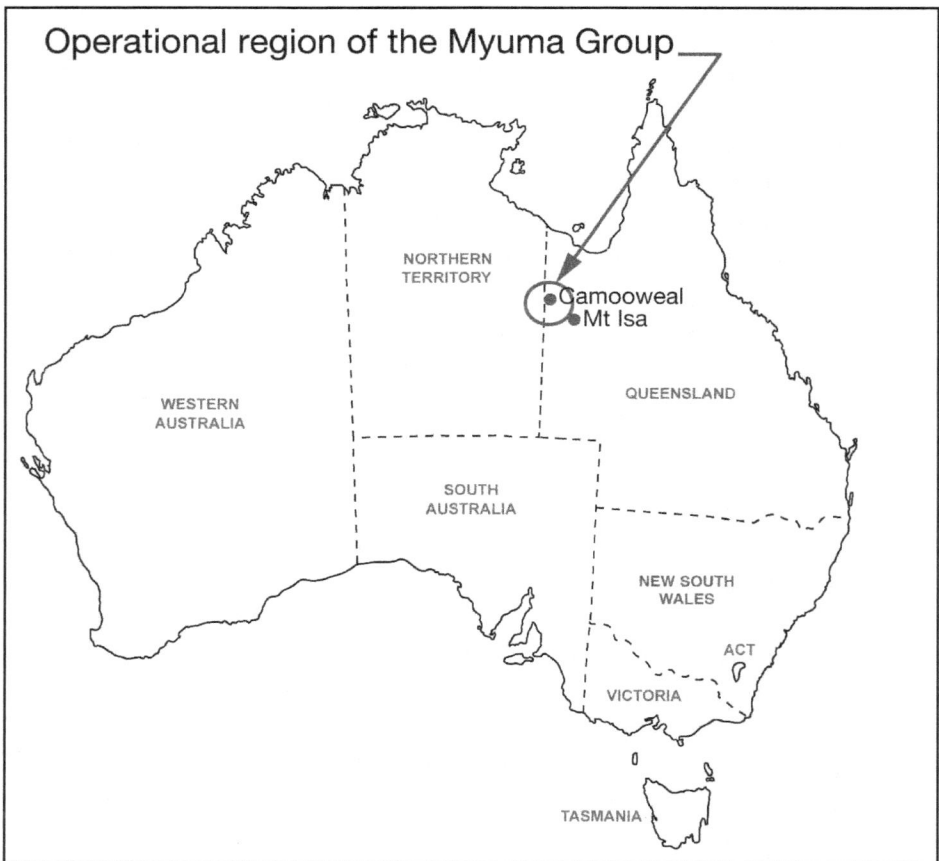

Map 14.1 Operational location of the Myuma Group

Source: Aboriginal Environments Research Centree, The University of Queensland.

---

2 The innovation and success of this group structure stimulated the author to profile it as a good-practice case study (Memmott 2010).

The Georgina River Frontier History

In the mid-nineteenth century, the Indjalandji-Dhidhanu people occupied the upper Georgina Basin and surrounding Barkly Tableland in far north-west Queensland. A young Dhidhanu man named Idaya, a forebear of the contemporary group, was alive at this time. The first impacts of colonisation were in December 1861, when the explorer William Landsborough encountered and renamed three sacred Indjalandji waterholes on the Georgina River as Lakes Mary, Francis and Canellan. His favourable report on the surrounding grasslands triggered several waves of pastoral occupation by colonists during 1864–84. The township of Camooweal was established beside Lake Francis in 1884 and was to flourish as a border customs post, a pastoral industry service town and a droving stop for the 'cattle barons' bringing cattle from the Barkly Tableland and the Kimberley to the eastern coastal markets.

Decimation of the Aboriginal groups of the Georgina occurred in parallel during the late nineteenth century and was largely attributable to frontier violence, as well as multiple infectious and contagious diseases. Only a few Indjalandji-Dhidhanu families survived, together with remnants of the neighbouring Kalkadungu, Bularnu and Waluwarra tribal groups, providing cheap labour for the pastoral industry. Partly in response to the widespread demographic collapse, the Queensland Government introduced the *Aboriginals Protection and Restriction of the Sale of Opium Act 1897*, which regulated, but also forced, Aboriginal people to labour in the pastoral industry (arguably an economic mode of internal colonialism; see White 2011). Uncooperative workers were sent to institutionalised penal settlements in the east of the State such as Cherbourg, Woorabinda and Palm Island.

The descendants of Idaya lived in the pastoral camps and town camps as they worked under 'the Act' and intermarried with spouses from these other tribal groups. The contemporary elder of the Myuma Group, Ruby Saltmere, was born in 1933 at a traditional birthing camp. Ruby's uncle Dijeru Jack (the grandson of Idaya) performed rainmaking rituals to green the country at the request of the local pastoralists, and maintained the group's link to the rainmaking site of Dugalunji. A sense of a Georgina River Aboriginal culture and community survived. Ruby Saltmere sums this up by saying 'as for the country part of it, well, we know the country because we been here all our life and worked on it'.

Levering up Myuma from Native Title

In 1998, the descendants of Idaya submitted a native title application under the *Native Title Act 1993* (Cwlth) over a part of the Georgina River around

Camooweal including Lakes Francis and Canellan. In 1999 the development progress of a proposed new Georgina River bridge by the Queensland Main Roads Department was stymied by two competing native title claims, but an independent review of the historical and contemporary ethnographic evidence indicated that the Indjalandji claimants were the appropriate traditional owners for the bridge site (Memmott and Stacy 1999), which allowed them to commence negotiation with Main Roads over progressing the bridge. A second issue was a strong objection by the elder Ruby Saltmere to sinking deep pier footings for the bridge within the riverbed, as she believed this would harm the Rainbow Serpent's back that had metamorphosed into the bedrock of the river (and which would unleash an environmental catastrophe). Main Roads engineers designed a system of pad footings such that the piers could sit on top of the river bedrock without penetrating it. A third issue was the implementation of additional environmental management principles required by the Indjalandji claimants to protect cultural heritage sites and other natural features (Archaeo and Dugalunji 2002).

The construction of the bridge was then able to proceed. The Indjalandji, using their native title claimant status, managed to negotiate outcomes and benefits from Queensland Main Roads, including employment and training for themselves and Aboriginal members of the wider community. In addition, a construction camp (the 'Dugalunji Camp') was established in 2001 by Main Roads within the Camooweal Town Common for use by the group. It was agreed that after the completion of the bridge, the site of the construction camp would be left in the hands of the Indjalandji group, to assist the groups to participate in the subsequent highway upgrades. The bridge was officially named Ilaga Thuwani, meaning 'The Camping Ground of the Rainbow Serpent'. The Queensland Government viewed the bridge project as a successful partnership (DATSIP 2005:24).

Profile of the Myuma Group[3]

By 2002, the Indjalandji-Dhidhanu Group of Traditional Owners at Camooweal established the Myuma Group of corporations to further the wellbeing, cultural maintenance and quality of lifestyle of their people as well as the Aboriginal people of their region. The Myuma Group came to consist of three corporate entities, each with a different function: Myuma Proprietary Limited, Dugalunji Aboriginal Corporation and Rainbow Gateway Limited (see Table 14.1). The group's leader, Colin Saltmere, progressed from being a pastoral 'ringer' to the Managing Director of Myuma.

---

3   This and some of the following sections have been edited from PMA (2007), 'The Myuma Story', and updated.

Myuma Proprietary Limited is a non-profit proprietary company, incorporated for the purposes of managing the business arm of the group's activities. Its constitutional objectives are to promote and benefit the welfare of the Aboriginal communities of the upper Georgina River region, but in recent years it has expanded geographically to assist people throughout the greater part of north-east Australia. Myuma Proprietary Limited runs an enterprise operation (including labour and plant hire) and also employs and delivers accredited training programs to local Aboriginal people in civil and mining construction and related support services (horticulture, hospitality and catering). At the time of writing, the number of workers employed by Myuma ranged between 40 and 80, 90 per cent of whom were Aboriginal. Myuma purposefully engaged people from their neighbouring traditional owner Aboriginal groups as employees and trainees in all projects (see Map 14.3).

The Dugalunji Aboriginal Corporation is a not-for-profit organisation whose core business is management of the group's native title and cultural heritage interests. This includes land and riverine management activities, and the provision and management of cultural heritage services to clients. Myuma Proprietary Limited assists Dugalunji to deliver employment/training outcomes to local Aboriginal people in cultural heritage practices. Rainbow Gateway Limited acts as a tax-deductible charity that receives and distributes any net incomes from Myuma Proprietary Limited and Dugalunji Aboriginal Corporation for use in addressing the charitable goals of the Indjalandji-Dhidhanu.

Table 14.1 The Three Corporate Vehicles of the Myuma Group and their Respective Spheres of Operation

Corporate vehicle	Sphere of operation
Myuma Pty Ltd	Economic enterprises, training
Dugalunji Aboriginal Corporation	Cultural heritage, native title, land and riverine management
Rainbow Gateway Ltd	Social, welfare and charitable projects

Training Delivery by the Myuma Group and Partners

From its early stages, Myuma's leaders recognised that ample employment opportunities for Aboriginal trainees existed within Myuma's own operations as well as within the many civil construction and mining companies operating in the region. The Myuma Group forged close working relationships with key industry stakeholders, including regional job network agencies and Community Development Employment Projects (CDEP) organisations, Australian Government agencies, State Government agencies, registered training organisations that were Australian Quality Framework (AQF) compliant and peak industry groups. From this network, a consultative committee[4] was formed to develop a training management model that emphasised a set of key learnings. First, the committee had to be proactive in scoping forthcoming onsite training opportunities and associated project proponents who would be willing to engage in an Aboriginal training program. Second was the need for the committee to take a collective approach to identifying and pooling available government resources for the respective costs incurred by trainees, training organisations and onsite employers. Third was the need for early engagement between the training agency and the identified project proponent and their project contractor on the issues of design, delivery and integration of training into the contract work onsite. A final learning was the importance of identifying the particular needs of trainees between exiting their training program and entering their available employment option; in some cases, this involves the provision of further short, specialised training packages.

During 2006, the Myuma Group and its partners designed and trialled a pre-vocational, accredited, individualised training program that delivered competencies specifically chosen to equip Aboriginal participants for pre-identified, full-time, entry-level industry positions. During 2007–08 the demographic profile of trainees broadened to take in both remote and urban communities throughout the Gulf of Carpentaria, Cape York, north Queensland and the far east of the Northern Territory. This broadened set of community sources facilitated a more careful selection process, maximising opportunities for those with high motivation and unfulfilled capacity, including from remote communities characterised as having dysfunctional traits. The geographic diversity ensured a stimulating multicultural interactive experience between trainees from diverse and different Aboriginal cultures. Some of them (for example, the Wik from Aurukun) were steeped in aspects of Aboriginal law, whilst other, urban trainees had largely missed out. At the end of 2009, informal agreements were in place with a number of Aboriginal community councils or non-governmental organisations (NGOs) from whom to regularly recruit trainees, including at Aurukun, Yarrabah, Palm Island, Mossman and Innisfail.

Participants were largely Aboriginal school-leavers or persons who were either long-term unemployed or at risk of long-term unemployment. Each training intake was largely made up of 30 young adults in the eighteen to twenty-six-year age range and with a mixture of men to women in the ratio of about five to one. Participants were usually recruited in groups of three, four or five from each targeted community such that upon arrival there were some familiar faces with whom one could interact. The social relatedness grew as individuals found themselves in different work teams and activity groups.

---

4   Myuma's consultative committee later transformed into the Mount Isa Region Industry and Infrastructure Key Managers Forum.

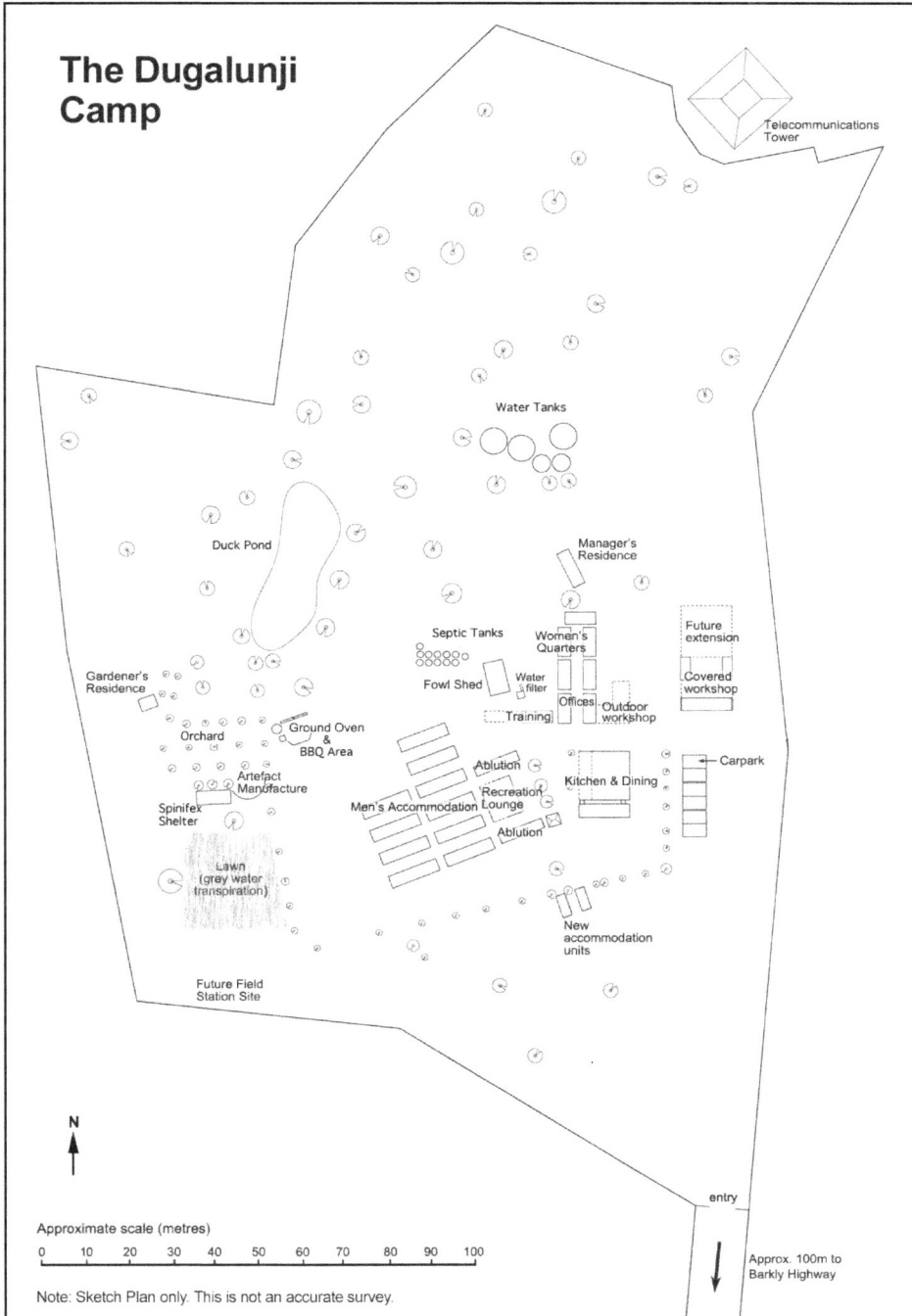

The Dugalunji Camp

Telecommunications Tower

Water Tanks

Duck Pond

Manager's Residence

Future extension

Septic Tanks

Women's Quarters

Covered workshop

Gardener's Residence

Fowl Shed

Water filter

Offices

Outdoor workshop

Training

Orchard

Ground Oven & BBQ Area

Carpark

Artefact Manufacture

Ablution

Kitchen & Dining

Spinifex Shelter

Men's Accommodation

Recreation Lounge

Ablution

Lawn (grey water transpiration)

New accommodation units

Future Field Station Site

N

Approximate scale (metres)

0 10 20 30 40 50 60 70 80 90 100

Note: Sketch Plan only. This is not an accurate survey.

entry

Approx. 100m to Barkly Highway

Map 14.2 Plan of Myuma Camp in 2006

Source: Aboriginal Environments Research Centree, The University of Queensland.

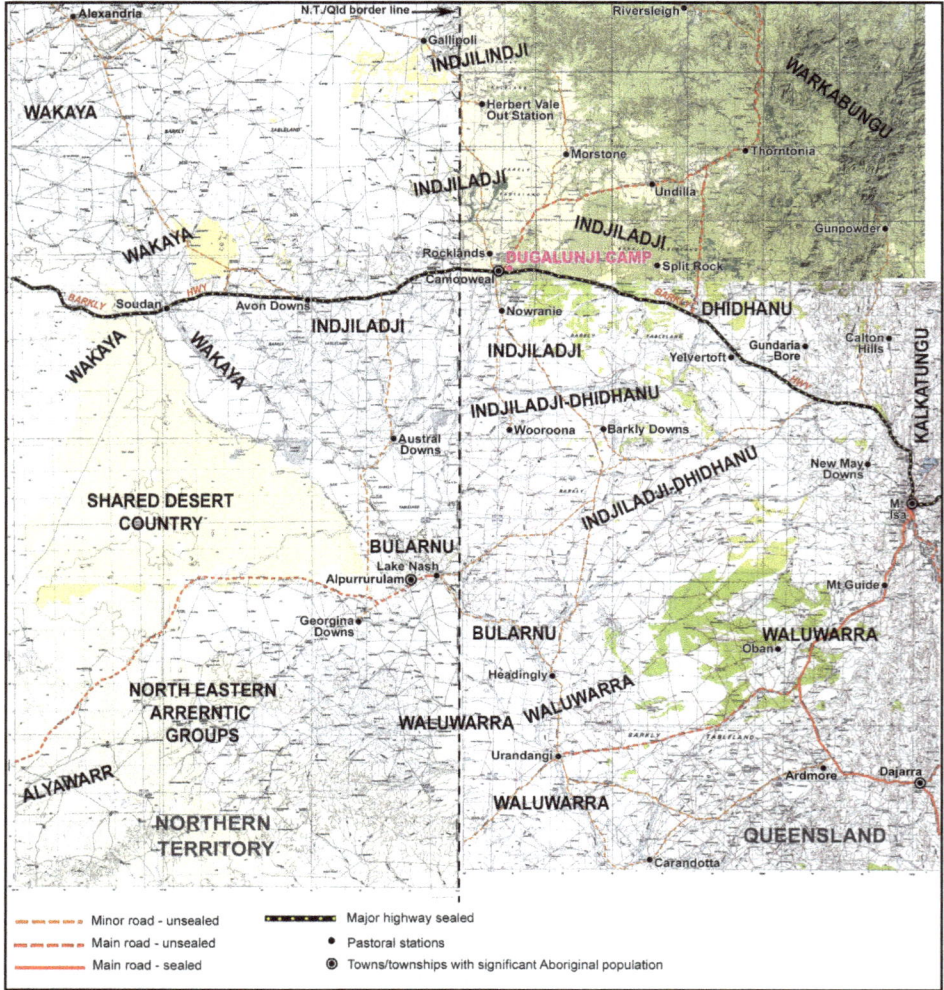

Map 14.3 Towns and pastoral stations in the vicinity of Camooweal, with the Indjaladji-Dhidhanu territory and neighbouring traditional owner groups

Source: Aboriginal Environments Research Centree, The University of Queensland.

The pre-vocational training curriculum involves three accredited streams: 1) civil construction, 2) mining, and 3) life skills. The program aims to foster an emergence of diverse Aboriginal identities within the trainee group based on Aboriginal values, to strengthen individual confidence, to express their particular identity and to be able to contrast their identity with those of others. Aboriginal cultural identity and religion workshops have enhanced Aboriginal values of relatedness to others as well as to country and sacred sites, whilst family violence workshops have addressed issues of having one's employment undermined by home family problems. All of these components aimed to provide a strong foundation for young Aboriginal adults in the workplace embracing physical, psychological and skills performance. On-the-job practical experience also occurred during the training through a series of short work-team placements. The trainees have assisted Myuma in the delivery of existing contracts and works, including the execution of a range of well-supported public infrastructure projects chosen to yield long-term benefits to the residents of the Camooweal region and the travelling public, of which the trainees were able to feel justly proud in terms of their role in improving community services.

The mode of running the Dugalunji Camp was a critical factor underlying the success of the training program. The Myuma Managing Director, Colin Saltmere, operated the camp like a boarding school for young Aboriginal adults, providing a set of life skills and industrial discipline for the trainees. Problems certainly have arisen, given that the trainee intake has often included individuals with substance abuse addiction, insecurity about their Aboriginality, and immaturity about adulthood, and who have sometimes engaged in violent behaviour and in living outside of the Australian law in various ways. Nevertheless, the Myuma training course has maintained a high retention of trainees during the course and a high rate of graduation (86 per cent). Of the 105 trainees who graduated during 2007–09, some 69 (66 per cent) obtained employment upon graduation;[5] about one-third then remained in continuous employment for at least six months (Memmott 2010:Table 4).

Myuma's Service Provision

Services to Aboriginal Workers and Trainees

Myuma Proprietary Limited provides a range of key services and facilities to its Aboriginal workers and trainees in response to their expressed needs. Many of these services and facilities have been built up with the economic gains from

---

5   In 2009, placements were occurring with Rio Tinto, Alcan, Xstrata, Cairns Earthmoving Company, Incitec Pivot, CDE Capital, Legend International Incorporated, Mount Isa City Council and the Myuma Labour Hire Pod.

Myuma's enterprise work. The Dugalunji camp environment is a substance-free Aboriginal living area with nutritious meals and some recreation facilities— for example, a sports field, pool table, television lounge and small gymnasium. Myuma provides a private room for each of its employees and trainees, which for a good number of them is the first fully private space they have ever occupied and personalised. At the Dugalunji Camp, Aboriginal leaders have chosen when to facilitate or broker particular forms of service delivery. This form of participation and engagement is viewed as being essential to obtain sustainable outputs from service delivery.

Myuma staff act as informal social workers, counsellors or 'errand runners' to maintain harmony and wellbeing in the Dugalunji Camp. Above all, the Dugalunji Camp provides workers and trainees with a calm residential setting, relatively free of problems or chaos, where people can feel at home in the world for a while, and where relatedness enfolds for many with their fellows in the camp (after Austin-Broos 2009). Camp harmony results from intra-group harmony, which in turn results from the requirement of a strong personal moral code conveyed through the camp rules and the authoritative guidance of Colin Saltmere as camp boss. The Myuma pre-vocational program has encouraged the development of a career narrative and a purpose in life. It has opened a window to alternative lifeways and career pathways that might not have been apparent or available in the home communities of the trainees.

Recognition of Myuma's Good Practice in Service Delivery

A range of indicators readily identifies Myuma's good practice as a service provider, specifically private-sector contracts for the supply of pre-vocational trainees to continue, including the production of a marketing video by the Queensland Department of Transport and Main Roads highlighting the good practice achieved in Myuma, for use in promoting reconciliation and upskilling via partnerships between Aboriginal communities and the Government. Colin Saltmere speaks on the film about 'building people', emphasising the holistic development of the individual, in addition to the other achievements of workplace alliances and skills development (DTMR 2009). Yet further indices of Myuma's good practice are: consistent and stable annual growth reflected in Myuma's annual gross turnovers;[6] the winning of a host of State and national industry awards for training, reconciliation and cultural heritage achievement; and a Commonwealth infrastructure grant of $3.8 million awarded to Myuma for the upgrading of its training facilities (Memmott 2010).

---

6   For example, the gross turnover of $8 million for 2007–08 increased to $10 million for 2008–09.

Myuma as a Complex Aboriginal Adaptive System within the Market

In contrast with directed consumption in many arid-zone communities whereby services are delivered unidirectionally downwards by government-sponsored agencies, the author's research aim was concerned with how demand-driven service delivery could be attained by Aboriginal communities, such that a more bidirectional and lateral (or transactional) relationship could be achieved between consumer communities and service providers, resulting in a better response of service supply to demand (or a demand-driven service delivery).

Due to its distinctive economic history, Myuma has become positioned in the market with complex supply and demand functions (or multiple diversified market interfacing). In the 2004–05 financial year, the Myuma Group contributed a total of $3.6 million to the local economy through its payment of wages for employment and training of local labour and the purchase of local services, supplies and products.[7] In the four subsequent financial years (to the end of June 2009), the contributions to the local economy did not fall below this amount and ranged upwards to $6.1 million (see Table 14.2). The total contribution over five financial years has been almost $21.7 million—an average of $4.34 million. These contributions have come via Myuma's enterprise and training contracts. Part of this monetary contribution (including charitable community-based services) goes into the township of Camooweal, assisting to reawaken its gentrified economy (decline occurred when its pastoral function was superseded by mechanised stock transport and mustering technology).

Table 14.2 Myuma's Contribution to its Regional Economy, 2004–09

Financial year	Contribution to local economy
2004–05	$3.6 million
2005–06	$4.2 million
2006–07	$6.1 million
2007–08	$3.6 million
2008–09	$4.2 million
Total (five years)	$21.7 million

The reader is thus asked to consider a market participation model in which there are complex demand and supply chains and networks (read in conjunction with Figure 14.1). Suppose I am to supply a service, X, in the market: in order

---

7   Myuma Proprietary Limited is a conventional consumer in that it buys in products and services. Ballpark figures for the costs of running Myuma include electricity at $56 000 per year, food at $300 000 per year and fuel at approximately $147 000 per year. A critical issue is whether there is a more sustainable consumption style possible for Myuma.

to do this, I have to demand Y goods and Z services. The entities that supply Y and Z, however, also want my supply of X, or alternatively want me to maintain the supply of X, which stimulates the trade of their goods and services in other parts of the market. Thus, demand is partly driven by the capacity to supply (not just to consume), as well as by the reciprocal appreciation of the mutual demands and needs for one another's services. Accountability becomes more lateralised with marketplace performance, with many interdependent players in the economic chain, as opposed to vertical accountability in a top-down service to bottom-up demand context—typical of many remote Aboriginal communities. In the theoretical literature on human consumption, this more complex set of market relationships is termed 'productive consumption'. The 'act of production is therefore in all its moments also an act of consumption... Production as directly identical with consumption, and consumption as directly coincident with production' (Marx 2001:32).

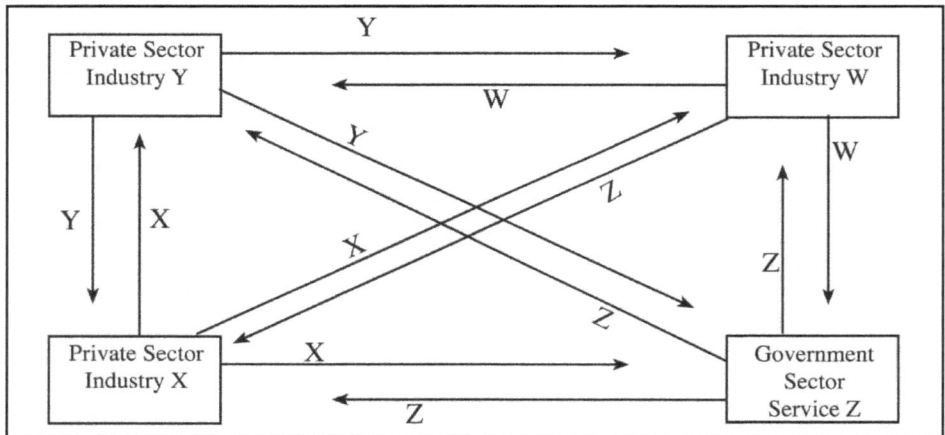

Figure 14.1 The market participation model: complex demand and supply chains and networks

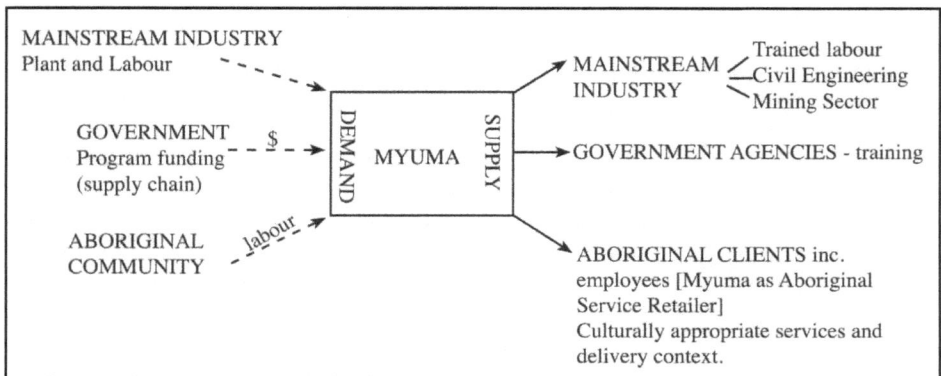

Figure 14.2 Myuma as the complex Indigenous adaptive system

A key challenge for Aboriginal groups is how to 'lever' themselves out of welfare dependency and to insert themselves into the market without substantial 'start-up' resources. The Myuma Group provides a case study of how to achieve this status. This positioning of Myuma in a complex network or field of supply and demand can be termed a 'transactional model of supply and demand'. In adjusting 'the playing field' of service delivery to be 'level' with a degree of demand-driven consumer choice, there was a need for Myuma to earn some power within market relationships and transactions, and for Myuma to take some control over information (informed consumerism) and decision-making capacity based on that information, thereby facilitating active engagement and negotiation on the terms of its Aboriginal consumers (trainees and workers).

A further critical method employed by Myuma to achieve this position is the design of the Dugalunji Camp as an 'Aboriginal service setting',[8] in contrast with a government service setting or a commercial service setting. An Aboriginal service setting can be defined as one that is largely controlled by Aboriginal people and is designed to be comfortable for Aboriginal consumers. There is a sense of identity with and even ownership of such a setting by Aboriginal people when the service is being delivered in an effective way.

A key role of the Aboriginal service setting is to 'level the playing field', so to speak, and alter the imbalance of power that has often characterised many transactions with Aboriginal people in government and commercial delivery settings, whereby delivery is one way with either no opportunity for Aboriginal negotiation as a consumer or the prospect of such negotiation being intimidated by discriminatory practices.[9] Although I have here employed the term 'Aboriginal service setting' to describe the Dugalunji Camp, it is more accurately an intercultural setting with a dominance of Aboriginal behavioural patterns and with ultimate Aboriginal control and management.

Critical Human Resources within the Myuma Group

Any profiling of Myuma and its achievements would be incomplete without some discussion of the role and calibre of the human resources that drive Myuma both from within and from outside its corporate framework. Foundational support is provided within the directorships of the Myuma Group by the Indjilandji-Dhidhanu group, and although some families are more active than others in the day-to-day company affairs and particular projects, they consistently gather for board meetings to make critical decisions. These decisions are not just restricted

---

8   This concept of 'the service setting' follows that of the 'behavioural setting' (Barker 1968; Barker and Wright 1955); see Memmott (2010:39–41).
9   Local historical examples that could be considered here are the Camooweal hotel and picture theatre as they were in the 1970s and 1980s, in which separatist settings were imposed upon the Aboriginal townspeople.

to new contract engagements or what to do with profits, but also encompass the wider concerns of the group, such as maintaining Indjalandji Aboriginal law and custom and matters of local Aboriginal community politics and social development. In this regard, Ruby Saltmere has played a dominant role as the group's elder and keeper of extensive cultural knowledge. Nevertheless, the day-to-day roles of being the 'focal driver' for Myuma and the lead negotiator with other communities, governments and industry are clearly taken by her son, Colin Saltmere, as Managing Director,[10] albeit assisted by his senior staff. Myuma's success is not just attributable to strong leadership, but also to a solid foundation of corporate teamwork, involving both staff and traditional-owner directors, as well as the supportive network of outside advisors and advocates for the Myuma Group, who come from diverse trades, professions and life paths.

The Relationship between Myuma's Activities and Aboriginal Law

The Myuma Group's practice is based on a strong commitment to Aboriginal law and culture. This is in defiance of the late Professor W. E. H. Stanner who asserted that the Dreaming and the market were incompatible: 'Ours is a market-civilisation, theirs not. Indeed, there is a sense in which The Dreaming and The Market are mutually exclusive' (Stanner 1979:58). Despite Stanner's views, the strong commitment to law and culture continues to permeate through the Dugalunji Camp on a daily basis via a number of mechanisms and behaviours that include: 1) the visitation and residence of regional elders at the Dugalunji Camp who engage in a variety of customary activities including hunting; 2) the regular contracting of cultural heritage services to industry by Dugalunji; 3) the running of cultural induction programs for regional industry workers; 4) the workshops on cultural identity strengthening for pre-vocational trainees from throughout north-east Australian cultural groups (numerous tribal identities); 5) the involvement of the Indjalandji in regional Aboriginal ceremonies; and 6) an ongoing program of Indjalandji sacred site recording in the region. The provision of cultural services to industry is one component of Myuma's hybrid economy along with road maintenance, fencing, land management and training contracts.

The Indjalandji elders' and leaders' respect of Aboriginal law and sacred sites gradually pervades into the awareness of staff, trainers and visitors. They become aware that they are in a cultural landscape of ancestrally created places and histories. There is thus a unique symbiotic relationship between the practice of Aboriginal law and the practice of commerce in the Dugalunji Camp

---

10   The significance of a 'focal driver' and effective negotiation as both being criteria for successful governance are outlined in Moran (2006:398).

whereby the two are mutually supportive of one another, generating a strong Aboriginality in the way that day-to-day 'business' is run by Myuma. This is directly projected on to the trainees who gain increased confidence in their own cultural identities and return to their home communities with a strengthened sense of their Aboriginality.

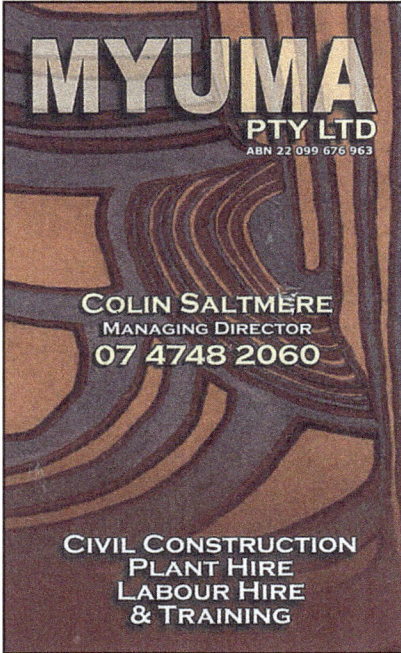

Figure 14.3 A Myuma business card with corporate logo designed by artist and Co-Director, Shirley Macnamara, using ground ochre sourced from the sacred site complex at Wuruna, which is believed to be the faeces of Picaninnies, left from the Dreaming

Conclusion: Summary of good practice

There is a range of significant good-practice strategies and methods underpinning Myuma's success. In historical order, the first was the use of a native title claim from which to obtain an initial set of economic assets (infrastructure, contracts). A second strategy was an inclusive (rather than exclusive) approach to spreading the enterprise benefits created by a small Indjilandji extended family group to a regional bloc of multiple language groups and to other beneficiaries in the wider community. This enabled the Myuma Group to project itself as a benefactor for the regional Aboriginal population (not simply as a nepotistic family-based firm)—an image that was essential to attract strong government support and local and regional legitimacy.

Acting as an Aboriginal host organisation, Myuma has accomplished a viable integration of economic enterprise activity and service provision, involving the following processes: 1) attracting a large-scale contract with government or private enterprise that can be fulfilled with largely Aboriginal labour; 2) hosting the Aboriginal labour onsite with accommodation, meals and a social and service environment that is culturally appropriate, so that the employees feel comfortable; 3) providing accessible training courses to the labour pool relevant to the work experience, so there is added value for the employees and so that the labour force acquires ongoing, diverse skill sets; and 4) attracting more enterprise and training contracts to achieve a stable continuity of employment, training and hence accompanying ongoing service provision. This has resulted in Myuma becoming part of the local and regional economic market, which partly explains its capacity to secure selected and culturally modified demand service needs from the government and business sectors.

Further critical factors underlie the Myuma success story. First is Colin Saltmere's leadership skill in being able to not only successfully influence and negotiate in the mainstream government and business world, but also simultaneously earn the respect of Aboriginal people by being a customary law authority and leader in the Barkly region. Second, Myuma has gained a reputation for professional levels of performance, generating widespread respect from both industry and government. Third is the pre-vocational training in an Aboriginal-run and controlled work camp, which doubles as an Aboriginal service setting, and in which most cross-cultural blockages and intimidations experienced by trainees can be worked through with a trusting training team. This results in 'closing the gap': 'not just job readiness, but having jobs ready' for the Aboriginal trainees—again, a function of Myuma's good standing in the economic market (Memmott 2010).

The value of the Myuma case study has thus been to profile an Aboriginal group which has been capturing both lateral (industry) and vertical (government) resource flows within its unique structure and integrating those resources to control service delivery in certain ways at the local level for the good of a regional Aboriginal collective. Such case studies are important in understanding techniques for creating a relatively stable socioeconomic position of both enterprise and service delivery under local political control, which is in turn partially insulated against any possible future fluctuations of either government or private resourcing.

In summary, it can be said that the Myuma experiment denies socioeconomic disadvantage as being an Aboriginal destiny. Myuma aims to lift young Aboriginal adults out of such disadvantage and 'provide for them, a prospect that they would otherwise not have, that their parents never had' (Pearson 2009). Through the device of the Aboriginal service setting, Myuma is able to provide its trainees and workers with a sense of 'at-homeness', of residential harmony and social relatedness of order and security—experiences that are often in contrast in particular ways with their home community life. Myuma, in light of the evidence at hand, is a nationally significant example of Indigenous people overcoming 'extraordinary hurdles to foster emergent social norms and new institutions' (Altman 2009) based on a culturally accommodating hybrid economy, a dialectic resolution that surmounts opposition between cultural idealism and economic pragmatism, overcomes mainstream left-wing and right-wing political myopias, and lands somewhere in 'the radical centre' to follow Pearson's recent prescribed position (Pearson 2009:248; Sutton 2009).

References

Altman, J. 2009. What 'liberal consensus'? [Book review of Sutton's *The Politics of Suffering*.] *New Matilda*, 16 July 2009. <http://newmatilda.com/2009/07/16/what-liberal-consensus>

Archaeo Cultural Heritage Services and the Dugalunji Aboriginal Corporation (Archaeo and Dugalunji) 2002. *Cultural Heritage Excavation and Collection: Georgina River Bridge Cultural Heritage Project, Camooweal, northwest Queensland*. Report to Department of Main Roads, EPA Permit N14/EIS/2000, October 2000 – December 2002.

Austin-Broos, D. 2009. Workfare, welfare and the hybrid economy: the Western Arrernte in Central Australia. Paper delivered at the Indigenous Participation in Australian Economies Conference, National Museum of Australia, Canberra, 10 November 2008.

Barker, R. 1968. *Ecological Psychology*. Stanford, Calif.: Stanford University Press.

Barker, R. and Wright, H. 1955. *Midwest and its Children. The psychological ecology of an American town*. New York: Row, Peterson & Company.

Department of Aboriginal and Torres Strait Islander Policy (DATSIP) 2005. *Partnerships Queensland: Future directions framework for Aboriginal and Torres Strait Islander policy in Queensland 2005–10*. Brisbane: Government Printer.

Department of Transport and Main Roads (DTMR) 2009. *Building Indigenous Capability—A remote employment and training partnership that works*. (Film.) Brisbane: Queensland Department of Transport and Main Roads.

Marx, K. 2001. Introduction. In D. Miller (ed.), *Consumption: Critical concepts in the social sciences*, pp. 32–6. London: Routledge.

Memmott, P. 2010. *Demand Responsive Services and Culturally Sustainable Enterprise in Remote Aboriginal Settings: A case study of the Myuma Group*. Alice Springs, NT: Desert Knowledge Cooperative Research Centre. [To be uploaded to DKCRC web site.]

Memmott, P. and Stacy, R. 1999. *Independent Anthropological Study on the Proposed Georgina River Bridge Site Camooweal, Qld*. Job No. 10/15C/2, Prepared for Main Roads, Queensland. St Lucia, Qld: Paul Memmott and Associates.

Moran, M. 2006. Practising self-determination: participation in planning and local governance in discrete Indigenous settlements. PhD thesis, School of Geography, Planning and Architecture, University of Queensland, Brisbane.

Paul Memmott and Associates (PMA) 2007. *The Myuma Group, Georgina River Basin—Aboriginal enterprise, training and cultural heritage*. Mount Isa, Qld: Myuma Proprietary Limited.

Pearson, N. 2009. *Up from the Mission: Selected writings*. Melbourne: Black Inc.

Sarra, C. 2009. New narrative tells of brighter future together. *The Weekend Australian*, 8-9 August, p. 23.

Stanner, W. E. H. 1979. Continuity and change among the Aborigines. In W. E. H. Stanner (ed.), *White Man Got No Dreaming: Essays 1938–1973*, pp. 41–66. Canberra: Australian National University Press.

Sutton, P. 2009. Here I stand: Noel Pearson's 'Up from the Mission'. [Book review.] *The Monthly* (46) (June).

White, J. 2011. Histories of Indigenous–settler relations: reflections on internal colonialism and the hybrid economy. *Australian Indigenous Studies* (1): 81–96.

15. Dugong Hunting as Changing Practice: Economic engagement and an Aboriginal ranger program on Mornington Island, southern Gulf of Carpentaria

Cameo Dalley

Introduction

Chapters in this volume and papers in a special edition of *The Australian Journal of Anthropology* in 2009 address the intersection of anthropology with economics. A particular focus has been the ways in which Indigenous cultures might relate to conceivably more foreign notions of market economies. One prominent example, which conceptualised Aboriginal engagements in economic enterprise, was the 'hybrid economy' model offered by Altman (2001). The model featured three intersecting realms: the 'market', the 'state' and the (Aboriginal) 'customary economy'. Important components of hybridity were the 'linkages', 'dependencies' and 'cleavages' between the various realms, which created particular opportunities, Altman (2001:5) argued, for economic development. Others, however, such as Martin (2003:3) and Merlan (2009:276), questioned the capacity of such sectors to exist in any way autonomously, instead pointing to their 'recursive' and 'interrelated' natures. These themes were similarly evident in the ethnographically rich analyses of local forms of economic relations by Austin-Broos (2003) and Smith (2003).

These explorations in economic anthropology draw heavily on broader discourses about the degree to which Aboriginal culture could be considered to exist autonomously from the culture of broader Australia. These discussions were particularly advanced by the contributions of Merlan (1998, 2005, 2006). Merlan's ethnography of the Aboriginal people of Katherine in the Northern Territory led her to propose a model of Aboriginal culture as having been transformed through interaction with others and, thus, having become thoroughly 'intercultural'. In Merlan's model, Aboriginal practice did not arise from an Aboriginal consciousness alone, but through its firm embedding within a broader cultural milieu (Merlan 2006:180). Merlan's work on the intercultural and the work of those who followed (for example, Hinkson and Smith 2005;

Holcombe 2005; Smith 2003) inform analysis of the case study presented here: Aboriginal hunting of dugong (*Dugong dugon*) in the remote Aboriginal community of Mornington Island in the southern Gulf of Carpentaria.

Indigenous hunting is particularly relevant to discussions about economic anthropology and the intercultural because of the obvious changes that have occurred to practice, as exemplified by hunting material culture (Altman 1987; Merlan 2009:277–8). In some instances at least, a range of handcrafted Aboriginal hunting implements and techniques has been replaced with the use of rifles, motor vehicles and aluminium dinghies with outboard motors. This situation is further complicated because some of the species targeted are considered rare or endangered but Aboriginal people's rights to hunt some of these species are recognised under the *Native Title Act 1993* (Cwlth). For some, hunting protected species is seen as incompatible with the ethos of the 'state'— in this case, the Australian Government—to preserve places and species of high environmental and biodiversity value (Department of the Environment, Water, Heritage and the Arts 2008). Aboriginal hunting is, therefore, an example of what Gudeman (2001:1) described as the unification of culture with economy—a 'shifting relation, filled with tension'.

In the case study from Mornington Island, I focus on two intersecting points. The first of these is a historical perspective on dugong hunting as an intercultural practice. This approach accords with the notion of economies as local and specific, informed by ongoing and iterative engagements between Aboriginal people and others. In this first portion of the chapter, I engage with the local and changing nature of hunting as a practice. In the latter half, I turn my attention to the 'social relationships and contextually defined values' (Gudeman 2001:1) of hunting in the more recent period, as crafted by the media, conservation biologists, the Australian Government and the Wellesley Islands Rangers, an Aboriginal Ranger program based on Mornington Island. I show that the Rangers' perceptions of issues in dugong management do not necessarily equate with those of the Australian Government, which provides funding for their employment (see also Yanner 2008). Using interviews undertaken between 2007 and 2009, I demonstrate how the Rangers' concerns about hunting relate to the management of social relations guiding hunting more than species conservation per se. In their positions as rangers, the men seek to mediate discontinuities between these socially derived concerns and those of a conservation ethic through the adoption of 'management speak' (Babidge et al. 2007:153) as a form of 'strategic engagement' (Martin 2003:8).

Dugong Hunting as an Intercultural Practice

In 1913 the Queensland Government approved an application from the Presbyterian Church to establish a mission on Mornington Island in the southern Gulf of Carpentaria (see Map 15.1). The application followed years of reports that the Aboriginal inhabitants of Mornington and the surrounding Wellesley Islands were being exploited by White traders seeking labour for their *bêche-de-mer* and pearl-shell enterprises (Harrison 1974; Loos 1982; White 1994:11). At the time, Mornington Island and the surrounding North Wellesley Islands were occupied by an estimated 400 Aboriginal people (Howard 1910) of the Lardil and Yankgaal language groups. In 1914, Reverend Robert Hall, who had been working in other Presbyterian missions on western Cape York, collected a ship from Thursday Island and sailed to Mornington to establish the first mission (Hall, 14 July 1914).

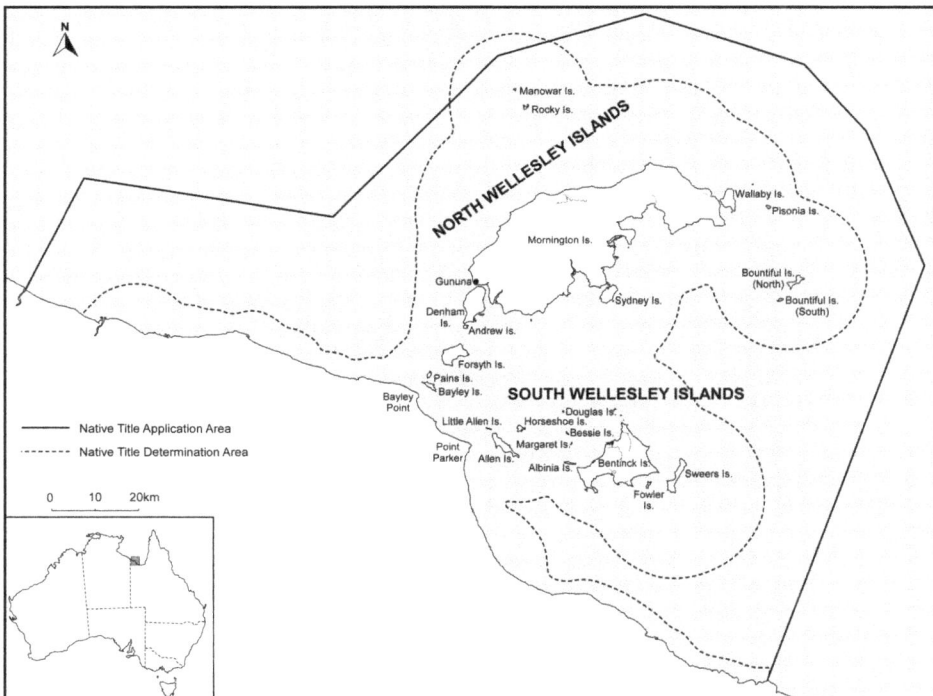

Map 15.1 Map of the southern Gulf of Carpentaria showing the areas in the application and those determined under the Wellesley Sea Claim (National Native Title Tribunal 2005). Note that the application and determination area extended only as far as the high-tide mark on land

Source: Sean Ulm.

During the journey, Hall acquired six Aboriginal staff from missions on western Cape York, who would serve both as crew on the mission sailboat and as staff and labourers in the establishment of the mission.[1] Within days of the party's arrival on Mornington Island, local Aboriginal people—primarily Lardil but also some Yangkaal people who journeyed across from neighbouring Denham Island—showed interest in the mission and began camping nearby (Hall, 2 June 1914, 23 July 1914). With little in the way of food, Hall set out to secure local Aboriginal labour to run a market garden. In order to pay local Aboriginal people for their work, Hall often sent the Cape York staff to hunt for dugong in the 12 ft (approximately 3.6 m) mission rowboat, shown in Figure 15.1 (Hall, 30 July 1914, 4 March 1915, 2 March 1916). In one such instance, after the mission had been operational for less than a month, more than 100 of the local Aboriginal residents came to work around the mission (Hall, 29 July 1914). Hall 'paid' the workers with a whole dugong, which the Cape York staff had hunted and cooked 'kapai Maori'[2] style (Hall, 30 July 1914). The hunting techniques and material culture used by the Cape York staff were markedly different from those of the local Lardil and Yangkaal Aboriginal people.

Figure 15.1 Dugong caught in the Appel Channel between Mornington Island and Denham Island, showing the mission rowboat used for hunting, 1916

Photo: Reverend Robert Hall, Hibberd Library collection.

---

1   Hall notes the first four crew members in his diary as Bertie, Bosin and Goodman (from Weipa) and Captain Henry Lewis (possibly a Torres Strait Islander) collected from Thursday Island (Hall, 9 April 1914, 20 April 1914). Along the journey from Thursday Island to Mornington Island, Hall also acquired another three crew members: Cockatoo and Wilkie (both from Batavia River) collected from Mapoon Mission (Hall, 25 April 1914) and Willie, an 'Aurukun boy', collected from the Aurukun Mission (Hall, 5 May 1914).
2   Hall was a New Zealander; however, there is no evidence to suggest that he undertook mission work with Maori.

Prior to Hall's arrival, large groups of Lardil and Yangkaal Aboriginal people hunted dugong (*dilmirrur*) and sea turtle (*bararun*) (McKnight 1999:128). A net, such as the one shown in Figure 15.2, was placed at the end of a channel at low tide with two supporting poles pushed deep into the ground. Men on *walbas* (see Figure 15.3), a raft made of small buoyant logs lashed together at one end using rope made from hibiscus-tree fibre, would herd the dugongs towards the net (Memmott 2010:12; Smart 1951:34). Other men ran through the shallows along the beach splashing the surface of the water (Memmott 1979:163). With its exit routes blocked, the dugong would be forced into the net, become entangled and drown and/or be speared by the men waiting in the shallows (Cawte 1972:17; Smart 1951:35). This hunting approach required a large, organised group of people, and specialised dugong and turtle-hunting camps were convened for this purpose at particular places along the coastline (Memmott 1983:52).

Figure 15.2 Brian Roughsey and Prince Escott (both deceased) with a modern reconstruction of a net used for catching dugong, 1976

Photo: George Heinsohn.

Along with this communal hunting approach came a structured system for the distribution of dugong meat for consumption, as recently described by Cyril Moon, a senior Lardil man:

But he fit for that camp, that one meat [dugong]. And them old people, he bin just know to slice'im and share the meat la one 'nother. That's before. He [the dugong hunter] bin cut'im dugong how he bin learn to cut'im that dugong, in his forefather time, great great [grandfather]. Same way, he cut'im like that, same way. He pass it [pieces of dugong meat] to people. He pass it lang his family, his countrymen. You can't tell him [what you want], bluff him. He no blind man when he pass'im. That 'un go right round that big whole camp. (Interview, 1 September 2007)

This system involved dedicated parts of the dugong being allocated to particular people, such as to those individuals (known as *dulmadas* in the Lardil language) who owned the country where the dugong was killed (Memmott and Trigger 1998:119).

Figure 15.3 *Walbas* in the Appel Channel between Mornington Island and Denham Island

Photo: Image 214, Fryer Library Pictorial Collection, UQFL477, Fryer Library.

The raft technology used in the Wellesley Islands differed substantially from the bark and dugout canoes used by Aboriginal neighbours on the adjacent mainland (Bradley 1997:273–302; Davidson 1935:138–9; Trigger 1987:80). There are no records suggesting that either bark or dugout canoes were in use or manufacture in the Wellesleys prior to the arrival of missionaries (Davidson 1935:73, 80). On his arrival on Mornington, Hall (6 June 1914) commented that 'some native men came out to the boat on a raft—their only boat'. In his summary of Australian Aboriginal watercraft, Davidson (1935:139, 143–4) suggests that the raft found in the Wellesleys was an older form of watercraft that in most other parts of Australia was superseded by either bark or dugout canoes. One potential explanation for retention of the raft is the limited availability of tree species in the Wellesleys suitable in size or bark type for the manufacture of other types of watercraft (Memmott 2010:91; Trigger 1987).

Hall's Aboriginal mission staff from western Cape York, however, were more familiar with dugong hunting from a dugout canoe or dugout outrigger[3] canoe (see Figure 15.4), as was ubiquitous in Cape York at this time (Davidson 1935:71–3). As detailed in Donald Thompson's (1934:243–4) *The Dugong Hunters of Cape York*, hunting from a dugout relied on the use of a *whap* (a generic term from Torres Strait): a spear with a detachable head of up to three prongs (referred to by Mornington Islanders as the *thartha*)[4] attached to a long rope. This approach involved a minimum of three people, usually men: one to row the canoe, one to use the *whap* and a third person to assist the others, arrange the rope and remove any entanglements (Hall 1986:93). The rigidity of the canoe formed a sturdy platform from which to force the *whap* into the back of the dugong and for the *thartha* to embed under the dugong's skin. The hunter could then hold onto the rope until the dugong tired, and it could be pulled beside the boat and drowned (Hall 1986:93; Thompson 1934:246). When Aboriginal people were introduced to wooden rowboats, the hunting method remained much the same.

Figure 15.4 Dugong caught by Robert Burns and George Dugong (both deceased), showing double outrigger canoe used for hunting, Mornington Island, circa 1921

Photo: UQ Anthropology Museum, University of Queensland.

During Hall's three years at the Mornington Island mission, local Aboriginal people accompanied the Cape York staff out on hunting trips, learning the methods themselves. Over a relatively short period from 1914, *whaps* and

---

3   An outrigger canoe has the same basic form as a dugout with the addition of either one (single outrigger) or two (double outrigger) steadying struts on either side, to assist the stability and buoyancy of the vessel (Davidson 1935:9).

4   The origin of this word is unclear, as it does not appear in either the Lardil or the Kaiadilt dictionaries.

dugout canoes replaced nets and *walbas* as the primary method of catching dugong in the Wellesley Islands.[5] There are a number of possible benefits to the *whap* and dugout canoe technique. Memmott (2010:43) noted that rafts were 'not very stable' and became waterlogged within a few hours of paddling (cf. Trigger 1987:80). *Whaps* and dugouts also required fewer participants for hunting while yielding a high rate of return.[6] In the Croker Island region off the coast of north-west Arnhem Land, archaeological evidence indicates that the introduction of dugout canoes (replacing bark canoes) was followed by a notable presence of dugong and turtle remains when compared with the period immediately preceding it (Peterson 2005:430).

On Mornington Island, the reliability of the hunting method became increasingly important as large numbers of Aboriginal people became sedentary around the mission and dependent on its food supply (Dalley and Memmott 2010:122). At the same time, there were also instances where Aboriginal people used mission equipment to hunt for dugong, the proceeds of which they then hid for their own consumption (Wilson, 8 September 1920, 15 May 1921).[7] Exercising personal autonomy in this way allowed individuals to meet their own responsibilities to kin through the provision of dugong meat. As more Aboriginal people learnt to build their own dugouts, they began approaching the mission with dugong and turtle meat that they had hunted themselves to exchange for flour, tea, sugar and other items such as fishing line and hooks (for example, Wilson, 1 December 1922).

Over the next 40 years, from the mid-1920s to the 1960s, hunting practices underwent little change. Aboriginal people on Mornington either used mission rowboats or manufactured their own dugout canoes and hunting materials using the techniques taught to them by Aboriginal staff from Cape York (Smart 1951:35). Gradually, the materials changed to include sharpened metal bolts in the *thartha* attached to rope and a light metal frame around the head of the *whap* (Marsh et al. 1980:258). In the 1960s, however, a significant shift occurred with the introduction and adoption of outboard motors and aluminium dinghies (Memmott 2010:92). One of the first such boats on Mornington was purchased by the artist Dick Roughsey, with money earned through the sale of his artworks

---

5   Reverend Wilson (24 June 1921, 22 December 1921), who replaced Hall in 1918, recorded instances where he destroyed canoes brought into 'prohibited waters' in proximity to the mission house. Wilson was concerned that fishing or cutting up dugong and turtle in these areas would attract sharks in the area where mission children swam for their daily bath.

6   Reverend Wilson recorded in his diary instances where the mission boat was sent out on hunting expeditions. With the exception of 1920, in the years 1919–25, the numbers of animals (dugong and turtle) caught were greater than the number of hunting expeditions.

7   Two of these recordings are as follows: 'The dinghy returned late last night with a nice dugong. I think William caught another + left it in the bush. There has been a general exodus in that direction this afternoon' (Wilson, 8 September 1920); and: 'Old man Peter's around cleared out on Friday with a dugong which William caught + planted. He got two + left the better one behind. I visited their plant + saw the remains' (Wilson, 15 May 1921).

in Cairns in 1964 (Roughsey 1971:137). Although outboard motors increased the range and frequency of hunting activities by reducing the physical exertion required for paddling, they did require a large initial outlay for purchase and ongoing funds for fuel and general repair (Memmott 1979:308; Memmott and Trigger 1998:121). In 1976, 1977 and 1978, Marsh et al. (1980) visited Mornington Island and provided a detailed recording of dugong hunting methods. At that time they recorded that 'hunting is carried out from 4–5 m aluminium dinghies; outboard motors ranging in size from 9 to 40 HP are used on all boats, the usual size being 18 to 25 HP' (Marsh et al. 1980:258). Dugong hunting methods were also shown in the Australian Museum film *Dugong! Dugong!*, recorded on Mornington Island in 1980 (Hughes 1980).

Between the 1960s and 1970s, Aboriginal people on Mornington moved into permanent, Western-style housing with electricity where the use of refrigerators and large freezers became possible (Brine 1980:4–5). While in principle these devices allowed meat to be preserved for longer and thus consumed by a single family over an extended period, the reality was somewhat more complex. Social responsibilities were such that hunters were still expected to share meat with others, particularly their family and the owners of the country from where the animal was taken. Other social conditions, such as the engagement of Mornington Islanders in employment on the Australian mainland, also mitigated against large numbers of dugong being caught (Marsh et al. 1980:264). Since that time gradual change has occurred, with larger boats and outboard motors becoming more common, and at the same time there has been (at least anecdotally) a decreasing reliance on bush foods for subsistence.

Changes to Dugong Hunting and Native Title, 1990s–2004

The impact and nature of change in hunting practice were brought to bear in native title proceedings. In 1996, Lardil, Kaiadilt, Yangkaal and mainland Ganggalida Aboriginal people lodged a native title claim over a large part of the seas of the southern Gulf of Carpentaria up to the high-tide mark on all of the Wellesley Islands and adjacent mainland coast (Behrendt 2004:14) (see Figure 15.1). *The Lardil Peoples v State of Queensland [2004] FCA 298* (now referred to as the 'Wellesley Sea Claim') followed a similar successful determination in the Croker Island sea claim off the Arnhem Land coast (*Mary Yarmirr and Others v the Northern Territory of Australia and Others FCA 771*) (Peterson 2005:428). The Croker case created an important legal precedent, which established the potential for Aboriginal marine tenure to be recognised in much the same way as Aboriginal land tenure. Part of this system of tenure was the requirement to ask permission to access sea country and to harvest marine resources within that country (Peterson 2005:438–9). It was this issue that played a similar role in the determination of the Wellesley Sea Claim. One avenue of questioning was about the changes in watercraft that had occurred in the Wellesleys during the mission period.

During the court process, lawyers for the State of Queensland, a respondent party to the claim, attempted to restrict the extent of the claim boundary by arguing that Aboriginal people had no knowledge of 'deep water'. Knowledge of 'deep water' beyond the inter-tidal zone, they argued, had arisen more recently with the advent of outboard motors and dugout canoes, which were better equipped than *walbas* to handle the rougher seas of deep water. Of particular importance to this line of questioning were those Aboriginal people who recalled the use of both *walbas* and dugout canoes. In this example, taken from the transcript of evidence, the lawyer for the State of Queensland questions a senior Yangkaal woman, Heather Toby, about changes in boat technology from about the 1920s.

> *When you were young you said how your father took you across from Forsyth to Denham on the raft, and you told us that you'd been fishing with your father on the raft when you were a young girl?* Yes.
>
> *And I think you said that you generally stayed close in to the shore?* Close to the shore.
>
> *And why is that?* Well, he couldn't go any further because the sea gets rough.
>
> *And the raft is not safe out that far?* It's not safe.
>
> *What about a canoe? Is a canoe any better for going out into the deep water?* Oh yes. (Transcript, 23 September 1999:437)

While not ignoring the impact of technological change, lawyers for the Aboriginal claimants argued that the *notion of hunting* as a practice remained consistent with Aboriginal tradition. This argument mirrored comments made in an earlier court case, *Yanner v Eaton [1999]*, lodged by Ganggalida man Murrandoo Yanner who was also one of the claimants in the Wellesley Sea Claim. The dispute, which was resolved in the High Court of Australia on appeal, concerned the legality of Yanner's hunting of a crocodile—a protected species under Queensland's *Fauna Conservation Act 1952* (Nicholls 2000). Although the case was as much about legal jurisdiction as the notion of tradition in native title rights, a number of comments were made during the court hearing regarding technological change in hunting. During the original trial in 1995, Dr David Trigger, an expert witness appearing on behalf of the defendant (Yanner), spoke about changes in boat and harpoon technology through the southern Gulf during the twentieth century

(Trigger 1996:26–7). In the High Court finding, the judge noted that 'although traditional hunting methods had changed over the years, the way in which the appellant [Yanner] hunted crocodiles was pretty much the same as the way his ancestors had' (Nicholls 2000:145).

In the Wellesley Sea Claim determination, however, Justice Cooper (2004:119) noted that 'with the present day availability of powered boats, particularly aluminium dinghies with outboard motors, access to sea Country for fishing and hunting is now more readily available than in times past'. He also noted that 'hunting of these animals [dugong and turtle] has continued throughout the recorded history of each of these peoples and it continues today' (Cooper 2004:125). Justice Cooper granted non-exclusive rights to the Aboriginal applicants within an area smaller than that originally claimed (see Figure 15.1) (Cooper 2004:107, 131). This did not include most of the area within the claim boundary where the water is greater than 15 m deep and thus considered 'deep water' (Cooper 2004:133). In spite of this, the non-exclusive rights included formal recognition of the Aboriginal right to hunt dugong and turtle within the designated Wellesley Sea Claim area (Cooper 2004:137), which was important for the Aboriginal claimants as it gave legal recognition to their own notions of ownership (Carpentaria Land Council Aboriginal Corporation 2006:13–15).

Dugong Hunting and Conservation Biology Discourses

The Wellesley Sea Claim determination occurred during a period of intensified interaction between Aboriginal people and the Australian Government in the management of land and sea resources (Buchanan et al. 2009). Over this same period, there has been increased media scrutiny of Indigenous hunting, particularly in northern Queensland. These reports have included alleged incidences of cruelty by Aboriginal hunters, the supposed sale of dugong and turtle meat on the 'black market' and examples where dead animals were found drowned in nets (for example, Bateman 2010; Schwarten 2010; Tapim 2011). Reports of this nature have led a range of politicians, media personalities and conservation organisations (sometimes including Indigenous people) to call for limits or bans on the taking of protected species (for example, Michael 2007; Ryan 2010; Viellaris 2009). Sometimes public comment has followed the release of research papers in conservation biology implicating Indigenous hunting in the decline of dugong populations.

Much of the conservation biology discourse coalesces around estimates of dugong populations and modelling of what might constitute a sustainable harvest of such populations (Heinsohn et al. 2004; Marsh et al. 1997, 1999, 2004). Despite considerable advances in understandings of dugong biology and reproduction, accurate quantifying of dugong populations remains problematic. Factors that influence survey methodology include

- reliance on aerial surveys that count only a fraction of the actual population in any location
- discrepancies in the mathematical model applied to extrapolate from aerially visible dugongs to the actual population
- mass dugong migrations across large geographic regions
- fluctuations of local populations based on a range of other unknown factors (Heinsohn et al. 2004:417; Kwan et al. 2006:169; Marsh et al. 1980, 2004:436–7).

In an earlier publication, Marsh (1996:139) concluded that 'unfortunately, existing survey methods are too inaccurate and imprecise to monitor dugong numbers at spatial and temporal scales useful to management'.[8] Just as populations have been difficult to quantify, so too has the impact of Indigenous hunting on dugong populations. In Torres Strait, for example, Kwan et al. (2006:169) noted that depending on the population modelling used, 'over harvest is difficult to prove empirically with the data available' (see also Heinsohn et al. 2004:417). *Sustainable Harvest of Marine Turtles and Dugongs in Australia—A national partnership approach* (Marine and Coastal Committee 2005) listed the negative impacts on dugong and turtle populations as including by-catch across a range of fishing activities, predation of turtle eggs by native and introduced species, coastal development, deteriorating water quality, marine debris, loss of habitat, boat strike and poaching by foreign nationals in Australian waters. Despite this, the disproportionate amount of academic research and media reports examining Indigenous hunting continues to position it as *the* major variable impacting the sustainability of dugong populations. As Yanner (2008:4) and others have noted, there has been much less willingness to discuss the impact or regulation of industries that negatively impact on dugongs, particularly commercial fishing.

Perhaps the most problematic aspect of some of the conservation biology literature, however, is that it misunderstands or misrepresents Aboriginal perspectives on hunting. For example, in a recent paper, the Aboriginal community of Hopevale on eastern Cape York was selected as a case study for a number of reasons, including that 'the thinking of both Aboriginal community members and management agency staff were likely to be representative of the entire Cape York region' (Nursey-Bray et al. 2010:370). This rendering of Aboriginal people and their perspectives on hunting as homogenous across a large geographical region ignores the diversity of historical and contemporary

---

8 Academics from other disciplines, such as archaeology, are also beginning to challenge the efficacy of such approaches, using data obtained from their own investigations (for example, McNiven and Bedingfield 2008).

experiences. As I have shown in the Mornington Island example, these factors are formative in developing Aboriginal perspectives on hunting, and, perhaps more importantly, impacting on hunting practice itself.

One of the Australian Government's responses to concerns about species sustainability has been to fund Aboriginal ranger groups across northern Australia. The 'Working on Country' program commenced in 2008[9] and its priorities were

- protecting biodiversity and natural icons
- protecting and rehabilitating coastal environments and critical aquatic habitats
- supporting natural resource management in northern Australia
- enhancing community skills, knowledge and engagement (Department of the Environment, Water, Heritage and the Arts 2008).

More broadly, the program aimed to 'train and employ up to 300 Indigenous Rangers to manage and conserve the natural and cultural features of Indigenous lands and waters' (Commonwealth of Australia 2008:44). The program identified three priorities, the second of which sought to support Indigenous people to undertake work to identify, conserve, maintain and manage sea country, threatened species and their habitats and culturally or regionally significant species and their habitats (Department of the Environment, Water, Heritage and the Arts 2008). One group to receive funding from Working on Country was the Wellesley Islands Rangers based on Mornington Island (Department of the Environment, Water, Heritage and the Arts 2008).

Wellesley Islands Rangers, Hunting and the Natural Resource Management Economy

The earlier success of the Wellesley Sea Claim in recognising Aboriginal native title rights aided the application of the Carpentaria Land Council Aboriginal Corporation (CLCAC) for Australian Government funding from the Working on Country grants program (Department of the Environment, Water, Heritage and the Arts 2008). In round three (funding commencing in 2008) of the Working on Country program, the CLCAC Wellesley Islands Rangers received funding to implement the Thuwathu/Bujimulla Sea Country Plan (CLCAC 2006). The

---

9 'Working on Country' is the Indigenous-specific program within the larger 'Caring for Our Country' program.

Sea Country Plan was devised by the Traditional Owners in collaboration with the CLCAC, and, amongst other things, prioritised the ongoing monitoring and sustainable use of dugong and sea turtle (CLCAC 2006:29–30).

Mornington Island is similar to most large, very remote Australian Aboriginal communities in that over the period of research (2007–09), very few Aboriginal Mornington Islanders were engaged in employment (Francis 2010).[10] In 2006, the median weekly income on Mornington Island was $209 (ABS 2006:Table B02), compared with the broader Australian median of $466. Prior to gaining employment as rangers, most of the eight men had been engaged two days per week as 'participants' in the Community Development Employment Projects (CDEP) scheme (Interview, Wellesley Islands Rangers, 19 June 2009). CDEP is fully funded by the Australian Government and on Mornington Island consists of a number of 'work gangs': groups of men undertaking basic tasks such as rubbish removal, fencing or general carpentry jobs around the community.[11] When employed in the ranger program, the men went from earning less than $200 per week in CDEP to more than $500 per week (Interview, Wellesley Islands Ranger A, 19 June 2009). This pay increase and the integration of the eight Mornington Island men into the natural resource management economy have had transformative social and economic effects on those men and their immediate families, as well as the broader community.

The most obvious of these changes has been the purchase of motor vehicles, with four of the eight rangers able to purchase a car or an additional car between 2008 and 2010 (Interview, Wellesley Island Rangers, 19 June 2009; Wellesley Islands Ranger B, Personal communication, 2010). On Mornington Island, owning a car, particularly a four-wheel-drive, facilitates access to remote parts of the Island, enabling families to travel the sometimes large distances 'out bush' to their traditional country to renew links, access bush food and participate in family activities. This is seen as particularly useful for many of the men who have large families with numerous young children. During a 2009 interview, the Rangers also commented on how they had greater capacity to afford 'household things' such as flat-screen TVs and freezers (Interview, Wellesley Island Rangers A, C and D, 19 June 2009). The men were also able to purchase items when they left the Island on work trips such as training exercises and ranger exchanges to other parts of Australia.

---

10   Although the 2006 Census recorded that more than 30 per cent of the Mornington Island community was employed, either in full-time or part-time positions, it seems likely that this figure includes CDEP participants (ABS 2006:Table B41). Although CDEP participation was not considered employment in the 2006 Census, my own experience suggests that Aboriginal Mornington Islanders would have been unlikely to make this distinction in completing the Census form. Taking into account the Mornington Shire Council's estimate of 60 full-time-equivalent positions in 2010 (Francis 2010), a more accurate estimation of fully funded employment (that is, excluding CDEP) might be 5–10 per cent of the total population of Mornington Island.

11   The program does include some women, particularly in a sewing 'gang'; however, the number of male participants greatly outweighs the number of women by my estimation at a ratio of three to one.

In 2009, the female partners of some of the Rangers also noted a decrease in reliance on other family members to loan them money between pay weeks (Interview, 12 June 2009). Despite the expenditure on large items such as cars and boats, all the Rangers and their partners also noted a greater access to cash and saving: 'we just got money sitting there all the time' (Interview, 12 June 2009; also Interview, Wellesley Islands Ranger E, 19 June 2009). This 'ready money' (Merlan 2009:277) was seen as particularly useful for unexpected costs, such as trips to the mainland for medical treatment or school trips off the Island for the Rangers' children. As well as economic benefits, the Rangers' partners commented on how the men's involvement created social cohesion because of their shared experience of work and greater economic prosperity. This meant that 'you don't have to…[hold a] grudge against families and [worry] who's better than who in the group because of one fella bought this and that, or they saving more money than this person' (Interview, 12 June 2009).

The type of work undertaken by the Rangers was seen to have broader community benefits. When undertaking work around the islands, one ranger noticed that 'if we do that then our countrymen from that area feel proud of us, for what we done for them, in their country' (Interview, Wellesley Islands Ranger F, 19 June 2009). Much of this work involved patrolling sea country, undertaking tasks such as observing dugong populations, recording turtle nesting sites, recording seagrass habitats and removing potential threats to dugong and turtle such as discarded commercial fishing nets known as 'ghost nets' (Wilson n.d.:3). Some of these tasks were undertaken in collaboration with researchers and external agencies that travelled to the Wellesley Islands to work with the Rangers. The Rangers also sometimes undertook hunting for funerals (for example, Field notes, 23 August 2007, 3 March 2010) or important community events such as the Gulf Dance Festival (for example, Field notes, 22 September 2008). When the ranger program first commenced on Mornington Island, parents sometimes reported that their children wanted to become a 'Bush Ranger' or a 'Power Ranger'—two of the nicknames given to the Wellesley Islands Rangers. The main attractions of the job were the access to cars, boats and quad bikes, wearing a uniform,[12] time spent out 'on country', trips off the Island and the derived income. Thus, as Buchanan et al. (2009:59) also concluded in their study of the Bardi Jawi Aboriginal Rangers in Western Australia, the social and economic benefits of being employed as a ranger were inextricably linked.

At the same time, there were undoubtedly discontinuities, which arose between governments' and the Wellesley Islands Rangers' discourses on hunting. Many of the Rangers' concerns relating to hunting pertained to the social mediation

---

12   Between 2007 and 2010, the Rangers were the only predominately Aboriginal positions that had an associated uniform. On the few occasions when the Rangers wore their uniforms, they were often described as 'too deadly' (impressive).

of practice and the move away from 'traditional' methods of hunting. One such example was the perception that some hunters, particularly young men, hunted in order to demonstrate their masculinity. The Rangers disliked the notion of 'big-noting yourself for hunting, want to be the main man, you want to be the gun player, you want to catch more dugong, more turtle than the next fella next to you...It's not about that' (Interview, Wellesley Islands Ranger F, 19 June 2009). The desire to undertake hunting for social status was partly attributed to greater access to larger, more powerful boat engines in recent decades: 'Now that we got outboards and big speedboats, some fellas think that they're ironman' (Interview, Wellesley Islands Ranger B, 19 June 2009).

At the same time, the rise in notoriety of an individual as a skilled hunter was seen as detracting from the communality of sharing meat among a large number of people: 'Hunters before just put one in a canoe cause that's all they could fit...That one would feed nearly the whole village. Those days, they used to cut it up traditional way where under the traditional way, it shares out a lot of meat and it was fair' (Interview, Wellesley Islands Ranger F, 19 June 2009). The Rangers described how some hunters eschewed this 'fairness':

> [T]here is some fellas on Mornington that kill today, they'll kill tomorrow, kill the next day and they'll kill the next day. They won't even give me or anyone else the chance to go. They've got two/three freezer full and they won't share it to the next-door neighbour or the bloke across the street. (Interview, Wellesley Islands Ranger F, 19 June 2009)

This was countered by the Rangers' use of contrary defining statements describing their own hunting practice, such as 'it's not about greed' and 'we share our meat' (Interview, Wellesley Islands Rangers F, 19 June 2009). Comments of this nature illustrated how the *social* responsibilities of hunting, particularly the distribution of meat, were particularly important to the Rangers.

When it came to implementing measures that might alter hunting practice, such as the adoption of a quota system to limit the number of dugongs killed, the Rangers were circumspect. One noted how changes to the current arrangements might be interpreted:

> [I]t is going to be hard to enforce because this is their comfort zone, this is what they've been doing for a long time, they're too used to it. They going to say, 'you can't tell me what to do!' But we say 'it's not telling you what to do, it's about managing it'. (Interview, Wellesley Islands Ranger F, 19 June 2009)

At the same time, they noted that the resource was important and that 'we need those things to be there for our grandchildren and great-grandchildren'. In the meantime, the Rangers undertook catch monitoring, surveyed dugong and turtle populations and talked in generalities about changing hunting practices in the future.[13] One described the approach as 'we just keep an eye on things' (Interview, Wellesley Islands Ranger A, 19 June 2009), but would not be drawn on what situations might require particular intervention.

The adoption of this kind of language might be considered as an example of Babidge et al.'s (2007:154) concept of 'management speak'. 'Management speak' is defined as a form of dialogue used by Aboriginal people when engaged in discussions over resources. In a candid interview in 2008, Murrandoo Yanner explained the problematic association between employment in the natural resource management economy and the adoption of particular approaches to dugong management. He (2008:5) noted:

> [P]rovided that we deliver on the environmental outputs we can say what we want politically, such as the dugong stuff, [we might say] 'We're not regulating dugongs, regardless of what government policy [is]'. But we can't say that because only the government is funding our rangers.[14] So we need to seek funding elsewhere so we can be staunch and make up our own minds and say what we want without the government jerking the chain on our neck.

Yanner's position and the Wellesley Islands Rangers' use of 'management speak' when discussing dugong management are also suggestive of Martin's use of the term 'strategic engagement'. For Martin (2003:8), strategic engagement is the 'process through which indigenous individuals, groups and communities are able to interact with, contribute to, draw from—and of course reject—the formal and informal institutions of the dominant Australian society'. Thus, the Rangers might be seen to benefit economically and socially from their involvement in the ranger program and undertake some works towards the overall goal of dugong management. At the same time, their own discourse about hunting focuses on the social and cultural changes to hunting rather more so than a conservation biology approach.

Conclusion

Through this chapter, I have charted the history of dugong hunting on Mornington Island as an intercultural practice, in much the same way that Merlan proposed. The arrival of missionaries and Cape York staff in the region in 1914 had a transformative impact on the techniques and material culture

---

13   This approach included involvement in seagrass habitat surveys—for example, Taylor et al. (2007:i).
14   It is unclear here what Yanner meant by 'our rangers', however, it might refer to the Wellesley Islands Rangers and the Moungabi (Burketown) Rangers, who are both auspiced by the CLCAC with which Yanner was closely associated. Alternatively, it might relate to all Indigenous rangers.

of dugong hunting. Observable changes also occurred from the 1960s with the introduction of aluminium dinghies and outboard motors. Through these periods of change, the sentiment of sharing dugong meat has persisted, while the number of people actually involved in a single hunt has decreased. The development of hunting through time is such that 'it can no longer be seen simply as a "traditional subsistence practice" insofar as such a label resists critical examination of contemporary intersecting values and resource streams' (Merlan 2009:278).

These intersecting values have come to the fore in the more recent period when the monitoring of dugong populations has become an integral part of the work of eight Aboriginal rangers based on Mornington Island. The program has had obvious economic and social benefits for the Rangers and their families. In employing the notion of 'strategic engagement' (Martin 2003) though, I have sought to explore the differing priorities of the Rangers and the Australian Government which employs them in much the same way that Yanner did. While Aboriginal people take up employment with agencies funded by the Australian Government, they do so with their own interpretations of key issues, as exemplified by the example of dugong hunting and management.

One question that remains, however, is the degree to which the adoption of 'management speak' and the mediation of governmental concerns might be considered strategic in the long term. As Martin (2003:8) noted, '"strategic engagement" should give Indigenous individuals and collectives…real choices as to where to go, and how to get there'. Looking to the future is a clear component in the successful implementation of strategic engagement. In the future it seems likely that governments, both State and Federal, are likely to desire more rather than less regulation of dugong hunting, particularly if dugong populations show continuing decline. Should this occur, the Rangers will have to develop new strategies for engaging with governments, particularly given that in other parts of Australia quota systems and/or bans on hunting have been established. Management speak has been utilised in the short term to mediate differing notions of dugong management, but in the absence of actual change to hunting practice, its effectiveness as a long-term strategy seems questionable.

One proposed solution has been for Aboriginal people to move away from government funding of ranger programs. In this scenario, Aboriginal people would enter into partnerships with private entities—to again quote Yanner (2008:5): 'so we're looking more at working with large companies and getting our own funding.' This approach is somewhat reminiscent of Altman's model of a hybrid economy where interaction might occur between the 'market', the 'state' and Aboriginal 'customary' realms. Yanner has suggested that this approach might provide Aboriginal people with the economic autonomy to make their own decisions in the management of country. This notion of attaining an autonomous decision-making position might be difficult to achieve given the embeddedness of Aboriginal people in the intercultural milieu, where rights and interests in natural resources are interconnected. As Smith (2003:88) concluded: 'Aboriginal people are neither truly autonomous in their relationship to wider Australian society, nor successfully refashioned as participants in the wider economy.' Despite this, forays such as the ranger program provide Aboriginal people with opportunities to gain skills and experience, particularly in developing relationships with governments, which bode well for the development of innovative responses to complex management issues. In-depth studies and those that explore the historical trajectory of practices such as hunting have the potential to meaningfully explore the complex ways in which Aboriginal people experience and seek to mediate such relationships.

References

Altman, J. C. 1987. *Hunter-Gatherers Today: An Aboriginal economy in north Australia*. Canberra: Australian Institute of Aboriginal Studies.

Altman, J. C. 2001. *Sustainable development options on Aboriginal land: the hybrid economy in the twenty-first century*. CAEPR Discussion Paper No. 226, Centre for Aboriginal Economic Policy Research, Australian National University, Canberra.

Austin-Broos, D. 2003. Places, practices and things: the articulation of Arrente kinship with welfare and work. *American Ethnologist* 30 (1): 118–35.

Australian Bureau of Statistics (ABS) 2006. *20010 BCP Gununa (L)- Qld Urban Centre-Locality*. Catalogue No. 2001.0, Community Profile Series. Canberra: Australian Bureau of Statistics.

Babidge, S., Greer, S., Henry, R. and Pam, C. 2007. Management speak: Indigenous knowledge and bureaucratic engagement. *Social Analysis* 51 (3): 148–64.

Bateman, D. 2010. State must do more to protect dugongs. *Cairns Post*, 29 April 2010: 11.

Behrendt, J. 2004. Lardil People v State of Queensland [2004] FCA 298. *Indigenous Law Bulletin* 6 (2): 14–17.

Blake, T. 1998. Historical report Wellesley Islands Sea Claim. Unpublished report prepared for the Carpentaria Land Council and the Claimants, Brisbane.

Bradley, J. J. 1997. Li-anthawirriyarra, people of the sea: Yanyuwa relations with their maritime environment. Unpublished PhD thesis, Faculty of Arts, Northern Territory University, Darwin.

Brine, J. 1980. After Cyclone Ted on Mornington Island: the accumulation of physical and social impacts on a remote Australian Aboriginal community. *Disasters* 4 (1): 3–10.

Buchanan, G., Altman, J., Arthur, B., Oades, D. and the Bardi Jawi Rangers 2009. *'Always part of us': the socioeconomics of Indigenous customary use and management of dugong and marine turtles—a view from Bardi and Jawi sea country, Western Australia.* Research Report Knowledge Series 001, North Australian Indigenous Land and Sea Management Alliance, Charles Darwin University, Darwin.

Carpentaria Land Council Aboriginal Corporation (CLCAC) 2006. *Thuwathu/ Bujimulla Sea Country Plan: Aboriginal management of the Wellesley Islands region of the Gulf of Carpentaria.* Burketown, Qld: Carpentaria Land Council Aboriginal Corporation.

Cawte, J. 1972. *Cruel, Poor and Brutal Nations: The assessment of mental health of an Australian Aboriginal community by short-stay psychiatric field team methods.* Honolulu: University of Hawai'i Press.

Commonwealth of Australia 2008. *Caring for Our Country: Outcomes 2008–2013.* Canberra: Commonwealth of Australia.

Cooper, J. 2004. Determination of *Lardil, Kaiadilt, Yangkaal and Gangalidda Peoples v State of Queensland & Others* [2004] Federal Court of Australia 298. Federal Court of Australia.

Dalley, C. and Memmott, P. 2010. Domains and the intercultural: understanding Aboriginal and missionary engagement at the Mornington Island Mission, Gulf of Carpentaria, Australia from 1914 to 1942. *International Journal of Historical Archaeology* 14: 112–35.

Davidson, D. S. 1935. The chronology of Australian watercraft. *The Journal of the Polynesian Society* 44 (173): 1–16; 44 (174): 69–84; 44 (175): 137–52; 44 (176): 193–207.

Department of the Environment, Water, Heritage and the Arts 2008. *Caring for Our Country—Working on country.* Canberra: Australian Government. Viewed 10 June 2010, <http://www.nrm.gov.au/funding/2008/woc.html>

Francis, C. 2010. Indigenous economic development: challenges for traditional owners, council and community. Paper presented at the Aligning Indigenous Land Management and Economic Development Conference, Darwin, 24 March 2010.

Gudeman, S. 2001. *The Anthropology of Economy: Community, market and culture.* Oxford: Blackwell.

Hall, R. H. 1914–17. Diaries. Unpublished copies of personal diaries held at the Hibberd Library, Weipa, Qld.

Hall, R. H. 1986 [1914–17]. *A Missionary Pioneer: Robert Hall of Mornington Island. His diaries.* R. Ian Hall (ed.). Waihola, New Zealand.

Harrison, J. 1974. Missionaries, fisheries and government in far north Queensland 1891–1919: a study of conflict and co-operation between the Presbyterian mission stations, commercial fishing interests and the Queensland Government on matters concerning the welfare of the Aborigines in Cape York and the Torres Strait 1891–1919. Unpublished BA(Hons) thesis, University of Queensland, St Lucia.

Heinsohn, R., Lacy, R. C., Lindenmayer, D. C., Marsh, H., Kwan, D. and Lawler, I. R. 2004. Unsustainable harvest of dugongs in Torres Strait and Cape York (Australia) waters: two case studies using population viability analysis. *Animal Conservation* 7: 417–25.

Hinkson, M. and Smith, B. 2005. Introduction: conceptual moves towards an intercultural analysis. *Oceania* 75 (3): 157–66.

Holcombe, S. 2005. Luritja management of the state. *Oceania* 75 (3): 222–33.

Howard, R. B. 1910. *Annual Report of the Chief Protector of Aboriginals for 1910, Queensland.* Brisbane: Government Printer.

Hughes, H. 1980. *Dugong! Dugong!* [Video recording.] Australian Museum film series, Sydney.

Hunt, J., Altman, J. C. and May, K. 2009. *Social benefits of Aboriginal engagement in natural resource management.* CAEPR Working Paper No. 60, Centre for Aboriginal Economic Policy Research, Australian National University, Canberra.

Kwan, D., Marsh, H. and Delean, S. 2006. Factors influencing the sustainability of customary dugong hunting by a remote indigenous community. *Environmental Conservation* 33 (2): 164–71.

Loos, N. 1982. *Invasion and Resistance: Aboriginal–European relations on the north Queensland frontier 1861–1897*. Canberra: Australian National University Press.

McKnight, D. 1999. *People, Countries and the Rainbow Serpent*. Oxford: Oxford University Press.

McNiven, I. J. and Bedingfield, A. C. 2008. Past and present marine mammal hunting rates and abundances: dugong (*Dugong dugon*) evidence from Dabangai bone mound, Torres Strait. *Journal of Archaeological Science* 35: 505–15.

Marine and Coastal Committee 2005. *Sustainable Harvest of Marine Turtles and Dugongs in Australia—A national partnership approach*. Canberra: Natural Resource Management Ministerial Council.

Marsh, H. 1996. Progress towards the sustainable use of dugongs by Indigenous peoples in Queensland. In M. Bomford and J. Caughley (eds), *Sustainable Use of Wildlife by Aboriginal Peoples and Torres Strait Islanders*, pp. 139–66. Canberra: Australian Government Publishing Service.

Marsh, H., Eros, C., Corkeron, P. and Breen, B. 1999. A conservation strategy for dugongs: implications of Australian research. *Journal of Marine and Freshwater Research* 50: 979–90.

Marsh, H., Gardner, B. R. and Heinsohn, G. E. 1980. Present-day hunting and distribution of dugongs in the Wellesley Islands (Queensland): implications for conservation. *Biological Conservation* 19: 255–67.

Marsh, H., Harris, A. N. M. and Lawler, I. R. 1997. The sustainability of the Indigenous dugong fishery in Torres Strait, Australia/Papua New Guinea. *Conservation Biology* 11 (6): 1375–86.

Marsh, H., Lawler, I. R., Kwan, D., Delean, S., Pollock, K. and Alldredge, M. 2004. Aerial surveys and the potential biological removal technique indicate that the Torres Strait dugong fishery is unsustainable. *Animal Conservation* 7: 435–43.

Martin, D. 2003. *Rethinking the design of Indigenous organisations: the need for strategic engagement*. CAEPR Discussion Paper No. 248, Centre for Aboriginal Economic Policy Research, Australian National University, Canberra.

Michael, P. 2007. Elders unhappy over dugong, turtle slaughter. *The Courier-Mail*, 9 October 2007: 7.

Memmott, P. 1979. Lardil properties of place: an ethnological study in man–environment relations. Unpublished PhD thesis, University of Queensland, St Lucia.

Memmott, P. 1983. Social structure and the use of space amongst the Lardil. In N. Peterson and M. Langton (eds), *Aborigines, Land and Land Rights*, pp. 33–65. Canberra: Australian Institute of Aboriginal Studies.

Memmott, P. 2010. *Material culture of the North Wellesley Islands*. AIATSIS Research Report Series, Aboriginal and Torres Strait Islander Studies Unit, University of Queensland, St Lucia.

Memmott, P. and Trigger, D. 1998. Marine tenure in the Wellesley Islands region, Gulf of Carpentaria. In N. Peterson and B. Rigsby (eds), *Customary Marine Tenure in Australia*, pp. 110–24. Oceania Monograph 48. Sydney: University of Sydney.

Merlan, F. 1998. *Caging the Rainbow: Place, politics and agency in a north Australian town*. Honolulu: University of Hawai'i Press.

Merlan, F. 2005. Explorations towards intercultural accounts of socio-cultural reproduction and change. *Oceania* 75 (3): 167–82.

Merlan, F. 2006. European settlement and the making and unmaking of Aboriginal identities. *The Australian Journal of Anthropology* 17 (2): 179–95.

Merlan, F. 2009. Introduction: recuperating economic anthropology. *The Australian Journal of Anthropology* 20: 269–84.

National Native Title Tribunal. 2005. *Native Title Determination: QC96/2 – QG207/97 (Wellesley Islands Sea Claim)*. Map created by Geospatial Services, National Native Title Tribunal. Canberra: NNTT.

Nicholls, F. G. 2000. Aboriginal hunting rights and fauna protection legislation. *Environmental Policy and Law* 30 (3): 143–6.

Nursey-Bray, M., Marsh, H. and Ross, H. 2010. Exploring discourses in environmental decision making: an Indigenous hunting case study. *Society & Natural Resources* 23: 366–82.

Peterson, N. 2005. On the visibility of Indigenous Australian systems of marine tenure. *Senri Ethnological Studies* 67: 427–44.

Roughsey, D. (Goobalathaldin) 1971. *Moon and Rainbow: The autobiography of an Aboriginal*. Brisbane: Rigby Books.

Ryan, B. 2010. MP attacks calls for dugong cruelty crackdown. *ABC News*, 21 December 2010.

Schwarten, E. 2010. Crackdown on illegal dugong hunting demanded. *Australian Associated Press General News*, 28 April 2010.

Smart, P. 1951. The dugong. *Walkabout* 17 (11): 34–5.

Smith, B. R. 2003. Pastoralism, local knowledge and Australian Aboriginal development in northern Queensland. *The Asia Pacific Journal of Anthropology* 4 (1–2): 88–104.

Stanner, W. E. H. 1979 [1958]. Continuity and change among the Aborigines. In W. E. H. Stanner (ed.), *White Man Got No Dreaming*, pp. 41–66. Canberra: Australian National University Press.

Tapim, F. 2011. Call to probe illegal dugong, turtle trade. *ABC News*, 6 September 2011.

Taylor, H. A., Rasheed, M. A. and Coles, R. 2007. *Seagrass Communities of the Wellesley Island Group*. Cairns, Qld: Queensland Department of Primary Industries and Fisheries.

Thompson, D. F. 1934. The dugong hunters of Cape York. *The Journal of the Royal Anthropological Institute of Great Britain and Ireland* 64 (July–December): 237–63.

Trigger, D. S. 1987. Inland, coast and islands: traditional Aboriginal society and material culture in a region of the southern Gulf of Carpentaria. *Records of the South Australia Museum* 20 (2): 69–84.

Trigger, D. S. 1996. Witness testimony of Dr David S. Trigger. Transcript of *Graham John Eaton v Murrandoo Bulanyi Mungabayi Yanner*, No. c/f 1692 of 1995, Magistrate's Court, Mount Isa, Qld: 21–32.

Viellaris, R. 2009. Crackdown urged on cruel trade in turtle, dugong meat. *The Courier-Mail*, 10 September 2009: 14.

White, F. D. 1994. Church and state in Presbyterian missions, Gulf of Carpentaria: 1937–1947. Unpublished MA thesis, University of Queensland, St Lucia.

Wilson, B. n.d. Dugong & marine turtle project update. *Carpentaria Land Council Aboriginal Corporation NRM Newsletter*: 3.

Wilson, R. H. 1918–26. Diaries. Unpublished copies of personal diaries held at the Australian Institute of Aboriginal and Torres Strait Islanders Studies Library, Canberra.

Yanner, M. 2008. Traditional owner comment. *Native Title Newsletter* 4 (July–August): 4–6. Canberra: Native Title Research Unit, Australian Institute of Aboriginal and Torres Strait Islander Studies.

Acknowledgments

Thanks to all Aboriginal research participants in the Wellesley Islands from 2006 to 2010, particularly the Wellesley Islands Rangers and their families. This research has been assisted by a grant, 'Fishing Through Time in the Wellesley Islands' (G2007/7292), from the Australian Institute of Aboriginal and Torres Strait Islander Studies. Additional assistance came from the Australian Research Council (ARC) Discovery Project 'Isolation, Insularity and Change in Island Populations—An interdisciplinary study of Aboriginal cultural patterns in the Gulf of Carpentaria' (DP0663047). The School of Architecture at the University of Queensland assisted with travel costs to attend the Indigenous Participation in Australian Economies Conference where this chapter was first presented. This chapter was further developed as a result of discussions with Geoff Buchanan of the Centre for Aboriginal Economic Policy Research (CAEPR) at The Australian National University and Dr David Martin. I extend particular thanks to Professor David Trigger, Wendy Asche, Dr Carla Meurk and Kelly Greenop for their comments on an earlier draft.

16. Environmental Conservation and Indigenous Development through Indigenous Protected Areas and Payments for Environmental Services: A review

Nanni Concu

Introduction

Payments for Environmental Services (PES) are instruments to promote conservation goals and development in rural and poor communities (Pagiola et al. 2008. The use of PES in Indigenous Australia has only recently emerged as a potential alternative to government funding. PES schemes are strongly linked to Indigenous natural resource management (NRM) carried out by traditional owners and custodians (hereinafter TOs) and Indigenous land and sea management groups, and increasingly formalised through Indigenous Protected Areas (IPAs).

Both PES and IPAs are hailed as alternatives to other forms of economic participation in the Australian economy. The Indigenous development discourse in Australia nowadays strongly emphasises participation in the mainstream economy as the fundamental element in overcoming the socioeconomic disadvantages of Indigenous communities (COAG 2009). Under this paradigm, economic participation is equated with entrepreneurship and employment, and government policies and public/private cooperation aim to provide job opportunities for Indigenous Australians in manufacturing, mining, agriculture, forestry, retail and other services (AEC 2010; COAG 2009). Reforms of the Community Development Employment Projects (CDEP) program, for instance, are meant to push Indigenous people into this sort of 'real' employment (Hudson 2009).

This model of economic participation might suit some Indigenous Australians. Others, particularly in remote areas,[1] might face different economic conditions that make employment in the mainstream economy a different challenge: in remote areas job opportunities are limited and economic participation would

---

1 For a definition of remote and very remote areas, see ABS (2007). Remoteness is measured by physical distance by road to the nearest urban centre. According to the Australian Bureau of Statistics, about 26 per cent of the Aboriginal and Torres Strait Islander population lives in remote and very remote regions (ABS 2010).

require relocation or increased mobility, potentially resulting in further economic disadvantage (Biddle 2009); job creation for Indigenous people in remote communities has also had limited success in and around mining leases (Altman and Martin 2009); the low agricultural potential in large parts of the Indigenous estate does not allow for investment in this sector (Luckert et al. 2007); furthermore, Indigenous Australians might also have different sets of incentives and cultural demands precluding direct transfer of non-Indigenous models of entrepreneurship and employment (Austin-Broos 2003; Lindsay 2005).

An alternative form of Indigenous economic participation is based on commercialisation of environmental goods and services through PES and government-supported NRM activities. This mix of market-based instruments and government funding is at the core of proposals for establishing Indigenous NRM-based economies (Altman and Whitehead 2003; Hill et al. 2007; Luckert et al. 2007; Woinarski et al. 2007). By trading environmental goods and services through market exchanges and public funding for NRM activities, Indigenous communities could access financial resources for the creation of culturally appropriate NRM employment and livelihoods.

Contrasted with other forms of employment, Indigenous NRM promotes the integration of economic growth with conservation goals in line with Indigenous aspirations to live on and care for their country (NLC 2006). By engaging Indigenous ecological knowledge and social capital, Indigenous NRM gives Indigenous landowners the possibility to match work obligations with cultural priorities, kin responsibilities and conservation goals (NLC 2006; Russel-Smith et al. 2009). Indigenous landowners in remote areas are also geographically well placed to address the complexities of many environmental issues in remote regions of the Australian continent (Luckert et al. 2007). Further, the Indigenous estate—covering about 20 per cent of the Australian landmass— has internationally significant environmental and cultural values (Altman et al. 2007). These factors—ecological knowledge, cultural and social capital, ownership of important environmental assets, location and low productive potential of the Indigenous estates—give Indigenous landowners a comparative advantage (if not an absolute advantage) in the provision of environmental services.

Examples of environmental services include fire management for carbon abatement, biodiversity conservation, and feral animal and invasive species control. These NRM activities have important indirect effects on other economic sectors such as tourism, commercial and recreational fishing, and agriculture. The Indigenous art market also benefits from Indigenous NRM, as it is dependent on the conservation of local environments and Indigenous NRM activities for the provision of natural products such as fibres, bark, timber and dyes for art production (see MAC 2008). Hence, Indigenous NRM generates environmental outcomes for the benefits of the Australian and international communities by creating bundles of private and public goods. Both government funding and PES are instruments to internalise—that is, turn them into private gains—the public benefits associated with Indigenous NRM, and to promote the private provision of environmental goods.

Indigenous NRM has become increasingly formalised through the establishment of IPAs. At the time of writing, there are 38 IPAs, comprising 23 per cent of Australia's protected areas or 2.8 per cent of the landmass of Australia (DEWHA 2010c). Market-based instruments for land management and environmental conservation are also increasingly being proposed and trialled. Muller (2008) and Greiner et al. (2009) advocate PES as an opportunity for Indigenous landowners to support their environmental and cultural management activities in northern Australia.

Dhimurru Aboriginal Corporation (hereinafter Dhimurru) and Djelk Rangers both have some experience of using PES schemes. They both also manage two important IPAs. I review their experience in order to assess the functioning of PES schemes as instruments to promote Indigenous conservation and development aspirations. This assessment highlights how Indigenous comparative advantage in NRM could be realised, what services Indigenous landowners are selling or providing through PES schemes and/or government support, and identify what is working and what is not. This would in turn inform both Indigenous NRM and potential buyers on best PES practices.

This chapter is organised in five sections, starting with a short introduction to Australia's IPAs. In section two, I discuss the theoretical framework for PES and its application to Indigenous NRM. Section three contains a description of Dhimurru and Djelk IPAs, the types of NRM activities both ranger groups routinely carry out, and estimates of resources allocated to each NRM activity. The review of PES schemes used by Dhimurru and Djelk to fund their NRM activities is in section four, and these schemes are discussed more broadly in section five.

Australia's Indigenous Protected Areas

The Indigenous Protected Area (IPA) program is the first national NRM program to specifically target Indigenous landowners. The IPA program was established in 1996 as part of the Federal Government's commitment to expand the National Reserve System (NRS), and thus meet Australia's obligations under Article Eight of the International Convention on Biodiversity Conservation (Gilligan 2006; Langton et al. 2005). IPAs are based on a voluntary agreement between TOs and the Federal Government through which Indigenous-owned land is assigned to the protection of biodiversity and the conservation of cultural resources. As such, IPAs have no legal basis—that is, they are not regulated by any Commonwealth, State or Territory legislation—but are managed as part of the NRS according to international conservation standards (Gilligan 2006). At the time of writing, there are 38 declared IPAs, with consultation projects under way for another forty. IPAs make up 23 per cent of Australia's NRS (DEWHA 2010c). Consultations are also under way to establish sea country IPAs (DEWHA 2010d).

The IPA program is generally reputed as an example of successful collaboration between governments and Indigenous landowners and as one of Australia's most successful conservation arrangements (Gilligan 2006). On the one hand, the Australian community has gained bio-regionally significant land as part of the NRS. The millions of hectares TOs voluntarily contribute to the NRS are acquired with little public expenditure. In its first 10 years (1996–2006), the IPA program received about $12 million in funding—equivalent to less than $1 per hectare of protected land—while making significant contributions to the NRS in terms of both area and biodiversity value (Gilligan 2006). As some of the land acquired by or returned to TOs had previously been exploited for pastoral or agricultural enterprises, it was often highly degraded. Indigenous landowners have taken it upon themselves to restore and conserve their traditional estates—again, with minimal investment from governments (Gilligan 2006; Langton et al. 2005). For Indigenous landowners, IPAs are an exercise of Indigenous governance. Control of the IPAs ultimately resides with senior traditional owners. IPAs are also a means to achieve a set of social, economic, environmental and cultural benefits (BAC 2009), and provide effective protection of Indigenous values (Dhimurru 2008). Gilligan (2006) reports that the majority of Indigenous communities living within IPAs received economic, educational, social and health benefits from the program.

Other national NRM initiatives have not been as successful. The National Landcare Program, the National Heritage Trust and the National Action Plan for Salinity and Water Quality provided more than $4.5 billion of public money to address land degradation (Kingwell et al. 2008). Indigenous participation in these NRM programs and access to funds have been relatively poor (Smyth et al. 2004). They also have not had relevant environmental outcomes, and taxpayers' money has not been used efficiently (Kingwell et al. 2008; Marsh and Pannell 2000).[2]

---

2   In 2008, the Federal Government scrapped the national programs and set up a new NRM framework: the Caring for Our Country initiative. This initiative integrates the Landcare, National Heritage Trust programs and Indigenous-specific programs such as Indigenous Protected Areas (IPAs) and Working on Country programs (Commonwealth of Australia 2010).

Payment for Environmental Services

The limited success of programs such as Landcare in Australia, or similar conservation projects in other countries (Wunder 2005), has spurred the development of instruments such as PES to address the global decline of biodiversity and poverty issues. PES are based on the idea that increasingly scarce environmental services can potentially be traded. Environmental service beneficiaries make direct, contractual and conditional payments to land managers for adopting management practices that secure ecosystem conservation and/or restoration (Wunder 2005). These contractual commitments have the potential to improve the livelihoods of economically disadvantaged communities. In other words, PES create markets where there is a market failure. The logic of PES is illustrated in Figure 16.1.

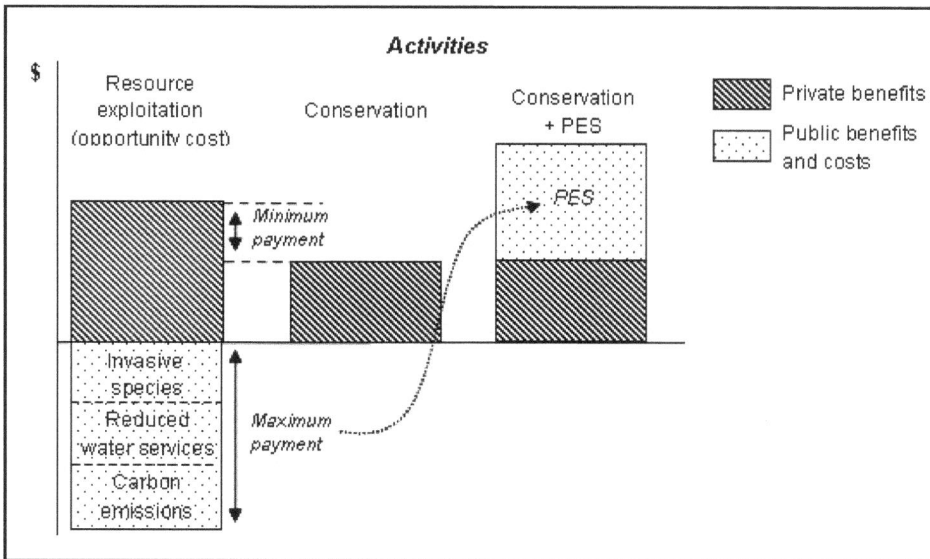

Figure 16.1 The logic of PES

Land managers often receive little financial benefit from conservation practices. When these benefits are less than the benefits from productive use of the land, such as agriculture or forestry, and when such productive activities impose costs on others (the global community, downstream populations, other land managers), PES could make conservation practices more attractive by paying land managers to adopt them.

Engel et al. (2008) list a set of conditions for the successful implementation of PES

- natural ecosystems are mismanaged because many of their benefits are externalities from the point of view of the owners

- buyers can be identified and are willing to pay for environmental services
- sellers of environmental services are also identified
- transactions are voluntary
- environmental services are well defined
- payments are conditional on effective service provision.

The first point describes the case of market failure. Arguably, this does not seem to apply to the Indigenous estate. Indigenous management practices are usually considered sustainable. Hunting and fishing according to Indigenous customs ensure that resources are not exhausted (Dhimurru 2006). Williams, for instance, describes a set of harvesting activities—including fire management, fish trapping and gathering bush products—that is meant to avoid waste, assure regeneration and maximise the productivity of the land (Williams 1986:93–4). The breakdown of pre-colonial Indigenous NRM and European models of agricultural exploitation are indeed some of the causes of environmental degradation on Indigenous lands. Alien species such as mission grass and buffaloes were introduced for commercial and agricultural purposes (Parson and Cuthberson 1992:119–21; Smith 1995:59). Depopulation is also a cause of declining environmental conditions in the Indigenous estate (Altman and Whitehead 2003). It can be argued that depopulation is partly a symptom of increasing opportunity costs for Indigenous people. Residing in remote or very remote areas requires forgoing economic opportunities that urban settings might offer. According to Biddle (2009), however, Indigenous people who move to urban areas do not do as well as those already residing there, and might do worse than those who stayed in remote centres.

All these causes of environmental degradation are direct consequences of policy distortions, rather than market failure. Addressing such distortions is an obvious first solution (Heath and Binswanger 1996). Once policy distortions are removed, it would be possible to adopt PES schemes that give incentives to Indigenous landowners to reside on their estates, improve traditional management practices by incorporating non-Indigenous science, and hence provide environmental services for the whole of Australia. Recent reforms by the Commonwealth and NT Governments of Indigenous policies are, however, further adding to such distortions by cutting support for Indigenous people living remotely (see COAG 2009).

Private and public benefits and costs on Indigenous-owned land are articulated in Figure 16.2. The low productive potential of most of the Indigenous estate implies that the private benefits of resource exploitation are lower than the private benefits owners gain in other parts of the Australian continent. There is a general agreement that Indigenous land managers have low opportunity costs, either because their land has low natural fertility (Greiner et al. 2009) or because of past agricultural practices, such as in the case of pastoral leases bought back by Indigenous organisations to set up IPAs (see Table 16.1). Low opportunity costs mean that Indigenous landowners potentially have a comparative advantage in environmental service provision. That is, they can provide environmental services with the highest *relative* efficiency in terms of the other goods and services that they extract from their land. Low opportunity costs also imply little bargaining power when negotiating PES. In many cases, the private benefits of Indigenous NRM can be assumed to be higher than benefits from other forms of resource use. This reflects the strong connection between Indigenous culture and the natural environment: Indigenous environmental conservation is strongly based on Indigenous cultural beliefs and philosophies (Williams 1986). In these circumstances, Indigenous landowners clearly would not be able to negotiate PES schemes by threatening, say, to exploit resources for agricultural enterprises. For instance, Muller (2008) mentions a Customs representative questioning the need to pay Indigenous rangers for something Customs gets for nothing.

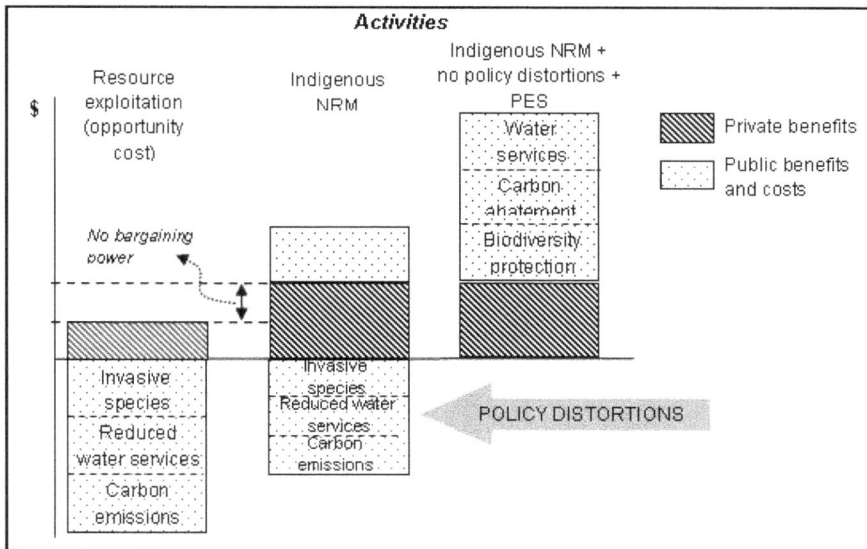

Figure 16.2 Benefits and costs from the Indigenous estate under different management options

Table 16.1 Sample of Indigenous Protected Areas

Name	State	Year	Size (ha)	Acquisition	Ownership	Previous use	IUCN cat.
Toogimbie	NSW	2004	46 000	Nari Nari Tribal Council	Nari Nari	Pastoral	4
Wattleridge	NSW	2001	480	ILC	Banbai	Wildlife refuge	6
Deen maar	Vic.	1999	453	Framlingham Ab. Trust	-	Agriculture	6
Tyrendarra	Vic.	2003	248	Winda-Mara AC	Gunditjmara		6
Guanaba	Qld	2000	100	ILC	Kombumerri	Agriculture and forestry	4
Kaanju Ngaachi Wenlock and Pascoe Rivers	Qld	2008	200 000	Chuulangun AC	Kaanju	-	5
Warul Kawa	Qld	2001	35 000	Torres Strait Island Coordinating Council	Boigu	-	6
Mount Willoughby	SA	2002	386 500	ILC for Tjyrilia AC	Tjyrilia	Pastoral	6 and 2
Nantawarrina	SA	1998	58 000	SA Indigenous Lands Trust	Adnyamathanha		2, 4, 5 and 6
Watarru and Walalkara	SA	2000	1 900 000	APY (Anangu Pitjantjatjara Yankunytjatjara) Land Management	Anangu	-	6
Yalata	SA	1999	456 300	SA Indigenous Lands Trust	Kokata, Antakarinja, Pindiini and Ngalea	-	5
Ninghan	WA	2006	48 000	ATSIC for Pindiddy AC	Badimaya, Nyoongar, Yamatji and Wongai	Pastoral	3 and 4

Name	State	Year	Size (ha)	Acquisition	Ownership	Previous use	IUCN cat.
Paruku	WA	2001	430 000	ALT	Walmajarri, Jaru and Kukatja	Pastoral lease	2 and 6
Warlu Jilajaa Jumu	WA	2007	1 610 000	Handed back after NT claim	Ngurrara	–	5
Preminghana	Tas.	1999	500	Tasmania Land and Sea Ab. Council (purchased by Tasmanian Government under ALA 95)	–	State reserve	6
Risdon Cove and Putalina	Tas.	1999	141	Tasmanian Ab. Centre (purchased by Tasmanian Government under ALA)	–	Agriculture and forestry	5
Mount Chappell and Badger Islands	Tas.	2000	1594	Tasmanian Ab. Centre (purchased by Tasmanian Government under ALA 95)	–	Agriculture and forestry	5
Angas Downs	NT	2009	320 000	Imanpa Development Association (now managed by Lisanote Pty Ltd)	Matutjara, Yankunytjara and Pitjantjatjara	Pastoral	6
Anindilyakwa	NT	2006	300 000	Indigenous Land Trust (ALRA 76)	Anindilyakwa-speaking clans	–	6
Dhimurru	NT	2000	92 000	Indigenous Land Trust (ALRA 76)	Yolngu clans	–	5
Djelk	NT	2009	673 200	Indigenous Land Trust (ALRA 76)	Bininj clans	–	6
Laynhapuy	NT	2006	690 000	Indigenous Land Trust (ALRA 76)	Yolngu clans	–	6
Northern Tanami	NT	2007	4 000 000	Indigenous Land Trust (ALRA 76)	–	–	6
Warddeken	NT	2009	1 394 951	Indigenous Land Trust (ALRA 76)	Bininj clans	–	6

Source: Department of Sustainability, Environment, Water, Population and Communities <http://www.environment.gov.au/indigenous/ipa/index.html>

There are significant differences between PES and government funding for NRM, as well as other forms of economic participation. PES schemes involve individual buyers and sellers of environmental services. As such PES are not constrained within an overarching framework as in the case of government programs, and could be tailored according to the needs and aspirations of each Indigenous NRM group. In this regard, PES are similar to agreements between mining companies and Indigenous landowners, and would pose the same challenge of overcoming weaknesses in the bargaining position of Indigenous people (see O'Faircheallaigh 2008). Unlike mining agreements, PES-related activities do not cause damage to cultural heritage and Indigenous environments, so are less likely to invoke opposition from Indigenous communities. They also require active involvement of Indigenous knowledge and labour, thus creating both tangible (that is, economic) and symbolic outcomes that are central to Indigenous cultural identity (Scambary 2009).

The Two Study Areas

The Dhimurru IPA

Dhimurru (formerly known as Dhimurru Land Management Aboriginal Corporation) was established in 1992. Yolngu (Indigenous people from east Arnhem Land) were concerned about the impact of an increasing non-Indigenous population that followed the establishment of a bauxite mine and processing plant on their traditional lands. TOs run and control the organisation through the Dhimurru Board (Wa:nga-Watangu Yolngu) that includes representatives of 17 clans with interests in the region. The board sets management and access to recreational-area requirements (Dhimurru 2008). Dhimurru currently employs 16 Indigenous and six non-Indigenous staff. In the financial year 2008–09, Dhimurru had a budget of about $1.7 million.

In 2000, Yolngu declared the Dhimurru IPA, covering about 92 000 ha of land and 9000 ha of adjacent marine areas in the Gove Peninsula (Map 16.1). The IPA contains areas of important cultural and environmental value, hosting a significant representation of Australia's Arnhem Coast sub-bioregion ARC-3 (DEWHA 2010a). Environmental values include high plant diversity, intact faunal assemblages, and significant feeding and nesting sites for threatened species of marine turtles and seabirds (Dhimurru 2008). Dhimurru IPA surrounds land leased to Rio Tinto Alcan (RTA) for bauxite mining and processing, and the townships of Nhulunbuy, Yirrkala and Gunyangara.

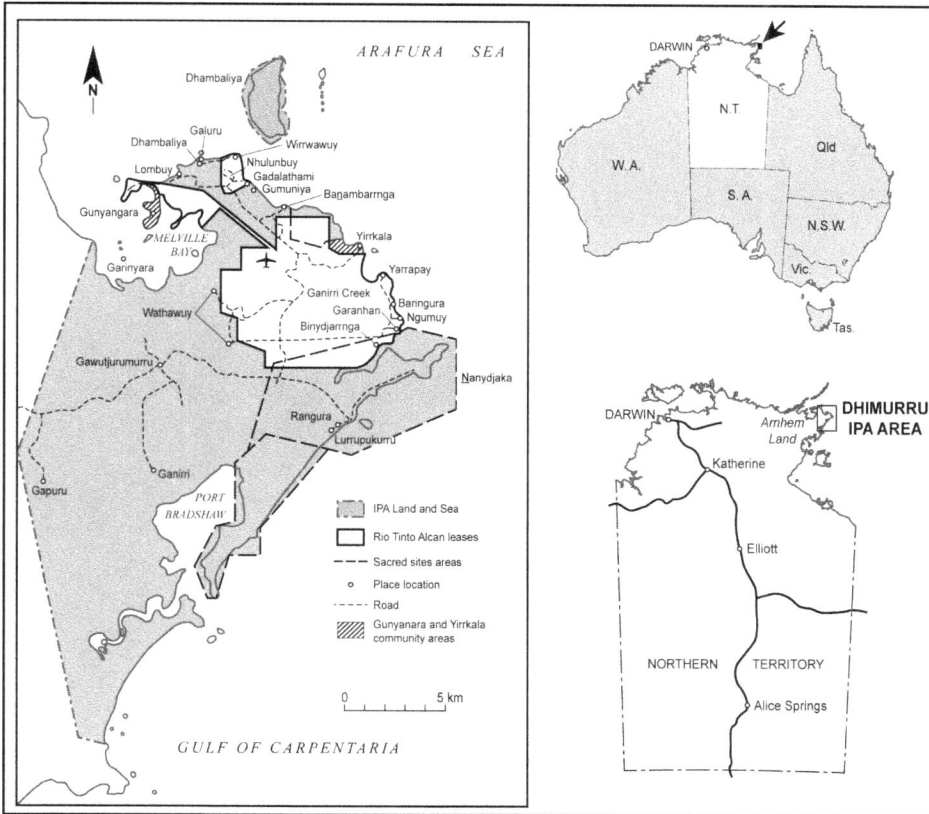

Map 16.1 The Dhimurru IPA

Source: Dhimurru (2008); map redrawn by Peter Johnson.

The primary focus of Dhimurru's activities is the protection of Yolngu values and conservation and enhancement of the natural and cultural values of the IPA. Dhimurru also fosters 'both-ways' management by integrating Yolngu and non-Indigenous sciences. The IPA is also managed according to International Union for Conservation of Nature (IUCN) Category V Guidelines for Protected Areas (Dudley 2008). Dhimurru's activities have interconnected goals: people management, environmental monitoring, conservation and restoration, heritage and cultural activities. People management includes permit checks, signs and sign maintenance, fencing, rubbish pick-ups, and campsite and track maintenance. These activities allow Dhimurru to limit and monitor use, compliance and access. Limits on use and access prevent conflict with local Indigenous communities. They also have important environmental and cultural outputs. Limiting access protects sites of cultural and environmental significance by avoiding damage caused by vehicle movements (weed and non-native ant spreading, fire scars, bush and tree damage, opening of new tracks, disturbance of fauna, damage to nesting sites, and so on) as well as by inappropriate behaviour (vandalism, extirpation of specimens, and so on). Alongside these preventive activities, Dhimurru Rangers carry out environmental management and conservation. This includes: crocodile trapping, tagging and relocating; weed monitoring, treatment and eradication; discarded ('ghost') fishing net recovery and turtle rescue; Australian Quarantine and Inspection Service (AQIS) contracted work (mosquito, ant and weed sampling and monitoring); marine debris and beach clean-ups.

The Djelk IPA

Djelk IPA was declared in 2009. It extends over 673 200 ha, stretching from the Central Arnhem Plateau to the Arafura Sea (Map 16.2) in the Arnhem Coast sub-bioregion ARC-2 (DEWHA 2010b). Even though the IPA has been declared only recently, Djelk Rangers were established under the auspices of Bawinanga Aboriginal Corporation (BAC) in 1991. Djelk IPA comprises a biodiversity-rich landscape, which is home to iconic species such as saltwater crocodiles, and the richest variety in the world of reptiles (DEWHA 2010b). It is also a landscape populated with the cultures of 107 clans representing more than 12 language groups. Senior TOs guide and control Djelk IPA management through the IPA Advisory Committee consisting of representatives of landowning clans. The committee also includes the BAC executive and a representative of the Federal Department of Environment, Water, Heritage and the Arts (DEWHA). Djelk currently employs 35 rangers, a Ranger Coordinator and a Special Project Officer. Rangers are divided into three groups (Sea, Land, and Women Rangers), each coordinated by a senior supervisor. Djelk's budget for the financial year 2008–09 amounted to about $1.7 million.

The major responsibilities of Land and Women Rangers include burning, feral animal control and weed treatment to maintain biodiversity and productivity of the land through the use and transfer of both Indigenous and Western knowledge. Sea Rangers undertake management and surveillance up to 3 nautical miles off the coast. They focus on the protection of cultural and natural resources. Under fee-for-service agreements with Australian Customs and the NT Department of Resources-Fisheries, Djelk Sea Rangers patrol 200 km of coast to detect illegal, foreign and Australian fishing vessels and illegal migration, and to monitor recreational fishing.

There are substantial differences between Dhimurru and Djelk IPAs. Dhimurru's main activities focus on people management. The proximity of a mining town and mine operation to the Dhimurru IPA and the large non-Indigenous population pose the greatest threats to the conservation of cultural and natural assets. It also means that Dhimurru has a direct relationship with the mining company, which is a buyer of environmental services, as discussed in section four. Djelk Rangers have also several partners who buy their environmental services. Aside from selling services to Australian Customs, Fisheries and AQIS, Djelk Rangers are also part of the West Arnhem Land Fire Abatement (WALFA) scheme through which they sell carbon credits to a international company (see the next section).

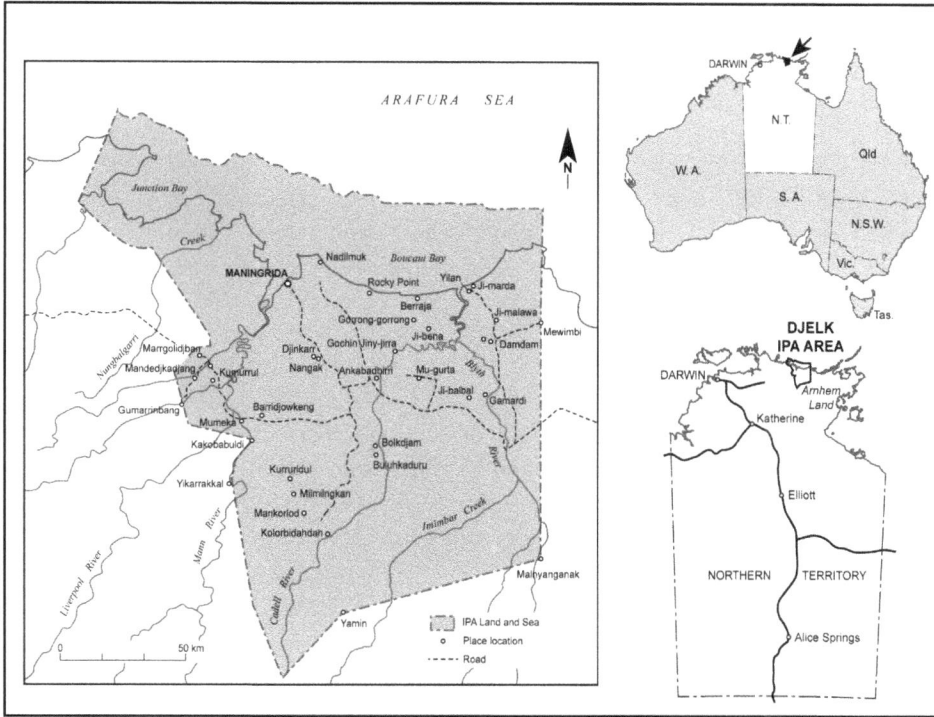

Map 16.2 The Djelk IPA

Source: Bawinanga (2009); map redrawn by Peter Johnson.

Indigenous NRM and PES

There are several contract-based arrangements currently operating in Indigenous Australia that have some or all of the characteristics of PES schemes.[3]

---

3   This does not include several additional PES or market-based schemes for environmental conservation that, in general, do not target Indigenous landowners or aim to address poverty issues (see, for instance, Yee and Clouston 2006).

The WALFA Scheme

The Western Arnhem Land Fire Abatement (WALFA) project is an outcome-based PES scheme involving Indigenous landowners in the Djelk and Warrdekken IPAs and Darwin Liquefied Natural Gas (DLNG) through a contractual agreement brokered by the NT Government and the Northern Land Council. It is the first large-scale commercial provision of environmental services in Indigenous Australia. According to this agreement, signed in 2005, Indigenous Rangers and TOs implement strategic fire management aimed at reducing the number of highly destructive, high in greenhouse gas (GHG) emission, late-season fires through prescribed early season burning across 28 million ha of western Arnhem Land. The reduction in GHG emissions and enhanced environmental protection offset the environmental impact of the liquefied natural gas plant in Darwin. In return, DLNG pays the TOs $1 million per year (in 2006 dollars) for 17 years. The target reduction of 100 000 tonnes of carbon dioxide equivalent per year relative to a 10-year baseline (1995–2004) has been regularly met (BAC 2007). The WALFA agreement is entirely voluntary, and carbon credits generated by the project are not tradable. The project's goals include environmental protection in the Arnhem Land Plateau, transfer of traditional ecological knowledge, assistance to TOs' return to country, as well as provision of economic benefits to the communities involved (Whitehead et al. 2009). While successfully delivering the expected outcomes, the project has also highlighted important issues relating to benefit sharing, potential conflicts between commercial versus customary use of natural resources, and lack of a national framework for carbon trading and emission abatement from fire management (Whitehead et al. 2009).

AQIS Fee-for-Service Program

Australian Quarantine Inspection Services (AQIS) and the NT Department of Primary Industries, Fisheries and Mines run an outcome-based or 'fee-for-services' program through which AQIS contracts Indigenous landowners and rangers to provide weed, insect and marine debris monitoring services (Muller 2008). AQIS pays for vehicle and vessel time, and provides full pay for up to two rangers to collect weed and insect samples, and patrol the coasts. There are few data about the outputs and outcomes of this program. Dhimurru earned about $8000 in 2008 from the AQIS contract (Dhimurru, Personal communication). As Dhimurru runs a $2 million operation, the AQIS fee-for-service scheme clearly has little financial impact. During informal talks with AQIS officers, it emerged that Indigenous male rangers are not always willing to take up weed and insect monitoring, but are usually eager to run marine debris patrols. One can speculate that the reason for this is that weeds and insect monitoring are not activities traditionally performed by Indigenous landowners. AQIS contracts run from year to year, and they offer no support for start-up costs, such as purchase of vehicles and vessels, so Indigenous rangers need to first access resources for these substantial initial investments.

Customs' Indigenous Rangers Program

A third PES-type scheme is the Indigenous Rangers Program run by Australian Customs and Border Protection Service. Under this program, Customs engages Indigenous rangers in maritime surveillance and biosecurity services. The program started as a pilot project in 2005 with a fee-for-services agreement between the Djelk Rangers and Customs. Under the agreement, Djelk Rangers initially received about $250 000 to employ two rangers in sea patrols. Djelk Rangers have intercepted several illegal fishing vessels and provided evidence for successful prosecution. In 2007 the scheme was extended to involve the Bardi Jawi Rangers in Western Australia and Aurukun Rangers in Queensland through a $623 000 commitment by the Federal Government (ACS 2007; FaHCSIA 2007).

Dhimurru and RTA Fee-for-Service Agreements

Since 2005 Rio Tinto Alcan (RTA) has contracted Dhimurru to carry out some ethno-ecology monitoring in Melville Bay, adjacent to the RTA bauxite refinery and shipping facilities, and bordering Dhimurru IPA. The contract requires Dhimurru to develop and provide ongoing maintenance of an ethno-ecological database, as well as supporting sampling activities in the bay by providing a vessel and crew. RTA committed to regular payments of about $40 000 per year. The contract expired last year, and has not been renewed, partly because of the global financial crisis, but also because Dhimurru has not delivered according to contractual requirements (Dhimurru, Personal communication).

Similarly, in 2008, RTA and Dhimurru initiated talks to contract archaeological surveying of the RTA mining area. Dhimurru proposed to take responsibility of TOs' inputs in cultural resource identification, recruit professional expertise and undertake field survey work. The project also had important training elements for Dhimurru. After Dhimurru undertook two trial surveys, however, RTA halted the project following the global financial crisis (Dhimurru, Personal communication).

While all these schemes meet the conditions for PES outlined above (voluntary in nature, payment on delivery, specified services, identified buyer and seller), there are some important differences among them that partially explain their different outcomes, as discussed in the next section.

Discussion

The success of the IPA program in Australia is based on several factors. Government funding has supported TOs focused on managing their traditional estates and protecting heritage. Strong Indigenous knowledge and governance have guided environmental conservation. Both Dhimurru and Djelk IPAs are outstanding examples of how to balance the needs of Indigenous landowners with the requirements attached to government funding. This balance is producing important environmental outcomes, as well as employment opportunities for Indigenous people living in remote Australia. Overall, the increasing number of IPAs and the renewed commitment of the Federal Government indicate that IPAs are seen as an instrument through which Indigenous groups can empower themselves and transform their marginalised status in Australia's economic and political space.

A critical area needing to be addressed is the coordination of the IPA program with other government programs and overarching policy frameworks. In particular, the Closing the Gap framework (COAG 2009) is in direct conflict with the efforts of Indigenous landowners to stay on and care for their country. Also, the voluntary nature of the IPA agreements means that governments are not required to provide any specific commitment, particularly in terms of revising existing policies with negative impacts on the environment. For instance, declaring an IPA does not preclude or extinguish mining rights: 30 per cent of the newly declared Djelk IPA is under mining exploration leases (Djelk Rangers, Personal communication). Indigenous rangers also have no control over activities that impact on the IPA but occur outside its boundaries. In the Gove Peninsula, for instance, bauxite mining and refining have a large ecological footprint, with likely negative effects on the surrounding Dhimurru IPA. Further, Indigenous rangers demand better recognition of the links between cultural and environmental management both at funding and at reporting levels (Dhimurru, Personal communication).

The review of the existing PES schemes involving Djelk and Dhimurru Rangers highlights weaknesses, constraints and opportunities. Some weaknesses relate to the TOs' ability (or lack of) to negotiate contractual agreements with buyers of environmental services. WALFA, for instance, is the result of a long process of government-funded research, information and negotiation that included every aspect of the arrangement. In comparison, the AQIS fee-for-service scheme is a take-it-or-leave-it arrangement. Indigenous landowners have no chance of negotiating compensation, length and methods of undertaking the activities, and hence no possibility of developing a contractual arrangement that best matches their cultural, social and environmental needs and responsibilities. Negotiations would guarantee a degree of autonomy in the implementation of contracted activities, so that they can fit around Indigenous cultural and environmental responsibilities. This might clash with canonical notions of contracted labour, where work requires a hierarchical structure of command, unlike Yolngu circular governance structures (see, for instance, Marika et al. 2009).

Negotiations should also ensure that activities required for the generation of the contracted environmental services match traditional management practices. Whenever this match does not occur, and when conflicting cultural priorities are apparent (see the case of water buffaloes described in Albrecht et al. 2009), negotiations should focus on making Indigenous and non-Indigenous interests converge prior to setting up any PES scheme. There seems to be a better match between Indigenous NRM activities, cultural priorities and contracted activity in the case of WALFA than with AQIS contracts and the RTA ethno-ecological survey. AQIS monitoring activities require skills and knowledge that, possibly, are not closely related to existing Indigenous knowledge and management practices. In the case of RTA ethno-ecological surveys, Dhimurru's IPA management demanded most of its resources, and Dhimurru could only partially fulfil the contract requirements.

Financial constraints and lack of skills are major limiting factors for PES schemes. Lack of skills for the execution of the contractual commitments requires PES schemes to provide the necessary training. For example, complex PES schemes such as the Customs Indigenous Rangers Program require training in several areas: coxswain, maritime safety, law compliance and enforcement. Potential environmental service buyers might find that investing in training is not feasible, or not even proper, as in the case of federal agencies relinquishing enforcement powers in favour of Indigenous landowners.

Further, Indigenous knowledge and management practices might not be suited to addressing new or emerging environmental trends and threats, such as weeds and feral animals, protection of threatened species and climate change (Garnett and Woinarski 2007), and hence limit the type of environmental services they can provide. As Luckert et al. (2007) state, there is a strong case for governments to invest in improving Indigenous landowners' skills in NRM, and to properly fund and support basic ecological and environmental research on Indigenous-owned land. Only such commitment would secure the long-term success of the IPA program on environmental and social grounds, and open new avenues for PES-type arrangements.

It also appears that financial elements limit the ability of Indigenous communities to participate in PES. One of these constraints is the need for up-front investments in vehicles, vessels or other assets. As the AQIS scheme does not provide sufficient resource for these start-up costs, it is plausible to say that some Indigenous groups willing to enter the scheme are not able for lack of basic capital. Indeed, in the case of WALFA, the project has been successful also because the Indigenous communities involved have a well-resourced ranger group and Outstation Resource Agency (ORA) that have been able to provide the necessary capital. It should also be noted that PES schemes could expose Indigenous landowners to the instability of international markets, especially in the mineral sector, as is the case of Dhimurru contractual relationships with RTA. These risks could deter some Indigenous landowners and organisations from making the initial investments necessary to provide environmental services.

Best-practice PES schemes are based on ongoing payments, both to ensure environmental service delivery and to signal serious commitment from buyers (World Bank 2009). It is common for the Federal Government to set up pilot schemes that go on for several years—such as the Customs Indigenous Ranger Program—without developing them into full-scale financial commitments that maximise environmental benefits and promote local development. Indeed, securing long-term funding has always been one of the major problems for Indigenous NRM groups. The success of the WALFA project seems to indicate the need for long-term agreements.

It should also be noted that, as Indigenous Australians might have different sets of incentives and cultural demands, one should not expect that PES are automatically taken up by traditional owners. Monetary incentives might not be enough to ensure the delivery of contracted service, undertake conservation work or change management practices. Weed and insect monitoring through AQIS fee-for-service, for instance, have not been particularly successful with Dhimurru Rangers.

Practitioners have also identified other problems with PES. Market exchange through PES can be realised only for environmental and cultural elements that can be commodified. This can limit the scope for PES applicability, as well as risk the conflation of a set of systemic cultural and environmental complexities in commercialised elements, with potentially detrimental effects on the system (Norgaard 2010). Indigenous rangers are indeed demanding that governments recognise the links between environmental and cultural practices, and the holistic approach driving their land management practices.

PES linked to offsetting schemes—while potentially positive for the local environment and culture—have zero effect on the global environment. For example, global GHG emissions are not decreasing as a result of the WALFA project, as required in order to reduce the probability of serious adverse effects as a result of climate change (IPCC 2007). Finally, the impact of PES in reducing poverty and addressing environmental issues cannot be assessed without considering the overall effects in the local economy and policy settings. There is evidence, for example, that some PES schemes create little gains for non-participants, and that some participants might not gain at all when the scheme is poorly linked to the rest of the economy (Bulte et al. 2008).

Opportunities exist to further engage Indigenous landowners as providers of environmental services. The NT Environmental Protection Agency (EPA), for instance, should consider collaborative arrangements with Indigenous rangers for monitoring the impacts of industrial and economic development. Recent industrial accidents in RTA mining facilities near Dhimurru IPA have highlighted the importance of constant environmental monitoring and public availability of the results. Establishing effective maritime surveillance and enforcement systems is also seen as an important way to engage Indigenous rangers and Indigenous knowledge, and to ensure respectful recognition of Indigenous rights to the sea (Dhimurru 2006).

While new opportunities are now developing for Indigenous NRM to sustain an integrated customary–market–state economy, it should be noted that Yolngu people, for example, have always made clear their aspirations. In the words of senior Yolngu landowners, they 'wish to contribute to regional and national economic development, in keeping with…time-honoured responsibilities to care for land and sea' (Dhimurru 2006).

References

Albrecht, G., McMahon, C., Bowman, D. and Bradshaw, C. 2009. Convergence of culture, ecology, and ethics: management of feral swamp buffalo in northern Australia. *Journal of Agricultural and Environmental Ethics* 22 (4): 361–78.

Altman, J. C. and Martin, D. (eds) 2009. *Power, culture, economy: Indigenous Australians and mining*. CAEPR Research Monograph No. 30, Centre for Aboriginal Economic Policy Research, Australian National University, Canberra, <http://online.anu.edu.au/caepr/mono.php>

Altman, J. C. and Whitehead, P. J. 2003. Caring for country and sustainable Indigenous development: opportunities, constraints and innovation. CAEPR Working Paper No. 20, Centre for Aboriginal Economic Policy Research, Australian National University, Canberra, <http://online.anu.edu.au/caepr/working.php>

Altman, J. C., Buchanan, G. J. and Larsen, L. 2007. *The environmental significance of the Indigenous estate: natural resource management as economic development in remote Australia*. CAEPR Discussion Paper No. 286, Centre for Aboriginal Economic Policy Research, Australian National University, Canberra, <http://online.anu.edu.au/caepr/discussion.php>

Austin-Broos, D. 2003. Places, practices, and things: the articulation of Arrernte kinship with welfare and work. *American Ethnologist* 30 (1): 118–35.

Australian Bureau of Statistics (ABS) 2007. *Australian Standard Geographical Classification*. Canberra: Australian Bureau of Statistics. Viewed 26 May 2010, <http://www.abs.gov.au/AUSSTATS/abs@.nsf/DetailsPage/1216.0Jul%20 2007?OpenDocument>

Australian Bureau of Statistics (ABS) 2010. *Australian Social Trends*. Canberra: Australian Bureau of Statistics. Viewed 26 May 2010, <http://www.abs.gov. au/ausstats/abs@.nsf/mf/4102.0>

Australian Customs Service (ACS) 2007. *Indigenous Ranger Program*. Canberra: Australian Customs Service. Viewed 4 October 2009, <http://www.customs. gov.au/webdata/minisites/annualReport0607/pages/page36.html>

Australian Employment Covenant (AEC) 2010. *Fifty Thousand Sustainable Indigenous Jobs*. Viewed 6 June 2010, <http://www.fiftythousandjobs.com.au/>

Bawinanga Aboriginal Corporation (BAC) 2007. *Annual Report*. Maningrida, NT: Bawinanga Aboriginal Corporation.

Bawinanga Aboriginal Corporation (BAC) 2009. *Djelk Indigenous Protected Area Management Plan*. Maningrida, NT: Bawinanga Aboriginal Corporation.

Biddle, N. 2009. *The geography and demography of Indigenous migration: insights for policy and planning*. CAEPR Working Paper No. 58, Centre for Aboriginal Economic Policy Research, Australian National University, Canberra, <http://online.anu.edu.au/caepr/working.php>

Bulte, E. H., Lipper, L., Stringer, R. and Zilberman, D. 2008. Payments for ecosystem services and poverty reduction: concepts, issues, and empirical perspectives. *Environment and Development Economics* 13 (3): 245–54.

Commonwealth of Australia 2010. *What is Caring for Our Country?* Canberra: Commonwealth of Australia. Viewed 3 February 2010, <http://www.nrm. gov.au/about/caring/index.html>

Council of Australian Governments (COAG) 2009. *National Indigenous Reform Agreement (Closing the Gap)*. Canberra: Council of Australian Governments. Viewed 10 March 2010, <http://www.coag.gov.au/intergov_agreements/ federal_financial_relations/docs/IGA_FFR_ScheduleF_National_ Indigenous_Reform_Agreement.pdf>

Department of the Environment, Water, Heritage and the Arts (DEWHA) 2010a. *Dhimurru Indigenous Protected Area*. Canberra: Commonwealth of Australia. Viewed 3 March 2010, <http://www.environment.gov.au/indigenous/ipa/declared/dhimurru.html>

Department of the Environment, Water, Heritage and the Arts (DEWHA) 2010b. *Djelk Indigenous Protected Area*. Canberra: Commonwealth of Australia. Viewed 3 March 2010, <http://www.environment.gov.au/indigenous/ipa/declared/djelk.html>

Department of the Environment, Water, Heritage and the Arts (DEWHA) 2010c. *Indigenous Protected Areas*. Canberra: Commonwealth of Australia. Viewed 10 May 2010, <http://www.environment.gov.au/indigenous/ipa/index.html>

Department of the Environment, Water, Heritage and the Arts (DEWHA) 2010d. *Sea Country Indigenous Protected Areas*. Canberra: Commonwealth of Australia. Viewed 3 March 2010, <http://www.environment.gov.au/indigenous/ipa/sea.html>

Department of Families, Housing, Community Services and Indigenous Affairs (FaHCSIA) 2007. *Illegal Foreign Fishing—Indigenous rangers trial*. Canberra: Commonwealth of Australia. Viewed 4 October 2009, <http://www.fahcsia.gov.au/about/publicationsarticles/corp/BudgetPAES/budget2007-08/budget2007-07_indigenous/Pages/budget2007-07_indigenous_19.aspx>

Dhimurru 2006. *Sea Country Plan*. Nhulunbuy, NT: Dhimurru Aboriginal Corporation.

Dhimurru 2008. *IPA Plan of Management 2008 to 2015*. Nhulunbuy, NT: Dhimurru Aboriginal Corporation.

Dudley, N. 2008. *Guidelines for Applying Protected Area Management Categories*. Gland, Switzerland: International Union for Conservation of Nature.

Engel, S., Pagiola, S. and Wunder, S. 2008. Designing payments for environmental services in theory and practice: an overview of the issues. *Ecological Economics* 65 (4): 663–74.

Garnett, S. T. and Woinarski, J. 2007. A case for Indigenous threatened species management. In M. K. Luckert, B. M. Campbell, J. T. Gorman and S. T. Garnett (eds), *Investing in Indigenous Natural Resource Management*. Darwin: Charles Darwin University Press.

Gilligan, B. 2006. *The National Reserve System Programme 2006 Evaluation.* Canberra: Department of the Environment and Heritage. Viewed 10 March 2010, <http://www.environment.gov.au/parks/publications/nrs/evaluation-2006.html>

Greiner, R., Gordon, I. and Cocklin, C. 2009. Ecosystem services from tropical savannas: economic opportunities through payments for environmental services. *The Rangeland Journal* 31 (1): 51–9.

Heath, J. and Binswanger, H. 1996. Natural resource degradation effects of poverty and population growth are largely policy-induced: the case of Colombia. *Environment and Development Economics* 1 (1): 65–84.

Hill, R., Harding, E. K., Edwards, D., O'Dempsey, J., Hill, D., Martin, A. and McIntyre-Tamwoy, S. 2007. *A cultural and conservation economy for northern Australia. Final report to Land and Water Australia.* Canberra: Land and Water Australia. Viewed 5 October 2009, <http://lwa.gov.au/products/pr071437>

Hudson, S. 2009. Out with the old: are the CDEP reforms enough? *Policy* (Summer 2008–09).

Kingwell, R., John M. and Robertson, M. 2008. A review of a community-based approach to combating land degradation: dryland salinity management in Australia. *Environment, Development and Sustainability* 10 (6): 899–912.

Intergovernmental Panel on Climate Change (IPCC) 2007. *Climate Change 2007: Synthesis report.* Valencia, Spain: Intergovernmental Panel on Climate Change.

Langton, M., Rhea, Z. M. and Palmer, L. 2005. Community-oriented protected areas for Indigenous people and local communities, *Journal of Political Ecology* 12: 23–50.

Lindsay, N. J. 2005. Toward a cultural model of Indigenous entrepreneurial attitude. *Academy of Marketing Science Review* 5: 1–15.

Luckert, M. K., Campbell, B. M., Gorman, J. T. and Garnett, S. T. (eds) 2007. *Investing in Indigenous Natural Resource Management.* Darwin: Charles Darwin University Press.

Maningrida Arts & Culture (MAC) 2008. *Annual Report 2007–08.* Maningrida, NT: Maningrida Arts & Culture.

Marika, R., Yunupingu Y., Marika-Mununggiritj, R. and Muller, S. 2009. Leaching the poison—the importance of process and partnership in working with Yolngu. *Journal of Rural Studies* 25 (4): 404–13.

Marsh, S. P. and Pannell, D. 2000. Agricultural extension policy in Australia: the good, the bad and the misguided. *The Australian Journal of Agricultural and Resource Economics* 44 (4): 605–27.

Muller, S. 2008. Indigenous payment for environmental service (PES). Opportunities in the Northern Territory: negotiating with customs. *Australian Geographer* 39 (2): 149–70.

Norgaard, R. B. 2010. Ecosystem services: from eye-opening metaphor to complexity blinder. *Ecological Economics* 69 (6): 1219–27.

Northern Land Council (NLC) 2006. *Celebrating Ten Years of Caring for Country. A Northern Land Council initiative*. Darwin: Northern Land Council.

O'Faircheallaigh, C. 2008. Negotiating cultural heritage? Aboriginal–mining company agreements in Australia. *Development and Change* 39 (1): 25–51.

Pagiola, S., Rios, A. R. and Arcenas, A. 2008. Can the poor participate in payments for environmental services? Lessons from the silvipastoral project in Nicaragua. *Environment and Development Economics* 13 (3): 299–325.

Parsons, W. and Cuthbertson E. 1992. *Noxious Weeds of Australia*. Melbourne and Sydney: Inkata Press.

Russel-Smith, J., Whitehead, P. and Cooke, P. 2009. *Culture, Ecology and Economy of Fire Management in North Australian Savannas: Rekindling the Wurrk tradition*. Collingwood, Vic.: CSIRO Publishing.

Scambary, B. 2009. Mining agreements, development, aspirations, and livelihoods. In J. Altman and D. Martin (eds), *Power, Culture, Economy: Indigenous Australians and mining*. CAEPR Research Monograph No. 30, Centre for Aboriginal Economic Policy Research, Australian National University, Canberra.

Smith, N. 1995. *Weeds of Natural Ecosystems: A field guide to environmental weeds of the Northern Territory*. Darwin: Environment Centre Northern Territory.

Smyth, D., Szabo, S. and George, M. 2004. *Case studies in Indigenous engagement in natural resource management in Australia*. Prepared for the Department of Environment and Heritage, Commonwealth of Australia, Canberra. <http://www.nrm.gov.au/publications/case-studies/pubs/indigenous-engagement.pdf>

Whitehead, P. J. 2007. A general case for natural resource management: market failure and government policy. In M. K. Luckert, B. M. Campbell, J. T. Gorman and S. T. Garnett (eds), *Investing in Indigenous Natural Resource Management*. Darwin: Charles Darwin University Press.

Whitehead, P. J., Purdon, P., Cooke, P. M., Russel-Smith, J. and Sutton, S. 2009. The West Arnhem Land Fire Abatement (WALFA) project: the institutional environment and its implications. In J. Russel-Smith, P. J. Whitehead and P. Cooke (eds), *Culture, Ecology and Economy of Fire Management in North Australian Savannas: Rekindling the Wurrk tradition*. Collingwood, Vic.: CSIRO Publishing.

Williams, N. M. 1986. *The Yolngu and their Land*. Stanford, Calif.: Stanford University Press.

Woinarski, J., Mackey, B., Nix, H. and Traill, B. 2007. *The Nature of Northern Australia*. Canberra: ANU E Press.

World Bank 2009. *Best Practice in PES Design*. Washington, DC: The World Bank. Viewed 5 October 2009, <http://go.worldbank.org/B8H9WA8W30>

Wunder, S. 2005. *Payments for Environmental Services: some nuts and bolts*. Occasional Paper No. 42, Center for International Forestry Research, Bogor, Indonesia.

Yee, S. and Clouston, B. 2006. *Round 1 Market Based Instruments Pilot Programs— Overview and implications for regional NRM groups in Queensland*. Brisbane: Department of Natural Resources, Mines and Water.

Acknowledgments

The author gratefully acknowledges the Tropical Rivers and Coastal Knowledge (TRaCK) research hub and the Australian Rivers Institute for funding this study. TRaCK receives major funding for its research through the Australian Government's Commonwealth Environment Research Facilities initiative, the Australian Government's Raising National Water Standards Program, Land and Water Australia, the Fisheries Research and Development Corporation and the Queensland Government's Smart State Innovation Fund.

Contributors

Jon Altman is a research professor in economic anthropology at the Centre for Aboriginal Economic Policy Research (CAEPR) at The Australian National University. From 1990 - 2010 he was foundation director of CAEPR. He is now an Australian Research Council Australian Professorial Fellow. His research focuses on issues of interculturality and economic hybridity in remote Indigenous Australia.

Gwenda Baker is an historian and a consultant. She has a PhD in history from Monash University where she has also been a Research Fellow. She is currently Adjunct Research Fellow at the Monash Indigenous Centre. She has a long association with the people on Elcho Island, the site of one of the early Methodist missions in North East Arnhem Land. Her research interests include Aboriginal contact history and the interactions between Aborigines, governments and missions; gender and religion; families and Yolngu value systems; cross-cultural intersections of religion, Aboriginal leadership and governance; and land rights and mining in the Northern Territory.

Giovanni (Nanni) Concu completed his doctorate in January 2005 at the University of Western Australia. He taught environmental economics at the Universita' di Sassari (Italy) for several years, held a posdoctoral fellowship at the University of Queensland, and conducted research in Arnhem Land through Charles Darwin University. From 2009 to 2011 he was a faculty member of the Centre for Aboriginal Economic Policy Research at The Australian National University, where he carried out research on the environmental needs and costs of environmental management in two IPAs (Djelk and Dhimurru) in Arnhem Land, funded by the Tropical Rivers and Coastal Knowledge (TRaCK) hub.

Cameo Dalley is an anthropologist based in Brisbane with experience working in native title and cultural heritage with Aboriginal groups in south-east Queensland, western Cape York and the Northern Territory. She has previously published on intercultural engagements centered around the Mornington Island mission in the early 20th century and on the concept of indigeneity both in Australia and internationally. As part of her doctoral research she undertook ethnographic fieldwork on the remote Aboriginal community of Mornington Island in north-west Queensland. Other research interests include race relations, periods of transition for Aboriginal youth, alcohol and violence in remote communities and the use of mobile phones and social networking sites by Mornington Islanders. She is currently Secretary of the Australian Anthropological Society.

Natasha Fijn is a College of the Arts and Social Sciences Research Fellow at The Australian National University (2011-2014). Her current research relates to the connections between Yolngu and culturally significant animals in north-east Arnhem Land. The research employs ethnographic film and other visual material as tools to investigate Yolngu connections with animals. She is the author of *Living with Herds: human-animal coexistence in Mongolia* (2011), which focuses on herders and their herd animals and their domestic co-existence. Natasha was a co-organiser of the conference on Indigenous participation in Australian Economies at the National Museum of Australia in 2009.

Andrew Gunstone is a Senior Lecturer in Australian Indigenous Studies in the School of Applied Media and Social Sciences at Monash University. His main research interests are in the politics of Australian reconciliation and the contemporary and historical political relationships between Indigenous and non-Indigenous peoples in Australia. He is also the founder and editor of the *Journal of Australian Indigenous Issues*.

Kristyn Harman completed her PhD in 2008 at the University of Tasmania where she lectures in Aboriginal Studies. Her research interests include cross-cultural contact on British colonial frontiers, frontier experiences of working class women, Indigenous life histories, and legal history. Kristyn is the author of *Aboriginal Convicts: Australian, Khoisan and Māori Exiles* (2012).

After training and working in the visual arts, **Ian Keen** gained a BSc in anthropology at University College London (1973) and a PhD in anthropology at The Australian National University (1979). He is the author of *Knowledge and Secrecy in an Aboriginal Religion* (1994), and *Aboriginal Economy and Society* (2004) as well as many articles in journals and edited books, and he edited *Being Black: Aboriginal Cultures in 'Settled' Australia*, as well as *Indigenous Participation in Australian Economies* (2010) and other collections of essays. His research interests have included Yolngu kinship and religion, Aboriginal land rights, Aboriginal economy, and language and sociality. He taught at the University of Queensland and The Australian National University, where he is now a Visiting Fellow.

A Queensland-based freelance consultant historian, Dr **Ros Kidd**'s five-year research into previously unseen State government files relating to the control of Aboriginal people was the basis of her 1997 book *The Way We Civilise* (1997). Her subsequent publications include *Black Lives, Government Lies* (2002), and *Trustees on Trial: recovering the stolen wages* (2006). Dr Kidd has worked for numerous native title claimants, and has written for the Stolen Generations Inquiry (1997), the Indigenous Crime Taskforce (1999), the Forde Inquiry into Abuse of Children in State Institutions (1999), and the Cape York Justice Study (2001). She acted as expert witness in the 1996 Human Rights inquiry into underpaid wages, and was instrumental in the establishment of the 2006 Senate Committee of Inquiry into the missing wages and entitlements of Aboriginal people during the 20th century. Her submission was published in 2007 as *Hard Labour, Stolen Wages* (2007).

Christopher Lloyd is Professor of Economic History at University of New England, Armidale, Australia, and Visiting Professor at the Nordwel Centre at Helsinki University, Finland. He studied at the Universities of New England, Sussex, and Oxford. His research interests have been in the methodology and theory of social science history, Australian historical political economy, comparative history of settler economies, comparative history of welfare states, and the long-run evolutionary geo-economic history of the past half millennium. Earlier books include *Explanation in Social History* (1986), *The Structures of History* (1993), and *Settler Economies in World History* (with Jacob Metzer and Richard Sutch) (2012). Recent articles have appeared in, among other places, *Australian Economic History Review*, *History and Theory*, *Journal of Australian Political Economy*, *Österreichische Zeitschrift für Geschichtswissenschaft*, *New Zealand Journal of History*, and *Australian Journal of Political Science*.

Paul Memmott is a multi-disciplinary researcher (architect/anthropologist) and the Director of the Aboriginal Environments Research Centre (AERC) at the University of Queensland, where he is Professor in the School of Architecture and the Institute of Social Science Research (ISSR). The AERC provides a focus for postgraduate research and applied research consultancy throughout Australia. Its field of research encompasses the cross-cultural study of the people-environment relations of Indigenous peoples with their natural and built environments. Services are provided to remote and urban Aboriginal groups across most States. Research interests encompass Aboriginal housing and settlement design, Aboriginal access to institutional architecture, Indigenous constructs of place and cultural heritage, vernacular architecture and Native Title, social planning in Indigenous communities, and issues of homelessness, crowding, mobility and family violence.

Maria Nugent is an ARC Future Fellow in the Australian Centre for Indigenous History in the School of History at The Australian National University. Before this, she was based at the Centre for Historical Research at the National Museum of Australia. She has been involved with the La Perouse Aboriginal community for over twenty-five years. Her books include *Botany Bay: Where Histories Meet* (2005) and *Captain Cook Was Here* (2009). She is currently working on a large research project on Aboriginal people's historical remembrance.

Alan O'Connor's working life has been spent in government, engaged in research and policy development in the fields of justice, housing, social justice, and data analysis. He worked for a decade as the Research Officer in the Department of State Aboriginal Affairs in South Australia with the main focus of monitoring and coordinating agency responses to the Royal Commission into Aboriginal Deaths in Custody. He is a life member of Habitat for Humanity Australia, where he has been involved for many years in building houses with low income families in Australia and Asia, working on boards and developing policy.

Michael Pickering is currently the Head of Curatorial and Research with the National Museum of Australia. He has a wide range of research interests and has published over 40 articles on topics ranging from political cartoons, material culture, cannibalism, settlement patterns, exhibitions, ethics, and repatriation.

Since 1994 **Anthony Redmond** has worked in the northern Kimberley region with Ngarinyin people and their neighbours, in Central Australia since 2002, and in Cape York Peninsula since 2005. During this time he has conducted ethnographic research into transformations in local economies, Indigenous relationships with pastoralists, traditional cosmology, sung traditions and bodily experiences of time and country, as well as conducting applied native title and lands rights research. His most recent work has been focused on death and grieving, the comic in everyday Ngarinyin life, the social and ritual importance of body fat, and a phenomenology of travelling in community trucks. Anthony is currently a Visiting Research Fellow at Centre for Aboriginal Economic Policy Research at The Australian National University, where he was an Australian Research Council Chief Investigator in a Linkage project on Indigenous participation in the Australia colonial economy (2007-11).

Fiona Skyring is a historian. While employed by the Kimberley Land Council from 1999 to 2005 as an expert witness, Fiona gave evidence on behalf of native title applicants in five trials in the Federal Court. Since then Fiona has worked for organisations representing native title applicants in Western Australia and Queensland, as well as contributing to community history projects and academic publications. She is the author of 'Justice: A history of the Aboriginal Legal Service of Western Australia'. Fiona was a research associate in the Australia Research Council funded Linkage project on Indigenous participation in the Australian economy.

Gretchen Marie Stolte is a doctoral candidate in anthropology at The Australian National University's School of Archaeology & Anthropology. She holds degrees in art history (BA honours, University of Oregon, USA) and anthropology (MAnth, ANU). Her research focuses on the relationship between images and identity among Aboriginal and Torres Strait Islander artists in urban and regional centres. As well as artworks such as paintings, linoprints, batiks, carvings and sculptures, Gretchen also researches contemporary dance, costumes and music.

Peter Thorley has been working on heritage projects with Western Desert Aboriginal communities since 1986. Since joining the National Museum of Australia in 2006, he has provided specialist curatorial advice on several of the Museum's exhibitions including "Papunya Painting: Out of the Desert", "Yiwarra Kuju: the Canning Stock Route" and "Warakurna: All The Stories Got Into Our Minds and Eyes". He is currently a partner investigator in the ARC Linkage project entitled *Pintupi Dialogues: Reconstructing Memories of Art, Land and Community Through the Visual Record*, and was partner investigator in the Australia Research Council funded Linkage project on Indigenous participation in the Australian colonial economy.

Petronella Vaarzon-Morel is an independent anthropologist with extensive experience working with Aboriginal people across central Australia. She has conducted research for Aboriginal land claims and native title claims in the Northern Territory, Western Australia and Queensland. She has also collaborated on interdisciplinary projects concerned with intercultural environmental issues for which she was a recipient of the Northern Territory Government's Desert Knowledge Research and Innovation Award in both 2008 and 2010. She studied anthropology at Indiana University, Bloomington, Indiana, and has written on a range of issues including Aboriginal history, housing, art and the environment. Her publications include peer reviewed reports, monographs and journal articles.

John White is a Visiting Fellow with the School of Archaeology and Anthropology at The Australian National University. His recently completed anthropology PhD thesis entitled *On the road to Nerrigundah: An historical anthropology of Indigenous-settler relations in the Eurobodalla region of New South Wales* draws on ethnographic and archival research. This research was part of the Australian Research Council Linkage project on Indigenous participation in the Australian colonial economy.

Index

www.ingramcontent.com/pod-product-compliance
Lightning Source LLC
Chambersburg PA
CBHW061242270326

41928CB00041B/3366